MW01141253

JOURNAL FOR THE STUDY OF THE OLD TESTAMENT SUPPLEMENT SERIES

341

Editors
David J.A. Clines
Philip R. Davies

Executive Editor
Andrew Mein

Editorial Board
Richard J. Coggins, Alan Cooper, J. Cheryl Exum, John Goldingay,
Robert P. Gordon, Norman K. Gottwald, John Jarick,
Andrew D.H. Mayes, Carol Meyers, Patrick D. Miller

Sheffield Academic Press
A Continuum imprint

Mesopotamia and the Bible

Comparative Explorations

edited by

Mark W. Chavalas and K. Lawson Younger, Jr

Journal for the Study of the Old Testament
Supplement Series 341

First published in 2002 by Sheffield Academic Press Ltd, an imprint of
Continuum.
This edition published in 2003 by T&T Clark International, an imprint of
Continuum.
The Tower Building, 11 York Road, London SE1 7NX
15 East 26th Street, New York, NY 10010

www.continuumbooks.com

British Library Cataloguing-in-Publication Data

A catalogue record for this book is available from the British Library

Typeset by Sheffield Academic Press
Printed on acid-free paper in Great Britain by Biddles Ltd.,
Guildford and King's Lynn

ISBN 0567-08231-8

CONTENTS

At the 1994 meeting of the Near East Archeological Society in Aurora, IL, Vice-President Bryant Wood asked Mark Chavalas to organize a panel noting the relationship of Mesopotamia to biblical studies. Thus, a double panel was organized, entitled 'Syro-Mesopotamia and the Bible' for the Near East Archeological Society, presented on 17 November 1995, in Philadelphia, PA. The panels were:

First Plenary Session
Wayne T. Pitard, University of Illinois:
'Whispers from the Dust: North Syrian Funerary Customs and their Relationship to Israel'

A. *The Early and Middle Bronze Ages*
Richard Averbeck, Trinity Evangelical Divinity School:
'Sumerians, Temple Building, and the Bible'

Mark W. Chavalas, University of Wisconsin-La Crosse:
'Inland Syria in the Third and Second Millennia BC'

David Deuel, The Masters Seminary:
'Administration by Mail in Fifteenth Century Assyria'

Second Plenary Session,
Wayne Pitard, University of Illinois:
'Voices from the Dust: The Bible and the Great Libraries from Ugarit'

B. *The Middle and Late Bronze Ages*
Daniel Fleming, New York University:
'Emar: On the Road from Harran to Hebron'

K. Lawson Younger, Jr, LeTourneau University:
'The Inscriptions of Sargon II in Light of Recent Research'

Bill Arnold, Asbury Theological Seminary:
'Light from Babylonia and the Rise of Israelite Literature'

It was decided to publish the proceedings in a slightly altered and expanded format, and thus William Schniedewind, Richard Hess, Edwin Yamauchi, Ronald Veenker, Steven Holloway, and Victor Matthews were asked to add papers on areas of Syro-Mesopotamia not addressed in the original panel. In addition, Wayne Pitard collapsed his two plenary sessions into one paper. Some might question the addition of papers concerning Ugarit and Alalakh (as well as information concerning Ebla) to a book devoted to Mesopotamia and the Bible. However, in this book we will take a very loose definition of Mesopotamia as encompassing some regions of Syria immediately west of the Tigris-Euphrates Valley that were obviously connected culturally to traditional Mesopotamia.

The contributors were given only the most general geographic and chronological parameters concerning their papers. They were not specifically asked per se to write on the relationship of their subject to biblical studies (e.g. 'Nuzi and the Bible'; although some did do this), but to write on their own interests (implicitly offering the reader an opportunity to either make comparisons/contrasts with the Bible, or to see how their particular subject sheds light [if any] on the biblical text). Thus, this volume is not intended to be an exhaustive overview of Mesopotamian civilization, but a description of certain aspects of that civilization that may (or may not) help the reader place the Bible in its greater ancient Near Eastern context. The emphasis, however, is placed primarily on Mesopotamia and its relationship to biblical studies.

Mark W. Chavalas
K. Lawson Younger, Jr

ABBREVIATIONS

AASOR	Annual of the American Schools of Oriental Research
AAA	*Annals of Archaeology and Anthropology* (University of Liverpool)
AAAS	*Annales archéologiques arabes syriennes*
AAT	Ägypten und Altes Testament
AB	Anchor Bible
ABC	A.K. Grayson, *Assyrian and Babylonian Chronicles* (Locust Valley, NY: J.J. Augustin, 1975)
ABD	David Noel Freedman (ed.), *The Anchor Bible Dictionary* (New York: Doubleday, 1992)
ABL	R.F. Harper, *Assyrian and Babylonian Letters* (London/Chicago, 1892–1914)
ActSum	*Acta Sumerologica*
AfO	*Archiv für Orientforschung*
AHI	G.I. Davies, *Ancient Hebrew Inscriptions: Corpus and Concordance* (Cambridge: Cambridge University Press, 1991)
AHw	Wolfram von Soden, *Akkadisches Handwörterbuch* (Wiesbaden: Harrassowitz, 1959–81)
AION	*Annali dell'istituto orientale di Napoli*
AJA	*American Journal of Archaeology*
AJBI	*Annual of the Japanese Biblical Institute*
AKA	E.A. Budge and L.W. King, *The Annals of the Kings of Assyria* (Volume 1; London: British Musuem, 1902)
AnBib	Analecta biblica
AnBoll	Analecta Bollandiana
ANET	James B. Pritchard (ed.), *Ancient Near Eastern Texts Relating to the Old Testament* (Princeton: Princeton University Press, 1950)
AnOr	Analecta orientalia
AnSt	*Anatolian Studies*
AO	*Aula Orientalis*. Revista de estudios del próximo oriente antiguo
AOSup	Aula Orientalis Supplementa
AOAT(S)	Alter Orient und Altes Testament (Sonderreihe)
AoF	*Altorientalische Forschungen*
AOS	American Oriental Series
AOTS	D. Winton Thomas (ed.), *Archaeology and Old Testament Study: Jubilee Volume of the Society for Old Testament Study 1917–1967* (Oxford: Clarendon Press, 1967)

AQ	*Anthropological Quarterly*
ARAB	D.D. Luckenbill, *Ancient Records of Assyria and Babylonia* (2 vols.; Chicago, 1926–27)
ARI	A.K. Grayson, *Assyrian Royal Inscriptions* (2 vols.; Wiesbaden: Otto Harrassowitz, 1972–76)
ARM	Archives royales de Mari
ArOr	*Archiv orientální*
AS	Assyriological Studies
Asarh	R. Borger, *Die Inschriften Asarhaddons Königs von Assyrien* (AfO Beiheft, 9; Graz: Ernst Weidner, 1956)
ASOR	American Schools of Oriental Research
ASORDS	American Schools of Oriental Research Dissertation Series
Assur	*Assur*. Monographic Journals of the Near East (Malibu: Undena, California)
Assyria 1995	S. Parpola and R.M. Whiting (eds.), Assyria 1995: Proceedings of the 10th Anniversary Symposium of the Neo-Assyrian Text Corpus Project, Helsinki, September 7–11, 1995 (Helsinki: The Neo-Assyrian Text Corpus Project, 1997)
AT	D.J. Wiseman, *The Alalakh Texts* (Occasional Publications of the British Institute of Archaeology at Ankara, 2; London: British Institute of Archaeology, 1953)
AUSS	*Andrews University Seminary Studies*
BA	*Biblical Archaeologist*
BAL[2]	R. Borger, *Babylonische-assyrische Lesestücke* (AnOr, 54; Rome, 1979, 2nd edn)
BaM	*Bagdader Mitteilungen*
BARev	*Biblical Archaeology Review*
BASOR	*Bulletin of the American Schools of Oriental Research*
BASORSup	*Bulletin of the American Schools of Oriental Research, Supplements*
BAT 1985	*Biblical Archaeology Today: Proceedings of the International Congress on Biblical Archaeology, Jerusalem, April, 1984* (Jerusalem: Israel Exploration Society, 1985)
BBR	*Bulletin for Biblical Research*
BBVO	Berliner Beiträge zum Vorderen Orient. Berlin
BCSMS	*Bulletin of the Canadian Society for Mesopotamian Studies*
BeO	*Bibbia e oriente*
Bib	*Biblica*
BibOr	Biblica et orientalia
BJRL	*Bulletin of the John Rylands University Library of Manchester*
BM	British Museum
BO	*Bibliotheca orientalis*
BR	*Bible Review*
BSac	*Bibliotheca Sacra*
BTB	*Biblical Theology Bulletin*
BWANT	Beiträge zur Wissenschaft vom Alten und Neuen Testament
BZAW	Beihefte zur *ZAW*
CAD	Ignace I. Gelb *et al.* (eds.), *The Assyrian Dictionary of the*

	Oriental Institute of the University of Chicago (Chicago: Oriental Institute, 1956–)
CANE	J.M. Sasson (ed.), *Civilizations of the Ancient Near East* (4 vols.; New York: Charles Scribner's Sons, 1995)
CBQ	*Catholic Biblical Quarterly*
CBQMS	*Catholic Biblical Quarterly*, Monograph Series
CH	R.F. Harper, *The Code of Hammurabi*
COS	W.W. Hallo and K.L. Younger (eds.), *The Context of Scripture* (3 vols.; Leiden: E.J. Brill, 1997–2002)
CTN	Cuneiform Texts from Nimrud
DDD	K. van der Toorn, B. Becking and P.W. van der Horst (eds.), *The Dictionary of Deities and Demons* (Leiden: E.J. Brill, 1995)
DOTT	D. Winton Thomas (ed.), *Documents from Old Testament Times* (London: Nelson, 1958)
EA	J.A. Knudtzon, *et al.* (eds.), *Die El-Amarna-Tafeln* (Vorderasiatische Bibliothek, 2; Leipzig, 1915)
Edom and Seir	D.V. Edelman (ed.), *You Shall Not Abhor an Edomite For He is Your Brother: Edom and Seir in History and Tradition* (Archaeology and Biblical Studies, 3; Atlanta: Scholars Press, 1995)
EEM	P. Bienkowski (ed.), *Early Edom and Moab: The Beginning of the Iron Age in Southern Jordan* (Sheffield Archaeological Monographs, 7; Sheffield: J.R. Collis Publications in association with National Museums and Galleries on Merseyside, 1992)
EI	*Eretz-Israel*
Emar	M.W. Chavalas, (ed.), *Emar: The History, Religion, and Culture of a Syrian Town in the Late Bronze Age* (Bethesda: CDL Press, 1996)
EvQ	*Evangelical Quarterly*
FAOS	Freiburger Altorientalische Studien
FAT	Forschungen zum Alten Testament
FTH	A.R. Millard, J.K. Hoffmeier and D.W. Baker (eds.), *Faith, Tradition, and History: Old Testament Historiography in its Near Eastern Context* (Winona Lake, IN: Eisenbrauns, 1994)
GAG	W. von Soden, *Grundriss der Akkadischen Grammatik* (AnOr, 33; Rome: Pontifical Biblical Institute, 1952)
HAR	*Hebrew Annual Review*
HANES	History of the Ancient Near East/Studies
HSM	Harvard Semitic Monographs
HSS	Harvard Semitic Studies
HSS 5	*Excavations at Nuzi 1*: E. Chiera, 'Texts of Varied Contents' (1929)
HSS 9	*Excavations at Nuzi 2*: R.H. Pfeiffer, 'The Archives of Shilwa-teshub Son of the King' (1932)
HSS 13	*Excavations at Nuzi 4*: R.H. Pfeiffer and E.R. Lacheman, 'Miscellaneous Texts from Nuzi' (1942)

HSS 14	*Excavations at Nuzi 5*: E.R. Lacheman, 'Miscellaneous Texts from Nuzi, Part II: The Palace and Temple Archives' (1950)
HSS 15	*Excavations at Nuzi 6*: E.R. Lacheman, 'The Administrative Archives' (1955)
HSS 16	*Excavations at Nuzi 7*: E.R. Lacheman, 'Economic and Social Documents' (1958)
HTR	*Harvard Theological Review*
HUCA	*Hebrew Union College Annual*
ICC	International Critical Commentary
IEJ	*Israel Exploration Journal*
IOS	*Israel Oriental Studies*
ISBE	Geoffrey Bromiley (ed.), *The International Standard Bible Encyclopedia* (4 vols.; Grand Rapids: Eerdmans, rev. edn, 1979–88)
JANES	*Journal of the Ancient Near Eastern Society*
JAOS	*Journal of the American Oriental Society*
JARCE	*Journal of the American Research Center in Egypt*
JBL	*Journal of Biblical Literature*
JCS	*Journal of Cuneiform Studies*
JEN	Joint Expedition with the Iraq Museum at Nuzi
JEN 2	Texts 101-221: E. Chiera, 'Declarations in Court' (Paris, 1930)
JEN 4	Texts 321-427: E. Chiera, 'Proceedings in Court' (Philadelphia, 1934)
JEN 5	Texts 428-559: E. Chiera, 'Mixed Texts' (Philadelphia, 1934)
JESHO	*Journal of the Economic and Social History of the Orient*
JJS	*Journal of Jewish Studies*
JNES	*Journal of Near Eastern Studies*
JNSL	*Journal of Northwest Semitic Languages*
JPOS	*Journal of the Palestine Oriental Society*
JRAS	*Journal of the Royal Asiatic Society*
JSOT	*Journal for the Study of the Old Testament*
JSOTSup	*Journal for the Study of the Old Testament*, Supplement Series
JSS	*Journal of Semitic Studies*
JSSSup	*Journal of Semitic Studies*, Supplement Series
JTS	*Journal of Theological Studies*
KAI	H. Donner and W. Röllig, *Kanaanäische und aramäische Inschriften* (3 vols.; Wiesbaden: Harrassowitz, 1962–64)
Khorsabad	A. Caubet (ed.), *Khorsabad, le palais de Sargon II, roi d'Assyrie. Actes du colloque organisé au musée du Louvre par le Service culturel les 21 et 22 janvier 1994* (Louvre conférences et colloques; Paris: La documentation Française, 1995)
KTU	M. Dietrich, O. Loretz, and J. Sanmartín, *Keilalphabetische Texte aus Ugarit einschliesslich der keilalphabetischen Texte außerhalb Ugarits. Teil 1 Transkription* (AOAT, 24/1; Kevelaer: Butzon & Bercker; Neukirchen–Vluyn: Neukirchener Verlag, 1976)

KTU[2]	M. Dietrich, O. Loretz and J. Sanmartín, *The Cuneiform Alphabetic Texts from Ugarit, Ras Ibn Hani, and Other Places* (*KTU*: Münster: Ugarit-Verlag, 1995, 2nd enlarged edn)
KUB	*Keilschrifturkunden aus Boghazköi* (Staatliche Museen zu Berlin, Vorderasiatische Abteilung; Berlin: Akademie Verlag, 1921–)
La Bible et l'orient	*La Bible et l'orient: travaux du première congrès d'archéologie et d'orientalisme biblique (Saint-Cloud, 23–25 Avril, 1954)* (Paris: Presses Universitaires de France, 1954)
LEC	Library of Early Christianity
MANE	Monographs of the Ancient Near East
MARI	*Mari, Annales de recherches interdisciplinaires*
Mari in Retrospect	G.D. Young (ed.), *Mari in Retrospect: Fifty Years of Mari and Mari Studies* (Winona Lake, IN: Eisenbrauns, 1992)
MDOG	Mitteilungen der deutschen Orient-Gesellschaft
Mesopotamien und seine Nachbarn	
	H.-J. Nissen and J. Renger (eds.), *Mesopotamien und seine Nachbarn: Politische und kulturelle Wechselbeziehungen im Alten Vorderasien vom 4. bis 1. Jahrtausend v. Chr.* (RAI 25; BBVO, 1; Berlin: Dietrich Reimer, 1982)
NABU	*Nouvelles assyriologiques brèves et utilitaires*
NBD	J.D. Douglas *et al.* (eds.), New Bible Dictionary (Leicester: Inter-Varsity Press, 2nd edn, 1982)
NEA	*Near Eastern Archaeology*
NEAEHL	E. Stern (ed.), *The New Encyclopedia of Archaeological Excavations in the Holy Land* (Jerusalem: The Israel Exploration Society & Carta, 1993)
NEASB	*Near East Archaeology Society Bulletin*
NHSAS	M.W. Chavalas and J. Hayes (eds.), *New Horizons in the Study of Ancient Syria* (Malibu: Undena, 1992)
NIDOTE	Willem A. VanGemeren (ed.), *New International Dictionary of Old Testament Theology and Exegesis* (5 vols.; Grand Rapids: Zondervan, 1997)
OA	*Oriens Antiquus*. Rivista del Centro per le Antichità e la Storia dell'Arte del Vicino Oriente
OEANE	E.M. Meyers (ed.), *The Oxford Encyclopedia of Archaeology in the Near East* (5 vols.; Oxford: Oxford University Press, 1997)
OBO	Orbis biblicus et orientalis
OCPR	E. Matsushima (ed.), *Official Cult and Popular Religion in the Ancient Near East: Papers of the First Colloquium on the Ancient Near East—The City and its Life, held at the Middle Eastern Culture Center in Japan (Mitaka, Tokyo), March 20-22, 1992* (Heidelberg: Winter, 1993)
OIP	The University of Chicago, Oriental Institute Publications
OLZ	*Orientalische Literaturzeitung*
Or	*Orientalia*
OrSu	*Orientalia Suecana*

PEQ	*Palestine Exploration Quarterly*
PKB	J.A. Brinkman, *A Political History of Post-Kassite Babylonia, 1158–722 B.C.* (AnOr, 43; Rome: Pontifical Biblical Institute, 1968)
PLAMAP	O. Bar-Yosef and A. Khazanov (eds.), *Pastoralism in the Levant: Archaeological Materials in Anthropological Perspectives* (Monographs in World Archaeology, 10; Madison, WI: Prehistory Press, 1992)
PNA	S. Parpola, K. Radner, H. Baker, *et al.* (eds.), *The Prosopography of the Neo-Assyrian Empire* (Helsinki: The Neo-Assyrian Text Corpus Project, 1998–)
POTW	A.J. Hoerth, G.L. Mattingly and E.M. Yamauchi (eds.), *Peoples of the Old Testament World* (Grand Rapids: Baker Book House, 1994)
Power and Propaganda	
	M.T. Larsen (ed.), *Power and Propaganda: A Symposium on Ancient Empires* (Copenhagen: Akademisk Forlag, 1979)
PPS	*Proceedings of the Prehistoric Society*
PRS	*Perspectives in Religious Studies*
PSBA	*Proceedings of the Society of Biblical Archaeology*
RA	*Revue d'assyriologie et d'archéologie orientale*
RAI	Recontre Assyriologique Internationale
RB	*Revue biblique*
RHR	*Revue de l'histoire des religions*
RIMA 1	*The Royal Inscriptions of Mesopotamia. Assyrian Periods.* Volume 1: A.K. Grayson, *Assyrian Rulers of the Third and Second Millennia BC (To 1115BC)* (Toronto: University of Toronto, 1987)
RIMA 2	*The Royal Inscriptions of Mesopotamia. Assyrian Periods.* Volume 2: A.K. Grayson, *Assyrian Rulers of the Early First Millennium BC (1114–859 BC)* (Toronto: University of Toronto, 1991)
RIMA 3	*The Royal Inscriptions of Mesopotamia. Assyrian Periods.* Volume 3: A.K. Grayson, *Assyrian Rulers of the Early First Millennium BC II (858–745 BC)* (Toronto: University of Toronto, 1996)
RIME 2	*Royal Inscriptions of Mesopotamia: Early Periods.* Volume 2: D. Frayne, *Sargonic and Gutian Periods* (Toronto: University of Toronto, 1993)
RIME 3.1	*The Royal Inscriptions of Mesopotamia: Early Periods.* Volume 3.1: D.O. Edzard, *Gudea and His Dynasty* (Toronto: University of Toronto Press, 1997)
RIME 3.2	*Royal Inscriptions of Mesopotamia: Early Periods.* Volume 3.2: D. Frayne, *Ur III Period (2112–2004 BC)* (Toronto: University of Toronto, 1997)
RIME 4	*Royal Inscriptions of Mesopotamia: Early Periods.* Volume 4: D. Frayne, *Old Babylonian Period (2003–1595 BC)* (Toronto: University of Toronto, 1990)

RivB	*Rivista biblica italiana*
RlA	E. Ebeling and B. Meissner *et al.* (eds.) *Reallexikon der Assyriologie*
RSP	L. Fisher and S. Rummel (eds.), *Ras Shamra Parallels: The Texts from Ugarit and the Hebrew Bible* (3 vols.; Rome: Pontifical Biblical Institute, 1975–81)
SAA	State Archives of Assyria
SAAB	*State Archives of Assyria Bulletin*
SAAS	State Archives of Assyria Studies
SANE	Sources from the Ancient Near East
SAOC	Studies in Ancient Oriental Civilizations. Chicago: The Oriental Institute
SBL	Society of Biblical Literature
SBLDS	SBL Dissertation Series
SBLMS	SBL Monograph Series
SBLRBS	SBL Resources for Biblical Study
SBLWAW	SBL Writings of the Ancient World
SCCNH	Studies on the Civilization and Culture of Nuzi and the Hurrians
SHCANE	Studies in the History and Culture of the Ancient Near East
ScrHier	Scripta Hierosolymitana
SEL	*Studi Epigrafici e Linguistici sul Vicino Oriente antico*
SHAJ	*Studies in the History and Archaeology of Jordan*
SIC 1	C.D. Evans, W.W. Hallo and J.B. White (eds.), *Scripture in Context: Essays on the Comparative Method* (Pittsburgh Theological Monograph Series, 34; Pittsburgh: Pickwick, 1980)
SIC 2	W.W. Hallo, J.C. Moyer and L.G. Perdue (eds.), *Scripture in Context*, II. *More Essays on the Comparative Method* (Winona Lake, IN: Eisenbrauns, 1983)
SIC 3	W.W. Hallo, B.W. Jones and G.L. Mattingly (eds.), *The Bible in the Light of Cuneiform Literature: Scripture in Context*, III. (Ancient Near Eastern Texts and Studies, 8. Lewiston: The Edward Mellen Press, 1990)
SIC 4	K.L. Younger, Jr, W.W. Hallo and B.F. Batto (eds.), *The Canon in Comparative Perspective: Scripture in Context*, IV. (Ancient Near Eastern Texts and Studies, 11; Lewiston, NY: The Edwin Mellen Press, 1991)
SJOT	*Scandinavian Journal of the Old Testament*
SMIM	J.A. Dearman (ed.), *Studies in the Mesha Inscription and Moab* (Atlanta: Scholars Press, 1989)
Studies Ahlström	W. Barrick and J. Spencer (eds.), *In the Shelter of Elyon: Essays on Ancient Palestinian Life and Literature in Honor of Gosta W. Ahlström* (Sheffield: JSOT Press, 1984)
Studies Albright	H. Goedicke (ed.), *Near Eastern Studies in Honor of William Foxwell Albright* (Baltimore: The Johns Hopkins University Press, 1971)

Studies Archer   W. Kaiser and R. Youngblood (eds.), *A Tribute to Gleason Archer* (Chicago: Moody Press, 1986)

Studies Astour   G.D. Young, M.W. Chavalas and R.E. Averbeck (eds.), *Crossing Boundaries and Linking Horizons: Studies in Honor of Michael C. Astour on His 80th Birthday* (Bethesda: CDL Press, 1997)

Studies Barr   S.E. Balentine and J. Barton (eds.), *Language, Theology, and the Bible: Essays in Honour of James Barr* (Oxford: Oxford University Press, 1994)

Studies Birot   J.M. Durand and J.R. Kupper (eds.), *Miscellanea Babylonica: Mélanges Offerts à Maurice Birot* (Paris: Editions Recherche sur les civilisations, 1985)

Studies Borger   S.M. Maul (ed.), *Festschrift für Rykle Borger zu seinem 65. Geburtstag am 24. Mai 1994: tikip santakki mala basmu* (Groningen: Styx, 1998)

Studies Bounni   P. Matthiae *et al.*, (eds.), *Resurrecting the Past: A Joint Tribute to Adnan Bounni* (Leiden: Nederlands Instituut voor het Nabije Oosten, 1990)

Studies Braidwood   T.C. Young *et al.* (eds.), *The Hilly Flanks and Beyond: Essays in the Prehistory of Southwestern Asia Presented to Robert J. Braidwood* (Chicago: University of Chicago Press, 1984)

Studies Cross   P.D. Miller, P.D. Hanson and S.D. McBride (eds.), *Ancient Israelite Religion: Essays in Honor of Frank Moore Cross* (Philadelphia: Fortress Press, 1987)

Studies Freedman   C.L. Meyers and M. O'Connor (eds.), *The Word of the Lord Shall Go Forth: Essays in Honor of David Noel Freedman in Celebration of His Sixtieth Birthday* (Winona Lake, IN: Eisenbrauns, 1983)

Studies Garelli   D. Charpin and F. Joannès (eds.), *Marchands, Diplomates et empereurs: Etudes sur la civilisation mésopotamienne offertes à P. Garelli* (Paris: Editions Recherche sur les Civilisations, 1991)

Studies Gibson   N. Wyatt, W.G.E. Watson and J.B. Lloyd (eds.), *Ugarit, Religion and Culture. Proceedings of the Inter-national Colloquium on Ugarit, Religion and Culture Edinburgh, July 1994. Essays Presented in Honour of Professor John C. L. Gibson* (UBL, 12; Münster: Ugarit-Verlag, 1996)

Studies Harrison   A. Gileadi (ed.), *Israel's Apostasy and Restoration: Essays in Honor of Roland K. Harrison* (Grand Rapids, MI: Baker Book House, 1988)

Studies Heltzer   Y. Avishur and R. Deutsch (eds.), *Michael. Historical, Epigraphical and Biblical Studies in Honor of Prof. Michael Heltzer* (Tel Aviv: Archaeological Center Publications, 1999)

Studies Kaufmann   M. Haran (ed.), *Studies in Bible and Jewish Religion: Yehezkel Kaufmann Jubilee Volume* (Jerusalem: Magnes Press, 1960)

Studies King   M.D. Coogan, J.C. Exum and L.E. Stager (eds.), *Scripture and Other Artifacts: Essays on Archaeology and the Bible in*

	Honor of Philip J. King (Louisville, KY: Westminster/John Knox Press, 1994)
Studies Kraus	G. van Driel *et al.* (eds.), *Zikir Šumim: Assyriological Studies Presented to F. R. Kraus on the Occasion of his Seventieth Birthday* (Nederlands Instituut voor het Nabije Oosten Studia Francisci Scholten Memoriae Dicata, 5; Leiden: E.J. Brill, 1982)
Studies Lacheman	M.A. Morrison and D.I. Owen (eds.), *In Honor of Ernest R. Lacheman on his Seventy-Fifth Birthday* (SCCNH, 1; Winona Lake, IN: Eisenbrauns, 1981)
Studies Landsberger	H.G. Güterbock and T. Jacobsen (eds.), *Studies in Honor of Benno Landsberger on his Seventy-fifth Birthday April 21, 1965* (AS, 16; Chicago: University of Chicago Press, 1965)
Studies Lambdin	D.M. Golomb (ed.), *'Working with No Data': Semitic and Egyptian Studies Presented to Thomas O. Lambdin* (Winona Lake, IN: Eisenbrauns, 1987)
Studies van Loon	O.M.C. Haex, H.H. Curvers and P.M.M.G. Akkermans (eds.), *To the Euphrates and Beyond: Archaeological Studies in Honour of Maurits N. van Loon* (Rotterdam/Brookfield: A.A. Balkema, 1989)
Studies Loretz	M. Dietrich and I. Kottsieper (eds.), *'Und Mose schrieb dieses Lied auf': Studien zum Alten Testament und zum Alten Orient. Festschrift für Oswald Loretz zur Vollendung seines 70. Lebensjahres mit Beiträgen von Freunden, Schülern und Kollegen* (AOAT, 250; Münster: Ugarit-Verlag, 1998)
Studies Mendenhall	H.B. Huffmon, F.A. Spina and A.R.W. Green (eds.), *The Quest for the Kingdom of God: Studies in Honor of George E. Mendenhall* (Winona Lake, IN: Eisenbrauns, 1983)
Studies Moran	T. Abusch, J. Huehnergard and P. Steinkeller (eds.), *Lingering over Words: Studies in Ancient Near Eastern Literature in Honor of William L. Moran* (Atlanta: Scholars Press, 1990)
Studies Pope	J. Marks and R. Good (eds.), *Love and Death in the Ancient Near East: Essays in Honor of Marvin H. Pope* (Guilford: Four Quarters Publishing Company, 1987)
Studies Sjöberg	H. Behrens *et al.* (eds.), *DUMU E₂ DU-BA-A: Studies in Honor of Ake W. Sjöberg* (Philadelphia: The University Museum, 1989)
Studies von Soden	M. Dietrich and O. Loretz (eds.), *Vom Alten Orient von Soden zum Alten Testament. Festschrift für Wolfram Freiherrn von Soden zum 85. Geburtstag am 19. Juni 1993* (AOAT; Kevelaer: Butzon & Bercker; Neukirchen–Vluyn: Neukirchener Verlag, 1995)
Studies Speiser	W.W. Hallo (ed.), *Essays in Memory of E.A. Speiser* (New Haven: American Oriental Society, 1968)
Studies Tadmor	M. Cogan and I. Eph'al (eds.), *Ah, Assyria,...Studies in Assyrian History and Ancient Near Eastern Historiography Presented to Hayim Tadmor* (ScrHier, 33; Jerusalem: The Magnes Press, 1991)

Studies Wright	F.M. Cross *et al.* (eds.), *Magnalia Dei: Essays on the Bible and Archaeology in Memory of G. Ernest Wright* (Garden City, NY: Doubleday, 1976)
Studies Young	J.E. Coleson and V.H. Matthews (eds.), *Go to the Land I Will Show You: Studies in Honor of Dwight W. Young* (Winona Lake, IN: Eisenbrauns, 1996)
TAD	B. Porten and A. Yardeni, *Textbook of Aramaic Documents from Ancient Egypt* (4 vols.; Jerusalem: The Hebrew University, 1986–1999)
TCS	Texts from Cuneiform Sources
TDOT	G.J. Botterweck and H. Ringgren (eds.), *Theological Dictionary of the Old Testament*
TFS	S. Dalley and J.N. Postgate, *The Tablets from Fort Shalmaneser* (CTN, 3; Oxford: British School of Archaeology, 1984)
TLZ	*Theologische Literaturzeitung*
TRu	*Theologische Rundschau*
TynBul	*Tyndale Bulletin*
TZ	*Theologische Zeitschrift*
UB	G.J. Brooke, A.H.W.Curtis and J.F. Healey (eds.), *Ugarit and the Bible: Proceedings of the International Symposium on Ugarit and the Bible. Manchester, September 1992* (UBL, 11; Münster: Ugarit-Verlag, 1994)
UBL	Ugaritisch-Biblische Literatur
UF	*Ugarit-Forschungen*
Unity and Diversity	H. Goedicke and J.J.M. Roberts (eds.), *Unity and Diversity: Essays in the History, Literature, and Religion of the Ancient Near East* (Baltimore: The Johns Hopkins University Press, 1975)
Ugarit in Retrospect	G.D. Young (ed.), *Ugarit in Retrospect: Fifty Years of Ugarit and Ugaritic* (Winona Lake, IN: Eisenbrauns, 1979)
VAB	Vorderasiatische Bibliothek
VT	*Vetus Testamentum*
VTSup	*Vetus Testamentum*, Supplements
WO	*Die Welt des Orients*
WZHB	*Wissenschaftliche Zeitschrift der Humboldt-Universität zu Berlin*
WZKM	*Wiener Zeitschrift für die Kunde des Morgenlandes*
YNER	Yale Near Eastern Researches
YOS	Yale Oriental Series. Babylonian Texts
ZA	Zeitschrift für Assyriologie
ZAH	*Zeitschrift für Althebraistik*
ZÄS	*Zeitschrift für ägyptische Sprache und Altertumskunde*
ZAW	*Zeitschrift für die alttestamentliche Wissenschaft*
ZDMG	*Zeitschrift der deutschen morgenländischen Gesellschaft*
ZDPV	*Zeitschrift des deutschen Palästina-Vereins*

LIST OF CONTRIBUTORS

Bill T. Arnold, Asbury Theological Seminary

Richard E. Averbeck, Trinity International University—Divinity School

Mark W. Chavalas, University of Wisconsin—La Crosse

David C. Deuel, Brandon, Florida

Daniel E. Fleming, New York University

Richard S. Hess, Denver Seminary

Steven W. Holloway, American Theological Library Association

Victor H. Matthews, Southwest Missouri State University

Wayne T. Pitard, The University of Illinois

William Schniedewind, University of California, Los Angeles

Ronald A. Veenker, Western Kentucky University

Edwin Yamauchi, Miami University

K. Lawson Younger Jr, Trinity International University—Divinity School

ASSYRIOLOGY AND BIBLICAL STUDIES:
A CENTURY AND A HALF OF TENSION

Mark W. Chavalas

> What is the reason for these efforts in remote, inhospitable, and dangerous lands? What is the reason for this expensive rooting through rubble many thousands of years old, all the way down to the water table, where no gold and no silver is to be found? What is the reason for the competition among nations to secure excavation rights to these deserted mounds, and the more the better? Moreover, what is the source of the ever-increasing, self-sacrificing interest, on both sides of the Atlantic, allotted to the excavations in Babylonia and Assyria?
>
> To these questions there is one answer, even if not the whole answer which points to what for the most part is the motive and the goal, namely, the Bible (Delitzsch 1906: 1).

So began F. Delitzsch's famous inaugural lecture for the German Oriental Society entitled, 'Babel und Bibel', 13 January 1902, in Berlin. However, those who believed that the excavations in Mesopotamia had the primary purpose of illuminating the Bible and verifying its historicity were to be disappointed with the remainder of Delitzsch's first and succeeding lectures, as he spoke from the standpoint of an Assyriologist who attempted to show the primacy and superiority of Babel (Mesopotamia) over the Bible. The tension between the two disciplines of Assyriology and biblical studies in the past century and a half has often been acute and has never adequately been defined. In fact, any comparative study of issues concerning the two has often been considered a hazardous affair.[1] Assyriology, of course, is by definition a new discipline, and has often been considered an intruder by biblicists (Kraus 1969: 69-73). On the other hand, the Assyriologist has often had to work under the shadow of the biblicists, who have for the most part considered Assyriology an auxiliary to biblical studies. They often have had to connect their work for relevance to biblical

---

1.   See the discussion by van der Toorn 1985: 1-8.

studies. Of course, many Assyriologists in the early period maintained a traditional doctrinal orthodoxy. Assyriology remains a subject for specialists; there never has been an assyriological equivalent to Egyptomania, except for the Amorite hypothesis. The Assyriologist must admit that ironically it was the Bible that helped illuminate the newly found cuneiform documents in the nineteenth century, as it provided transcriptions of five of the names of the Assyrian kings.[2] For some biblical scholars, the impact of Assyriology upon biblical studies has been minimal, an untenable position for those of us who attempt to bridge both fields.[3] When one scrapes away the superficial similarities, however, the two disciplines have thus developed almost wholly independent of each other. In some respects, scholars of the two disciplines are not always properly trained or well suited to do comparative studies.[4] Too often scholars have taken 'inventorial' approach to comparisons, listing various parallel phenomena without making clear their significance (Malul 1990: 32). Although it is certainly legitimate to look for parallels (Veenhof 1995), the methodological criteria for studying Mesopotamia and the Bible have not been adequately articulated. There needs to be a systematic manner in the approach to the comparative method.[5] Most would agree that the biblical scholar must examine the immediate and wider biblical context before resorting to searching for external evidences from Mesopotamia, and the general context of those external sources also. One must also ask whether or not the phenomenon in question existed outside the stream of the ancient Near Eastern tradition, of which both the biblical and Mesopotamian cultures were a part (Malul 1990: 93-97).

On the whole, the biblical scholars have made but superficial use of Assyriological research, mainly because of the high degree of specialization needed to work with its data (Millard 1989: 24). Furthermore, a great number of Assyriologists neither have an interest in biblical studies, nor do they see many obvious and direct connections to the Old Testament, while Old Testament scholars are often too concerned with theological matters to become interested in immersing themselves in technical

2.   Also, see the discussion by Tadmor 1985: 262.

3.   Notice the lack of attention to ancient Near Eastern matters in some of the major works devoted to the history of Old Testament scholarship; Kraeling 1955; Hahn 1956; Kraus 1956; Greenslade 1963.

4.   See the discussion of this issue in regards to biblical scholars studying Ugaritic religion; see Hillers 1985.

5.   This is one of the themes of Barr 1987.

matters (in fact, some biblical scholars were drawn to Assyriology because of its comparative lack of theological controversies; this has certainly been the case in Great Britain and North America). The cuneiform material accessible to the biblical scholar is limited to the relatively few fully edited and annotated texts. At any rate, it is not surprising to see a tension between the two disciplines. In spite of this, it is strongly urged that the two disciplines continue to interact, as long as they retain their own methodology and autonomy (see Tadmor 1985: 266).

In this introduction, I will attempt to trace some of the major developments of the relationship between the two fields since the discovery and subsequent decipherment of 'Babylonic' cuneiform in the mid-nineteenth century.

The two disciplines are very different. Assyriology studies a dead civilization. When Xenophon, the Greek general and historian, traversed the boundaries of Assyria at the beginning of the fourth century BCE, he traveled past both Nimrud and Nineveh. Although he noticed both of these cities, he called them by their Greek names, and assumed that the region was part of Media, and that the two cities were destroyed by the Persians. Thus, he was unaware that they were two of the great Assyrian capitals, which had become abandoned mounds in the preceding two centuries.[6] The Bible and various Greek sources became powerful factors in keeping alive the memory of Mesopotamian civilization. Yet it was not simply the interest in biblical studies that drove the Europeans to the Tigris-Euphrates Valley in the early nineteenth century. France and Great Britain were looking for land routes to India and took great efforts to exert their influence on these areas. Archeology was thus an unconscious extension of European imperialism.

Because of the spiritual connections with the Old Testament, those in the West are the remote descendants of the Mesopotamians.[7] Assyriology's importance to world history is only now being discussed by Assyriologists.[8] However, Assyriologists have rarely been able to synthesize their massive data base for the public. Furthermore, biblical scholars have been much

---

6.   Xenophon, *Anabasis* I.4.6-12. Other classical period authors, including Herodotus and Ptolemy were better versed about this area. I thank Michael C. Astour for the preceding observation.

7.   See Bottéro (1992: 15-25) who argues that Assyriology should be at the center of the social sciences, since it contains our cultural 'family documents'.

8.   See, for example, Hallo 1996.

more prone to search for comparative data than have Assyriologists.[9] The two civilizations of Mesopotamia and Israel must be studied independently of each other, while recognizing the intimate relationship of the two (Saggs 1978: 5). Comparisons between the two were often done early on in regards to polemic.[10] The two traditions should be seen as two contemporary systems in the ancient Near East, and not necessarily exclusively in context with each other. Searching for direct comparisons can be methodologically unsound, causing one to omit great amounts of relevant data. Clearly, Mesopotamia and Israel (including Syria) were part of a greater cultural continuum (van der Toorn 1996: 4).

The study of Syro-Mesopotamian civilization has advanced greatly in the past 25 years. Of special import is the renewed interest in Eastern or 'Mesopotamian' Syria, where new archeological finds have radically altered our understanding of not only the ancient Near East, but of the Bible as well. Although there have recently been some brief descriptions of Mesopotamian connections and the Bible,[11] there has been no detailed synthesis in English of the Tigris-Euphrates region in regards to the Bible in many years.[12]

From the beginning, scholars were intrigued by the possibilities of studying the two disciplines, and either emphasized the similarities or stressed differences.[13] At the outset of the nineteenth century the Anglican Church retained a supremacy over biblical studies that was not seen in either Germany or France. Thus, when German and French historical and literary criticism of the Bible began to filter into Great Britain there was a sharp reaction. These 'Germanisms' as they were called (the propensity to view many Old Testament stories as mythical and to de-emphasize the importance of the Old Testament) were considered a threat to the understanding of the divine inspiration of Scripture (Chadwick 1966: 628). There was a fear that the Bible would be 'polluted' by being too close to a

9.   Sjöberg (1984: 217) found it necessary to state that he comes to the Old Testament with 'the eyes of an Assyriologist'.

10.   E.g. in terms of religion, see Vriezen 1968.

11.   E.g. Hoerth, Mattingly and Yamauchi 1994.

12.   E.g. Larue 1967; Parrot 1955; 1958. A number of Assyriologists have worked on comparative themes of Mesopotamia and the Bible late in their career; see now von Soden 1985 (this is not in fact a synthesis but a collection of some of von Soden's previously published works on biblical and assyriological themes) and Bottéro 1986–92; 1993a; and 1994.

13.   Talmon 1978a: 332; for a critique of finding comparisons as a modern variation of the long history of the effort to deny Israel any innovation, see Greenspahn 1991.

pagan tradition (i.e. Mesopotamia). Ironically, the British and French Enlightenment which had been imported to Germany had now returned in an altered form to a country was had previously been cool to biblical criticism. However, the fact that historical criticism was presently being done in Homeric studies made it easier for scholars to be open to the 'Germanisms' (Kraeling 1955: 89-97). However, the first impressions of the cuneiform tablets had little impact on nineteenth-century biblical criticism.

The first major excavations were done by the French, under P.E. Botta, who had knowingly begun working at Nineveh in 1842.[14] Of course, the ancient name of the mound was Ninua, a fact which was known by the Medieval Arab geographers and Jewish travelers (e.g. Benjamin of Tudela in the twelfth century AD), but not to the European travelers or, for the most part, the European adventurers (Grayson 1997: 106). Though Botta soon left Nineveh, he directed his attentions to Khorsabad, where he found the palace of the Assyrian king Sargon II. Ironically, he mistakenly thought he had discovered Nineveh (see Budge 1925: 67). Botta's discoveries at Khorsabad, though, created an immense interest in Mesopotamian antiquities in Europe. Although the French government sponsored work on drawing the reliefs that had been brought to Paris, Botta never received the public recognition afforded many other adventurers to the Middle East. Nonetheless, the French government subsidized the magnificent volumes produced by Botta, although they were only accessible to a small number of persons (not including Layard!) (McCall 1998: 198). At any rate, A. de Longpérier was able to read the name Sargon, King of Assyria on one of the monuments, identifying him with the same mentioned in Isa. 20.1, the first name of a Mesopotamian king to be read by a modern scholar from outside the biblical text.[15] Furthermore, V. Place succeeded Botta at Khorsabad and found more of the layout of the city of Sargon II (Place 1867–70).

Soon thereafter the Englishman, A.H. Layard, began work at Nimrud in 1845.[16] Like Botta, he also thought he had found Nineveh, and his famous work, *Nineveh and its Remains* is in fact primarily a discussion of material

14. Botta and Flandin 1849–50; Botta 1843–44. For a recent discussion of the French involvement in the mid-nineteenth century, see Fontan (ed.) 1994.

15. Moorey 1991: 8. For French interest in Mesopotamian and biblical connections, see Vigouroux 1877.

16. Layard 1849; 1849–53; 1853. A compendium of Layard's (and Botta's) work was done by Bonomi 1852.

from Nimrud. Layard found at Nimrud the first dramatic sculptural link to the Old Testament, the Black Obelisk of Shalmaneser III and the citation concerning Jehu of Israel. This, of course, was not proven until the obelisk was deciphered years later. At this early date there was a general understanding that the Assyrians and Babylonians led away the Israelites and Judahites captive (Sennacherib and Nebuchadnezzar were household names to the European public).[17] Layard's finds were quickly disseminated and became topics for newspapers and popular journals. They impressed British and American societies who were still immersed in Old Testament piety. They not only hoped that Layard's investigations would help provide the correct understanding of Scripture, they were convinced that the Bible had been vindicated by his finds, especially since they believed that it confirmed the destruction of the Assyrian cities as foretold by the biblical prophets. Thus, Layard had to step very carefully as he came to conclusions about the finds and their relevance to the Old Testament, knowing that controversies were brewing back home. But, as long as the texts could not be read with any certainty, nothing could be firmly established.[18] Others, however, were more cynical and supposed that if Layard attached biblical importance to his discoveries, he would become more famous and receive the backing of the religious public.[19] Thus, Layard created a sensation with his books, both in Europe and America.[20] Many of the responses by theologians about the finds were premature and often irresponsible, as they tried to appeal to religious sensibilities (Kildahl 1959: 2-20). However, much of the hoopla about theological fears of the budding discipline of Assyriology was soon displaced with Darwin's revolutionary ideas.

Although both Botta and Layard knew their Bible as well as their classics, neither appeared to be interested in trying to prove the historical

17. Hincks in 1849 had deciphered the names of Esarhaddon and Sennacherib in the Layard's reliefs (1851b: 977); and Grotefend read Shalmaneser (Moorey 1991: 10). See Hincks 1851b; 1852; and H.C. Rawlinson found the names of the Israelite and Judahite kings of Jehu and Menahem in the Assyrian annals, e.g., see Rawlinson 1850. Also see Hincks 1853; 1850.

18. See the discussion in Larsen 1996: 155-64.

19. See Saggs 1984: 306; and Barnett 1960. Layard did not hesitate to make biblical correlations, e.g., 1849 I: 75-76. Unfortunately, many of his preliminary ideas were preached from British pulpits, giving rise to widespread 'logorrhea', according to Kildahl 1959: 55-59, 147-49.

20. Others quickly followed with works of the same ilk; see Vaux 1855; Bonomi 1869. For Layard's influence in Britain and the US, see Kildahl 1959.

veracity of either traditions in regards to Mesopotamia. Of course, the public was interested in the elucidation of the Old Testament, while academics saw in their work an interesting specimen for understanding the evolution of the arts through sculpture and the like (Larsen 1996: 68). But the academic world was somewhat slow in incorporating the material uncovered by them.

In 1852, now ten years after the first excavations in the Tigris-Euphrates region, J.C. Hoefer published *Chaldée, Assyrie, Médie, Babylonie, Méso-potamie, Phénicie, Palmyrène*,[21] where he collected all of the biblical and classical references to Mesopotamia, as well as descriptions of the area by travelers from medieval times to his present. Little, however, was discussed about the new finds. In the same year, E. Hincks and H.C. Rawlinson were able to partially decipher Sennacherib's account of the invasion of Judah, which appears to be remarkably similar to the biblical account in 2 Kgs 18.13-16.[22] At last, many thought there was now convincing proof of the connections of Assyria and Israel, and that the Assyrian texts really did contain information that would help explain Old Testament passages. Although there was initial enthusiasm from the religious community, theologians were not able to explain the discrepancies in the two accounts. Ten years later Rawlinson published a provisional chronology of Assyrian history that provided a datum point for comparing it with biblical history. He also was able to figure out an account of Shalmaneser III's war with Jehu of Israel, which provoked great interest in Great Britain.[23] However, even Rawlinson's brother George, an Anglican clergyman, felt that the investigation of the Assyrian palaces had to be stopped because they came 'uncomfortably close to the holy text'.[24] Henry saw this as 'downright rot'.[25] At any rate, the decipherment of Assyrian cuneiform caused Assyriology to be acknowledged as a legitimate discipline.[26] Although there were apparent contradictions in the Assyrian and

21. Paris: Firmin Didot Frères, 1852.

22. See the discussion by Hincks and Rawlinson in Layard 1853: 118-24.

23. His magnum opus was H. Rawlinson 1860–84.

24. Although he came to see the usefulness of Mesopotamian studies on shedding light upon the Old Testament world; see G. Rawlinson 1862: vi; 1859; 1871.

25. British Library 38977, 219-24, 31 March 1847 (as listed in Larsen 1996: 366); but see G. Rawlinson 1885. At any rate, Hincks was more open to stating biblical connections than was Rawlinson: see Hincks 1862a; 1862b.

26. The decipherment became official when Rawlinson, Talbot, Hincks and Oppert (1857) independently translated an inscription of Tiglath Pileser I.

biblical records, the two disciplines were intertwined, and continued to retain close ties, at least for the time being. By this time, over 50 personal and place names from the Bible had been identified in the Assyrian records (Layard 1849: 626-28). In fact, the natural link between the two disciplines was recognized by the founding of the Society of Biblical Archaeology in London in 1870. The Society's goal was to investigate the archeology and history of Assyria, as well as other biblical lands.

Arguably, the most sensational find of the early periods was made by George Smith, who had been enthralled with the Bible since he was a youth, and was almost obsessed with knowing more about the historical books of the Old Testament (Smith 1875: 9). On 3 December 1872, Smith addressed the Society of Biblical Archaeology and revealed a Babylonian account of the flood story, causing an ecclesiastical and scientific sensation in both Britain and France, even greater than that of Layard's time. Public interest in Mesopotamia was renewed. The flood texts were viewed by the public at the British Museum with great interest. Assyriology was now viewed as a sword to pierce the emerging German school of 'Higher Criticism', which was seen to be undermining the authority of the Old Testament.[27] Smith was offered funding to find the missing portion of the tablet back in northern Iraq. Although the Bible had had priority as having the oldest records of humanity, this new-found deluge text clearly delineated a problem.[28] How was there an earlier version of the Holy Text? Did it no longer have chronological priority? Smith refrained from providing his own interpretation. Was this just a later perverted version from a different religious system, or the origin of all flood stories? In retrospect, these issues ultimately caused the public to be wary of the Assyriology, a discipline which was not regarded as being encumbered with the authority of Scripture. It is at this point that the two disciplines began to drift further apart (Tadmor 1985: 265). Hebrew scholars began to suspect many of the Assyriologist's translations of texts. Based upon the cumulative effect of Assyriological discoveries and finds in other fields, the British resistance to biblical criticism was weakened (Kraeling 1955: 92).

27. Wiseman 1962: 11; Saggs 1999: 78. Many of these scholars, such as J. Wellhausen and R. Smith, were Semiticists who were drawn to biblical comparisons with Arabic studies, rather than Assyriology.

28. Smith 1876. B. Denys, in a review of Smith's work (*The Chaldean Account of Genesis* [London: Thomas Scott, 1877]), was one of the few who appreciated the seriousness of the issue.

Smith's successors in the British Museum continued in his tradition of looking for biblical parallels. W. Boscawen caused a public excitement by claiming that many of the difficulties in the book of Daniel, including the identity of Darius the Mede, had been cleared up.[29] Another Assyriologist interested in biblical connections was A.H. Sayce, an Anglican priest who was a prolific writer who periodically attempted to prove historical details of the Old Testament from Assyrian and Babylonian sources.[30] Sayce identified Nimrod with Gilgamesh, and while others identified from cuneiform sources the kings who fought with Abraham in Genesis 14. Others who were influenced by Smith were T. Pinches (1902), and indirectly S.R. Driver (1904), C.H.W. Johns (who became interested in Assyriology as a boy by reading the works of G. Smith [see Johns 1914]), A.T. Clay (1915; 1922), and L.W. King.[31] We are even told by Wallis Budge that one wealthy banker paid an Assyriologist a retaining fee to look for biblical parallels (Budge 1925: 271). Many imaginary parallels concerning creation (see Delano 1985), paradise,[32] the fall of man, Cain and Abel, and the Tower of Babel were reputedly found.[33] At any rate, by the end of the nineteenth century, Sayce was confident to say that the 'wave of historical skepticism' was ending before its spirit and principles had influenced popular thought (Sayce 1894b).

American involvement (which was slow in manifesting itself)[34] in the Near East stemmed profoundly from its interest in the historical veracity of the Bible and its interest in Semitic studies (see Brown 1888–89; 1909). In fact, the American Oriental Society was formed in 1842, just about the

29. Boscawen's best known work was Boscawen 1903.

30. E.g. see Sayce 1885; 1888; 1891; 1894a; 1895; 1907.

31. King 1918. For a study of King's impact on biblical and Assyriological studies, see Smith 1968.

32. E.g. see Neuman 1876: 66-67. Neuman, an American doctor of divinity, was convinced that 'disentombing' the dead past would go far to strengthen the faith of the weak and to dissipate the doubts of others (see Larsen 1992).

33. Observe the full title of Smith's work; *The Chaldean Account of Genesis containing the Description of the Creation, Fall of Man, the Deluge, the Tower of Babel, the Times of the Patriarchs, and Nimrod; Babylonian Fables, and Legends of the Gods; from the Cuneiform Inscriptions* (Smith 1876).

34. Kildahl (1959: 194-212) argues that the Americans were too preoccupied with domestic concerns until after the Civil War. There were only a handful of works describing the relationship of the new finds to the Bible; e.g. Davis 1852; Kidder 1851; Ward 1870; Tufton 1874; Merrill 1885. For an recent overview of American involvement in the Near East, see Kuklick 1996.

same time as Botta's excavations. A large number of relics were sent to
the US by American missionaries who lived in the Near East. Many of
these items ended up in religious institutions, which provided a religious
context for their interpretation.[35] Nathaniel Schmidt, a professor at Colgate
Divinity School, was actually put on trial for heresy and dismissed, as
many of his translations and interpretations of cuneiform texts were
considered contrary to Scripture.[36]

Many Americans went to Germany to study Assyriology with F.
Delitzsch, since there was no chair of Assyriology in either America or
Great Britain. These included Hilprecht (1903),[37] F. Brown (the first to
teach Akkadian in America),[38] G. Barton,[39] and M. Jastrow (1914), while
W.F. Albright[40] and R.W. Rogers (1908) studied with the German P.
Haupt in the US[41]; all wrote of the connections of the two fields. Brown,
along with Driver, took issue with Sayce's uncritical view that Scripture
had been confirmed by the findings of archeology (Brown 1896: 67;

35. E.g. Andover Theological Seminary, Episcopal Seminary (Alexandria, VA),
and Auburn Theological Seminary; see Merrill 1885. Other religious schools which
taught Akkadian included Baptist Theological Seminary (Newton Centre, MA),
Protestant Episcopal Seminary (Philadelphia, PA), and the Summer School of Hebrew
(Chicago, IL); see Adler 1887.

36. Schmidt left Colgate for Cornell in 1896, where he was able to flourish under
markedly different circumstances; see Bishop 1962: 327. Later on during his tenure at
Cornell, Schmidt suffered persecution, not because of 'heretical' Assyriological views,
but because he refused to buy Liberty bonds during World War I (p. 429).

37. Hilprecht taught Old Testament theology at the University of Erlangen in
Germany and came to Philadelphia in 1886 to become the editor of the *Sunday School
Times* (see the discussion in Meade 1974: 35-37).

38. At Union Theological Seminary at New York, beginning in 1880. For his work
on bridging the two disciplines, see Brown (1891), where he warned theologians not to
discount the factual discoveries made by Assyriology nor to cause these facts to be fit
into the corresponding biblical model. Brown, like W.F. Albright later, eventually
devoted more time to Hebrew studies.

39. Barton 1916 was immensely popular and was reprinted many times.

40. It will be remembered that the great orientalist Albright began his career in
Assyriology, and was somewhat skeptical of the historicity of the biblical traditions:
see Long 1993. His unpublished doctoral dissertation was on the Assyrian flood
account (1916a). Many of his early articles were assyriological in nature; e.g. 1915;
1916b.

41. See Meade 1974. Haupt was editor of *The Sacred Books of the Old Testament*
(Leipzig: J.C. Hinrichs, 1893–1904), where he assembled scholars to do critical
editions of Old Testament books.

Driver 1909; Sayce 1894a). Brown, however, was a positivist when it came to the historicity of Scripture in its relationship with the Assyrian texts:

> When an Assyrian statement can be equally well explained in two different ways, we have the right, and are bound, as we should be in all historical study, to take that explanation which harmonizes with a corresponding Biblical statement (Brown 1891: 23).

With the impetus of de Sarzec's spectacular finds at Tello in the 1880s, the American Oriental Society, Archeological Institute of America, and the Society of Biblical Literature all began lobbying for an American expedition to Babylonia. A number of scholars (acting on their own, and not as representatives of any of the societies) came together to organize an expedition that would find material that supported contemporary interpretations of the Old Testament (Ward 1886: 5). A team was assembled to dig at Nippur in southern Mesopotamia, headed by the Reverend J. Peters and the German trained Assyriologist H.V. Hilprecht. Though the two did not always see eye to eye, the expeditions (1889–1900) collected thousands of texts which continue to be housed at the University Museum of the University of Pennsylvania and studied by Assyriologists.[42] The French finds at Susa of the Code of Hammurabi about this time also spurred interest in biblical parallels (see Cook 1904). Assyriology was also beginning to flourish in the late nineteenth century in Italy, Scandinavia, and Holland (Budge 1925: 241-44).

The Germans also showed an interest in making biblical connections with the Near East by at least 1880.[43] E. Schrader published *Die Keilinschriften und das Alte Testament* (1885–88), a model of thorough scholarship that helped lead to the founding of the Deutsche Orient Gesellschaft (German Oriental Society) in 1898,[44] which led to the German excavations in Babylon and Assur. We are told that 'every student of Hebrew or of Assyrian consulted it, every Old Testament commentator quoted from it or made reference to it' (see Rogers 1912: xvii). Thus, it led many to be interested in biblical comparisons. In particular, H. Gunkel attacked the recent arguments of J. Wellhausen for the late dating of

42. See Hilprecht 1908; and Peters 1899. See the recent evaluation of the controversy in Kuklick 1996: 123-40.

43. For German (esp. in Berlin) work in the Near East, see Renger 1979. Schrader published a volume on Israelite prehistory as early as 1863. Also see Delitzsch 1881.

44. One of its purposes was to elucidate the world of the Bible; see Larsen 1987: 102.

Genesis 1 by showing close parallels with it and Babylonian mythology,[45] while F. Hommel (1897) studied comparative traditions of Israel and Babylonia.[46]

By the end of the nineteenth century Old Testament scholars still ignored much of the textual material that might have put Babylonian civilization in a good light. They naively argued for the great superiority of Hebrew monotheism. But the Assyriologists fought back and defended the ethical and spiritual system of Babylonia, and even its ethical superiority. F. Delitzsch[47] argued against the high-handed manner with which his subject was viewed by Old Testament scholars.[48] Some argued that many Hebrew ideas actually originated in Mesopotamia and were borrowed by Israel. Much of this is understandable, if one realizes that before this, Assyriology had been seen as less than an auxiliary science of Old Testament and classical antiquity studies (see Zimmern 1889). The idea of Babylonian primacy was perfected by Delitzsch in 1902–1903.[49] In his lectures, he argued that Israel could only be studied in light of Babylonia, and in fact Israelite civilization was derived from Babylonia. Thus, comparative analysis was ultimately not productive, since Babylonia was the source of Hebrew civilization. He then argued that many Babylonian features were still clung to by the Judeo-Christian religious tradition (by way of the Old Testament). Thus, in a series of lectures, Assyriology went from an innocent scholarly pursuit to a discipline that had direct relevance to modern religion. Delitzsch also claimed that the divine name Yahweh was found in the Hammurabi code.[50] In the second lecture, Delitzsch argued against the divine inspiration of Scripture, went so far as to say that the Old Testament had dubious relevance for Christianity, and claimed

45. Gunkel 1885. Gunkel took issue with Wellhausen's isolationist view, as he refused to recognize the influence of Egypt and Mesopotamia upon Israelite literature.

46. Also done by the Dutch; e.g. Eerdmans 1891.

47. Budge (1925: 289) tells us that Delitzsch 'had heard a supernatural voice which assured him that he was to be George Smith's successor'. One can only assume that it was Enki, the friend of humankind.

48. He also had an antipathy for the Old Testament; see the discussion by Finkelstein 1958: 432.

49. Delitzsch 1902. There have been numerous discussions by Assyriologists and others of Delitzsch's famous lectures. In the early years, see e.g., Kittel 1903; Hommel 1902; Jensen 1902; and D. Gunkel 1903. For more recent reviews, see e.g., Finkelstein 1958; Reventlow 1983; Ebach 1986: 26-44; Huffmon 1987; Johanning 1988; Lehnmann 1994; and Larsen 1995.

50. Since disproved, see Huffmon 1971.

that Jesus was a Galilean and not even a Semite.[51] He also countered that the Old Testament was intellectually inferior to the Babylonian tradition. Predictably, the religious communities in Germany, Great Britain, and the US reacted negatively to his lectures. H. Gunkel (1904) complained about his naivety in knowledge of biblical interpretation and the history of religion. However, biblical scholars could not argue with him concerning Assyriological matters. Others vehemently argued against the idea of the ethical inferiority of the Old Testament, but primarily from doctrinal rather than strictly academic grounds.[52] The third lecture bordered on anti-Semitism, as Delitzsch emphasized the non-Semitic roots of Mesopotamian civilization. Delitzsch went so far as to say that, since the Old Testament was entirely superfluous to the Christian church, one should rather read German cultural folk epics. He even advocated replacing the Old Testament with W. Schwaner's *Germanen-Bibel aus heiligen Schriften germanischer Volker*, which was a compilation of German folk traditions and theological ideas (Schwaner 1910). In fact, the Israelite Scriptures should no longer be considered as stemming from divine revelation, since they did not stand up to the scrutiny of science and scholarship. Those who continued to believe in the Scriptures were steeped in ignorance and apathy. Moreover, he was explicit in his defense of German nationalism, and the fact that those Germans who studied the tablets and excavated on the mounds of Mesopotamia did it for 'Germany's honor'. Most scholars, however, did not argue with his thesis directly. Delitzsch did show that the Babylonians had reached a high level of ethical and spiritual thought. Although many of his arguments can easily be refuted today (e.g. the Babylonian connections with the Hebrew Sabbath), they could not be so at the turn of the century because of an imprecise knowledge of Akkadian. The biblical scholars refused to appreciate Babylonian religion on its own terms and merits (see Finkelstein 1958: 438). The famous German New Testament scholar A. Harnack (1903) said that Delitszch had said nothing new, although the general public was now part of the debate.

The response of the Assyriologists was to be very cautious and circumspect; in fact, most withdrew from the public scene. Delitzsch, however, was profoundly influential in the field because he trained many German, British, and American Assyriologists, including, R.F. Harper, D.G. Lyon, R.W. Rogers (1912), P. Haupt, C. Bezold, P. Jensen, and H. Zimmern.

---

51. For this treatment, see Davies 1975.

52. See Skinner 1910; even the Assyriologist Heidel (1946) indirectly hinted at the inferiority of Babylonian religion.

Delitzsch's lectures had an impact not only on Assyriology and biblical studies but on critical theology as well (Larsen 1995: 97). The triumphant view that Assyriology and its discoveries had vindicated the biblical record and its historicity had been permanently marred. After all, Israel was only a small part of a much larger ancient Near Eastern world that had constant interaction with each other (see Winckler 1906a: 15).

Delitzsch made public the views of many Assyriologists, who now espoused to a school of thought called 'Pan-Babylonianism', championed by H. Winckler, who argued that all world myths were reflections of Babylonian astral religion which had developed about 3000 BCE.[53] H. Zimmern argued that the Babylonian creation epic was an older version of the New Testament and that the story of Christ's passion was nothing but a repetition of the 'myth of Bel-Marduk of Babylon'.[54] P. Jensen argued that the Mesopotamian myths (Gilgamesh in particular) were the foundation for all world folk tales, including the Bible (Jensen 1890; 1906; 1924). Israelite history was simply a series of repetitions of the Gilgamesh story. Even the story of Jesus of Nazareth was simply a retelling of Gilgamesh. In fact, the Kaiser himself jumped on the 'Babel bandwagon' and argued that Jesus was a non-Jew who actually opposed the message of the Old Testament. Other German scholars at the turn of the century argued for all cosmology and other items coming from Babylon.[55] Delitzsch himself continued to hold to his views (Delitzsch 1920; 1921). The Pan-Babylonians, however, were considered indiscriminate in their hypotheses, and most of their extreme ideas were rejected by both biblical and Assyriological scholars.[56] Pan-Babylonism did leave its mark to some extent on biblical studies. For example, Old Testament scholars such as H. Gunkel[57] and A. Jeremias (1911) began to examine literary types in the Old Testament in the light of Mesopotamian literature. Biblical scholars now

53. Evidently first coined by Jeremias (1906) in his preface; also see 1904. Jeremias (1903) also commented on Delitzsch's famous lectures. Pan-babylonianism was spread largely through the efforts of Winckler 1901; 1905; and 1907a.

54. Zimmern 1906–18; 1901; 1910. Also see Radau 1908.

55. Winckler also discussed Pan-Babylonianism, *Babel und Bibel*, and other issues in 1906b; 1906c; 1907b.

56. E.g. Schmidt 1908 and Kugel 1910. Clay (1890) led the charge to discredit Pan-Babylonism in America.

57. Though Gunkel complained about the extreme methods of Delitzsch, he took advantage of using Mesopotamian literary themes to understand the Old Testament; see Gunkel 1904.

began to accept the fact that the Bible could be studied in the context of the ancient Near East (see Kittel 1921; Gressman 1924). Thus, the massive corpus of Assyriological literature began to be used to illuminate the entirety of ancient Near Eastern culture, not just ad hoc Old Testament literary and historical problems.[58]

By the 1920s Assyriologists began to de-emphasize the theme of origins, and were now intent to stress the distinctive elements of Mesopotamian civilization.[59] Thus, they attempted to assert their autonomy,[60] calling for the study of Mesopotamia for its own sake.[61] B. Landsberger argued that any culture is conceptually autonomous (like the great German thinker Johann Herder)[62] and would be misunderstood if viewed from the concepts of another culture.[63] But Landsberger understood that because of the sheer amount of textual material the Assyriologist has at his/her disposal, they have rarely been afforded the time to reflect upon their discipline and determine its long-term goals. At any rate, the Assyriologist has left undefined its relationship with biblical studies, let alone its relationship to world history (Wiseman 1962).

Ur

The 1920s also saw a flurry of spectacular discoveries in Mesopotamia that appeared to have relevance to the Bible. At the site of Ur (the biblical Ur of the Chaldees), C.L. Woolley, a follower of Sayce (rather than S.R. Driver), was not only convinced he had found the city of Abraham (Woolley 1936), but also believed he had found the biblical flood, which he announced to the world in 1929. He was contrasted by the Assyriologist S. Langdon, who argued that the flood deposits found at Kish more closely resembled that mentioned in the Gilgamesh epic (Woolley 1930). These

58. See the discussion by Saggs 1969: 13.

59. Although see Hehn 1913; Stummer 1922; and Bonkamp 1939.

60. Still, some comparative studies of Israel and Mesopotamia continued: e.g. Ermoni 1910 and Castellino 1940.

61. E.g. Landsberger 1926; even Landsberger (1967) occasionally wrote on biblical comparisons; as did his colleague, Poebel 1932.

62. Even Herder had dreamt of the rediscovery of the ancient Near East for the purposes of understanding the origins of European civilization; see the discussion in Larsen 1987: 96-97.

63. Oppenheim (1977: 21-22) has echoed this concern about scholars who have attempted to connect Assyriological data with the Old Testament in some acceptable way, and others who find haphazard comparisons.

ideas have spawned many articles which have discussed the flood's historicity (or lack thereof).[64]

Nuzi

The cuneiform texts discovered at the excavations at Nuzi (1925–31) have long been a mine of comparative information for the Old Testament.[65] E. Chiera, the first director of the Nuzi excavations had received a Bachelor of Divinity and Master of Theology from Crozer Theological Seminary, and was thus sensitive to these issues. Furthermore, R.H. Pfeiffer, also one of the Nuzi directors, was educated at the Theological School of Geneva and received a Bachelor of Divinity from the University of Geneva in 1915. Very soon after their discovery, there was a flurry of scholarship observing the striking putative parallels to the biblical Patriarchs in the socio-economic and legal spheres.[66] The consensus was that the two also must have shared the same chronological proximity.

However, in the past generation there has been no consensus as to the relative importance of the Nuzi material for biblical studies, especially with the impetus of the publication of other Nuzi texts.[67] There has been a re-evaluation,[68] and some have rejected any Nuzi connections to the Bible altogether.[69] However, the academic pendulum has swung back to the middle, with what B. Eichler calls a 'more sobering and responsible attitude toward the usefulness and importance of the Nuzi tablets and the Bible' (Eichler 1989: 107-19). Though the Nuzi–biblical parallels cannot solve chronological issues, they are a source of documentation for the socio-economic practices in Mesopotamia, which will help illuminate biblical law and practices (Selman 1983; Eichler 1989: 107-19). Thus, many have agreed with the rules of comparative method listed by W.M. Clark (1977: 143), although there are still many concerns about biblical

64. See Mallowan 1964; Raikes 1966. However, there are skeptics (Lenzen 1964) and those who hold to the symbolic meaning of the flood (Kilmer 1972; Carter 1977).

65. View the preliminary statements by S. Smith 1926.

66. E.g. S. Smith 1932; Chiera 1932–33; Ginsberg and Maisler 1933; Mendelsohn 1935; Gordon 1935a; 1935b; 1935c; 1935d; 1936; 1937; 1940; Burrows 1937; 1940; Lewy 1938; 1939; 1940; Speiser 1938; 1940; 1964; 1955; 1967; Albright 1961.

67. See the discussion in Eichler 1989: 112.

68. Beginning with de Vaux 1949; Greenberg 1962; Van Seters 1968; 1969; Mullo-Weir 1967–68; 1967; and Freedman 1970.

69. Van Seters 1975: 65-103; Thompson 1974: 196-297; 1978. Also, see Thompson's most recent work 1999.

connections (Morrison 1983). Other text collections (e.g. from Alalakh and Emar) show that the Nuzi customs may have been common throughout a wide chronological and geographic range, while others have argued that first millennium BCE customs are more relevant for the biblical sphere (or not relevant at all).[70]

Ugarit

Arguably, over the past 70 years there has been more written concerning the relationship of Ugarit and the Bible than any other single Syro-Mesopotamian site. The first generation saw a flurry of activity to show numerous parallels with Ugarit and the Bible, both real and imagined, as P. Craigie has noted.[71] There was the usual novelty of studying newly found materials that led to hasty conclusions (Craigie 1979a), but on the whole there was not much excess in comparative studies.[72] There were, however, specific studies that elucidated comparisons between Psalm 29 and selections of Ugaritic poetry,[73] although many have seen these connections as more complicated than first supposed (Fensham 1963a; Craigie 1972; 1979b). Ginsberg (1945) also saw a comparison with Deut. 14.21 and an Ugaritic text that had a line that Virolleaud translated 'cook a kid in milk' (Virolleaud 1933), although some have argued that this connection is tenuous (Craigie 1977a). By the 1960s new developments arose. New mythical and liturgical texts from Ugarit were discovered that initially raised excitement among comparative scholars (see Gray 1978). However, some argued that the connections between the two were ambiguous at best, and problematic (see Smith 1952). M. Dahood argued that the Hebrew language had to be relearned in light of new data from Ugarit.[74] But, over the years, many have claimed that a 'Pan-Ugaritism' has

---

70. Again, see Van Seters 1968; 1975; and Thompson 1974.

71. Albright (1966: 6-7) was at the forefront of this.

72. See Jack 1935; de Vaux 1937; Baumgartner 1938; 1940; 1941; 1947; Dussaud 1937; de Langhe 1945; Patton 1944; Ginsberg 1945; and Coppens 1946. Later surveys include Rainey 1965; Kapelrud 1965; Jacob 1960; Pfeiffer 1962; Gray 1957; 1978; Barker 1976; Mihalic 1981; Cazelles 1985; O'Connor 1987; and Loretz 1990a.

73. Ginsberg (1938) theorized about the idea that Ps. 29 was originally a Phoenican hymn. This was substantiated by Gaster 1946–47; Cross 1950; Freedman 1972.

74. Dahood 1962; 1966–70; 1968; and numerous articles in 1972–81. For a recent critique of Dahood's comparisons, see Loretz 1972; 1987; 1990b; Talmon 1978b; Schroer 1980; Caquot 1988; Curtis 1994; and Barr 1994.

resulted,[75] primarily because of the large Claremont project directed by L. Fisher (Fisher *et al.* 1972–81) and the large amount of works by Dietrich and Loretz.[76]

The past 30 years has seen a reasoned analysis of comparisons in many areas.[77] Craigie has argued that the literary comparisons of Ugarit and Israel are flawed since the two traditions used different literary forms (Fisher and Knutson 1969; Craigie 1971). Others have argued against the comparative school of Dahood (Stuart 1976). Still, comparative analysis of poetic imagery (e.g. Watson 1976; Cross 1973: 112-44; Craigie 1974; 1978), parallel word pairs (Cassuto 1971: 25-32), and poetic meter continue (Gibson 1978: 140; Loretz and Kottsieper 1987). J. Barr (1968) has urged caution for the use of Ugaritic to establish new etymologies for Hebrew. Others have argued a connection of feudalism in Ugarit and in the Bible (see Gray 1952). There have been many comparisons of Ugaritic and Hebrew religion, most of which emphasized the undeniable contrasts between the two, but later studies have shown a continuity between them.[78] Hebrew Poetry and Ugaritic connections have been studied by Albright (1944) and his students.[79] At any rate, the recent works on Ugarit and the Bible are numerous.[80]

Mari

Mari is a prime example of the need of caution of the use of the comparative method, since interesting comparisons can often lead to shallow or extreme conclusions. Both W.F. Albright (1956: 256) and A. Parrot, the great excavator of Mari (the son of a Lutheran minister and devout in his own right), succumbed to making direct but ultimately unconvincing connections between the Mari population and the Patriarchs, and the tribe

75. Criticized by de Moor and van der Lugt 1974; Craigie 1977b; Donner 1967; and Held 1974.

76. *Ugarit Forschungen and Alter Orient und Altes Testament.*

77. For a comparison of the literary relationships, see Craigie 1971; and Healey 1984.

78. Kaiser 1962; Habel 1964; Clifford 1972; Schmidt 1966; Miller 1973; Albright 1968; van der Toorn 1991; L'Heureux 1974; de Moor and Sandars 1991.

79. Cross and Freedman 1948; 1950; Cross 1955; 1968; 1973; Freedman 1976; and Robertson 1972.

80. Curtis 1985; Craigie 1983; Brooke, Curtis and Healey 1994; Pope 1994; and Petersen 1998. A recent ASOR Plenary Session in Orlando, Florida (18 November 1998) featured A.R. Millard and D. Pardee speaking on the subject of 'Ugarit and the Bible'.

Benjamin, in particular.[81] Parrot, however, did revitalize biblical archeology for the French-speaking public in a way not seen since Botta.

Since the commencement of the publication of Mari texts after World War II, and because of the connection of Mari being in the reputed homeland of the patriarchs (Gibson 1962; Mathews 1981; 1986), there have been numerous examples of comparative research in the field of personal names (e.g. Jean 1954), tribal organization (Malamat 1962; 1968), rituals (Speiser 1958), and other various Israelite customs (Cazelles 1967; Malamat 1973). One of the most discussed comparisons are the Mari prophetic texts.[82] However, E. Noort has argued that the relationship between the two prophetic traditions is ambiguous at best.[83] But the Israelite and Mari material need to be seen as two separate corpora, even if similar (Malamat 1989: 27-29). He advocates a typological or phenomoenological method. Efforts should be concentrated on examining typical phenomena, seeking out common sets of concepts and practices and institutions. One must not forget the immense chronological gap between the two corpora. When such similarities are seen in aggregate, they cannot simply be seen as representing common patterns of human nature.[84] Proper comparisons also involve the contrasting approach. The very nature of the source material is fundamentally different, as the Mari texts are first hand daily material, while the biblical text has been processed, and composed later than its events (see Malamat 1983). As with Ugarit, there are many current studies on the relationship of Mari and the Bible.[85]

Alalakh

When Woolley began working at Alalakh in 1937, he was interested in finding evidence of cultural connections between Syria and the eastern Mediterranean area.[86] Though not directly related to the Bible, the Alalakh

---

81. Parrot 1950; 1954; 1962; 1967. Mari had been a site of major concern for biblical scholars soon after the commencement of the excavations; see Bea 1940.

82. Among the more recent are: Schult 1966; Huffmon 1968; Buss 1969; Moran 1969; Ross 1970; Craghan 1975; Ellermeier 1977; Schmitt 1982; Sasson 1983; Malamat 1987; Parker 1993; and Barstad 1993.

83. Noort 1977; and the review by Sasson 1980.

84. On the comparative approach, see Gelb 1980; Millard 1983; and Lemaire 1985.

85. See the 'Table ronde sur Mari et la Bible', in *RA* 92.1-2 (1998) and 93.1 (1999); and Malamat 1998.

86. The excavations were from 1937–39 and 1946–49; see Woolley 1955, and a more popular account, Woolley 1953.

material has been considered to shed light on the greater Syro-Palestinian context of the Bible (see Tsevat 1958). The ubiquitous Habiru have also been found there, but are viewed as an important mercenary class in the Alalakh texts. This term, of course, has been compared to the biblical term Hebrew on many occasions.[87] Moreover, some Assyriologists have argued that the biographical inscription of Idrimi appears to anticipate the biographical stories of Joseph and David (Oppenheim 1955; Buccellati 1962), and has even been compared to the Jepthah story in Judges 11.[88] At any rate, the Alalakh material has been considered a valuable source of comparative (and contrastive) material (see Wiseman 1967). Like Nuzi, the customs (e.g. marriage contracts) at Alalakh have been compared to the Patriarchal periods, although it is admitted that the parallels from Alalakh are less clear (Hess 1994: 204). Certainly the connection of Alalakh *hupsu* ('poor') with Hebrew *hopsi* ('poor') is vague at best (Hess 1994: 208-209). As with Nuzi, J. Van Seters has rejected the Alalakh comparisons with the Patriarchal narratives (Van Seters 1975: 100-103). R. Hess in this volume argues that the cumulative weight of comparisons with the Bible shows a common cultural milieu for both. He argues that we need to view Alalakh comparisons on a case by case basis (Hess 1994: 199-215).

Ebla

No Syro-Mesopotamian site in recent memory has appealed to the religious sensibilities of those interested in biblical studies more than Tell Mardikh/Ebla.[89] The Italians under, P. Matthiae, labored there for over 12 years before they uncovered a large cache of cuneiform tablets in the room of a palace (1974–76).[90] The epigrapher G. Pettinato (1980) called the script used there 'proto-Canaanite', a potential ancestor to biblical Hebrew. For the next five years many exceptional and unsubstantiated claims were made about the significance of the Ebla texts and their relationship to the Bible, many of which came from those who had never seen the texts, or were not familiar with cuneiform. Nonetheless, there was also much

87. There are numerous studies concerning the Habiru; Bottéro 1954; Greenberg 1955; Loretz 1984a; and Na'aman 1986.

88. Greenstein and Marcus 1976: 76-77. At any rate, the Alalakh material has been considered a valuable source of comparative (and contrastive) material.

89. For an overview of the controversies of Ebla and the Bible to 1979, see Bermant and Weitzman 1979.

90. General works on Ebla include, Matthiae 1981; and Pettinato 1981.

speculation among the scholarly world (Pettinato 1976; 1980; Freedman 1978). D.N. Freedman made his conclusions about the earlier historical context for the biblical patriarchs based upon unpublished Ebla tablets, which were preliminarily read by M. Dahood and Pettinato.[91] Dahood made many preliminary statements concerning the connection between Ugaritic forms and Eblaite (e.g. the fact that Ebla sheds light on the Minor Prophets).[92] The present consensus is that Ebla has no bearing on the Minor Prophets, the historical accuracy of the biblical Patriarchs, Yahweh worship, or Sodom and Gomorrah (see Merrill 1983). Many of these preliminary analyses came into the popular press as truth, and thus great amounts of misinformation leaked to the public.[93]

The second epigrapher, A. Archi spent some effort in refuting many of the premises of Dahood and Pettinato, ignoring most of the sensationalism, primarily from the American press (Archi 1979; 1981). He argued that the supposed evidence for Yahweh at Ebla was questionable and ambiguous, and that the kings of Ebla were not anointed like the kings of Israel (contra Pettinato 1977), the function of Eblaite judges does not appear to be like that of Israel, there is no Genesis creation story (Pettinato 1977: 231-32), and Ebla place names do not easily correspond to the Bible names or the 'cities of the plain'.[94] The Eblaite connections with the Hebrew language are unclear.[95]

The excitement concerning the Ebla material has somewhat died down. In Pettinato's more recent works there is still a discussion concerning biblical connections, primarily in the field of geography (Pettinato 1991: 179-80; Hallo 1992). The trend has been to exhibit the fact that Ebla has an importance all of its own as an incipient Old Syrian civilization at the advent of urbanism. Thus, in the past 15 years, only a miniscule amount of effort has been put to comparisons of Ebla and the Bible, compared to the large amount of work on the civilization of Ebla itself. This is preferable.[96]

---

91. Dahood and Pettinato 1982 (a large bibliography of newspaper and popular articles was compiled by M. O'Connor: 331-35); Dahood 1978; 1979; 1981a; 1982; 1984; and 1987.

92. Dahood 1983a; and Shea 1983. Greenfield (1988) argues that a little restraint would have stopped some of these extraordinary theories.

93. With the help of H. Shanks, editor of *BARev*.

94. Echoed by Biggs 1980.

95. Dahood 1978: 81-112. For a reasoned view of Ebla in its Palestinian context, see Vigano and Pardee 1984.

96. See for language, Dahood 1982; 1984; Müller 1984; Baldacci 1987; Althann 1983. For religion, see Dahood 1981b; 1983b; Müller 1981; and Loretz 1984b.

Emar

Although it has not had the publicity of either Ebla, Mari, or for that matter Ugarit, the texts of Emar may shed more light on biblical customs than do the other textual corpora. Emar is physically closer to Israel than any of the others. Emar was fated to be in the background of the Ebla controversies of the late 1970s and 1980s. The construction of the Tabqa Dam in Syria caused the Middle Euphrates site of Emar to be regarded as a salvage project, commenced by a French team in 1972 (see Margueron 1995). Six seasons of work were sandwiched into five years (1972–76; see Pitard 1996: 14). Nearly 2000 texts were found, most of which were published a decade later by D. Arnaud (1985–86). Thus, the excitement surrounding the other textual corpora has been slow in coming with Emar. The research concerning Emar and biblical studies has thus far been reasoned and tentative (see, e.g., Arnaud 1979; 1981; Tsukimoto 1989; Fleming 1995). This, however, in light of past experience, is likely to change. Emar was evidently not ever a great kingdom in its own right. The site of Imar was mentioned in both the Ebla and Mari archives, and later became a Hittite protectorate in the Late Bronze Age. The relationship of Emar to biblical studies is, as D. Fleming says in this volume, most striking in the religious sphere. The concept of anointing is found at Emar, as the NIN.DINGER priestess is anointed on the first day of the festival (Fleming 1992). The Emar festivals have various requirements that may be compared to the Levitical regulations (Fleming 1995: 144), and the elements of the biblical festival system have some correspondence to the *zukru* calendar (Fleming 1995: 144; and his essay in this volume, see below). Emar also has the prophetic office of *nabu*, already well known at Mari (Fleming 1995: 145). Others have argued that the Emar inheritance texts bear a resemblance to the Nuzi material, and thus to Genesis 31 (see Huehnergard 1985), while still others claim that Emar 'provides an empirical model for the Mesopotamian textual tradition, exemplifying the possibilities of transmission to Iron Age Israel' (Hoskisson 1991: 21-32). B. Schmidt has recognized connections concerning the care of the dead at Emar and Israel (Schmidt 1992). Fleming concludes that Emar's mixed urban and small-town Syrian communal life offers a closer social comparison for Israel that even Ugarit (Fleming 1995: 147). At any rate, Emar's indigenous ritual texts represent a unique source of understanding ancient Syrian religions, with texts that are distinct from the Ugaritic corpus.

Synthesis

The tendency in the last 30 years has been to overemphasize the importance of new discoveries to the Old Testament, and then when the flaws become obvious, approach comparative data from the standpoint of skepticism, causing many to completely ignore comparative material altogether (Roberts 1985: 96). Scholars have had difficulty between 'paralellomania' and isolating the culture in question. The comparative method has been attacked as a form of 'pseudorthodoxzy'.[97] One scholar who has attempted the middle ground between the comparative and contrastive methods is W.W. Hallo, who espouses a contextual method, which emphasizes both similarities (comparative) and differences (contrastive), also looking for diachronic and synchronic variations.[98] Hallo's goal, 'is not to find the key to every biblical phenomenon in some ancient Near Eastern precedent, but rather to silhouette the biblical text against its wider literary and cultural environment' (Hallo 1991: 24). Thus, we must not succumb either to 'parallelomania'[99] or to 'parallellophobia'.[100]

Since World War II there has been an explosion of comparative studies of Israel and Mesopotamia from scholars of both fields. There have been a number of collections of primary source materials from the ancient Near East and their relationships to the Bible.[101] The primary English volumes were compiled by J. Pritchard and others.[102] Other works include general studies (Müller 1991), literature,[103] pictoral studies (Keel 1974; 1977;

97. M. Smith 1969 and even advocating a 'contrasting' method; Hallo 1977 but see the caveat by Roberts 1976.

98. Apparently first coined by Parker (1979–80) who emphasizes both similarities (comparative) and differences (contrastive), also looking for diachronic and synchronic variations (Hallo 1980). Hallo has led four National Endowment for the Humanities Summer Seminars which have had this as its primary theme: *SIC* 1; *SIC* 2; *SIC* 3; *SIC* 4. See the review of *SIC* 1 by Pardee 1985; also see van der Toorn 1985.

99. Sandmel (1962) describes it as 'that extravagance among scholars which first overdoes the supposed similarity in passages and then proceeds to describe source and derivation as if implying literary connection flowing in an inevitable or predetermined direction', p. 1.

100. See the discussion of Ratner and Zuckerman 1986.

101. Since the publication of Winckler 1892; Gressman 1909; and Galling 1950.

102. Since 1945, see, *DOTT*; *ANET*; Beyerlin 1978; *COS*; and Matthews and Benjamin 1997.

103. Lambert 1954; Kramer 1959; Lowenstam 1980; Soll 1988; Walton 1989; and Gordon and Rendsberg 1997.

1978), women (Frymer-Kensky 1989; 1992; van der Toorn 1994), sacrifice (Hallo 1987), religion,[104] prophecy (H. Weippert 1985; Millard 1985), cosmology (Heidel 1946; 1951; Lambert 1965; Saggs 1978), law,[105] treaties,[106] hymns and psalms,[107] wisdom,[108] death and the afterlife (Lewis 1989; Tropper 1989; 1994), genealogies (Malamat 1968; Wilson 1977), and historical literature (Speiser 1957; Albrektson 1967; Younger 1990; and various contributions in *FTH*).

Many have viewed the past century and a half of relations of Mesopotamia and the Bible to be cyclical in nature.[109] Typically, there was a furor because of the announcement of a rumor that a large archive was found that had the potential of verifying the biblical text. Often, unverified statements were made by conservative Old Testament scholars who were concerned about the historicity of the text (which is not to say that the subject of historicity has no place in biblical studies). Of course, the publication of a selected portion of an archive causes excitement because of the supposed biblical parallels. However, the publication of a larger corpus permits the more precise contexts for many of these parallels, but the Assyriologist then shows the uniqueness of the area in question. The philologist begins to show that the linguistic parallels are superficial. It often takes time for the biblical scholar interested in parallels to appreciate the Assyriologist's contributions. J. Sasson has promoted some goals that should be set forth before making biblical connections; what are the

104. de Fraine 1954; Draffkorn 1957; de Jonge 1959; Moran 1965; Gamper 1966; Weippert 1972; McKay 1973; Cogan 1974; Wright 1987; Gammie and Perdue 1990; Dietrich and Loretz 1992; Bottéro 1993b; and van der Toorn 1997.

105. Szlechter 1954; Mendenhall 1954; Greenberg 1960; Yaron 1970; Paul 1970; Lambert 1972; Boecker 1980; van der Toorn 1985; Westbrook 1985; and Epstein 1986.

106. Other than Mendenhall (1955), most biblical scholars have either ignored or paid scant attention to Wiseman's publication of the vassal treaties of Esarhaddon (Wiseman 1958). Mendenhall wrote before their discovery. This is in spite of the fact that Assyriologists have shown stark similarities between the treaties and Deut. 28 (Borger 1961; and Frankena 1965). See Fensham 1962; 1963b; Hillers 1964; 1969; Weinfeld 1970; 1973; and McCarthy 1978.

107. A few works were devoted to this before World War II, e.g., Driver 1926; and Widengren 1936. More recent works include Dalglish 1962; Hallo 1968; Gerstenberger 1971; and Ferris 1992.

108. Noth and Winton Thomas 1955; Gray 1970; Cooper 1971; Sasson 1973; Waltke 1979; and Weinfeld 1988.

109. Sasson 1980: 128-30. Much of the remainder of the paragraph comes from Sasson, and Greenspahn 1991: 6.

differences in contexts? Are the texts in question the same literary genre? Is etymological kinship always useful in helping to make comparisons (Sasson 1980: 129)?

I end this survey with an admonition from a prominent Assyriologist:

> We shall always have with us the third- and fourth-hand popularizers who will pound and mash significant additions to the fund of knowledge into an amorphous and misleading pabulum for the consumption of the semi-literate. The field of biblical history and archeology has had more than its fair share of treatment. But it is quite another thing for reputed scholars in the field to lend their own prestige and authority to similar endeavors... I believe that the first responsibility of such scholars after the requirements of their own researches is to inform the truly literate portion of the general public...of the very substantial gains made in recent decades toward our understanding of the Bible, and the world of which it was a part. And this must be done in a way that can inspire the confidence of the educated lay public in the methods and critical standards of biblical scholarship (Finkelstein 1958: 349).

BIBLIOGRAPHY

Adler, C.
1887 'Review of *Les Langues perdues de la perse et de l'Assyrie*', *Andover Review* 8: 44.

Albrektson, B.
1967 *History and the Gods* (Lund: C.W.K. Gleerup).

Albright, W.F.
1915 'The Conclusion of Esarhaddon's Broken Prism', *JAOS* 35: 391-93.
1916a 'The Assyrian Deluge Epic' (PhD dissertation, The Johns Hopkins University).
1916b 'The Eighth Campaign of Sargon', *JAOS* 36: 226-32.
1944 'The Oracles of Balaam, *JBL* 63: 207-33.
1956 *The Archaeology of Palestine* (Harmondsworth: Penguin Books).
1961 'Abram the Hebrew: A New Archaeological Interpretation', *BASOR* 163: 36-54.
1966 *New Horizons in Biblical Research* (London: Oxford University Press).
1968 *Yahweh and the Gods of Canaan* (Garden City, NY: Doubleday).

Althann, R.
1983 'Psalms 58,10 in the Light of Ebla', *Bib* 64: 123-25.

Archi, A.
1979 'The Epigraphic Evidence from Ebla and the Old Testament', *Bib* 60: 556-66.
1981 'Further Concerning Ebla and the Bible', *BA* 44: 145-54.

Arnaud, D.
1979 'Meskéné-Emar et l'Ancien Testament', *RHR* 116-19.

1981   'La religion à Emar', *Le Monde de la Bible* 20: 34.
1985–86   *Recherches au pays d'Aštata: Emar VI* (Paris: Editions Recherche sur les Civilisations).

Baldacci, M.
1987   'The Eblaite PN ish-ta-mar ᵈda-gan and Micah 6,16a', *AO* 5: 144-46.

Barker, K.
1976   'The Value of Ugaritic for Old Testament Studies', *BSac* 133: 119-30.

Barnett, R.
1960   'Canning and Cuneiform: A Century of Assyriology', *The Museum Journal* 60.8: 192-200.

Barr, J.
1968   *Comparative Philology and the Text of the Old Testament* (Oxford: Clarendon Press).
1987   *Comparative Philology and the Text of the Old Testament* (Winona Lake, IN: Eisenbrauns, 2nd edn).
1994   'Philology and Exegesis: Some General Remarks, with Illustrations from Job 3', in C. Brekelmans (ed.), *Questions disputées d'Ancien Testament* (Leuven: Leuven University Press): 39-61.

Barstad, H.
1993   'No Prophets? Recent Developments in Biblical Prophetic Research and Ancient Near Eastern Prophecy', *JSOT* 57: 39-60.

Barton, G.
1916   *Archeology and the Bible* (Philadelphia: American Sunday-School Union).

Baumgartner, W.
1938   'Ras Shamra Mythologie und biblische Theolgie', *TLZ* 63: 153-56.
1940   'Ras Schamra und das Alte Testament', *TRu* 12: 163-88.
1941   'Ras Schamra und das Alte Testament', *TRu* 13: 1-20, 85-102.
1947   'Ugaritische Probleme und ihre Tragwiete für das Alte Testament', *TZ* 3: 81-100.

Bea, A.
1940   'Die Texte von Mari und das Alte Testament', *Bib* 21: 188-96.

Bermant, C., and M. Weitzman
1979   *Ebla: A Revelation in Archeology* (New York: Times Books).

Beyerlin, W. (ed.)
1978   *Near Eastern Religious Texts Relating to the Old Testament* (trans. J. Bowden; Philadelphia: Westminster Press).

Biggs, R.
1980   'The Ebla Tablets: an Interim Perspective', *BA* 43: 76-87.

Bishop, M.
1962   *A History of Cornell* (Ithaca, NY: Cornell University Press).

Boecker, H.
1980   *Law and the Administration of Justice in the Old Testament and Ancient East* (London: SPCK; trans. of *Recht und Gesetz im Altes Testament und in altes Orient*, 1976).

Bonkamp, B.
1939   *Die Bibel im Lichte der Keilschriftforschung* (Recklinghausen: G.W. Wisarius).

Bonomi, J.
    1852   *Nineveh and its Palaces: The Discoveries of Botta and Layard, Applied to*
                the Elucidating of Holy Writ (London: Office of the Illustrated London
                Library).
    1869   *Nineveh and its Palaces: The Discoveries of Botta and Layard, applied to*
                the Elucidation of Holy Writ (London: Bell & Daldy, 2nd edn).
Borger, R.
    1961   'Zu den Asarhaddon-Verträgen aus Nimrud', *ZA* 54: 173-96.
Boscawen, W.
    1903   *The First of Empires: Babylon and the Bible in the Light of Latest Research*
                (London: Harper).
Botta, P.E.
    1843–44   *Lettres sur ses découvertes à Nineve* (Paris: Imprimerie Royale).
Botta, P.E., and M.E. Flandin
    1849–50   *Monument de Ninive* (5 vols.; Paris: Imprimerie Nationale).
Bottéro, J.
    1954   *Le problème des Habiru* (Paris: Imprimerie Nationale).
    1986–92   *Naissance de Dieu: La Bible et l'historien* (Paris: Gallimard).
    1992   *Mesopotamia: Writing, Reasoning, and the Gods* (trans. Z. Bahrani and M.
                van de Mieroop; Chicago: University of Chicago Press).
    1993a   *Initiation à l'Orient ancient: De Sumer à la Bible* (Paris: Gallimard).
    1993b   'Le modèle babylonien de la Genèse biblique', *L'Histoire* 164: 14-22.
    1994   *Babylone et la Bible: entriens avec Hélène Monsacré* (Paris: Hachette).
Brooke, G.J., A.H.W. Curtis and J.F. Healey (eds.)
    1994   *UB.*
Brown, F.
    1888–89   'Semitic Studies in the Theological Seminary', *Hebraica* 5: 86-88.
    1891   *Assyriology: Its Use and Abuse in Old Testament Study* (New York: Charles
                Scribner's Sons).
    1896   'Old Testament Problems', *JBL* 15: 67.
    1909   'Semitic Studies in America', *Johns Hopkins University Circular* 3: 240-59.
Buccellati, G.
    1962   'La "carriera" di David e quella di Idrimi, re di Alalah', *BeO* 4: 95-99.
Budge, E.A.
    1925   *The Rise and Progress of Assyriology* (London: Martin Hopkinson & Co.,
                Ltd).
Burrows, M.
    1937   'The Complaint of Laban's Daughters', *JAOS* 57: 259-76.
    1940   'The Ancient Oriental Background of the Hebrew Levirate Marriage',
                BASOR 77: 1-15.
Buss, M.
    1969   'Mari Prophecy and Hosea', *JBL* 88: 338.
Caquot, A.
    1988   'Psaume LXXII 16', *VT* 38: 214-18.
Carter, E.
    1977   'The Babylonian Story of the Flood: An Archaeological Interpretation',
                Bibliotheca Mesopotamica 7: 9-15.

Cassuto, U.
    1971   *The Goddess Anath: Canaanite Epics of the Patriarchal Age* (Jerusalem: Magnes Press).

Castellino, G.
    1940   *Le lamentazioni indiviuali e gli inni in Babilonia e in Israele* (Torino: Societa Editrice Internazionale).

Cazelles, H.
    1967   'Mari et l'ancien Testament', *La civilisation de Mari* (RAI 15; Liege: G. Miegiers): 73-90.
    1985   'Ugarit et la Bible', *BAT 1985*: 244-47.

Chadwick, O.
    1966   *The Victorian Church* (London: A. & C. Black).

Chiera, E.
    1932–33   'Habiru and Hebrews', *American Journal of Semitic Languages* 49: 115-24.

Clark, W.M.
    1977   'The Patriarchal Traditions', in J. Hayes and J.M. Miller (eds.), *Israelite and Judean History* (Philadelphia: Westminster Press): 120-48.

Clay, A.T.
    1890   *Amurru: The Home of the Northern Semites: A Study Showing that the Religion and Culture of Israel were not of Babylonian Origin* (Philadelphia: Sunday School Times).
    1915   *Light on the Old Testament from Babylon* (Philadelphia: The Sunday School Times Co., 4th edn).
    1922   *A Hebrew Deluge Story in Cuneiform and Other Epic Fragments in the Pierpont Morgan Library* (YOS, 3/V; New Haven: Yale University Press).

Clifford, R.
    1972   *The Cosmic Mountain in Canaan and the Old Testament* (Cambridge, MA: Harvard University Press).

Cogan, M.
    1974   *Imperialism and Religion: Assyria, Judah, and Israel in the Eighth and Seventh Centuries B.C.E.* (Missoula: Scholars Press).

Cook, S.A.
    1904   *The Laws of Moses and the Code of Hammurabi* (New York: Macmillan, 1904).

Cooper, J.
    1971   New Cuneiform Parallels to the Song of Songs', *JBL* 90: 157-62.

Coppens, J.
    1946   'Les parallèles du Psautier avec les textes de Ras Shamra-Ougarit', *Bulletin d'histoire et d'exegesis de AT* 18: 113-42.

Craghan, J.
    1975   'Mari and its Prophets: The Contributions of Mari to the Understanding of Biblical Prophecy', *BTB* 5: 32-55.

Craigie, P.C.
    1971   'The Poetry of Ugarit and Israel', *TynBul* 22: 3-31.
    1972   'Psalm XXIX in the Hebrew Poetic Tradition', *VT* 22: 143-51.
    1974   'The Comparison of Hebrew Poetry: Psalm 104 in the Light of Egyptian and Ugaritic Poetry', *Semitics* 4: 10-21.
    1977a   'Deuteronomy and Ugaritic Studies', *TynBul* 28: 155-69.

1977b	'Three Ugaritic notes on the Song of Deborah', *JSOT* 2: 33-49.
1978	'Deborah and Anat, A Study of Poetic Imagery (Judges 5)', *ZAW* 90: 374-81.
1979a	'Ugarit and the Bible: Progress and Regress in 50 Years of Literary Study', in G.D. Young (ed.), *Ugarit in Retrospect: Fifty Years of Ugarit and Ugaritic* (Winona Lake, IN: Eisenbrauns): 99-111.
1979b	'Parallel Word Pairs in Ugaritic Poetry: A Critical Evaluation of their Relevance for Psalm 29', *UF* 11: 135-40.
1983	*Ugarit and the Old Testament* (Grand Rapids: Eerdmans).

Cross, F.M.

1950	'Notes on a Canaanite Psalm in the Old Testament', *BASOR* 117: 19-21.
1955	'The Song of Miriam', *JNES* 14: 237-50.
1968	'Song of the Sea and Canaanite Myth', *JTS* 5: 1-25.
1973	*Canaanite Myth and Hebrew Epic* (Cambridge: Harvard University Press).

Cross, F.M., and D.N. Freedman

| 1948 | 'The Blessing of Moses', *JBL* 67: 191-210. |
| 1950 | *Studies in Ancient Yahwistic Poetry* (Missoula: Scholars Press). |

Curtis, A.H.W.

| 1985 | *Ugarit: Ras Shamra* (Grand Rapids: Eerdmans). |
| 1994 | 'The Psalms since Dahood', *UB*: 1-10. |

Dahood, M.

1962	'Ugaritic Studies and the Bible', *Gregorianum* 43: 55-79.
1989	*Ugaritic-Hebrew Philology: Marginal Notes on Recent Publications* (Rome: Biblical Institute Press).
1966–70	*The Psalms* (3 vols.; Garden City, NY: Doubleday).
1968	*Ugaritic and the Bible* (Paris: Desclee de Brouwer).
1975–81	in L. Fisher, *et al.*, *RSP*, 1975–81.
1978	'Ebla: Ugarit, and the Old Testament', in J.A. Emerton (ed.), *Congress Volume: Göttingen, 1977* (VTSup, 29; Leiden: E.J. Brill): 81-112.
1979	'The Ebla Tablets and Old Testament Theology', *Theology Digest* 27: 303-11.
1981a	'Ebla, Ugarit, and the Bible', in G. Pettinato, *The Archives of Ebla: An Empire Inscribed on Clay* (Garden City, NY: Doubleday): 81-121.
1981b	'The God JA at Ebla', *JBL* 100: 607-608.
1982	'Eblaite and Biblical Hebrew', *CBQ* 44: 1-24.
1983a	'The Minor Prophets and Ebla', in *Studies Freedman*: 47-67.
1983b	'The Divine Designation <hu> in Eblaite and the Old Testament', *AION* 43: 193-99.
1984	'Hebrew Hapax Legomena in Eblaite', in L. Cagni (ed.), *Il bilinguisimo a Ebla* (Naples: Istituo Universitario Orientale): 439-70.
1987	'Love and Death at Ebla and their Biblical Reflections', *Studies Pope*: 93-99.

Dahood, M., and G. Pettinato

| 1982 | 'Ebla and the Old Testament', in T. Ishida (ed.), *Studies in the Period of David and Solomon and Other Essays* (Winona Lake, IN: Eiseubrauns): 309-35 (bibliography by M. O'Connor, pp. 331-35). |

Dalglish, E.

| 1962 | *Psalm Fifty-One in the Light of Ancient Near Eastern Patternism* (Leiden: E.J. Brill). |

Davies, A.T.
1975   'The Aryan Christ: A Motif in Christian Anti-Semitism' *Journal of Ecumenical Studies* 12: 569-79.

Davis, A.
1852   *Lecture on the Remarkable Discoveries Lately made in the East: as those of Nineveh, Persia, etc.* (Buffalo: Phiriney).

Delano, J.
1985   'The "Exegesis" of Enuma Elish and Genesis 1—1875–1975: A Study in Interpretation' (PhD dissertation, Marquette University).

Delitzsch, F.
1881   *Wo Lag das Paradies? eine biblisch-assyriologisch Studie* (Leipzig: J.C.Hinrichs).
1902   *Babel und Bibel* (Leipzig: J.C. Hinrichs; trans. *Babel and Bible* [Chicago: The Open Court Publishing Co.]).
1906   *Babel and Bible: Three Lectures on the Significance of Assyriological Research for Religion, Embodying the Most Important Criticisms and the Author's Replies* (Chicago: The Open Court Publishing Co.).
1920   *Die Grosse Täuschung*, I (Stuttgart: Deutsche Verlags-Anstalt).
1921   *Die Grosse Täuschung*, II (Württemberg: Karl Rohm in Lorch).

Dietrich, M., and O. Loretz
1992   *'Jawhe und seine Aschera': Anthropomorphes Kultbild in Mesopotamien, Ugarit und Israel. Das biblische Bildverbot* (Münster: Ugarit-Verlag).

Donner, H.
1967   'Ugaritismen in der Psalmenforschung', *ZAW* 79: 322-50.

Draffkorn, A.
1957   'Ilani-Elohim', *JBL* 76: 341-49.

Driver, G.R.
1926   'The Psalms in the Light of Babylonian Research', in D.C. Simpson (ed.), *The Psalmists* (Oxford: Oxford University Press): 109-73.

Driver, S.R.
1904   *The Book of Genesis* (London: Metheun).
1909   *Modern Research as Illustrating the Bible* (London: Oxford University Press).

Dussaud, R.
1937   *Les découvertes de Ras Shamra (Ugarit) et l'Ancien Testament* (Paris: P. Geuthner; revised 1941).

Ebach, J.
1986   'Babel und Bibel oder: Das "Heidenische im Alten Testament"', in R. Farber and R. Schleisier (eds.), *Die Restauration der Götter: Antike Religion und Neo-Paganismus* (Würzburg: Königshausen & Neumann): 26-44.

Eerdmans, B.D.
1891   *Melekdienst en verering van hemellischamen in Israel's Assyrische periode* (Leiden: Eduard Ijdo).

Eichler, B.
1989   'Nuzi and the Bible: A Retrospective', in *Studies Sjöberg*: 107-19.

Ellermeier, F.
1977   *Prophetie in Mari und Israel* (Göttingen: Norten-Hardenberg; 2nd edn).

Epstein, L.
1986   *Social Justice in the Ancient Near East and the People of the Bible* (London: SCM Press; trans. of *La justice sociale dans le Proche-Orient ancient et le peuple de la Bible*).

Ermoni, N.
1910   *La Bible et l'assyriologie* (Paris: Bloud, 1910).

Fensham, F.C.
1962   'Malediction and Benediction in Ancient Near Eastern Vassal Treaties and the Old Testament', *ZAW* 74: 1-9.
1963a   'Psalm 29 and Ugarit', *Studies on the Psalms* (Potchefstroom: Pro Rege): 84-99.
1963b   'Common Trends in Curses of the Near Eastern Treaties and Kudurru Inscriptions Compared with Maledictions of Amos and Isaiah', *ZAW* 75: 155-75.

Ferris, P.W.
1992   *The Genre of Communal Lament in the Bible and the Ancient Near East* (Atlanta: Scholars Press).

Finkelstien, J.J.
1958   'Bible and Babel: A Comparative Study of the Hebrew and Babylonian Religious Spirit', *Commentary* 26: 431-44.

Fisher, L., and F.B. Knutson
1969   'An Enthronement Ritual at Ugarit', *JNES* 28: 157-67.

Fisher, L., and S. Rummel (eds.)
1975–81 *RSP*.

Fleming, D.
1992   *The Installation of the Baal's High Priestess at Emar: A Window on Syrian Religion* (Atlanta: Scholars Press).
1995   'More Help from Syria: Introducing Emar to Biblical Study', *BA* 58: 139-47.

Fontan, E. (ed.)
1994   *De Khorsabad à Paris: le découvertes des Assyriens* (Paris: Réunion des Musées Nationaux).

Fraine, J. de
1954   *L'aspect religieux de la royaute israelite: L'institution monarchique dans l'Ancien Testament et dans les textes mésopotamiens* (Rome: Pontifical Biblical Institute).

Frankena, H.
1965   'The Vassal-Treaties of Esarhaddon and the Dating of Deuteronomy', *OTS* 14: 122-54.

Freedman, D.N.
1970   'A New Approach to the Nuzi Sisterhood Contract', *JANESCU* 2: 77-85.
1972   'Psalm XXIX in the Hebrew Poetic Tradition', *VT* 22: 144-45.
1976   'Divine Names and Titles in Early Hebrew Poetry', *Studies Wright*: 55-102.
1978   'The Real Story of the Ebla Tablets: Ebla and the Cities of the Plain', *BA* 41: 143-64.

Frymer-Kensky, T.
1992   *In the Wake of the Goddesses: Women, Culture, and the Biblical Transformation of Pagan Myth* (New York: Fawcett Columbine).

1989   'The Ideology of Gender in the Bible and the Ancient Near East', *Studies Sjöberg*: 185-91.

Galling, K.
1950   *Textbuch zur Geschichte Israels* (Tübingen: J.C.B. Mohr).

Gammie, J., and L. Perdue (eds.)
1990   *The Sage in Israel and the Ancient Near East* (Winona Lake, IN: Eisenbrauns).

Gamper, A.
1966   *Gott als Richter in Mesopotamien und in Alten Testament: zum Verständnis einer Gebsbirte* (Innsbruck: Universitätsverlag Wagner).

Gaster, T.
1946–47   'Psalm 29', *JQR* 37: 55-65.

Gelb, I.J.
1980   'Comparative Method in the Study of the Society and Economy of the Ancient Near East', *Rocznik Orientalistyczny* 41: 29-36.

Gerstenberger, E.
1971   *Der bittende Mensch: Bittritual und Klageleid des Einzelnen im alten Testament* (Heidelberg: Habil-Schrift).

Gibson, J.C.L.
1962   'Light from Mari on the Patriarchs', *JSS* 8: 44-62.
1978   *Canaanite Myths and Legends* (Edinburgh: T. & T. Clark, 2nd edn).

Ginsberg, H.
1938   'A Phoenician Hymn in the Psalter', *Atti del XIX Congresso Internazionale degli Orientalisti, 23–29 Settembre, 1935* (Rome: G. Bardi): 472-76.

Ginsberg, H., and B. Maisler
1933   'Semitized Hurrians in Syria and Palestine', *JPOS* 13: 243-67.

Ginsberg, J.
1945   'Ugaritic Studies and the Bible', *BA* 8: 41-58.

Gordon, C.H.
1935a   'A New Akkadian Parallel to Deuteronomy 25.1-12', *JPOS* 15: 29-34.
1935b   '*'lhim* in its Reputed Meaning of Rulers, Judges', *JBL* 54: 139-44.
1935c   'Fratriarchy in the Old Testament', *JBL* 54: 223-31.
1935d   'Parallels nouziens aux lois et coutumes de l'Ancien Testament', *RB* 44: 34-41.
1936   'An Akkadian Parallel to Deuteronomy 21.1ff', *RA* 33: 1-6.
1937   'The Story of Jacob and Laban in the Light of the Nuzi Tablets', *BASOR* 66: 25-27.
1940   'Biblical Customs and the Nuzi Tablets', *BA* 3: 1-12.

Gordon, C.H., and G. Rendsberg
1997   *The Bible and the Ancient Near East* (New York: W.W. Norton & Co., 4th edn).

Gray, J.
1952   'Feudalism in Ugarit and Early Israel', *ZAW* 64: 49-55.
1957   *The Legacy of Canaan* (VTSup, 5; Leiden: E.J. Brill; 2nd rev. edn 1965).
1970   'The Book of Job in the Context of Ancient Near Eastern Literature', *ZAW* 82: 251-69.
1978   'Canaanite Religion and Old Testament Study in the Light of New Alphabetic Texts from Ras Shamra', *Ugaritica* 7: 79-108.

Grayson, A.K.
1997   'The Resurrection of Ashur: A History of Assyrian Studies', *Assyria 1995*:
            105-14.
Greenberg, M.
1955   *The Hab/piru* (New Haven: American Oriental Society).
1960   'Some Postulates of Biblical Criminal Law', *Studies Kaufmann*: 5-28.
1962   'Another Look at Rachel's Theft of the Teraphim', *JBL* 81: 239-48.
Greenfield, J.
1988   'Review of *Studies Freedman*', *BASOR* 262: 93-94.
Greenslade, S. (ed.)
1963   *The Cambridge History of the Bible. III. The West from the Reformation to
            the Present Day* (Cambridge: Cambridge University Press).
Greenspahn, F.
1991   'Introduction', in F. Greenspahn (ed.), *Essential Papers on Israel and the
            Ancient Near East* (New York: New York University Press): 7-8.
Greenstein, E., and D. Marcus
1976   'The Akkadian Inscription of Idrimi', *JANESCU* 8: 76-77.
Gressman, H.
1924   'Die Aufgaben der alttestamentlichen Forschung', *ZAW* 42: 1-33.
Gressman, H. (ed.)
1909   *Altorientalische Texte und Bilder zum Alten Testament* (2 vols.; Berlin: W.
            de Gruyter; 2nd edn 1926).
Gunkel, D.
1903   'Babylonische und biblische Urgeschichte', *Die Christliche Welt* 17: 121-34.
Gunkel, H.
1885   *Schöpfung und Chaos in Urzeit und Endzeit: eine religionsgeschichtliche
            Untersuchung über Gen. 1 und AP Joh. 12* (Göttingen: Vandenhoeck &
            Ruprecht).
1904   *Israel and Babylon: The Influence of Babylon on the Religion of Israel*
            (Philadelphia: J. McVey; trans. of *Israel und Babylon: der Einfuss
            Babylonien auf die israelitische Religion*, 1903).
Habel, N.
1964   *Yahweh versus Baal* (New York: Brookman Associates).
Hahn, H.
1956   *The Old Testament in Modern Research* (London: SCM Press).
Hallo, W.W.
1968   'Individual Prayer in Sumerian: The Continuity of a Tradition', *JAOS* 88:
            71-89.
1977   'New Moons and Sabbaths', *HUCA* 48: 1-2.
1980   'Biblical History in its Near Eastern Setting: The Contextual Approach', *SIC*
            1: 1-26.
1987   'The Origins of the Sacrificial Cult: New Evidence from Mesopotamia and
            Israel', in *Studies Cross*: 3-13.
1991   *The Book of the People* (Atlanta: Scholars Press).
1992   'Ebrium at Ebla', *Eblaitica* 3: 139-50.
1996   *Origins: The Ancient Near Eastern Background of Some Modern Western
            Institution* (Leiden: E.J. Brill).

Harnack, A.
  1903   *Letter to the Preussiche Jahrbuch on the German Emperor's Criticism of Prof. Delitzsch's Lectures on Babel und Bibel* (London: Williams & Norgate).
Healey, J.
  1984   'The Immortality of the King: Ugarit and the Psalms', *Or* 53: 245-54.
Hehn, J.
  1913   *Die biblische und die babylonische Gottesidee* (Leipzig: J.C. Hinrichs).
Heidel, A.
  1946   *The Gilgamesh Epic and Old Testament Parallels* (Chicago: University of Chicago Press).
  1951   *The Babylonian Genesis* (Chicago: University of Chicago Press).
Held, M.
  1974   'Hebrew Ma'gal: A Study in Lexical Parallelism', *JANESCU* 6: 107-14.
Hess, R.S.
  1994   'Alalakh Studies and the Bible: Obstacle or Contribution?', in *Studies King*: 199-215.
Hillers, D.
  1964   *Treaty-Curses and the Old Testament Prophets* (Rome: Pontifical Biblical Institute).
  1969   *Covenant: The History of a Biblical Idea* (Baltimore: The Johns Hopkins University Press).
  1985   'Analyzing the Abominable: Our Understanding of Canaanite Religion', *JQR* 75: 253-69.
Hilprecht, H.V.
  1903   *Explorations in Bible Lands* (Philadelphia: A.J. Holman).
  1908   *The So-Called Peters-Hilprecht Controversy* (Philadelphia: A.J. Holman, 1908).
Hincks, E.
  1850   *On the Khorsabad Inscriptions* (Dublin: H. Gill).
  1851   'Assyrian Antiquities', *The Athenaeum* 1246: 977.
  1851   'Nimrud Obelisk', *The Athenaeum* 1251: 1384–85.
  1852   'Nimrud Inscriptions', *The Athenaeum* 1262: 26.
  1853   in Layard, *Discoveries in the Ruins of Nineveh and Babylon* (London: J. Murray): 139.
  1862a   'Bible, History, and the Rawlinson Canon', *The Athenaeum* 1810: 20-22.
  1862b   'Bible, History, and the Rawlinson Canon', *The Athenaeum* 1813: 115-16.
Hoefer, J.C.
  1852   *Chaldée, Assyrie, Médie, Babylonie, Mésopotamie, Phénicie, Palmyrène* (Paris: Firmin Didot Frères).
Hoerth, A., G. Mattingly, and E. Yamauchi (eds.)
  1994   *POTW*.
Hommel, F.
  1897   *The Ancient Hebrew Traditions as Illustrated by the Monuments: A Protest Against the Modern School of Old Testament Criticism* (New York: E. & J.B. Young, trans. from German).
  1902   *Die altorientalischen Denkmäler und das Alte Testament: eine Erwiderung auf Prof. Fr. Delitzsch's 'Babel und Bibel'* (Berlin: Deutsche Orient Mission).

Hoskisson, P.
1991   'Emar as an Empirical Model of the Transmission of the Canon', *SIC* 4: 21-32.

Huehnergard, J.
1985   'Biblical Notes on Some New Akkadian Texts from Emar (Syria)', *CBQ* 47: 428-34.

Huffmon, H.
1968   'Prophecy in the Mari Letters', *BA* 31: 101-24.
1971   'Yahweh and Mari', in *Studies Albright*: 283-90.
1987   'Babel und Bibel: The Encounter Between Babylon and the Bible', in M. O'Connor and D.N. Freedman (eds.), *The Backgrounds for the Bible* (Winona Lake, IN: Eisenbrauns): 125-36.

Jack, J.W.
1935   *The Ras Shamra Tablets: Their Bearing on the Old Testament* (Edinburgh: T. & T. Clark).

Jacob, E.
1960   *Ras Shamra-Ugarit et l'Ancien Testament* (Neuchatel: Delechaux & Niestlé).

Jastrow, M.
1914   *Hebrew and Babylonian Traditions: The Haskell Lectures Delivered at Oberlin College in 1913* (London: T. Fisher Unwin).

Jean, C.
1954   'Les noms propres de personnes dans les lettres de Mari et dans les plus anciens textes du Pentateuque', in *La Bible et l'orient*: 121-28.

Jensen, P.
1890   *Assyrische-babylonische Mythen und Epen* (Berlin: Reuther & Reichard).
1902   'Babel und Bible', *Die Christliche Welt* 16: 487-94.
1906   *Das Gilgamesch-Epos in der Weltliteratur* (Strassburg: K.J. Trubner).
1924   *Gilgamesch-Epos, jüdische Nationalsagen, Ilias und Odysee* (Leipzig: E. Pfeiffer).

Jeremias, A.
1903   *Kampfe um Babel und Bibel: ein Wort zur Verstandigung und Abwehr* (Leipzig: J.C. Hinrichs).
1904   *Die Panbabylonisten der alte Orient und die aegyptische Religion* (Leipzig: J.C. Hinrichs).
1906   *Das Alte Testament im Lichte des alten Orients* (Leipzig: J.C. Hinrichs).
1911   *The Old Testament in the Light of the Ancient East* (London: Williams & Norgate; trans. of *Das Alte Testament im Lichte des Alten Orients*).

Johanning, K.
1988   *Der Babel-Bibei-Streit: Eine forschungsgeschichtliche Studie* (Frankfurt am Main: Peter Lang).

Johns, C.H.W.
1914   *The Relations between the Laws of Babylonia and the Law of the Hebrew Peoples* (London: H. Milford).

Jonge, H. de
1959   *Demonische ziekten in Babylon ed de Bijbel* (Leiden: E.J. Brill).

Kaiser, O.
1962   *Die mythische Bedeutung des Meeres in Aegypten, Ugarit und Israel* (Berlin: Alfred Töpelmann).

Kapelrud, A.
1965   *The Ras Shamra Discoveries and the Old Testament* (Oxford: Basil Black-
            well).
Keel, O.
1974   *Wirkmächtige Siegeszeichen im Alten Testament* (Göttingen: Vandenhoeck
            & Ruprecht).
1977   *Jahwe-Visionen und Siegelkunst* (Göttingen: Vandenhoeck & Ruprecht).
1978   *The Symbolism of the Biblical World* (New York: Seabury).
Kidder, D.
1851   *Nineveh and the River Tigris* (New York: Lane & Scott).
Kildahl, P.
1959   'British and American Reactions to Layard's Discoveries in Assyria (1845–
            1860)' (PhD dissertation, University of Minnesota).
Kilmer, A.
1972   'The Mesopotamian Concept of Overpopulation and its Solution as Reflected
            in the Mythology', *Or* 41: 160-77.
King, L.W.
1918   *Legends of Babylon and Egypt in Relation to Hebrew Tradition* (London: H.
            Milford).
Kittel, R.
1903   *Die babylonischen Ausgrabungen und die biblische Urgeschichte* (Leipzig:
            A. Deichert).
1921   'Die Zukunft der alttestamentlichen Wissenschaft', *ZAW* 39: 84-99.
Kraeling, E.
1955   *The Old Testament since the Reformation* (London: Lutterworth Press).
Kramer, S.N.
1959   'Sumerian Literature and the Bible', *AnBib* 12: 185-204.
Kraus, H.
1956   *Geschichte der historisch-kritischen Erforschung des Alten Testaments*
            (Neukirchen: Erziehungsverein).
1969   *Geschichte der historisch-kritischen Erforschung des Alten Testaments*
            (Neukirchen–Vluyn: Neukirchener Verlag, 2nd edn).
Kugel, F.
1910   *Im Bennkreis Babels: Panbabylonische Konstruktionen und Religions-
            geschichtliche Tatsachen* (Münster: Verlag der Aschendorfschen Buchhand-
            lung).
Kuklick, B.
1996   *Puritans in Babylon: The Ancient Near East and American Intellectual Life
            1880–1930* (Princeton: Princeton University Press).
L'Heureux, C.
1974   'The Ugaritic and Biblical Rephaim', *HTR* 67: 265-74.
Lambert, M.
1954   'De quelques thèmes littéraires en Sumérien et dans la Bible, in *La Bible et
            l'orient*: 4-15.
Lambert, W.
1965   'A New Look at the Babylonian Background of Genesis', *JTS* 16: 287-300.
1972   'Destiny and Divine Intervention in Babylon and Israel', *OTS* 17: 65-72.

/Landsberger, B.
1926   'Die Eigenbegrifflichkeit der babylonischen Welt', *Islamica* 2: 355-72.
        Reprinted and translated as *The Conceptual Autonomy of the Babylonian World* (Malibu: Undena, 1976).
1967   'Akkadisch-Hebräisch Wortgleichungen', VTSup 17: 176-204.
Langhe, R. de
1945   *Les textes de Ras Shamra-Ugarit et leurs rapports avec le milieu biblique de l'Ancien Testament* (2 vols.; Louvain: Bibliotheque de l'université).
Larsen, M.
1987   'Orientalism and the Ancient Near East', *Culture and History* 2: 96-102.
1992   'Seeing Mesopotamia', *Culture and History* 11: 116-20.
1995   'The "Babel/Bible" Controversy and its Aftermath', *CANE* 1: 95-106.
1996   *The Conquest of Assyria: Excavations in an Antique Land* (London: Routledge).
Larue, G.
1967   *Babylon and the Bible* (Grand Rapids: Baker Book House).
Layard, A.H.
1849   *Nineveh and its Remains* (London: J. Murray).
1849-53 *The Monuments of Nineveh* (London: J. Murray).
1853   *Discoveries in the Ruins of Nineveh and Babylon* (London: J. Murray).
Lehnmann, R.G.
1994   *Friedrich Delitzsch und der Babel-Bibel Streit* (Freiberg: Universitäts-verlag).
Lemaire, A.
1985   'Mari et la Bible et le monde nord-ouest sémitique', *MARI* 4: 549-58.
Lenzen, H.
1964   'Zur Flutschicht in Ur', *BaM* 3: 52-64.
Lewis, T.J.
1989   *Cults of the Dead in Ancient Israel and Ugarit* (Atlanta: Scholars Press).
Lewy, J.
1938   'Influences hurrites sur Israel', *Revue des études sémitiques*: 49-75.
1939   'Habiru and Hebrews', *HUCA* 14: 587-623.
1940   'A New Parallel between Habiru and Hebrews', *HUCA* 15: 47-58.
Long, B.
1993   'Mythic Troupe in the Autobiography of William Foxwell Albright', *BA* 56: 36-45.
Loretz, O.
1972   'Die Ugaritistik in der Psalmeninterpretation. Zum Abschluss des Kommentars von M. Dahood', *UF* 4: 167-69.
1984a   *Habiru-Hebräer: eine sozio-linquistische Studie über die Herkunft des Getiliziums 'Ibri vom Appellativum Habiru* (Berlin: W. de Gruyter).
1984b   'Hebräer in Ebla? Eine Fehlanziege zu 'ibri "Hebräer" und dem "Hebräer Abram" (Gen 14,13)', in P. Fronzaroli (ed.), *Studies on the Language of Ebla* (Florence: Istituto de Linguistica e di Lingue Orientali): 253-79.
1987   'Textologie des Zephanja-buches. Bemerkungen 10 als Parallelen zu Ps. 29, 10', *ZAW* 99: 219-28.
1990a   *Ugarit und die Bibel: Kanaanäische Götter und Religion im Alten Testament* (Darmstadt: Wissenschaftliche Buchgesellschaft).

      1990b   'KTU 1.101.1-30 und 1.2 IV kanaanäischer Literatur in Psalm 6', *UF* 22:
               195-220.
Loretz, O., and I. Kottsieper
      1987   *Colometry in Ugaritic and Biblical Poetry: Introduction, Illustrations and
               Topical Bibliography* (UBL, 5; Altenberge: CIS-Verlag).
Lowenstam, S. (ed.)
      1980   *Comparative Studies in Biblical and Ancient Oriental Literatures* (Neuckir-
               chen–Vluyn: Neukirchener Verlag).
Malamat, A.
      1962   'Mari and the Bible: Some Patterns of Tribal Organization and Institutions',
               JAOS 82: 143-50.
      1968   'King Lists of the Old Babylonian Period and Biblical Genealogies', *JAOS*
               88: 163-73.
      1973   *Mari and the Bible: A Collection of Essays* (Jerusalem: Jerusalem University
               Press).
      1983   'The Proto-History of Israel: A Study in Method', in *Studies Freedman*:
               303-13.
      1987   'A Forerunner of Biblical Prophecy: The Mari Documents', in *Studies
               Cross*: 33-52.
      1989   *Mari and the Early Israelite Experience* (Oxford: Oxford University Press).
      1998   *Mari and the Bible* (Leiden: E.J. Brill).
Mallowan, M.
      1964   'Noah's Flood Reconsidered', *Iraq* 26: 62-82.
Malul, M.
      1990   *The Comparative Method in Ancient Near Eastern and Legal Studies*
               (AOAT, 227; Kevelaer: Verlag Butzon & Bercker).
Margueron, J.-Cl.
      1995   'Emar: The Capital of Aštata in the Fourteenth Century B.C.E.', *BA* 58: 126-
               38.
Mathews, V.H.
      1981   'Pastoralists and Patriarchs', *BA* 44: 215-18.
      1986   'The Walls of Gerar', *BA* 49: 118-26.
Matthews, V.H., and D. Benjamin
      1997   *Old Testament Parallels: Laws and Stories from the Ancient Near East*
               (New York: Paulist Press, 2nd edn).
Matthiae, P.
      1981   *Ebla: An Empire Rediscovered* (Garden City, NY: Doubleday).
McCall, H.
      1998   'Rediscovery and Aftermath', in S. Dalley (ed.), *The Legacy of Mesopotamia*
               (Oxford: Oxford University Press): 181-98.
McCarthy, D.
      1978   *Treaty and Covenant* (Rome: Pontifical Biblical Institute).
McKay, J.
      1973   *Religion in Judah under the Assyrians 732–609 B.C.* (London: SCM Press).
Meade, C.
      1974   *Road to Babylon: Development of U.S. Assyriology* (Leiden: E.J. Brill).

Mendelsohn, I.
1935   'The Conditional Sale into Slavery of Free-born Daughters in Nuzi and the
            Law of Ex. 21.7-11', *JAOS* 55: 190-95.
Mendenhall G.
1954   'Ancient Oriental and Biblical Law', *BA* 17: 26-46.
1955   *Law and Covenant in Israel and the Ancient Near East* (Pittsburgh: Biblical
            Colloquium).
Merrill, E.
1983   'Ebla and Biblical Historical Inerrancy', *BSac* 140: 302-21.
Merrill, S.
1885   'Assyrian and Babylonian Monuments', *BSac* 32: 320-49.
Mihalic, I.
1981   'Ugarit and the Bible (a Question still unanswered)', *UF* 13: 147-50.
Millard, A.R.
1983   'Methods of Studying the Patriarchal Narratives as Ancient Texts', in A.R.
            Millard and D.J. Wiseman (eds.), *Essays on the Patriarchal Narratives*
            (Winona Lake, IN: Eisenbrauns): 43-92.
1985   'La prophétie et l'écriture: Israel, Aram, Assyrie', *RHR* 202: 125-45.
1989   'Mesopotamia and the Bible', *Aram* 1: 1-24.
Miller, P.D., Jr
1973   *The Divine Warrior in Early Israel* (Cambridge, MA: Harvard University
            Press).
Moor, J.C. de, and P. van der Lugt
1974   'The Spectre of Pan-Ugaritism', *BO* 31: 3-26.
Moor, J.C., de, and P. Sandars
1991   'An Ugaritic Expiation Ritual and its Old Testament Parallels', *UF* 23: 283-
            300.
Moorey, P.
1991   *A Century of Biblical Archeology* (Louisville, KY: Westminster/John Knox
            Press).
Moran, W.
1965   'The Ancient Near Eastern Background of the Love of God in Deuteronomy',
            CBQ 25: 77-87.
1969   'New Evidence from Mari on the History of Prophecy', *Bib* 50: 15-56.
Morrison, M.A.
1983   'The Jacob and Laban Narrative in Light of Ancient Near Eastern Sources',
            BA 46: 155-64.
Müller, H.-P.
1981   'Gab es in Ebla einem Gottesnamen Ja?', *ZA* 70: 70-92.
1984   'Ebla und das althebräische Verbalsystem', *Bib* 65: 145-67.
Müller, H.-P. (ed.)
1991   *Babylonien und Israel: historische, religiöse und sprachliche Beziehungen*
            (Darmstadt: Wissenschaftliche Buchgesellschaft).
Mullo-Weir, C.J.
1967-68   'The Alleged Hurrian Wife-Sister Motif in Genesis', *Transactions of the
            Glasgow University Oriental Society* 22: 14-25.
1967   'Nuzi', *AOTS*: 73-86.

Na'aman, N.
    1986   'Habiru and Hebrews: The Transfer of a Social Term to the Literary Sphere',
                JNES 45: 271-88.

Neuman, J.
    1876   *The Thrones and Palaces of Babylon and Nineveh* (New York: Harper &
                Bros).

Noort, E.
    1977   *Untersuchungen zum Gottesbescheid in Mari: Die 'Mariprophetes' in der
                alttestamentlichen Forschung* (Kevelaer: Butzon & Bercker).

Noth, M., and D. Winton Thomas (eds.)
    1955   *Wisdom in Israel and the Ancient Near East* (Leiden: E.J. Brill).

O'Connor, M.
    1987   'Ugarit and the Bible', in M. O'Connor and D.N. Freedman (eds.), *Back-
                grounds for the Bible* (Winona Lake, IN: Eisenbrauns): 151-64.

Oppenheim, A.L.
    1955   'Review of S. Smith, *The Statue of Idrimi* (London: British Institute of
                Archaeology at Ankara)', *JNES* 15: 199-200.
    1977   *Ancient Mesopotamia: Portrait of a Dead Civilization* (Chicago: University
                of Chicago Press, 2nd edn).

Pardee, D.
    1985   'Review of *SIC* 1', JNES 44: 220-22.

Parker, S.B.
    1979–80   'Some Methodological Principles in Ugaritic Philology', *Maarav* 2: 7-41.
    1993   'Official Attitudes toward Prophecy at Mari and in Israel', *VT* 43: 50-68.

Parrot, A.
    1950   'Les tablettes de Mari et l'Ancien Testament', *RHR* 30: 1-11.
    1954   'Mari et l'Ancient Testament', in *La Bible et l'orient*: 117-20.
    1955   *Nineveh and the Old Testament* (London: SCM Press).
    1958   *Babylon and the Old Testament* (London: SCM Press).
    1962   *Abraham and his Times* (Philadelphia: Fortress Press; trans. W.J. Farley).
    1967   'Mari', *AOTS*: 136-44.

Patton, J.H.
    1944   *Canaanite Parallels in the Book of Psalms* (Baltimore: The Johns Hopkins
                University Press).

Paul, S.
    1970   *Studies in the Book of the Covenant in the Light of Cuneiform Law* (Leiden:
                E.J. Brill).

Peters, J.
    1899   *Nippur, or Excavations and Adventures on the Euphrates* (2 vols.; New
                York: G.P. Putnam's Sons).

Petersen, A.R.
    1998   *The Royal God: Enthronement Festivals in Ancient Israel and Ugarit?* (CIS,
                5; JSOTSup, 259; Sheffield: Sheffield Academic Press).

Pettinato, G.
    1976   'The Royal Archives of Tell-Mardikh/Ebla', *BA* 39: 44-52.
    1977   'Gli archivi reali di Tell-Mardikh-Ebla: riflessioni e prospettive', *RivB* 25:
                231-35.
    1980   'Ebla and the Bible', *BA* 43: 203-16.

1981	*The Archives of Ebla: An Empire Inscribed on Clay* (Garden City, NY: Doubleday).
1991	*Ebla: A New Look at History* (Baltimore: The John Hopkins University Press; trans. from Italian, 1986).

Pfeiffer, C.
1962	*Ras Shamra and the Bible* (Grand Rapids: Baker Book House).

Pinches, T.
1902	*The Old Testament in the Light of the Historical Records and Legends of Assyria and Babylonia* (London: SPCK).

Pitard, W.
1996	'The Archaeology of Emar', in *Emar*: 13-23.

Place, V.
1867–70	*Ninive et l'Assyrie, avec des essais de restauration par Félix Thomas* (3 vols.; Paris: Imprimerie Impériale).

Poebel, A.
1932	*Das appositionell bestimmte der I. Pers. Sing. im den Westsemitisch Inschriften und im Alten Testament* (Chicago: University of Chicago Press).

Pope, M.
1994	*Probative Pontificating in Ugaritic and Biblical Literature: Collected Essays* (UBL, 10; Münster: Ugarit-Verlag).

Radau, H.
1908	*Bel, the Christ of Ancient Times* (Chicago: The Open Court Publishing Co.).

Raikes, R.
1966	'The Physical Evidence for Noah's Flood', *Iraq* 28: 52-63.

Rainey, A.
1965	'The Kingdom of Ugarit', *BA* 28: 102-25.

Ratner, R., and B. Zuckerman
1986	'A Kid in Milk...? New Photographs of KTU 1.23, Line 14', *HUCA* 57: 15-60.

Rawlinson, G.
1859	*Historical Evidences of the Truth of the Scripture Records* (London: John Murray).
1862	*The Five Great Monarchies of the Ancient Eastern World* (New York: Dodd, Mead, & Co.).
1871	*The Alleged Historical Difficulties of the Old and New Testaments* (London: Harper & Bros.).
1885	*Egypt and Babylon: From Scripture and Profane Sources* (London: Hodder & Stoughton).

Rawlinson, H.C.
1850	'On the Inscriptions of Babylonia and Assyria', *JRAS* 12: 401-83.
1860–84	*Cuneiform Inscriptions of Western Asia* (5 vols.; London: R.E. Bower).

Rawlinson, H.C., W.H.F. Talbot, E. Hincks, and J. Oppert
1857	*Inscription of Tiglath Pileser I, King of Assyria* (London: Royal Asiatic Society).

Renger, J.
1979	'Die Geschichte der Altorientalisk und der vorderasiatischen Archäologie in Berlin von 1875–1945', in W. Arenhövel and C. Schreiber (eds.), *Berlin und die Antike* (Berlin: Deutsches Orient Archäologiches Institut): 151-92.

Reventlow, H.G.
    1983   *Hauptprobleme der alttestamentlichen Theologie im 20. Jahrhundert* (Darm-
                stadt: Wissenschaftliche Buchgesellschaft, 1983; trans. as *Problems of
                Biblical Theology in the Twentieth Century*, 1985).
Roberts, J.J.M.
    1976   'Myth vs. History', *CBQ* 38: 1-13.
    1985   'The Ancient Near Eastern Environment', in D. Knight and G. Tucker (eds.),
                The Hebrew Bible and its Modern Interpreters (Philadelphia: Fortress
                Press): 89-96.
Robertson, D.
    1972   *Linguistic Evidence in Dating Early Hebrew Poetry* (Missoula: Scholars
                Press).
Rogers, R.W.
    1908   *The Religion of Babylonia and Assyria, Especially in its Relations to Israel*
                (New York: Eaton & Mains).
    1912   *Cuneiform Parallels to the Old Testament* (New York: Eaton & Mains).
Ross, J.
    1970   'Prophecy in Hamath, Israel, and Mari', *HTR* 63: 1-28.
Saggs, H.W.F.
    1969   *Assyriology and the Study of the Old Testament* (Cardiff: University of
                Wales Press).
    1978   *The Encounter with the Divine in Mesopotamia and Israel* (London: The
                Athlone Press).
    1984   *The Might that was Assyria* (London: Sidgwick & Jackson).
    1999   'Assyriology and Biblical Studies', *Dictionary of Biblical Interpretation*
                (Nashville: Abingdon Press): 69-78.
Sandmel, S.
    1962   'Parallelomania', *JBL* 81: 1-13.
Sasson, J.
    1973   'A Further Cuneiform Parallel to the Song of Songs', *ZAW* 85: 359-60.
    1980   'Two Recent Works on Mari', *AfO* 27: 127-35.
    1983   'Mari Dreams', *JAOS* 73: 283-93.
Sayce, A.H.
    1885   *The Witness of the Monuments to the Old Testament Scriptures* (London:
                Religious Tract Society).
    1888   *Fresh Light from the Ancient Monuments: A Sketch of the Most Striking
                Confirmations of the Bible* (London: Religious Tract Society).
    1891   *The Races of the Old Testament* (London: The Religious Tract Society).
    1894a   *The Higher Criticism and the Verdict of the Monuments* (London: SPCK).
    1894b   'The Archaeological Witness to the Literary Activity of the Mosaic Age', in
                R.V. French, *Lex Mosaica, or the Law of Moses and the Higher Criticism*
                (London: Eyre & Spottiswoode): 1-17.
    1895   *The Bible and the Monuments: The Primitive Hebrew Records in the Light of
                Modern Research* (London: Eyre & Spottiswoode).
    1907   *The Archaeology of the Cuneiform Inscriptions* (London: SPCK).
Schmidt, B.
    1992   'The Gods and the Dead of the Domestic Cult at Emar', in *Emar*: 141-63.

1994   *Israel's Beneficent Dead: Ancestor Cult and Necromancy in Ancient Israelite Religion and Tradition* (FAT, 11; Tübingen: J.C.B. Mohr).

Schmidt P.W.

1908   'Panbabylonismus und ethnologischer Elementargedanke', *Mitteilungen der anthropologischen Gesellschaft in Wien* 38: 73-9.

Schmidt, W.

1966   *Königtum Gottes in Ugarit und Israel* (Berlin: Alfred Töpelmann, 2nd edn).

Schmitt, A.

1982   *Prophetischer Gottesbescheid in Mari und Israel: Eine Strukturuntersuchung* (Stuttgart: Kohlhammer Verlag).

Schrader, E.

1863   *Studien zur Kritik und Erklärung der biblischen Urgeschichte* (Zurich: Verlag von Meyer & Zeller).

1885–88   *Die Keilinschriften und das Alte Testament* (London: Williams & Norgate, trans. as *The Cuneiform Inscriptions and the Old Testament*).

Schroer, S.

1980   'Psalm 65-Zeugnis eines integrativen JHWH Glaubens?', *UF* 22: 285-301.

Schult, H.

1966   'Vier weitere Mari-Briefe "Prophetischen Inhalts"', *ZDPV* 82: 228-32.

Schwaner, W.

1910   *Germanen-Bibel aus heiligen Schriften germanischer Volker* (Schlachtensee: Volkerzieher Verlag, 3rd edn).

Selman, M.J.

1983   'Comparative Customs and the Patriarchal Age', A.R. Millard, and D.J. Wiseman (eds.), *Essays on the Patriarchal Narratives* (Winona Lake, IN: Eisenbrauns): 91-139.

Shea, W.

1983   'Two Palestinian Segments from the Eblaite Geographical Atlas', in *Studies Freedman*: 589-612

Sjöberg, A.

1984   'Eve and the Chameleon', in *Studies Ahlström*: 217-25.

Skinner, J.

1910   *A Critical and Exegetical Commentary on Genesis* (ICC; Edinburgh: T. & T. Clark).

Smith, C.C.

1968   'The Impact of Assyriology upon Old Testament Study, with Special Reference to the Publications of Leonard William King' (PhD dissertation, University of Chicago).

Smith, G.

1875   *Assyrian Discoveries* (London: S. Low, Marston, Low & Searle).

1876   *The Chaldean Account of Genesis* (London: S. Low, Marston, Searle & Rivington).

Smith, M.

1952   'The Common Theology of the Ancient Near East', *JBL* 71: 49-50.

1969   'The Present State of Old Testament Studies, *JBL* 88: 19-35.

Smith, S.

1926   in C. Gadd, 'Tablets from Kirkuk', *RA* 23: 127.

1932   'What were the Teraphim?', *JTS* 33: 33-36.

Soden, W. von
    1985   *Bibel und alter Orient: altorientalische Beitrage zum Alten Testament*
                (Berlin: W. de Gruyter).
Soll, W.
    1988   'Babylonian and Biblical Acrostics', *Bib* 69: 305-23.
Speiser, E.A.
    1938   'The Nuzi Tablets Solve a Puzzle in the Books of Samuel', *BASOR* 72: 15-
                17.
    1940   'Of Shoes and Shekels: (I Samuel 12.3, 13.21)', *BASOR* 77: 15-20.
    1955   'I Know not the Day of my Death', *JBL* 74: 252-56.
    1957   'The Biblical Idea of History in its Common Near Eastern Setting', *IEJ* 7:
                201-16.
    1958   'Census and Ritual Expiation in Mari and Israel', *BASOR* 149: 17-25.
    1964   *Genesis* (AB; Garden City, NY: Doubleday).
    1967   'The Wife-Sister Motif in the Partriarchal Narratives', in J.J. Finkelstein and
                M. Greenberg (eds.), *Oriental and Biblical Studies* (Philadelphia: University
                of Pennsylvania Press): 62-82.
Stuart, D.
    1976   *Studies in Early Hebrew Meter* (Missoula: Scholars Press).
Stummer, F.
    1922   *Sumerisch-akkadische Parallelen zum Aufbau alttestamentlicher Psalmen*
                (Paderborn: F. Schoningh).
Szlechter, F.
    1954   'Le prat dans l'Ancien Testament et dans les codes Mésopotamiens d'avant
                Hammourabi', in *La Bible et l'orient*: 16-25.
Tadmor, H.
    1985   'Nineveh, Calah, and Israel', *BAT*: 253-64.
Talmon, S.
    1978a   'The Comparative Method', J.A. Emerton (ed.), *Congress Volume:
                Göttingen, 1977* (VTSup, 29; Leiden: E.J. Brill): 320-56.
    1978b   'On the Emendation of Biblical Texts on the Basis of Hebrew parallels', *EI*
                14: 117-24 (in Hebrew).
Thompson, T.L.
    1974   *The Historicity of the Patriarchal Narratives* (BZAW, 133; Berlin: W. de
                Gruyter).
    1978   'A New Attempt to Date the Patriarchal Narratives', *JAOS* 98: 76-84.
    1999   *The Bible in History: How Writers Create a Past* (London: Jonathan Cape).
Toorn, K. van der
    1985   *Sin and Sanction in Israel and Mesopotamia: A Comparative Study* (Assen:
                Van Gorcum).
    1991   'Funerary Rituals and Beatific Afterlife in Ugaritic Texts and in the Bible',
                BO 48: 40-66.
    1994   *From her Cradle to her Grave: The Role of Religion in the Life of the
                Israelite and Babylonian Woman* (The Biblical Seminar, 23; Sheffield: JSOT
                Press).
    1996   *Family Religion in Babylonia, Syria, and Israel: Continuity and Change in
                the Forms of Religious Life* (Leiden: E.J. Brill).

Toorn, K. van der (ed.)
1997   *The Image and the Book: Iconic Cults, Aniconism, and the Rise of Book Religion in Israel and the Ancient Near East* (Leuven: Peeters).

Tropper, J.
1989   *Nekromantie, Totenbefragung in alten Orient und im Alten Testament* (Kevelaer: Verlag Butzon & Bercker).

Tsevat, M.
1958   'Alalakhiana', *HUCA* 29: 109-43.

Tsukimoto, A.
1989   'Emar and the Old Testament: Preliminary Remarks', *AJBI* 15: 3-24.

Tufton, O.
1874   'Progress and Result of Cuneiform Decipherment', *Baptist Quarterly* 8: 191-208.

Van Seters, J.
1968   'The Problem of Childlessness in Near Eastern Law and the Patriarchs of Israel', *JBL* 87: 401-408.
1969   'Jacob's Marriages and Ancient Near Eastern Customs: A Reexamination', *HTR* 62: 387-95.
1975   *Abraham in History and Tradition* (New Haven: Yale University Press).

Vaux, R. de
1937   'Les textes de Ras Shamra et l'Ancien Testament', *RB* 46: 526-55.
1949   'Les patriarches Hébreux et les découvertes modernes', *RB* 56: 34-35.

Vaux, W.
1855   *Nineveh and Persepolis* (London: Arthur Hall, Virtue & Co.).

Veenhof, K.H.
1995   'Seeing the Face of God: The Use of Akkadian Parallels', *Akkadica* 94.5: 33-37.

Vigano, L., and D. Pardee
1984   'Literary Sources for the History of Palestine and Syria: The Ebla Tablets', *BA* 47: 6-16.

Vigouroux, F.
1877   *La Bible et le découvertes modernes en Egypte et en Assyrie* (Paris: Berche et Tralin).

Virolleaud, C.V.
1933   'La naissance des deux gracieux et beaux: poème phénicien de Ras Shamra', *Syria* 14: 128-51.

Vriezen, C.
1968   'The Study of the Old Testament and the History of Religion', VTSup 17: 1-24.

Waltke, B.
1979   'The Book of Proverbs and Ancient Wisdom Literature', *BSac* 136: 221-38.

Walton, J.
1989   *Ancient Israelite Literature in its Cultural Context* (Grand Rapids: Zondervan).

Ward, W.H.
1870   'Assyrian Studies-Textbooks', *BSac* 27: 184-91.
1886   *Report on the Wolfe Expedition to Babylonia, 1884-5* (Boston: Archeological Institute of America).

Watson, W.G.E.
1976   'The Pivot Pattern in Hebrew, Ugaritic, and Akkadian Poetry', *ZAW* 88: 239-53.
Weinfeld, M.
1970   'The Covenant of Grant in the Old Testament and in the Ancient Near East', *JAOS* 90: 184-203.
1973   'Covenant Terminology in the Ancient Near East and its Influence in the West', *JAOS* 93: 190-99.
1988   'Job and its Mesopotamian Parallels', in W. Claassen (ed.), *Text and Context* (JSOTSup, 48; Sheffield: JSOT Press): 217-26.
Weippert, H.
1985   *Beiträge zur prophetischen Bildsprache in Israel und Assyrien* (Freiburg: Göttingen).
Weippert, M.
1972   '"Heiliger Krieg" in Israel und Assyrien', *ZAW* 84: 469-93.
Westbrook, R.
1985   'Biblical and Cuneiform Law Codes', *RB* 92: 247-64.
Widengren, G.
1936   *The Accadian and Hebrew Songs of Lamentation as Religious Documents* (Uppsala: Almqvist & Wiksell).
Wilson, R.
1977   *Genealogy and History in the Biblical World* (New Haven: Yale University Press).
Winckler, H.
1892   *Keilschriftliches Textbuch zum Alten Testament* (Leipzig: E. Pfeiffer).
1901   *Himmels-und Weltenbild der Babylonier als Grundlage der Weltanschaung und Mythologie aller Völker* (Leipzig: J.C. Hinrichs).
1905   'Die Weltanshaung des Alten Orients', *Ex Oriente Lux* 1: 1-50.
1906a   'Der alte Orient und die Bibel', *Ex Oriente Lux* 2: 15.
1906b   *Die babylonische Weltschöpfung* (Leipzig: J.C. Hinrichs).
1906c   *Der Alte Orient und de Bible uebst einemänhang Babel und Bibel-Bibel und Babel* (Leipzig: E. Pfeiffer).
1907a   *Die babylonische Geisteskultur in ihren Beziehungen zur Kulturentwicklung der Menscheit* (Leipzig: Quelle & Meyer).
1907b   *Die jungsten Kampfer wider den Pmnhabylonismus* (Leipzig: J.C. Hinrichs).
Wiseman, D.J.
1958   'The Vassal Treaties of Esarhaddon', *Iraq* 20: 1-99.
1962   *The Expansion of Assyrian Studies: An Inaugural Lecture Delivered on 27 February, 1962* (London: School of Oriental and African Studies, University of London).
1967   'Alalakh', *AOTS*: 119-35.
Woolley, C.L.
1930   'The Biblical Deluge: An Ascertained Fact', *Illustrated London News* 8 February.
1936   *Abraham: Recent Discoveries and Hebrew Origins* (London: Faber & Faber).
1953   *Forgotten Kingdom* (Harmondsworth: Penguin Books).

1955   *Alalakh: An Account of the Excavations at Tell Atchana in the Hatay, 1937–49* (London: Society of Antiquaries).

Wright, D.P.
1987   *The Disposal of Impurity: Elimination Rites in the Bible and in Hittite and Mesopotamian Literature* (Atlanta: Scholars Press).

Yaron, R.
1970   'Middle Assyrian Law Codes and the Bible', *Bib* 51: 77-85.

Younger, K.L., Jr
1990   *Ancient Conquest Accounts: A Study in Ancient Near Eastern and Biblical History Writing* (JSOTSup, 98; Sheffield: JSOT Press).

Zimmern, H.
1889   *Die Assyriologie als Hilfswissenschaft für das Studium den Alten Testaments und des klassischen Altertums* (Königsberg: W. Koln).

1901   *Biblische und babylonische Urgeschichete* (Leipzig: J.C. Hinrichs, trans. *The Babylonian and Hebrew Genesis,* London: David Nutt, 1901).

1906–18   *Zum babylonischen Neujahrsfest* (2 vols.; Leipzig).

1910   *Zum Streit um die 'Christusmythe': Das babylonische Material in seinen Hauptpunkten dargestellt* (Berlin: Reuther & Reichard).

The Quest for Sargon, Pul and Tiglath-Pileser in the Nineteenth Century*

Steven W. Holloway

Prior to 1847, scholars interested in establishing a history of Assyria were entirely dependent on the Old Testament and classical authors. Prenineteenth century accounts of Assyria and Babylonia, routinely relying on Archbishop Ussher's chronological framework,[1] 'found' Assyria around 2783 *Anno Mundi* by Ninus and Semiramis. They then jump down to the second Assyrian dynasty and King Pul who received Menahem's tribute sometime between 770 and 745, followed by Tiglath-Pileser,[2] Shalmaneser, Sennacherib and Esarhaddon, and conclude with the fall of Nineveh in the time of Sarakos during the reign of Josiah.[3] 'Sargon, King of Assyria' appears only in Isa. 20.1; the name was not preserved in

---

* An outline of this essay originally appeared as a poster presentation at the XLVe Rencontre Assyriologique Internationale, exhibited at Harvard University, 5–8 July 1998.

1. For an overview of Archbishop Ussher's chronological schema and influence, see Barr 1984; Hughs 1990: 261-63.

2. Writing under the influence of the Old Testament translations, most nineteenth-century authors either capitalized the second element of the name (Tiglath-Pileser) or treated it as a single word: Tiglathpileser. The modern convention that the non-theophoric elements in Akkadian sentence names are to be represented by lower case letters did not take hold until the twentieth century. Since this essay deals with nineteenth-century scholarship, I shall spell the royal Assyrian names accordingly.

3. E.g. Schroeer 1726: 467-71; Koopmans 1819; Fraser 1842: 41-67. Several scholars working in the first half of the nineteenth century, especially dubious of the legendary quality of Ctesias's Assyria, limited their historical coverage to king Pul and later monarchs; see Niebuhr 1857: 37-39. Virtually any post-Enlightenment pre-1850 encyclopedia article on Assyria reproduces the traditional two-dynasty schema of Assyrian history; see, e.g., Anonymous 1817: 4-5; Kanngiesser 1820: 151-53; Anonymous 1842: 717-18; for brief modern summaries see Drews 1965: 141-42; and Larsen 1996: 170-72.

classical sources. Since biblical Sargon[4] did not trouble the kingdoms of Israel or Judah, in contrast to the momentous careers of Shalmaneser, Sennacherib and Esarhaddon in Scripture, many pre-assyriological commentators believed that Sargon was merely an alias for one of the better-known Assyrian rulers mentioned in 2 Kings and Isaiah. For instance, a head count of eighteenth-century authors who identified Sargon with Shalmaneser include Prideaux (Prideaux 1716: 20) and Vitringa.[5] The writers Hugo Grotius (1776: 35) and Marsham (1649: 41) in the seventeenth century and Schroeer (1726: 151-53, 62-63) and Robert Lowth[6] in the eighteenth century identified Sargon with Sennacherib, while the eighteenth century writers Perizonius (1711: 256-57), Kalinsky (1748: 79-88) and the

4.   In this brief essay I shall refer to three overlapping yet self-contained Assyrias: 'biblical Assyria', 'classical Assyria', and 'historical Assyria'. 'Biblical Assyria' corresponds to the severely truncated and sinister cameo appearance of the Neo-Assyrian empire in the Hebrew Scriptures; its custodians are generations of biblical apologists and exegetes. 'Classical Assyria' is the Assyria that emerges from the pages of the Loeb Classical Library. Legend and fiction abound, though there are relics of authentic historical details. Significant studies of 'classical' Assyria include Eilers 1971; Piccaluga 1982; Nagel 1982; Pettinato 1985; Capomacchia 1986. From the standpoint of the universal historian, the distinction between 'biblical' and 'classical' Assyria is an artificial one. Prior to the nineteenth century, historical treatments of Assyria amalgamated the names and events of the two sources into a seamless web stretching from Nimrod to Sardanapalus or Sarakus, usually conforming the whole to an overarching schema of the four world empires. While the Julian dating of the biblical events and the objectivity of the various classical authors were subject to debate, confidence that the enterprise would yield historically credible information was never seriously in doubt. 'Historical Assyria' is, at least in theory, the Assyria created by the modern science of assyriology fueled by primary texts and artifacts. All three of these Assyrias derive from discrete sources or realia, yet they are all intellectual constructs subject to elaboration and revision, in accordance with the dominant schools of thought among contemporary biblical specialists, classicists, and assyriologists, respectively.

5.   Campegius Vitringa, *Observationes Sacrae*, 1711, cited in Winer 1849: 383. Winer's lucid, encyclopedic presentation of biblical scholarship poised on the brink of the decipherment of Akkadian and the European excavation of Mesopotamia is a superb resource for investigating the modern pre-assyriological academic study of the Bible and its environment.

6.   Lowth (1834 [1799]: 244) defending his surmise with the observation of Jerome that Sennacherib was known by seven different names (cf. *Tobit*). Jerome's interpretation is surely due to his exposure to traditional rabbinic exegesis which collapses all of the scriptural names of Assyrian kings into that of the *Unheilsherr* Sennacherib; cf. *Sanh.* 94a.

great Michaelis[7] identified the chameleon king with Esarhaddon.

Prior to the excavation of Khorsabād and the identification of its builder with Sargon, early nineteenth-century biblical exegetes tended to be puzzled by the obscure Sargon.[8] As the mysteries of the biblical world fell under the secular dissection of early modern historical investigation, however, the often vague chronological syncretisms and historicizing patterns that satisfied generations of biblical apologists began to be challenged.[9] Between 1800 and 1850, a chorus of brave voices that accepted Sargon as a bona fide king in his own right burst forth from the German academy, situating him between Shalmaneser and Sennacherib: Rosenmüller, Gesenius, Maurer, Knobel, Ewald, and Winer.[10] Sargon's 26 centuries of obscurity were jeopardized by the French excavations at Khorsabād. In 1845, Löwenstern, more by bizarre accident than philological acumen, deduced that the builder of the Khorsabād palace was identical with the king in Isa. 20.1—but, as everyone knows, that king was *really* Esarhaddon. Longpérier confirmed the reading of 'Sargon' in 1847, and Henry C. Rawlinson[11] gave it his reluctant blessing in 1850.[12] Although a handful

---

7.   Cited in Winer 1849: 383, s.v. Sargon.

8.   Eichhorn 1824: 387-89. Fletcher (1850: 250) one of many learned travelogues made during the first spate of excavations in Mesopotamia, guessed that Sargon, the builder of Khorsabād, was the same as the biblical Sennacherib; Milman 1870 [1866; 1829 original]: 425-26 n. 1 relegates Sargon to a footnote, observing that 'The moderns insist that he was a distinct king: but there is much difficulty about the chronology. He was, it is agreed, builder of the splendid palace at Khorsabad...'

9.   The highly influential study Movers (1841–56) was symptomatic of this intellectual movement, and acted as a powerful catalyst in the German academy.

10.   Rosenmüller 1825: 107; Gesenius 1828, s.v. Sargon; Maurer 1835: 324; Knobel 1837: 114; Ewald 1847: 333-34; and Winer 1849: 383, s.v. Sargon. Newman (1847: 270) argued that Sargon probably succeeded Tiglath-pileser, yet '[i]t must be confessed that Rosenmüller, Gesenius, Winer, and all leading authorities, interpose Sargon in the latter interval [between Shalmaneser and Sennacherib]'. Once the historicity of Sargon had been firmly established, one historian overcompensated by concluding that Shalmaneser was the Jewish name for Sargon! (he was abetted in this by the inability of the cuneiform decipherers to identify the expected name of Shalmaneser); see Niebuhr 1857: 160.

11.   On the imposing figure of Henry Creswicke Rawlinson (1810–1895), see Flemming 1894; G. Rawlinson 1898; Smith, Stephen, and Lee 1921–22: 771-74; Couture 1984: 143-45; and most notably Larsen (1996: 79-361) who makes detailed use of the heretofore unpublished correspondence exchanged between A.H. Layard and Rawlinson between 1846–55, currently housed in the British Museum.

12.   On a Khorsabād relief of a seaside city under Assyrian attack, Löwenstern,

of biblical exegetes would remain agnostic regarding Sargon's independent existence, the Louvre exhibits from the 'French Nineveh' and
translations of the Khorsabād inscriptions signaled a complete victory for
Sargon (II) as a textbook entity by the 1860s.[13]

apparently working from Isa. 20.1, concluded that the siege of Ashdod was the subject
matter of the relief. In the accompanying inscription, he erroneously read Ashdod, but
isolated the signs of the royal name, which he guessed, on the basis of their
resemblance to Hebrew characters, to represent *r s k*, which he understood as a
metathesis for 'Sarak', a variant form of Sargon. The basis of the analysis was wrong
at every step—yet Sargon was indeed the royal name of the inscription. Unfortunately,
Löwenstern, like most early nineteenth-century exegetes, convinced that the biblical
Sargon was an alias for a better-known Assyrian monarch, concluded that the author of
the inscription was actually Esarhaddon. For the reasoning involved, see Booth 1902:
355-57, and Pallis 1965: 140-41; the original work, Isidor Löwenstern, *Essai de
déchiffrement de l'écriture assyrienne*, 1845, is unavailable to me. Löwenstern was
quite familiar with the earlier correlations of biblical and classical Assyrian kings:
Schalmanasser = Schalman; Sanherib = Jareb; Assaradon = Assaredin and Sargon;
Nabuchodonoser of Judith = Saosduchin or Chiniladan of the Ptolemaic canon; see
Löwenstern 1851: 557. By 1850, H.C. Rawlinson would confirm the reading of Sargon
and cite a passage in the Arabic geographer Yāqūt that Khorsabād, a village east of the
Tigris, a dependency of Nineveh, adjoined the ancient ruined city of Sarghun, 'where
treasure to a large amount had been found by excavating'; H. Rawlinson 1850: 19 n. 2.
In H. Rawlinson 1851: 902-903, while agreeing that Sargon is the name of both the
Khorsabād king and of Scripture, he reasserts the time-honored exegetical feint that
Sargon = Shalmaneser of the Bible.

   13. Hincks (1854: 393-410) represents one of the earliest efforts to synchronize the
reigns of biblical, Assyrian and Babylonian kings based on cuneiform sources, shortly
thereafter popularized by G. Rawlinson 1862: 248, 358-80 and *passim*; Robio de La
Tréhonnais 1862: 187-90; Lenormant 1868: 455-64 ('Sargin'); Wattenbach 1868: 23-
24, 27-28; Finzi 1872: 42-47 ('Sarukina'); Schmidt 1872: 406-18. Smith (1869a: 92-
100, 106-12) is a masterful pioneering chronological history of Sargon, utilizing
limmu-dates from administrative and economic texts in conjunction with the historical
inscriptions. No small role in the legitimation of this heretofore shadowy king was
played by the anonymous article on Assyria in the 8th edition of the *Encyclopaedia
Britannica* (1853) that argued for the independent existence of Sargon (III, 778) and, a
much larger stick, the essay by the famous Austen Henry Layard, in which he based his
certainty that Sargon (= the king in Isa. 20) followed the reign of Shalmaneser and
preceded that of Sennacherib on the newly deciphered inscriptions; Layard 1858: 275.
Sargon has his own entry in the 9th edition of the *Encyclopaedia Britannica* (1886). At
the turn of this century, Sayce would write a sophisticated essay on the king's reign
with no allusion to the earlier exegetical uncertainty surrounding Sargon's identity.
Sargon had become as solidly respectable a member of the royal 'biblical Assyria'
pantheon as Tiglath-Pileser or Sennacherib (Sayce 1901a). I would like to thank Ms

The inconclusive but correct identification in 1847 of the name Sargon in the Khorsabād inscriptions with the Sargon mentioned in Isa. 20.1 was the first time an Assyrian royal name was read in an extra-biblical document;[14] Sennacherib and Esarhaddon followed in 1848.[15] The conventions of the logograms by which most Assyrian royal names were represented were only haltingly understood until the great Sumero-Akkadian syllabaries began to be systematically investigated in the late 1850s, hence, colorful trial efforts like 'Dimmanu-Bara' (Hincks 1853) and 'Temen-Bar' (H. Rawlinson 1850: 22-23). The cuneiform signs of the name 'Shalmaneser' frustrated the decipherers and convinced many skeptics that the decipherment of Akkadian was a scholarly hoax. So, although a translation of the Black Obelisk inscription of Shalmaneser III appeared in 1850 and the captioned image of 'Jehu son of Omri' was correctly identified in 1851,[16] the Obelisk itself would not be associated with Shalmaneser until the late 1850s, when the royal name was accurately transcribed.[17] By the

Shanta Uddin, Corporate Librarian for Encyclopedia Britannica, Inc., for permitting me to consult the crucial 8th edition of the *Encyclopaedia Britannica*.

14. Longpérier (1848) building on Botta's phonetic realization of the MAN sign as 'sar'.

15. Hincks 1848: 439-40 ('Sankirib' and 'Assaradin'); 1855: 30-36 (read 25 June 1849), involved substantial guesswork: the identification of Sennacherib was right: the reading *San-ki-ram* was not. On the figure of the remarkable rector Dr Edward Hincks (1792–1866), whose role as a decipherer of Akkadian has been eclipsed in most earlier secondary studies by that of H.C. Rawlinson, see Davidson 1933; Lane-Poole 1921–22; Cathcart 1994; Daniels 1994; and Larsen 1996: 178-79, 211, 213, 215-27, 231, 293-305, 333-37, 356-59.

16. H. Rawlinson 1850: 22-48. Rawlinson's translation, an astounding feat at the time, used the limited syllabary at his disposal and so missed identifying Jehu of Israel and the kings of Damascus; his dating of the Black Obelisk to the twelfth century added to the obscurity. Hincks (1851) correctly observed that 'Yau, son of Humri' = Jehu of Israel.

17. In a brief response to Rawlinson's translation of the Black Obelisk, Georg Friedrich Grotefend, reasoning from the series of Syro-Palestinian campaigns enumerated in the text, concluded that the best historical fit for the author's profile is the Shalmaneser of Josephus—and hence rejects Rawlinson's Temen-Bar for Shalmaneser; Grotefend 1850. There is no evidence that Hincks or Rawlinson knew of Grotefend's proposal—the author of the Black Obelisk would remain a mystery for the next five years. The case is similar to Löwenstern's 'reading' of Sargon/Esarhaddon. In the absence of a convincing reading based on phonetic sign values, even good guesswork went begging. Oppert's work with the syllabaries S^a and S^b presumably allowed him to identify accurately the author of the Black Obelisk with Shalmaneser

year 1853, with the publication of the results of Layard's second campaign in *Discoveries among the Ruins of Nineveh and Babylon*, Layard could boast that the progress of decipherment had yielded over 50 cuneiform names of kings, nations, cities, peoples, and gods found in the Old Testament, including Sargon, Sennacherib, and Esarhaddon.[18]

Curious to relate, 'Pul', the Assyrian king who received tribute from Menahem of Israel in 2 Kgs 15.19-20, posed no special difficulty prior to the decipherment of the royal Assyrian annals. The name also appears in Berossos, Josephus, and the Ptolemaic canon—how could such venerable authorities possibly be mistaken?[19] Among biblical commentators and historians of the ancient world writing prior to 1850, Pul was universally recognized as the first Assyrian conqueror to trouble Israel, followed immediately by Tiglath-Pileser.[20] Hincks's reading in 1852 of 'Menahem of Samaria' as tributary to the king whose sculptures had been reused in the Southwest Palace of Nimrūd[21] permitted Layard a year later to publish

---

III; unfortunately, he did not publish his phonetic reading of the name; Oppert 1856. In the same publication he read *Tiglat-pallou-sir*, *Sin-akhi-irib* and *Assour-akh-iddin* for, respectively, Tiglath-Pileser, Sennacherib, and Esarhaddon, and contemptuously dismissed Rawlinson's equation of biblical Pul with the false reading of 'Phal-lukha' as an example of a researcher conforming his evidence to fit the hypothesis. In Oppert's opinion, no monuments of biblical Pul had yet been found, the unspoken assumption being that Pul was a genuine historical personage different from Tiglath-Pileser, and that inscriptional evidence would eventually vindicate the Bible.

On the life and scholarship of Jules Oppert (1825–1905), see Muss-Arnolt 1894; Anonymous 1905; Lehmann-Haupt 1905. Born in Hamburg, Oppert's route to academic placement in France entailed naturalization as a French citizen.

18. Layard 1853: 626-28, table 2. The list included Jehu, Omri, Menahem, Hezekiah, Hazael, Merodach-baladan, Ashdod, Lachish, Damascus, Hamath, Hittites, Ur, Harran. On the colorful career of Sir Austin Henry Layard, consult Layard 1903; Waterfield 1963; Saggs 1970: 1-64 (Saggs's excellent introduction); Fales and Hickey 1987; Bohrer 1989; Larsen 1996; Russell 1997: 1-128.

19. פּוּל (2 Kgs 15.19, MT); φουλ (2 Kgs 15.19, LXX); Phulos (Berossos); φουλος (Josephus); Πωρος (Ptolemaic Canon). Cuneiform [m]*pu-lu* also occurs in Kinglist A iv 8, though the *editio princeps* of this text would not be published until the 1880s; Pinches 1883-84: 193-98 (Rm 3,5 = BM 33332 = CT 36, pls. 24-25). For all forms and sources of the royal name Pul, see Brinkman 1968: 240-41 n. 1544.

20. See Schroeer 1726: 144, 468-69; Winer 1849: II, 259-60 ('Phul'), and 611-12 ('Thiglath pileser'); Kenrick 1855: 374-75 (wholly untroubled by recently published inscriptions); Milman 1870: 302-305.

21. Hincks 1852: 26. G. Rawlinson (1859: 375 n. 2) disturbed by the unbiblical collocation of Rezin of Damascus with Menahem of Samaria, assented to Hincks's

an engraving of an Assyrian king on his chariot with the caption 'Bas-relief, representing Pul, or Tiglath-Pileser'.[22] The identification, made before the cuneiform name of the king could actually be read, proved to be correct, a striking instance of 'biblical Assyria' opening the threshold to 'historical Assyria'. While the events enumerated in the translations of the badly mutilated inscriptions of Tiglath-Pileser (III) seemed to corroborate the military history of 'biblical Assyria', 'King Pul' proved too entrenched in the scholarly imagination for the first assyriologists *not* to find him in the 'monuments'. For example, through a false reading of the royal name Adad-nārārī (III) as 'Phal-lukha', and by equating this with biblical Pul (Rawlinson 1854a), Rawlinson one month later in 1854 was able to link the name Semiramis of Greek legend with Israelite history, a wonderful if evanescent example of 'biblical' and 'classical' Assyria stealing a march on 'historical Assyria'.[23]

reading but proposed that the Assyrian scribe mistook Menahem for Pekah. His brother George Rawlinson, whose fidelity to the 'received literal history' of the Old Testament led him to adopt several forced synchronizations, observed that 'The comparative chronology of the reigns of Sennacherib and Hezekiah is the chief difficulty which meets the historian who wishes to harmonize the Scriptural narrative with the Inscriptions' (p. 384 n. 2). In spite of the silence of Sennacherib's annals, H.C. Rawlinson, who had read the Taylor and Bellino prisms, maintained the traditional exegetical position that Sennacherib had campaigned twice in Palestine; H. Rawlinson 1851: 903. George Rawlinson loyally followed his brother's lead in this matter; G. Rawlinson 1859: 383; 1868: 119-21.

22. Layard 1853: 619. In his text Layard asserts that '[t]his Assyrian king must, consequently, have been either the immediate predecessor of Pul, Pul himself, or Tiglath Pileser, the name on the pavement-slab not having yet been deciphered' (p. 617).

23. The mother—not the wife!—of Adad-nārārī III was Sammu-râmat, the origin of the legendary Greek Semiramis: the name of mother and son figured together in a votive inscription described by H. Rawlinson 1854b: 465. Rawinson repeats this correlation in H. Rawlinson 1859: 519. Herodotus (1.184) believed Semiramis lived some five generations before Nitocris, a date that corresponds roughly (very roughly) to the Ussherite dating of Pul; hence, Rawlinson's chain of associations. George Rawlinson, to his credit, dismissed Ninus and his wife, Semiramis, as real historical personages; G. Rawlinson 1859: I, 364; on Semiramis as the wife of Iva-lush, 'perhaps the Pul of the Hebrew Scriptures, the Phaloch or Phalôs of the Septuagint, and the Belochus of Eusebius and others', see H. Rawlinson in G. Rawlinson 1859: I, 373 (written in 1857 or earlier). George Vance Smith, writing during the brief time that H.C. Rawlinson's theory of the identity of 'Phal-lukha' attracted any adherents, grapples with the Old Testament, the classical sources, and the 'monuments' (G.V. Smith 1857: 19-23, 65-67). Layard, in his authoritative essay on Nineveh in the 8th

The industrious Rawlinson, beginning in 1862 in a series of articles devoted to Assyrian and Babylonian chronology,[24] believed himself capable of providing the means for solving the vexatious puzzle of the lengths of the reigns of the Assyrian kings. During the Neo-Assyrian era, calendar years were named after a fixed rota of officials, comparable to the use of the names of Greek archons and Roman consuls for the same purpose. These eponyms were systematically recorded in lists, or canons, sometimes with parenthetical notices of events of military or political importance. Rawlinson had access to four overlapping canon lists; combined, they covered what we now know to have been the late tenth century through the beginning of Assurbanipal's reign in the seventh century.[25] The Assyrian eponym canon not only made it possible to demonstrate conclusively the sequence of kings from the heretofore obscure ninth-century monarchs to the resplendent Assurbanipal of the lion-hunt sculptures, but it also enabled students of history to state how many years, say, Tiglath-Pileser (III) and Shalmaneser (III) occupied the throne. The *editio princeps* of the Akkadian texts appeared in the *Cuneiform Inscriptions of Western Asia* series in 1866 and a final edition in 1870;[26] Schrader published an accurate synoptic transliteration of the canons complete with BCE dating as an appendix to his *Keilinschriften und Alte Testament* (1872). The indefatigable George Smith would canvass the brief but contentious history of interpretation in his 1875 monograph entitled *The Assyrian Canon; Containing Translations of the Documents, and an Account of the Evidence,*

edition of the *Encyclopaedia Britannica* (1858), follows H.C. Rawlinson in his equation of Pul = ?Phal-lukha, complete with prefixed question mark. With some reservation, Rawlinson still maintained the identity of the inscriptions of 'Vul-lush' (= ^{d}10-ÉRIN.TÁḪ, Adad-nārārī [III]) and Pul in 1861, followed by W.H.F. Talbot; H. Rawlinson 1861 I R 35 nn 1-3; Talbot 1862: 181-86; I R 35 pl. 35 no. 1 (= *RIMA* 3 A.0.104.8). Rawlinson abandoned his identification of 'Iva-lush III' with Pul in 1862, a revision based on his work with the eponym canon; H. Rawlinson 1862a: 725.

24. 'I am glad to be able to announce to those who are interested in the comparative chronology of the Jewish and Assyrian kingdoms, the discovery of a Cuneiform document which promises to be of the greatest possible value in determining the dates of all great events which occurred in Western Asia between the beginning of the ninth and the latter half of the seventh century B.C.', H. Rawlinson 1862a: 724. [Rawlinson originally believed that the 'canon' consisted of a list of the annual high priests of Assyria]; Rawlinson 1862b; 1863; 1867a; 1867b.

25. For a modern edition see now Millard 1994; and the useful discussion of the Neo-Assyrian eponym system in Finkel and Reade 1995.

26. II R, 68-69; III R, 1.

on the Comparative Chronology of the Assyrian and Jewish Kingdoms, from the Death of Solomon to Nebuchadnezzar.[27]

In cuneiform script, Tiglath-Pileser's name usually required five or more different characters for its representation.[28] Tukultī-apal-É.šar.ra ≠ Pul, as even the most enthusiastic assyriological tyros were forced to admit. Publication of the Assyrian eponym canon, begun in 1862, failed to break the suspense. No Pul. Historicist denials of missing King Pul include:

1.   The Assyrian eponym canon is flawed—Pul was skipped in a 40-odd year hiatus (Oppert continued to campaign for this well into the 1880s).[29]
2.   'The compiler of the [Assyrian eponym] canon was a blunderer' (Hincks).[30]
3.   Pul was a Chaldean suzerain whose reign was skipped by the Assyro-phile canon authors (Bosanquet).[31]
4.   Pul is to be identified with an eighth-century monarch preceding

27.   Smith 1875. '…I believe myself that that the [Assyrian eponym] canon is a complete and accurate document' (1875: 72). On the brilliant but brief career of George Smith, 'the intellectual picklock', see Sayce 1876; Seccombe 1921–22; Hoberman 1983; Evers 1993.

28.   For all the options, see Brinkman 1968: 240 n. 1544.

29.   The professional assyriologist Oppert and his followers, in the face of the Assyrian eponym canon's conclusive evidence against it, would doggedly maintain a biblically-based conviction in Pul's reality, a parade example of the authority of biblical Assyria over historical Assyria; Oppert 1868; 1887. Finzi 1872: 35-37, follows Oppert, but uneasily leaves open the possibility that Pul = Tiglath-Pileser. George Rawlinson, in his review of Lenormant's *Manuel*, would spend almost a quarter of his essay fulminating over Oppert's pernicious legacy in the matter of Pul's non-appearance in the Assyrian eponym canon; G. Rawlinson 1870: 95-99.

30.   Hincks, *Journal of Sacred Literature*, January 1863, quoted in Bosanquet 1874: 2.

31.   Bosanquet 1865: 152-53. 'Such appears to be the simple explanation of a difficulty, which has led Dr. Hincks and M. Oppert to suggest, that the names of not less than thirty or forty archons at Nineveh have been omitted from the Assyrian Canon, between the reigns of Asshur-zallus [= Aššur-nārārī V] and Tiglathpileser, in order to make room for the supposed reign of Pul' (1865: 153). Also see Bosanquet 1874: 58-61. Bosanquet's 'methodology' entailed the utmost freedom in juggling Assyrian regnal dates to match his preconceptions of Israelite and Judahite timelines. Smith, with fatal courtesy: 'The chronological system of Mr. Bosanquet is impossible; but assyriologists are under great obligations to him for the noble manner in which he supports their labours' (Smith 1875: 11).

Tiglath-Pileser whose name appears in the Assyrian eponym canon (G. Smith).[32]

5. Pul and Tiglath-Pileser are identical (H.C. Rawlinson and Schrader).[33]

The American semiticist Francis Brown in his prophetic monograph *Assyriology: Its Use and Abuse in Old Testament Study* archly summed up the mindset behind the biblical apologists' stubborn clinging to Pul:

> The vice of this method of handling the inscriptions lies here: that it involves a playing fast-and-loose with well-attested historical documents; hailing them eagerly when they say at once what you want them to say, but discrediting them with all your might when their utterances are troublesome to you....[34]

Schrader's identification in the 1870s of the scriptural and Ptolemaic canon entity Pul with the scriptural and cuneiform entity Tiglath-Pileser (III, generally known as II at the time) wins almost universal acceptance. In truth, this identification was anticipated a decade earlier by H.C. Rawlinson.[35] Unlike Schrader, however, Rawlinson never expressed his opinion about the positive correlation as an unqualified statement, leaving open the possibility that biblical Pul was a 'general' of Tiglath-Pileser.[36]

---

32. Smith (1869b: 9-10) while conceding that 'Sir Henry Rawlinson has suppressed the Biblical Pul king of Assyria, who took tribute from Menahem', nevertheless advocates that Vul-nirari (Aššur-nārārī V) = Pul since, according to Smith, he ascended the throne in 755, thus providing a plausible synchronism with Menahem of Israel. The phonetic similarity between Vul- and Pul satisfactorily accounted for the form of the biblical citation in Smith's opinion.

33. In 1872 Schrader skillfully marshaled the evidence for his hypothesis '...daß Phul und Pör und widerum Phul und Tiglath-Pileser ein und dieselbe Person sind', Schrader 1872: 133, and 124-28, 131-33; 1875: 321-23; 1878: 422-23, 458-60; 1880: 3-4. On the life of Eberhard Schrader (1836–1908), see Meyer 1908; and Renger 1979; and see the remarks in Cooper 1991: 52-56.

34. Brown 1885: 27-28.

35. A point of nationalistic honor defensively raised by Smith (1875: 13) who was well aware of Schrader's position.

36. Rawlinson 1863: 245. Although the eponym canons left no room for Pul's reign, a fact that the doggedly logical Rawlinson could not ignore, his discomfort with the notion of abandoning Pul is patently evident: 'But even if the separate name of Pul be thus eliminated from the royal Assyrian lists, our difficulties are not ended. There is much still to be done before we can fully reconcile the Hebrew accounts of this period of history with the contemporary cuneiform annals' (1863: 245). In subsequent articles in the *Athenaeum* which deal with Assyrian chronology, he avoids mentioning the

Schrader's lucid prose exposition, on the contrary, left no room for tergiversation. The interregnum of Pul 'hat in Wirklichkeit nie existiert'.[37] Since Pul = Tiglath-Pileser (III), the historical integrity of the Bible is perceived as intact, and the Assyrian eponym canon will be used by biblical pundits fearlessly, and hence recklessly, to date biblical and related historical events.

Within two decades of the time that biblical Sargon gained recognition as a genuine historical personage, Pul dislimned into a biblical and classical alias of Tiglath-Pileser. Sound familiar? The history of exegesis often repeats itself. The scholarly consensus from 1875 to the present, that Pul was another name by which the contemporaries of Tiglath-Pileser knew him,[38] may well be 'correct', that is, biblical and classical Assyria ≈ historical Assyria. On the other hand, one must pause to wonder what the exegetes of the nineteenth and twentieth centuries might have done with Sargon, had his name stubbornly refused to be read in the cuneiform inscriptions of Assyria.

Classical Assyria, ignorant of Sargon, and biblical Assyria, with a single ambiguous and minor reference to the king, resulted in centuries of learned speculation regarding the 'real' identity of this king. The assyriological *communis opinio* that the builder of the great Khorsabād palace was the very king mentioned in Isa. 20.1 acted as a balm laid upon the wounds of Victorian-era scholars inflicted by radical challenges to the historical veracity of the Bible.[39] The failure of assyriology to confirm the

name Pul altogether. That Rawlinson's notions regarding the identity of Pul and Tiglath-Pileser gained the attention of other scholars is borne out by Wattenbach (1868: 23), who asserted that '...es scheint, daß er [Pul] nicht verschieden ist vor Tiglath-Pilesar II, der Name verstümmelt aus Pulitser, der assyrischen Form des Namens'.

37. Hommel 1880: 19. Sayce conceived of Pul as a mere copyist's error for Tiglath-Pileser in his groundbreaking essay on Babylonia (that encompasses Assyria) in the 9th edition of the *Encyclopaedia Britannica*; Sayce 1886: 187. By the turn of the century, however, he had moderated his views in keeping with the consensus that Pul was the name by which Tiglath-Pileser was known in Babylonia; Sayce 1901b.

38. To be sure, the defense of the independent historicity of biblical Pul (Pul ≠ Tiglath-Pileser) continues to the present. Most of the proponents are motivated by the summons of biblical inerrancy, and utilize arguments that, for the most part, pit them against the academic study of assyriology and the Bible. See, e.g., McIntyre 1992; and his refutation, Storck 1992.

39. See, for example, G. Rawlinson 1868: 118-19. The entire work is aggressively apologetic in purpose, dedicated to combating 'German Neology', 'the latest phase of

independent reality of King Pul, on the other hand, touched a raw nerve in a Bible-fearing Europe,[40] sparking over 20 years of industrious textual and archeological excavation for the missing king.[41] Schrader's elegant solution, essentially a harmonization of biblical higher criticism and assyriological spadework, established a durable pattern for reconciling the dissonant claims of overlapping but distinct interest groups warring over their intellectual rights to the Bible.

BIBLIOGRAPHY

Anonymous
    1817   'Assyria', *Encyclopaedia Britannica: Or, a Dictionary of Arts, Sciences, and Miscellaneous Literature*, III (Edinburgh: Encyclopedia Press, 5th edn): 4-5.

Anonymous
    1842   'Assyria', *The Encyclopaedia Britannica or Dictionary of Arts, Sciences, and General Literature*, III (Edinburgh: A. & C. Black, 7th edn): 717-18.

modern unbelief' (p. 11). On the complex social issue of biblical literalism in the nineteenth century, see Shaffer 1975; Cameron 1987; and Rogerson 1984. On the evangelical hunger for biblical confirmation from the 'monuments' that crossed all classes and denominations in Victorian England, see Kildahl 1959: 147-94, and Bohrer 1989: 262-82. The Protestant pilgrimage to Palestine was born of this anxiety to lay one's hands on those mute stones: 'Biblical literalism and the efforts to corroborate the status of Scriptures as revealed texts precipitated certain changes in the approach to Palestine as a geographical and historical place ... The landscape itself was a sacred text to be read and interpreted literally, rather than allegorically or symbolically. Travel itself, the pilgrimage to the Holy Places, became a weapon with which to fight skepticism, the new Biblical criticism, Positivism and, from the 1870s, Darwinism' (Melman 1992: 168-69).

    40. On the relative omnipresence of Bibles in Victorian households, irrespective of whether the owners were dissenters, Anglicans, or even literate, see Knight 1995: 36-46. The ideological mission of Victorian imperialism cherished by many evangelicals, the edification of the globe through the spread of progressive Christian civilization on the British model, had its domestic correlate: in the period between 1840 and 1876, an unprecedented 7,144 Anglican churches were restored and an additional 1,727 were built at a cost of £25 1/2 million, a sum amassed mostly by private donation. Hyam 1993: 90; Gibson 1994.

    41. Including an anti-modernist imprimatur by the Catholic Church. Massaroli (1882) expanding on a series of essays that originally appeared in *Civiltà Cattolica*, self-consciously endeavors to defend the truth of scripture by arguing that Pul and Tiglath-Pileser are two distinct individuals (1882: 1-59) as well as maintaining the (by then) bravely reactionary claim that Sargon and Shalmaneser V are identical (pp. 60-143), flaunting or dismissing inscriptional evidence as the need arose.

Anonymous
    1905   'Oppert, Jules (1825–1905)', *Wer ist's? Unsere Zeitgenossen*, I (Berlin: Arani): 620.
Barr, J.
    1984   'Why the World was Created in 4004 BC: Archbishop Ussher and Biblical Chronology', *BJRL* 67: 575-608.
Bohrer, F.N.
    1989   'A New Antiquity: The English Reception of Assyria' (PhD dissertation, University of Chicago).
Booth, A.J.
    1902   *The Discovery and Decipherment of the Trilingual Cuneiform Inscriptions* (London: Longmans, Green & Co.).
Bosanquet, J.W.
    1865   'Assyrian and Hebrew Chronology Compared, with the View Showing the Extent to Which the Hebrew Chronology of Ussher Must Be Modified, in Conformity with the Assyrian Canon', *JRAS* NS 1: 145-80.
    1874   'Synchronous History of the Reigns of Tiglath-Pileser..and Azariah. Shal-manezer.." ..Jotham. Sargon.." ..Ahaz. Sennacherib.." ..Hezekiah. From B.C. 745 to 688', *Transactions of the Society of Biblical Archeology* 3: 1-82.
Brinkman, J.A.
    1968   *PKB*.
Brown, F.
    1885   *Assyriology: Its Use and Abuse in Old Testament Study* (New York: Charles Scribner's Sons).
Cameron, N.M.D.S.
    1987   *Biblical Higher Criticism and the Defense of Infallibilism in 19th Century Britain* (Texts and Studies in Religion, 33; Lewiston, NY: Edwin Mellen Press).
Capomacchia, A.M.G.
    1986   *Semiramis: una femminilità ribaltata* (Storia delle Religioni, 4; Rome: 'L'Erma' di Bretschneider).
Cathcart, K.J.
    1994   'Edward Hincks (1792–1866): A Biographical Essay', in Cathcart (ed.), 1994: 1-29.
Cathcart, K.J. (ed.)
    1994   *The Edward Hincks Bicentenary Lectures* (Dublin: University College Press).
Cooper, J.S.
    1991   'Posing the Sumerian Question: Race and Scholarship in the Early History of Assyriology', *AO* 9: 47-66.
Couture, P.G.
    1984   'Sir Henry Creswicke Rawlinson: Pioneer Cuneiformist', *BA* 47: 143-45.
Daniels, P.T.
    1994   'Edward Hinck's Decipherment of Mesopotamian Cuneiform', in Cathcart (ed.), 1994: 30-57.
Davidson, E.F.
    1933   *Edward Hincks: A Selection from his Correspondence, with a Memoir* (Oxford: Oxford University Press).

Drews, R.
1965 'Assyria in Classical Universal Histories', *Historia: Zeitschrift für alte Geschichte* 14: 129-42.

Eichhorn, J.G.
1824 *Einleitung in des Alte Testament*, IV (Göttingen: Karl Eduard Rosenbusch, 4th edn).

Eilers, W.
1971 *Semiramis: Entstehung und Nachhall einer altorientalischen Sage* (Österreichische Akademie der Wissenschaften philosophisch-historische Klasse; Minutes, Bd. 274, Abh. 2; Vienna: Herman Böhlaus).

Evers, S.M.
1993 'George Smith and the Egibi Tablets', *Iraq* 55: 107-17.

Ewald, H.
1847 *Geschichte des Volkes Israel bis Christus* III/1 (Göttingen: Dieterich).

Fales, F.M., and B.J. Hickey (eds.)
1987 *Austen Henry Layard tra l'Oriente e Venezia* (La Fenice, 8; Rome: 'L'Erma' di Bretschneider).

Finkel, I.L., and J.E. Reade
1995 'Lots of Eponyms', *Iraq* 57: 167-72.

Finzi, F.
1872 *Ricerche per lo studio dell' antichità Assira* (Turin: Ermanno Loescher).

Flemming, J.P.G.
1894 'Sir Henry Rawlinson und seine Verdienste die Assyriologie', *Beiträge zur Assyriologie und vergleichenden semitischen Sprachwissenschaft* 2: 1-18.

Fletcher, J.P.
1850 *Notes from Nineveh, and Travels in Mesopotamia, Assyria, and Syria* (Philadelphia: Lea & Blanchard).

Fraser, J.B.
1842 *Mesopotamia and Assyria, from the Earliest Ages to the Present Time; with Illustrations of their Natural History* (Edinburgh: Oliver & Boyd, 2nd edn).

Gesenius, W.
1828 *Hebräisches und chaldäisches Handwörterbuch über das Alte Testament* (Leipzig: Friedrich Christian Wilhelm Vogel, 3rd rev. edn).

Gibson, W.
1994 *Church, State and Society, 1760–1850* (British History in Perspective; New York: St. Martin's Press).

Grotefend, G.F.
1850 'Das Zeitalter des Obelisken aus Nimrud', in *Nachrichten von der Georg-Augusts-Universität und der Königl. Gesellschaft der Wissenschaften zu Göttingen* XIII (Göttingen: [np]): 177-86.

Grotius, H.
1776 *Hvgonis Grotii Annotationes in Vetvs Testamentvm emendativs edidit, et brevibvs complvrivm locorvm dilvcidationibvs avxit Georgivs Ioannes Ludov. Vogel, post mortem B. Vogelii continvavit Iohannes Christophorvs Doederlein* II (Halae: Io. Iac. Curt.).

Hincks, E.
1848 'On the Inscriptions at Van', *JRAS* 9: 387-449.
1851 'Nimrud Obelisk', *Athenaeum* 1261: 1384-85.

| 1852 | 'Nimrud Inscriptions', *Athenaeum* 1262: 26. |

1853　'The Nimrûd Obelisk', *Dublin University Magazine* 42 250: 420-26.

1854　'Chronology of the Reigns of Sargon and Sennacherib', *Journal of Sacred Literature* NS 6: 393-410.

1855　'On the Khorsabad Inscriptions', *The Transactions of the Royal Irish Academy* 22.2: 3-72.

Hoberman, B.

1983　'George Smith (1840–1876): Pioneer Assyriologist', *BA* 46: 41-42.

Hommel, F.

1880　*Abriß der babylonisch-assyrischen und israelitischen Geschichte von der ältesten Zeiten bis zur Zerstörung Babel's in Tabellenform* (Leipzig: J.C. Hinrichs).

Hughs, J.

1990　*Secrets of the Times: Myth and History in Biblical Chronology* (JSOTSup, 66; Sheffield: Sheffield Academic Press).

Hyam, R.

1993　*Britain's Imperial Century, 1815–1914: A Study of Empire and Expansion* (Cambridge Commonwealth Series; Lanham, MD: Barnes & Noble, 2nd edn).

Kalinsky, J.G.

1748　*Vaticinia Chabacvci et Nachvmi itemque nonnvlla Iesaiae, Micheae, et Ezechielis oracvla observationibvs historico-philologicis ex historia Diodori Sicvli circa res Sardanapali ea methodo illustrata, vt Libro priore historia vetervm scriptorvm de Sardanapalo vindicetvr; et defectio Medorvm ab Assyriis non ad Assarhaddonis initivm; sed ad regni finem revocetvr: posteriore vero Oracvla Prophetica eadem historia dvce explicentvr, qvibvs appendicis loco adiicitvr commentatio historico-philologica de lessv Ieremiae in obitvm Iosiae Ier. VIII, 18. ad finem cap. IX. qvaerendo* (Vratislaviaev: Impensis Ioh. Iacobi. Kornii).

Kanngiesser, P.F.

1820　'Assyrii', in J.S. Ersch and J.G. Gruber (eds.), *Allgemeine Encyclopädie der Wissenschaften und Künste in alphabetischer Folge von genannten Schrifts* V (Leipzig: Johann Friedrich Gleditsch): 151-53.

Kenrick, J.

1855　*Phoenicia* (London: B. Fellowes).

Kildahl, P.A.

1959　'British and American Reactions to Layard's Discoveries in Assyria, 1845–1860' (PhD dissertation, University of Minnesota).

Knight, F.

1995　*The Nineteenth-Century Church and English Society* (Cambridge: Cambridge University Press).

Knobel, A.W.

1837　*Der Prophetismus der Hebräer vollständig dargestellt*, II (Breslau: Josef Max und Komp.).

Koopmans, W.C.

1819　*Disputatio historico-critica de Sardanapalo* (Amsterdam: Vid. G. Warners et Fil.).

Lane-Poole, S.
1921–22   'Hincks, Dr. Edward (1792–1866)', in L. Stephen and S. Lee (eds.),
           Dictionary of National Biography: from the Earliest Times to 1900, IX (22
           vols., London: Oxford University Press): IX, 889b-90a.

Larsen, M.T.
1996   *The Conquest of Assyria: Excavations in an Antique Land 1840–1860*
           (London: Routledge).

Layard, A.H.
1853   *Discoveries in the Ruins of Nineveh and Babylon; with Travels in Armenia,*
           Kurdistan and the Desert: Being the Result of a Second Expedition under-
           taken for the Trustees of the British Museum (London: John Murray).

1858   'Nineveh', *The Encyclopaedia Britannica, or Dictionary of Arts, Sciences,*
           and General Literature XVI (Edinburgh: A. & C. Black, 8th edn): 272-77.

1903   *Sir A. Henry Layard, G.C.B., D.C.L., Autobiography and Letters from his*
           Childhood until his Appointment as H.M. Ambassador at Madrid, Edited by
           the Hon. William N. Bruce, with a Chapter on his Parliamentary Career by
           the Rt. Hon. Arthur Otway (London: John Murray).

Lehmann-Haupt, C.F.
1905   'Oppert, Julius', in A. Bettelheim (ed.), *Biographisches Jahrbuch und*
           deutscher Nekrolog, X (Berlin: Georg Reimer): 86-92.

Lenormant, F.
1868   *Manuel d'histoire ancienne de l'Orient jusqu'aux guerres médiques*. I.
           Israélites—Égyptiens—Assyriens (Paris: A. Levy Fils).

Longpérier, H.A.P.D.
1848   'Lettre à M. Isidore Löwenstern sur les inscriptions cunéiformes de l'Assyrie',
           Revue archéologique 4: 501-507.

Löwenstern, I.
1851   'Lettre à l'éditeur de la Revue Archéologique sur l'écriture assyrienne',
           Revue archéologique 8: 555-65.

Lowth, R.
1834   *Isaiah: A New Translation, with a Preliminary Dissertation and Notes, Criti-*
           cal, Philological, and Explanatory (Boston/Cambridge: William Hilliard/
           James Munroe & Co., 10th edn, 1834 [1799]).

Marsham, J.
1649   *Diatriba chronologica Johannis Marshami* (London: Jacobi Flesher).

Massaroli, G.
1882   *Phul e Tuklatpalasar II; Salmanasar V, e Sargon: questioni biblio-assire*
           (Rome: Tipografia poliglotta della S. C. di Propaganda).

Maurer, F.J.V.D.
1835   *Commentarius Grammaticus Criticus in Vetus Testamentum*, I (Leipzig:
           Fridericus Volckmar).

McIntyre, A.P.
1992   'Tiglath-pileser versus Pul—A Challenge to the Accepted View', *Cata-*
           strophism and Ancient History 14.2: 168-73.

Melman, B.
1992   *Women's Orients—English Women and the Middle East, 1718–1918:*
           Sexuality, Religion, and Work (Ann Arbor: University of Michigan Press).

Meyer, E.
1908   'Schrader, Eberhard', in A. Bettelheim (ed.), *Biographisches Jahrbuch und deutscher Nekrolog* XIII (Berlin: Georg Reimer): 156-63.

Millard, A.R.
1994   *The Eponyms of the Assyrian Empire, 910–612 B.C.* (SAAS, 2; Helsinki: Helsinki University Press).

Milman, H.H.
1870   *The History of the Jews, from the Earliest Period Down to Modern Times*, I (New York: W.J. Widdleton, rev. edn, 1870 [1866; 1829 original]).

Movers, F.K.
1841–56   *Die Phönizier* (Bonn: Eduard Weber).

Muss-Arnolt, W.
1894   'The Works of Jules Oppert', *Beiträge zur Assyriologie und vergleichenden semitischen Sprachwissenschaft* 2: 523-56.

Nagel, W.
1982   *Ninus und Semiramis in Sage und Geschichte: iranische Staaten und Reiternomaden vor Darius* (Berliner Beiträge zur Vor- und Frühgeschichte, NS, 2; Berlin: Spiess).

Newman, F.W.
1847   *A History of the Hebrew Monarchy from the Administration of Samuel to the Babylonian Captivity* (London: John Chapman).

Niebuhr, M.V.
1857   *Geschichte Assur's und Babel's seit Phul aus der Concordanz des Alten Testaments, des Berossos, des Kanons der Könige und der griechischen Schriftsteller* (Berlin: Verlag Von Wilhelm Hertz).

Oppert, J.
1856   'Rapport adressé à Son Excellence M. le Ministre de l'Instruction publique et des Cultes, par M. Jules Oppert, chargé d'une mission scientifique en Angleterre (15 My 1856)', *Archives des missions scientifiques et littéraires* 5: 221.

1868   'Le chronique biblique fixée par les éclipses des inscriptions cunéiformes', *Revue archéologique* 18: 308-28, 379-88.

1887   'Assyrie', *La Grande encyclopédie, inventaire raisonné des sciences, des lettres et des arts, par une société de savants et de gens de lettres*, IV (Paris: H. Lamirault et cie): 338-44.

Pallis, S.A.F.D.
1965   *The Antiquity of Iraq: A Handbook of Assyriology* (Copenhagen: Munksgaard).

Perizonius, J.
1711   *Jac. Perizonii Origines babylonicae et aegyptiacae, tomus II...* (Lugduni Batavorum: Johannem van der Linden).

Pettinato, G.
1985   *Semiramide* (La Storia; Milan: Rusconi).

Piccaluga, G.
1982   'La mitizzazione del Vicino Oriente nelle religioni del mondo classico', in H.-J. Nissen and J. Renger (eds.), *Mesopotamien und seine Nachbarn*: 573-612.

Pinches, T.G.
1883-84   'Communications', *PSBA* 6: 193-98.

Prideaux, H.
1716   *The Old and New Testament Connected in the History of the Jews and Neighbouring Nations, from the Declension of the Kingdom of Israel and Judah to the Time of Christ*, I (London: R. Knaplock, 2nd edn).

Rawlinson, G.
1859   *The History of Herodotus*, I (New York: D. Appleton & Company).
1862   *The Five Great Monarchies of the Ancient Eastern World; or, the History, Geography, and Antiquities of Chaldaea, Assyria, Babylonia, Media, and Persia, Collected and Illustrated from Ancient and Modern Sources*, I (London: John Murray).
1868   *The Historical Evidences of the Truth of the Scripture Records Stated Anew, with Special Reference to the Doubts and Discovereis of Modern Times. In Eight Lectures Delivered in the Oxford University Pulpit, in the Year 1859, on the Bampton Foundation* (Boston: Gould & Lincoln).
1870   'Early Oriental History [review of F. Lenormant, *Manuel d'histoire ancienne de l'Orient jusqu'aux guerres médiques*]', *The Contemporary Review* 14: 80-100.
1898   *A Memoir of Major-General Sir Henry Creswicke Rawlinson* (London: Longmans, Green & Co.).

Rawlinson, H.C.
1850   *A Commentary on the Cuneiform Inscriptions of Babylonia and Assyria; Including Readings of the Inscription of the Nimrud Obelisk, and a Brief Notice of the Ancient Kings of Nineveh and Babylon* (London: John W. Parker, 1850).
1851   'Assyrian Antiquities', *Athenaeum* 1243: 902-903.
1854a   'Babylonian Discoveries', *Athenaeum* 1377: 341-43.
1854b   'Babylonian Discovery: Queen Semiramis', *Athenaeum* 1381: 465-66.
1859   'On the Religion of the Assyrians and the Babylonians', in G. Rawlinson (ed.), *The History of Herodotus*, I (New York: D. Appleton & Company): 475-522.
1861   *The Cuneiform Inscriptions of Western Asia, Copied by E. Norris* (London: R.E. Bowler).
1862a   'Assyrian History', *Athenaeum* 1805: 724-25.
1862b   'Bible History and the Rawlinson Canon', *Athenaeum* 1812: 82-83.
1863   'Assyrian History and Chronology', *Athenaeum* 1896: 243-48.
1867a   'The Assyrian Canon Verified by the Record of a Solar Eclipse, B.C. 763', *Athenaeum* 2064: 660-61.
1867b   'The Assyrian Canon', *Athenaeum* 2080: 304-305.

Renger, J.
1979   'Die Geschichte der Altorientalistik und der vorderasiatischen Archäologie in Berlin von 1875 bis 1945', in W. Arenhövel and C. Schreiber (eds.), *Berlin und die Antike: Architektur, Kunstgewerbe, Malerei, Skulptur, Theater und Wissenschaft vom 16. Jahrhundert bis heute* (Berlin: Deutsches Archäologisches Institut): 151-57.

Robio de La Tréhonnais, F.M.L.J.
1862   *Histoire ancienne des peuples de l'Orient jusqu'au début des guerres*

médiques, mise au niveau des plus récentes découvertes, à l'usage des établissements d'instruction secondaire (Paris: Charles Douniol).

Rogerson, J.W.
1984   *Old Testament Criticism in the Nineteenth Century: England and Germany* (London: SPCK).

Rosenmüller, E.F.K.
1825   *Handbuch der biblischen Alterthumskunde*, I/2 (Leipzig: Baumgartner).

Russell, J.M.
1997   *From Nineveh to New York: the Strange Story of the Assyrian Reliefs in the Metropolitan Museum and the Hidden Masterpiece at Canford School* (New Haven: Yale University Press; New York: The Metropolitan Museum of Art).

Saggs, H.W.F. (ed.)
1970   *Nineveh and its Remains: Austen Henry Layard* (London: Routledge & Kegan Paul).

Sayce, A.H.
1876   'George Smith', *Nature* 14: 421-22.
1886   'Babylonia', *The Encyclopaedia Britannica or Dictionary of Arts, Sciences, and General Literature*, III (New York: Charles Scribner's Sons, 9th edn): 182-94.
1901a   'Sargon', in J. Hastings (ed.), *A Dictionary of the Bible, Dealing with its Language, Literature, and Contents Including the Biblical Theology* (New York: Charles Scribner's Sons; Edinburgh: T. & T. Clark, 1901): IV, 406b-407a.
1901b   'Tiglath-Pileser', in J. Hastings (ed.), *A Dictionary of the Bible, Dealing with Its Language, Literature, and Contents Including the Biblical Theology* (New York: Charles Scribner's Sons; Edinburgh: T. & T. Clark): IV, 761.

Schmidt, V.
1872   *Assyriens og Aegyptens gamle historie; eller, Historisk-geographiske undersøgelser om det gamle testamentes lande og folk*, I (Copenhagen: Wøldikes Forlag).

Schrader, E.
1872   *Die Keilinschriften und das Alte Testament* (Giessen: J. Ricker, 1st edn).
1875   'Assyrisch-Biblisches (2)', *Jahrbucher für protestanische Theologie* 1: 321-23.
1878   *Keilinschriften und Geschichtsforschung: Ein Beitrag zur monumentalen Geographie, Geschichte und Chronologie der Assyrer* (Giessen: J. Ricker).
1880   *Zur Kritik der Inschriften Tiglath-Pileser's II, des Asarhaddon und des Asurbanipal* (Berlin: Buchdruckerei der Königl. Akademie der Wissenschaften [ATLA Preservation microfiche 1986-1738]).

Schroeer, J.F.
1726   *Imperivm Babylonis et Nini ex monimentis antiqvis* (Francofvrti et Lipsiae: Georg. Marc. Knochivm).

Seccombe, T.
1921–22 'Smith, George (1840–1876)', in G. Smith, L. Stephen, and S. Lee (eds.), *Dictionary of National Biography: from the Earliest Times to 1900* (Oxford: Oxford University Press): XVIII, 447-49.

Shaffer, E.S.
1975   *'Kubla Khan' and The Fall of Jerusalem: The Mythological School in Biblical Criticism and Secular Literature, 1770–1880* (Cambridge: Cambridge University Press).

Smith, G., L. Stephen and S. Lee (eds.)
1921–22   *The Dictionary of National Biography. XLVI. From the Earliest Times to 1900* (22 vols.; Oxford: Oxford University Press).

Smith, G.
1869a   'Assyrian History: Additions to the History of Tiglath Pileser II', *ZÄS* 7: 92-100, 106-12.
1869b   'The Annals of Tiglath Pileser II', *ZÄS* 7: 9-17.
1875   *The Assyrian Canon; Containing Translations of the Documents, and an Account of the Evidence, on the Comparative Chronology of the Assyrian and Jewish Kingdoms, from the Death of Solomon to Nebuchadnezzar* (London: Samuel Bagster & Sons).

Smith, G.V.
1857   *The Prophecies Relating to Nineveh and the Assyrians: Translated from the Hebrew, with Historical Introduction and Notes, Exhibiting the Principal Results of the Recent Discoveries* (London: Longman, Brown, Green, Longmans & Roberts, 1857).

Storck, H.A.
1992   'Tiglath-Pileser versus Pul—Who is Pulling Whose Leg?', *Catastrophism and Ancient History* 14.2: 175-85.

Talbot, W.H.F.
1862   'Assyrian Texts Translated no. III: Inscription of Pul', *JRAS* 19: 181-86.

Waterfield, G.
1963   *Layard of Nineveh* (New York: Frederick A. Praeger).

Wattenbach, W.
1868   *Ninive und Babylon* (Heidelberg: Fr. Bassermann).

Winer, G.B.
1849   *Biblisches Realwörterbuch zum Handgebrauch für Studirende, Candidaten, Gymnasiallehrer und Prediger*, II (Leipzig: Carl Heinrich Reclam; New York: Rudolph Garrigue, 3rd rev. edn).

SUMER, THE BIBLE, AND COMPARATIVE METHOD: HISTORIOGRAPHY AND TEMPLE BUILDING

Richard E. Averbeck

When I was first asked to write on this topic a friend of mine, who is also a biblical scholar and, in fact, relatively well-informed about the ancient Near Eastern world, asked: 'How is it that you would attempt to show connections between the Bible and the Sumerians when they are so far removed historically, geographically, and linguistically from the world of ancient Israel. Sumerian isn't even a Semitic language'?![1] He thought that the goal was to establish some sort of direct connection between the Sumerians and ancient Israelite culture. His skepticism was well founded. Even Samuel Noah Kramer, who went so far as to endorse the very unlikely view of his teacher (Arno Poebel) that the biblical name 'Shem' (see Gen. 10–11) derives from 'Sumer' (Kramer 1959: 202-204),[2] readily acknowledged the *in*direct connectedness between Sumerian literature and the Hebrew Bible (Kramer 1959: 190). This, however, does not diminish the fact that the level of indirect influence was indeed quite significant (Bodine 1994: 19-21).

Given that there are special issues that arise in this instance, nevertheless, there are basic principles of comparative method that apply to all comparative work. Over 20 years ago Shemaryahu Talmon published what has become a classic essay on the principles and problems of using the comparative method in biblical interpretation (Talmon 1978). He isolated

---

1. I thank Mark Chavalas for inviting me to read an earlier and much shorter version of this paper at the symposium on Syro-Mesopotamia and Bible of the Near Eastern Archeological Society, November 17 1995 in Philadelphia. I also thank him and Lawson Younger for including this expanded version in the present volume.

2. For a good brief introduction to the Sumerian history, culture, and literature, and its significance for the biblical world see Bodine 1994. For helpful summaries of comparisons between Sumer and the Bible see esp. Kramer 1959: 189-204 and Hallo 1988.

four major principles: proximity in time and place, the priority of inner biblical parallels, correspondence of social function, and the holistic approach to texts and comparisons. These four categories will provide the framework for this study of methodology in the comparative study of Sumer and the Bible.

The first section of this essay will deal with Talmon's first two principles: proximity in time and place, and the priority of inner biblical parallels. These require relatively little explanation, so simple and brief illustrations will be sufficient. The principle of the priority of inner biblical parallels, in particular, will provide an occasion for preliminary consideration of the two main topics that will follow: historiography and temple building. These two topics provide the main substance for the more in depth treatments of Talmon's third and fourth principles: correspondence of social function, and the holistic approach to texts and comparisons, respectively.

With regard to correspondence of social function, much of the recent scholarly discussion about biblical and ancient Near Eastern historiography relates to its function in society. My own continuing research suggests that a comparison of the pre-Sargonic Sumerian historical inscriptions with the biblical historiographic literature offers a promising way forward in the ongoing debate. These are the earliest historiographic texts we have, and we know that Sumerian historiography was formative in the cuneiform world of the ancient Near East.

I have chosen to illustrate the principle of the holistic approach to texts and comparisons by comparing the biblical accounts of temple building with that of Gudea in the Gudea Cylinders. The composition inscribed on Gudea Cylinders A and B is renowned as one of the lengthiest, most skillful, and most difficult masterpieces in the corpus of extant Sumerian literature. It is also one of the most important ancient Near Eastern temple building texts and continues to receive considerable scholarly attention in that regard.[3]

1. *Time, Place, and Inner-Biblical Priority*
in the Study of Sumer and the Bible

Two major approaches have been taken to cataloging the various parallels between Sumerian culture and literature and that of the Hebrew Bible.

---

3.   See now especially Hurowitz 1992 and Averbeck 2000 and the literature cited in those places.

Already in 1959 Kramer isolated 15 themes or motifs that occur in both the Bible and Sumerian literature: creation out of a primeval sea that existed before the creation, mankind fashioned out of clay and granted the 'breathe of life', creation by both command and 'making' or 'fashioning', paradise stories, the flood, rivalry motifs like that of Cain and Abel, the Tower of Babel, organization of the earth, the personal god, law and law codes, ethics and morals, divine retribution, the plague motif, the suffering of the righteous, and the bleakness of the nether world.[4] After highlighting these points of correspondence he pointed out that they only 'scratches the surface' of what is there, and suggests that further work would most certainly expand upon his list especially in regard to the books of Psalms, Proverbs, Lamentations, and the Song of Songs.

Of course, since 1959 the work of isolating and explaining these and other parallels has continued. One can begin with Genesis 1–11 and move progressively through the biblical canon. For example, beginning with Genesis 1–11, the dual accounts of the creation of man in Genesis 1 and 2 has a parallel in the myth of 'Enki and Ninmah' (Klein 1997). The 120 year limit on a person's longevity in Gen. 6.3 surfaces also in 'Enlil and Namzitara' (Klein 1990). The combination of the creation of man and animals, the antediluvian culture, and the flood story in Genesis 1–9 has its parallel in a single Sumerian composition as well, 'The Eridu Genesis' (Jacobsen 1997). Work is continuing on the relationship between the Babylonian ziggurat and the tower of Babel in Genesis 11 (see most recently Walton 1995). Various Sumerian epics could be compared and contrasted with the patriarchal stories, the law codes of Urnammu and Lipitishtar are most certainly important sources for the early development of ancient Near Eastern case law, there are multitudes of hymns to gods (and temples) that could be compared to various Psalms in the Bible, laments that compare to laments in the Psalms and the book of Lamentations, love songs of the Dumuzi-Inanna cycle to be compared with the biblical Song of Songs and referenced in Ezek. 8.14, 'Weeping for Tammuz', and so on.[5]

Along the way, as the work on parallel themes and motifs has continued, scholars have sometimes raised concerns about the pick and choose nature of this method of comparison. Although much good work has been done by good scholars in this way, some of which has already been cited

---

4.   See Kramer 1959: 190-98 and the literature cited there.

5.   See well-rendered examples of these and other Sumerian texts in *COS*: I, 509-99; and *COS*: II, 385-438 and the literature cited in those places.

here, there is no doubt that the pick and choose method can lend itself to the misuse or misrepresentation of the texts themselves from the point of view of their own native literary and cultural context. Therefore, the well-known Sumerologist and comparativist William Hallo, advocates an approach based on genre comparability. Regarding comparisons between Sumerian literary compositions and the Bible, for example, he has collected and organized them according to genre categories based on their subjects: gods, kings, and common mortals (Hallo 1988: 30-38).

Common mortal texts fall largely into the category of what is called wisdom literature in the Bible (Job, Proverbs, Qoheleth). These include, for example, riddles, proverbs, instructions, disputations, and righteous sufferer accounts. Royal literature includes stories and traditions about heroic Sumerian kings before and after the flood, casuistic law codes, royal hymns, and prayers. In general, biblical correspondences here include the patriarchal accounts in Genesis, the laws in Exodus through Deuteronomy, and the Psalms, respectively. Literature that focusses on the gods includes incantations and divinatory texts, the exaltation of the patron deity, lamentations for destroyed cities, and erotic poetry. In the Bible, Yahweh is indeed exalted (Psalms and prayers), the fall of Jerusalem is lamented (Lamentations), and physical love is acclaimed as a wondrous thing (Song of Songs), but incantation and divination are forbidden.[6]

Throughout his discussion Hallo is just as concerned with contrasts between the Bible and Sumerian literature as he is with comparisons. This is not to say that Kramer and others were not aware of this issue. They also sometimes highlighted them in their writings, but Hallo and others have taken this to another level. Hallo's recent emphasis on genre as an organizing principle and on contrasts being as important as comparisons will effect how the reader engages with Talmon's four principles.[7] In general, one must keep in mind that the Bible is both in its world and against its world, and both sides of the discussion are equally important.

---

6. It is important to add here that, in the Bible, not only are all the various occultic divinatory procedures forbidden (Deut. 18.9-14), but they are replaced by prophets who were to speak clearly for Yahweh as Moses had done (Deut. 18.15-22).

7. See most notably Hallo 1990: 1-30, esp. 2-3. Most recently, see Hallo 1997: xxiii-xxviii, esp. xxv-xxvi; 2000: xxi-xxvi and the literature cited in those places. Talmon himself was already deeply concerned with a balance between comparison and contrast (see, e.g., Talmon 1978: 345).

2. *The Principle of Proximity in Time and Place*

First, we should limit ourselves to societies that lie within the 'historical stream' of biblical Israel while avoiding comparisons on a 'grand scale' (Talmon 1978: 356 with pp. 322-26, 329-32). This dictum is currently well-received. Few scholars of the ancient Near East and the Bible place much confidence in geographically and especially chronologically distant comparisons, except as they reflect a certain commonality in human experience quite apart from all the profound differences between cultures.

Sumer itself, of course, was far removed both geographically and chronologically from ancient Israel as a nation and culture. The Sumerian culture and the earliest precursors of the writing system that it spawned extend far back at least into the pre-historic Uruk period of Mesopotamian culture before 3000 BCE. The new consensus that has been emerging among Syro-Mesopotamian archeologists in the last decade is that, in the early Uruk period (i.e. 4000–3500 BCE), the kind of organized societies associated with the early development of civilization (advanced chiefdoms, cities with massive walls, etc.) were developing in northeastern Syria and southeastern Turkey without the influence of the highly urbanized city-state Uruk culture that was developing during the same period of time in the Sumerian homeland of southern Mesopotamian. Then in the later part of the Uruk period (i.e. 3500–3000 BCE, especially after 3200 BCE) there was an Uruk expansion that made contact with and influenced the peripheral regions east, north, and west of the Mesopotamian alluvial valley, including the already established chiefdoms and their cities in northern Syria.[8]

This new consensus, however, does not undermine the fact that,

---

8.   With regard to the history of writing and the Sumerian writing system see esp. Schmandt-Besserat 1995; and Vanstiphout 1995: 2182. For archeological, sociological, economic, and political dimensions of this pre-historic Sumerian presence and its contacts with regions outside of the central Mesopotamian valley see the proposal in Algaze 1993; and Astour 1992: 14-18. As reported, for example, in the *New York Times* of May 23 2000, § D p. 5 (John Noble Wilforn, 'Ruins Alter Ideas of How Civilization Spread'), the new excavations at Tell Hamoukar in northeastern Syria are reinforcing these conclusions from other recent archeological work at Tell Brak in northeastern Syria and at Hacinebi and Arslantepe in southeastern Turkey. The work by Algaze cited above, which argues that civilization started only in the south and then moved from there to the north, now needs revision in light of this new emerging consensus.

although the northern and western regions were much more advanced than previously thought and developed independently of southern Mesopotamia during the first part of the Uruk period, they did not achieve the high level of cultural development that we know from the Sumerians in southern Mesopotamia, the so-called 'cradle of civilization'. The following third millennium was the time of the development of the Sumerian language and literature in written form. By the end of the third millennium (c. 2000 BCE) the Sumerians had lost all political influence, but their language, literature, and culture had left an indelible mark that would be carried down into the second and first millenniums through the linguistic and literary conventions of the cuneiform scribal schools. In fact, many early Sumerian literary compositions are known only from their preservation in the Old Babylonian scribal canon (c. 1800–1600 BCE), and some were actually composed for the first time during the Isin-Larsa (c. 2000–1800) and Old Babylonian periods (c. 1800–1600).

As for the relationship between Sumer and the Bible, Sumer for all practical purposes lies within and, in fact, chronologically and literarily, at the beginning of the 'historical stream' of biblical Israel. In spite of the lack of linguistic similarity between the Semitic languages, of which Hebrew is one, and the non-Semitic Sumerian language, the Sumerians were nevertheless the progenitors of the cuneiform writing system, literature, and culture which deeply impacted the entire ancient Near East from very early days at least down to the middle of the first millennium BCE.

I am not arguing here for what Gelb ridiculed as a cultural 'Pan-Sumerianism' that does not recognize the early development of other high cultures both inside and outside of Sumer in proto-historical times (Gelb 1992: 121-22). The remarks above on the fourth millennium Uruk period are evidence of that. Moreover, in the third millennium the West Semitic world was more highly developed and connected within itself and with the Southern Mesopotamian world than once was thought. Gelb's proposal of a mid-third millennium Semitic 'Kish Civilization' that extended from the region of Akkad westward through Mari to Ebla and beyond is well-conceived (Gelb, 1992: 123-25, 200-202),[9] and others have argued that Akkadian was more predominant even in Sumer itself in these early days than has been commonly recognized.[10]

9. See also Astour 1992: 3-10; Archi 1987: 125-40.

10. See the rather provocative analysis of Sumerian and Akkadian language and culture in Presargonic Sumer in Cooper 1973.

These factors suggest that the cultural ingenuity and influence of the Sumerians had already been felt even in those early days in the Semitic world beyond the confines of the Mesopotamian valley. Moreover, there were later periods of time during which the level of international connectedness by means of cuneiform culture was indeed impressive. I am thinking here especially of the Amarna period (c. 1500–1200 BCE) (Lambert 1982: 314-15).[11] Again, even though the Sumerian people and their culture were long gone by that time, the origin of many cuneiform institutions and ideas went back to the Sumerian culture and its literary traditions.

The Sumerian world was mediated to the later biblical world through other languages and cultures, especially Akkadian, which became the *lingua franca* of the ancient Near East for a millennium and a half, as well as other forms of early Semitic cuneiform (e.g. Ebla in northern Syria and Presargonic Mari and Abu Salabikh in Mesopotamia), and the later cuneiform culture at large. This cuneiform culture was responsible for establishing and maintaining a longstanding underlying connectedness in the ancient Near East—a certain kind of overall 'common cultural foundation' that informed without undermining the various local cultures with which it came into contact (Hallo 1988: 38).

In light of the above, I would argue that the connections between Sumer and the Bible are *in*direct. Nevertheless, some of them are quite significant and revealing. An apt lexical illustration is the well-known but clearly non-Semitic word in the Hebrew Bible, *hêkāl*, 'palace, temple', which derives originally from Sumerian É-GAL, 'big house', via the Sumerian loanword in East Semitic Akkadian, *ekallu*. True, the connection from Sumerian to Hebrew is indirect here, but it is clearly a Hebrew word that has its ultimate origin in Sumerian.

With regard to clause syntax, the verb last word order of the Sumerian clause seems to have influenced Akkadian word order so that the verb is usually last in Akkadian clauses as well. It is true that the predominant verb first order in the normal biblical Hebrew prose may have been due in part to the nature of the *waw*-consecutive as a clause connector and the associated requirement of putting the verb first. The verb first word order common in other Semitic languages, nevertheless, suggests an underlying Sumerian causation for the verb last order in Akkadian. Here there is a contrast between Hebrew and Akkadian probably due to the fact that

---

11. Lambert also makes some important observations about influence in the other direction, from Syria-Palestine to southern Mesopotamia (1982: 311-14).

Sumerian had such a significant impact on the development of Akkadian.

As I have already observed, the early Sumerian hegemony in southern Babylonia had deep and abiding influence in the ancient Near Eastern world long after and far beyond the boundaries of direct Sumerian influence.

3. *The Priority of Inner-Biblical Parallels*

Talmon's second methodological principle is that 'The interpretation of biblical features...with the help of inner-biblical parallels should always precede the comparison with extra-biblical materials' (Talmon 1978: 356 with pp. 338-51). For example, assuming that one has analyzed a particular text comprehensively on its own merits, one needs to do careful analysis of and comparisons between the various biblical accounts of temple building (see esp. Exod. 25–40, the tabernacle construction account; 1 Kgs 5.1[15]–8.66; 2 Chron. 2–7; Ezek. 40–48) *before* comparing them with other ancient Near Eastern temple building texts, such as the Gudea Cylinders.

I would also argue, however, that this is just as important for the non-biblical comparative material. The Gudea Cylinders, for example, also need to be analyzed in comparison with other texts of their type from within their own immediate cultural and literary milieu. Fortunately, Victor Hurowitz and Jacob Klein have already done much of this work. Klein has shown that there is a particular subgenre of Sumerian royal hymns known as 'building and dedication hymns', which includes the Gudea Cylinders and three other compositions (Klein 1989: 27-67). Hurowitz has taken this subgenre of Sumerian texts as well as other (temple) building texts from the ancient Syro-Mesopotamian world, analyzed them, and in the context of that kind of analysis, has then compared them with the two major sanctuary construction accounts in the Bible, Exod. 25–40 and 1 Kgs 5–9 (Hurowitz 1985; 1992). As it turns out, there is one especially important point of contrast. The Gudea Cylinders present the temple building and dedication process as essentially a step by step ritual process. Ritual actions and processes saturate the text and, in fact, structure it. This is not the case in the parallel biblical accounts. It is true that the dedication procedures for the tabernacle and temple in the Bible involved elaborate ritual procedures, but that in no way compares with the obsessive concern for ritual guidance and confirmation in the Cylinders. I will come back to the details of this in the final section of this article.

Much of this overbearing ritual concern in the Cylinders reflects the need on the part of the ruler, Gudea, to virtually pry the specific desires and plans for the temple out of the heart of the deity for whom the temple was to be built (i.e. Ningirsu, the patron deity of Lagash). There is no ready revelation as is found in the Bible (Exod. 25–40). This feature of the Gudea Cylinders has gone relatively unnoticed in the comparative discussion and will be treated in greater detail below. Another example is historiography and history writing in Sumer and the Bible. Although much has been written on this subject, it seems to me that a good deal of it is defective, and a considerable amount of foundational work still remains to be done on both sides of the comparison. Moreover, there is far too much confusion about the very nature of the comparative enterprise as it has been applied to this subject.

4. The Corresponding Social Function of Compared Texts: Historiography in Sumer and the Bible

The third methodological principle that Talmon emphasizes is the need to treat societal phenomena by paying close attention to their 'function in the developing structure of the Israelite body politic *before* one engages in comparison with parallel phenomena in other societies' (Talmon 1978: 356 with pp. 324, 328-29, 333-38, 351-55). Texts and the phenomena that they describe or recount are integrally related to other phenomena in the community from which they derive, and superficial comparisons of isolated phenomena that appear to be similar are often misleading and counterproductive. With regard to texts in particular, which is what I am especially concerned with here, the point is that if a certain (kind of) text has a specific function in a society, comparative work should see to it that the corresponding (kind of) text in the other society has a similar function in that society.

This principle is actually a plea for paying due attention to the literary *Gattung* of the composition and its concomitant *Sitz im Leben*, and using that as one of the major criteria for comparison with other compositions within its historical stream (Talmon 1978: 351-52). This, of course, goes hand in hand with the study of textual *genres* and their production and use in societies as part of the 'form critical' enterprise. In other words, to the degree that the sociology of a text or text-type is known, this too should be considered when it is used in comparative work.

5. *The Current Discussion*

The past two or three decades of scholarship have seen increased debate over the subject of biblical history writing and historiography, much of it based on comparative ancient Near Eastern historiography. One of the major stimuli has been John Van Seters' book *In Search of History* (1983),[12] in which he argued that the so-called 'Deuteronomist', the exilic writer of the 'Deuteronomistic History' (i.e. Deut. 1–4 plus the substance of Joshua–Kings stripped of its later additions), was the earliest author to perform the task of true 'history writing' in the Bible and, in fact, in the entire ancient Near East (Van Seters 1983: 209-362).[13] He argues that the similarities between the Deuteronomistic History and the history writing of the Greek historian Herodotus show that there was an indirect connection between the two. The connection was supposedly mediated historically through the Phoenicians, who were seafaring Semites that had longstanding contact with the Aegean (Van Seters 1983: 8-54, esp. 53-54).

For Van Seters, 'history writing' is to be distinguished from 'historiography' and from texts that are 'historiographic' in nature but do not rise to the level of 'history writing' (Van Seters 1983: 1-7). Before the time of the Deuteronomist in ancient Israel and in the whole ancient Near East there was no true 'history writing', although there were 'historiographic' texts, according to Van Seters. Any pre-existing sources, native or foreign, that were used by the Deuteronomist and later by the 'Yahwist' to compose their histories do not qualify as 'history writing'. The implications of all this for the Yahwist's history in the Tetrateuch is worked out in two more recent volumes, one on Genesis and the other on Exodus through Numbers (Van Seters 1992; 1994).[14]

So Van Seters went 'in search of history' and found it in Genesis through 2 Kings. However, not all scholars are willing to accept the notion

12. There have been numerous reviews of this book and reactions to its arguments by scholars from all the various strands of biblical scholarship, some of which will be referred to in the following discussion.

13. The last sentence of his book reads, '...I hope I have demonstrated that the first Israelite historian, and the first known historian in Western civilization truly to deserve this designation, was the Deuteronomistic historian' (1983: 362).

14. He argues for a Yahwist that post-dates the Deuteronomist, contrary to common historical critical scholarly opinion. As for the work of the 'Priestly Writer', he considers it to be 'a secondary supplement to that of J and not an independent composition' (1992: 4).

that what he has found in Genesis through 2 Kings is 'history writing' in any meaningful way. Thomas L. Thompson, for example, has become unwilling to call anything in Genesis through Kings 'history writing' and, instead, thinks of it as an account of 'the mythic past'. It is a collection of old stories and legends about the past that was put together specifically to create a mythic past for the Israel of Persian and Hellenistic days. He argues that the Bible has been misunderstood as history and, in fact, we currently have 'no viable history for what we used to call "ancient Israel"' (Thompson 1999: 7). This is so, according to him, because the only sources we could use to write such a history are extra-biblical, and we have precious few of those. The Bible, after all, is disqualified for historical reconstruction because of its essentially mythological character.

I find myself agreeing in some respects and at the same time disagreeing in other respects with both of these men. On the one hand, Thompson is right to demand that history writing must be well-anchored in the truth about what actually happened in the past. If, therefore, one says that Genesis through 2 Kings is 'history writing', one needs to hold to a high degree of historicity in what it says about Israel's past. But I simply disagree with his almost totally negative assessment of the historical reliability of the biblical text. Van Seters, on the other hand, is right to emphasize the fact that 'history writing' was in ancient times, as it is today, a literary endeavor that not only records past situations and events but also imposes a certain form upon them. Thus, the way in which the ancients wrote history needs to be taken into account when one makes a judgment about whether or not Genesis through 2 Kings can properly be called ancient 'history writing'. I disagree, however, with his limited definition of 'history writing', his conclusion that it does not appear in the ancient Near East until the writing of Genesis through 2 Kings, and his proposal that the latter could have developed only under the influence of early Greek 'history writing' such as that of Herodotus.

It seems to me that one of the major problems in this discussion is that Talmon's third methodological principle of comparative analysis (sociological analysis) has been ignored. History writing is a general category of writing into which several different kinds of texts might fit. For example, to begin with Johan Huizinga's well-worn definition of history: 'History is the intellectual form in which a civilization renders account to itself of its past' (Huizinga 1963: 9).[15] This is primarily a *sociological* definition of

---

15. This is, in fact, the same definition that Van Seters uses to start with (1983: 1-2).

history and, in my opinion, in the present environment it is one of the best places to start when dealing with history writing, whether ancient or modern. Any text that functions sociologically in this way for a particular civilization constitutes history writing for that civilization. Whether it does it in the same way or with the same level of sophistication as a text from another place or another time is irrelevant.

> Every civilization creates its own form of history, and must do so. The character of the civilization determines what history shall mean to it, and of what kind it shall be. If a civilization coincides with a people, a state, a tribe, its history will be correspondingly simple. If a general civilization is differentiated into distinct nations, and these again into groups, classes, parties, the corresponding differentiation in the historical form follows of itself (Huizinga 1963: 7).

In a previous study I began an investigation of ancient Sumerian history writing based on the Presargonic Sumerian royal inscriptions from Lagash (c. 2500–2350 BCE) (Averbeck 1994).[16] I analyzed the most comprehensive and helpful exemplar of the set, and demonstrated how this analysis contributes to our understanding of history writing in the Bible. Even in the Presargonic inscriptions, which are the earliest historiographic documents available, one reads things like:

> Enlil, king of all lands, father of all the gods, by his authoritative command, demarcated the border between Ningirsu and Shara. Mesalim, *king of Kish*, at the command of Ishtaran, measured it off and erected a monument there (Cooper 1986: 54).[17]

This suggests that the predominantly Semitic kingdom of Kish in the north (see the remarks on this above) might have dominated Sumer politically in the mid-third millennium. The royal title 'king of Kish' was used in later times as a claim of sovereignty in the whole region of Sumer and Akkad and beyond (Hallo 1957: 23, 26). One can also compare the Sumerian King List, which says, 'After the flood swept over (the earth) (and) when kingship was lowered (again) from heaven, kingship was (first) in *Kish*'.[18] But even if in some cases the innovations they are credited with derive

---

16. Perhaps it is his view of royal inscriptions as only biographical that led Van Seters to overlook the significance of the Presargonic Sumerian royal inscriptions (c. 2500–2350 BCE).

17. Regarding influence from Syria-Palestine to southern Mesopotamia in the later second millennium BCE, see Lambert 1982: 311-14.

18. *ANET* 265.

ultimately from other pre- or proto-historic civilizations, the Sumerians were the ones that mediated them in literary form to later cuneiform cultures which, in turn, mediated them to the Israelite world in one way or another.

This is not the place to take the analysis of Sumerian historiography further. The goal on this occasion is to expand on its comparability to biblical history writing and the importance of that for the critical discussion outlined above. As Kirk Grayson once wrote:

> Although there were some differences between the earlier and later cultures as a result of ethnic and linguistic change, in many respects Assyrian and Babylonian ideas and institutions are Sumerian ideas and institutions in new garb, the new garb being a different language, Akkadian. Ideas about the past in Assyria and Babylonia were inherited from the Sumerians and, despite some alteration, their essential Sumerian character continued to be recognizable. In the discussion of historiographical genres we shall find only a few innovations in Assyrian and Babylonian times (Grayson 1980: 142).

I am fully aware that by taking the *earliest* ancient Near Eastern historical texts as the comparative base for understanding biblical historiography I am starting at the opposite end of the ancient Near Eastern history from Herodotus, upon whom Van Seters bases his comparative work. But that is part of the point. Although the Sumerians were far removed from ancient Israel in time and place, in some important ways at least, these inscriptions served the same basic sociological function in their time, place, and historical situation as Genesis through Kings did in ancient Israel. Moreover, the connection between Herodotus and the biblical history writers is, if anything, more tenuous than the comparison with Mesopotamian historiography to be articulated here (see more on this below). Comparing these Sumerian texts with the Bible from a sociological point of view provides a badly needed framework for properly handling three basic questions: the nature of history writing, the question of historicity, and the connection between history and mythology (or theology).

6. *History and the Nature of History Writing*

Many of the Presargonic royal inscriptions contain or consist almost entirely of historical narratives. These narratives recount and reflect on specific events, especially regarding the longstanding boundary conflict between Lagash and its competing city-state, Umma.[19] The Enmetena cone, in particular, 'provides the most comprehensive preserved recitation of the boundary history, beginning with Mesalim's arbitration, and ending with Enlil and Ninhursag, the great god of Sumer and his consort, supporting Enmetena against a contemporary ruler of Umma who claimed part of the territory of Lagash' (Cooper 1983: 15).[20] From this inscription we can discern some basic principles of historiography in Sumer, or at least in Presargonic Sumer at Lagash.[21]

First, the Enmetena cone begins by recounting how Enlil, who was conceived of in all of Sumer (not just Lagash) as the chief god of the Sumerian pantheon, first established the boundary between Lagash and Umma (literally, between the god of Lagash, Ningirsu, and the god of Umma, Shara). Second, in an early generation Mesalim, 'king of Kish' (see the remarks on this above), had measured it all off and set up a monument on the border. Third, the text recounts the previous history of the border conflict between Lagash and Umma over the fertile agricultural territory of the plain, covering at least three previous generations. Fourth, there is a relatively full description of the conflict between Enmetena himself and two successive rulers of Umma.

Fifth, Enmetena built a new boundary channel from the Tigris to the Nun-canal and re-established the proper boundary between Lagash and Umma. Finally, there is a blessing/prayer addressed on behalf of Enmetena to Shulutul, his personal god, followed by a conclusion in which the inscription calls upon Enlil and Ningirsu to destroy any ruler of Umma, or anyone else for that matter, who would dare violate the boundary channel. This final portion of the text, therefore, looks forward into the future days of Enmetena or perhaps even later generations.

Now, Van Seters admits that there are several different genres of extant historiographic texts from the ancient Near East, but argues that, ulti-

---

19. See the historical reconstruction of this conflict in Cooper 1983: 18-37.

20. There are two quite similar exemplars of this particular composition on clay cones (designated Cones A and B), and some fragmentary duplicates on jars (see the publications listed in the next footnote and the literature cited in them). None of them were found *in situ*, so one cannot discern their function or significance from the archeological context with any certainty. See the helpful discussion in Ellis 1968: 114-20.

21. See the short quotations and historiographic analysis in Averbeck 1994: 93-98. For a full English translation with notes see Cooper 1986: 54-57, and for a transliteration with German translation and commentary see Steible and Behrens 1982: I, 230-45 and II, 112-22.

mately, 'history writing' *per se* must be comprehensive and creative from the point of view of national identity. Thus, he writes in his conclusion:

> Dtr's purpose, above all, is to communicate through this story of the people's past a sense of their identity—and that is the *sine qua non* of history writing. No other historical work of the ancient Near East reveals so broad a purpose as this (Van Seters 1983: 359).

He has a legitimate point about the Joshua–Kings history, but the immediate question is whether it is appropriate to so strictly limit the concept of 'history writing' to exclude what he calls 'historiographic texts'. I do not think this is an acceptable way of handling the material.

It is hard for me to understand why the Enmetena inscription should not be called 'history writing'. There is no 'accidental accumulation of traditional material' here, 'the reason for recalling the past and the significance given to past events' is clearly evident, and the document most certainly 'examines the causes of present conditions and circumstances'.[22] One could even argue that it is 'national or corporate in character'. Even though it reports 'the deeds of the king', it does so from a corporate perspective, was part of the literary tradition, and played an important role in the official 'corporate tradition of the people' of Lagash, although it is hard to be sure how much these inscriptions reflect the views of the commoners or any other levels of the society.[23] In any case, the Enmetena

---

22. I am referring here to the first three of the five 'criteria by which to identify history writing in ancient Israel' according to Van Seters 1983: 4-5. With regard to the last two criteria, see below.

23. See Van Seters' fourth and fifth criterion of history writing (1983: 5). In point of fact, his emphasis on the importance of the 'national' character of true 'history writing' in ancient Israel does not really fit Huizinga's definition of history (cited above).

For example, in his review of *In Search of History*, Lawson Younger (1988: 110-17) rightly criticizes the manner in which Van Seters misapplies Johan Huizinga's definition of history as 'nationalistic' (see more on this below), his rather far-fetched connection between Herodotus and the Deuteronomist (is Israel really in the 'historical stream' of Greece? See Talmon's first principle above), and his use of genre as a 'magic wand' (Younger's term) by which he attempts to disqualify all other ancient Near Eastern historiographic texts as 'history writing' (p. 113).

With regard to the latter point, Younger cites the earlier review by Halpern (1985: 506-509), who writes, 'Here is the form-critic shaking an impotent fist at the refractory ancient who wrote to suit his own selfish ends: mixed forms, or mixed themes...reflect long development' (p. 508). Halpern continues, 'Van Seters sets out with a limited sensibility about history-writing and ends by discovering virtually none of it before the

cone is a carefully constructed purposeful composition that represents a long tradition, although admittedly not nearly as long and comprehensive as that of Genesis through 2 Kings. I will come back to the distinctiveness of biblical history writing in this regard later.

7. *History, Historicity, and Tradition*

The Enmetena inscription has a relatively sound foundation in historical fact. There are inter-textual parallels between the compositions from the several different generations represented by the inscriptions. Sometimes later inscriptions refer to events that are attested in earlier ones closer to or contemporary with the events themselves.[24] Now it is obvious that the Enmetena composition was written from the point of view of Lagash as opposed to Umma. Similarly, Genesis through 2 Kings was also written from a certain point of view, as is all history writing both ancient and modern.[25] This does not mean that we should necessarily deny any historical factuality to this section of the Hebrew Bible. Even the most critical of scholars do not take such a position, for example, regarding the Enmetena composition.

About 25 years ago Thompson and Van Seters wrote two separate volumes, both challenging the then current consensus of the relative historicity of the patriarchal narratives (Van Seters 1975: 1-122; Thompson 1974). Both men articulated their proposals and arguments very well. Each in their own way has contributed much to the development of what is sometimes called the 'minimalist' view of biblical historicity, which has moved far beyond doubting the historicity of the patriarchs. Today minimalism also includes David, Solomon, and in its most extreme forms almost all of what had previously been widely considered the history of Israel in the Old Testament period.[26]

6th century BCE. The book thus amounts to a procrustean definition and the assertion, possibly correct, that nothing before Dtr. fits it' (p. 508). See also the reviews by Roberts 1984; Rogerson 1986.

24. See the footnotes in Cooper 1986: 56-57 and the extensive discussion in Cooper 1983: 22-37.

25. For a careful discussion of this point as it relates to the philosophy of history and history writing see Younger 1990: 25-47.

26. For example, Thompson (1999: 190) writes: 'In short, the only historical Israel to speak of is the people of the small highland state which, having lost its political autonomy in the last quarter of the eighth century, has been consistently ignored by historians and Bible scholars alike. This is the Israel whose people, understanding

As I have already explained, the Enmetena cone clearly refers to earlier traditions about the boundary disputes between Lagash and Umma, and there are some earlier narrative inscriptions that independently verify those traditions. Unfortunately, theories rather than facts tend to become the overriding force in highly polemical discussions such as the one surrounding historicity in the Hebrew Bible.[27] The point is that, no matter what one's theoretical stance may be, one should always be willing to submit their theoretical framework to verifiable data, whether biblical or extra-biblical. The trick is to distinguish between what is truly verifiable data as opposed to scholarly interpretation or theoretical (re)construction of or about the data, or the absence of data. One should at least be willing to say that their theory is not currently confirmed in this or that detail by the data we have, if that is in fact the case.

How should one respond to such a state of affairs? Historical critical investigation of the history of Israel is a legitimate scholarly endeavor, and archeology and epigraphy have something significant to offer those who engage in it. All history writing is selective, and if the Bible does include history writing, as I believe it does, the history that it presents is also selective and incomplete. The nature of history writing necessarily leads to purposeful selection in order to draw out the significance of past events from the point of view of the civilization for which the history is written (see the definitions and remarks). This was certainly part of the purpose and rationale of the writing of the Enmetena cone in Presargonic Lagash and the various elements of the attested written tradition about the past referred to in it.

themselves as "Israelites", return to the light of history as the same highland farmers they had been for millennia. They are referred to in the stories of Ezra 4 as enemies of Benjamin and Judah. Their offence: they wish to help in the building of a temple to "the God of Israel" in Jerusalem. They are rejected in the story by Ezra's Jews and given a sectarian identity as "Samaritans" by historians. This Israel is not the Israel that biblical scholars who write "histories of Israel" have been interested in. It is not the Israel that we find in our biblical narratives. It is historical Israel'.

27. This is the sense one gets when reading, for example, Thompson's most recent discussion of the Tel Dan inscription, in which we find the expression *bytdwd* (Thompson 1999: 203-205). Certainly the most reasonable rendering is 'the house of David' in spite of all the objections that have been raised against it by those who, like Thompson, are committed to the non-historicity of David. The objections amount to so much special pleading and, I am sorry to say, the not so shrouded accusations of fraud and forgery in the discovery of the inscription are a disgrace (see, e.g., Thompson 1999: 205). See the remarks and literature cited in Schniedewind 1996; Dion 1999.

There is no space for an examination of all the textual and archeological details of this discussion here. The current state of affairs suggests, however, that scholars should back up and ask whether or not the account of Israelite history given in Genesis through 2 Kings would have made sense in the world of the ancient Near East. As Huizinga put it:

> In reality history gives no more than a particular representation of a particular past, an intelligible picture of a portion of the past...The idea of history only emerges with the search for certain connexions (*sic*), the essence of which is determined by the value which we attach to them.
>
> History is always an imposition of form upon the past, and cannot claim to be more...
>
> If history as an intellectual activity is an imposition of form, then we may say that as a product it is a form—an intellectual form for understanding the world, just as philosophy, literature...[i]ts purpose is to understand the world *in* and *through* the past (Huizinga 1963: 5, emphasis original).

As noted above, one needs to resist imposing modern standards and criteria for history writing on the ancients. Therefore, one must also resist denying their literary productions the status of 'history writing' simply because they do not correspond in some respects to the way in which we generally do historical research and write history today (Van Seters 1992: 1-7, 20-44, 328-33; 1994: 1-12, 457-58, 468). It may be true for some that 'a history adequate to our civilization can only be scientific history', which supposedly demands scientific certainty and accepts only natural causes (Huizinga 1963: 8). But such was most certainly not the case in either ancient Sumer or Israel.

This does not mean, however, that the ancients were not concerned to know the truth about what actually happened in their past and what caused those things to happen. This carries the notion of imposition of form on the past to its ultimate extreme. Such a view leads some scholars to the conclusion that since history writing is by nature literary, therefore, it does not necessarily have any substantial correspondence to the actual realities of the past. On the contrary, history writing that is worthy of the name cannot be purely fictional or propagandistic. As Huizinga puts it, although history writing must take a perspective on the past:

> Every civilization and every sectional civilization must hold *its own* history to be the true one, and is entitled to do so, provided that it constructs this history in accordance with the critical requirements imposed by its conscience as a civilization, and not according to the cravings for power in the interests of which it imposes silence upon this conscience (Huizinga 1963: 9, emphasis original).

Thus, for historical traditions to be truly historical they must have a substantial relationship to the actual reality of the past. At this point I would agree with Thompson against Van Seters in principle as it relates to the Bible. The degree to which Genesis through 2 Kings is accurate about what actually happened in the history recorded in them is an essential factor in determining whether or not they should be labeled 'history writing'. To put it the other way, to whatever degree these books do not recount accurately what happened in the past when it purports to do so, to that degree they are 'myth', or 'fiction', or 'legend', or perhaps 'propaganda'.

This brings us to the subject of pre-existing sources actually mentioned in the Hebrew Bible, as opposed to historical critical theories about hypothetical sources. First, the postexilic author(s) of Chronicles probably used the pre-exilic history written in Samuel and Kings as part of their source material. The latter may even be cited by name in certain places. Specific reference is made to 'the book of the kings of Israel' (1 Chron. 9.1; 2 Chron. 20.34; cf. 2 Chron. 20.34, 'the annals of Jehu son of Hanani, which are recorded in the book of the kings of Israel'), 'the records of Samuel the seer' (1 Chron. 29.29), 'the book of the kings of Israel and Judah' (or '...Judah and Israel'; see 2 Chron. 16.11; 25.26; 27.7; 28.26; 32.32; 35.27; 36.8), or simply 'the annotations on the book of the kings' (2 Chron. 24.27). Compare also: 'written in the vision of the prophet Isaiah son of Amoz in the book of the kings of Judah' (2 Chron. 32.32) and 'the book of the annals' (Neh. 12.23; note the word 'annals' = Hebrew lit. 'the words of the days', which is the Hebrew name for the books of 'Chronicles').

There are also references to other sources that probably do not correspond to the pre-exilic canonical historical books: 'the records of Nathan the prophet and the records of Gad the seer' (1 Chron. 29.29), 'the prophecy of Ahijah the Shilonite...the visions of Iddo the seer' (2 Chron. 9.29), 'the annotations of the prophet Iddo' (2 Chron. 13.22), 'the records of Shemaiah the prophet and of Iddo the seer that deal with genealogies' (2 Chron. 12.15), 'written in the records of the seers' (2 Chron. 33.19), 'written in the Laments' (2 Chron. 35.25). There are even references to the annals of foreign kings and kingdoms (e.g. Est. 2.23; 6.1-2; 10.2).

Second, and even more importantly, according to the pre-exilic historical books themselves (and one particular verse in the Pentateuch), even in the pre-exilic period some important written sources were used that, by and large, seem to have been completely lost to us. The names given to such sources include: 'the Book of the Wars of the LORD' (Num. 21.14), 'the Book of Jashar' (Josh. 10.13; 2 Sam. 1.18), 'the book of the annals of Solomon' (1 Kgs 11.41), 'the book of the annals of the kings of Israel' (1 Kgs 14.19; 15.31; 16.5, 14, 20, 27; 22.39; 2 Kgs 1.18; 10.34; 13.8, 12; 14.15, 28; 15.11, 15, 21, 26, 31), 'the book of the annals of the kings of Judah' (1 Kgs 14.29; 15.7, 23; 22.45; 2 Kgs 8.23; 12.19; 14.18; 15.6, 36; 16.19; 20.20; 21.17, 25; 23.28; 24.5).

The sheer number of sources and references to them must be taken into consideration when assessing the concern for historicity in ancient Israelite history writing. I would argue that this comes as close to our standards of reference as we could expect them to come in the ancient Near East. Yes, their history writing does not suit the modern positivistic and naturalistic sensibilities and methodologies of some modernist scholars. For such scholars the presumed mixture of 'myth' and 'legend' in the pre-exilic historical books utterly eliminates them as sources for learning about what happened in history.

8. *History, Historiography, and Mythography*

This brings me to the relationship between historiography and mythography. The latter refers to the critical study of mythological materials, and here I am concerned with how such study of myth relates to critical study of history writing in the Hebrew Bible. Over against Thompson, although Van Seters (1975: 1-122) has long since given up on historicity as a matter of any great concern to the biblical history writers, he still holds that Genesis through Kings is indeed 'history writing' rather than simply 'story' or 'myth'. Some might think that this difference between Thomson and Van Seters is just a matter of semantics—one man's history may be another man's myth, depending on how they define their terms. But there is something of substance here as well.

A modern positivist form of history writing will not admit myth into its consideration, except as a matter of correctly representing what people believed in the past about the past. According to the standard definition, *legend* stands 'somewhere between' myth and history, but more in the realm of myth because it is 'about heroes and eponymic forefathers'. So, 'It is the presence of either myth or legend in a historical work that requires some explanation' (Van Seters 1992: 25).

There are actually two different kinds of 'myth'. 'Founding myth' refers to origins, or at least divine intervention outside of time, 'when new patterns are established and old ones reformulate —times that need not be chronologically distant but usually are' (Doty 1986: 8). 'Permeating myth' refers to divine intervention that takes place within human time. For example, from the perspective of what is and is not expressed in the Enmetena cone, Enlil's demarcation of the original boundary is to be considered 'founding myth'. Enlil's founding moment was the perspective from which all the conflicts over the boundary were to be understood.[28]

'Permeating myth' does, in fact, 'permeate' the remainder of the composition. When 'Mesalim, king of Kish' measured off the boundary and set up a monument there, he did it 'at the command of [the god] Ishtaran'. When Ush smashed Mesalim's monument and invaded the plain of Lagash, 'Ningirsu, warrior of Enlil, at his [Enlil's] just command, did battle with Umma. At Enlil's command, he [apparently referring to the god Ningirsu] cast the great battle-net upon it, and set up burial mounds for it on the plain'. No ruler of Lagash is mentioned in this portion of the account. The victory is attributed to Ningirsu alone. When Il, a later ruler of Umma, attempted to shift 'the boundary-levee' to give Umma a larger portion of the plain, 'Enlil and Ninhursag did not allow him [to do] this'. It is not exactly clear how to interpret this line, but the outcome is once again attributed to divine intervention.[29] When Enmetena constructed the boundary channel 'from the Tigris to the Nun-Canal', he did it 'at the just command of Enlil, at the just command of Ningirsu'. Finally, if the future leader of Umma or anyone else should transgress upon the plain of Lagash, 'may Enlil destroy him! May Ningirsu, after casting his great battle-net upon him, bring down upon him his giant hands and feet!'

I have been using the term 'myth' to refer to the rationale of divine intervention in the Bible and the ancient Near East. One could just as easily use the term 'theology', as some do.[30] The difference is that for most people the term 'mythology' brings to mind 'fiction',[31] whereas this is not necessarily so with 'theology'. From the point of view of most modernists and positivist historians, Genesis 1–11 is 'founding myth' and Genesis 12 through 2 Kings is saturated with 'legend' and 'permeating myth'. But it must be recognized that, even in the case of the Enmetena

28. See the remarks and literature cited in Averbeck 1994: 92-93, 95-96.

29. For discussion of the problem here see Cooper 1983: 32-33.

30. See also, for example, Cooper 1983: 11, where he refers to the '*theological* rationale of all Mesopotamian imperialism' (emphasis mine).

31. See the helpful discussion of definitions in Doty 1986: 1-40, and compare also the discussion of myth, legend, and history in the Bible in Averbeck 1994: 93-100.

cone and other ancient Near Eastern compositions of its kind, the ancients themselves did not see this as 'fiction'. The 'theology' of the composition was simply treated as an essential part of their true 'history' (in the sense of historically accurate 'history writing'). In fact, there is no doubt that much of what is recounted in this inscription is historically accurate even if it is shaped according to the perspective of one side as opposed to the other, which is true of all history writing, ancient and modern. One would find comparable differences of perspective in histories of the 1950s or 60s CE written in the United States as opposed to the Soviet Union.

Similarly, in the Hebrew Bible Genesis 1–11 is presented as 'history', not 'myth' or 'fiction'. Van Seters himself is willing to include Genesis 1–11 in his category of 'history writing' (although he would argue that it is a case of 'mythologization of history') (Van Seters 1992: 26-27, 188-93). Part of the reason for this is the genealogical framework that runs through the entire book. By taking this framework of Genesis seriously, including the *toledot* ('generations') formula that runs through the book (Gen. 2.4; 5.1; 6.9; 10.1; 11.10, 27; 25.12, 19; 36.1, 9; 37.2) as well as the more substantial horizontal (Gen. 4.17-24; 10.1-32; 25.12-18; 36.1-43) and vertical genealogies (Gen. 5.1-32; 11.10-26) that periodically (re)capture the overall structure of its history, one is able to show that Genesis 1–11 is presented as an integral part of the history of Israel. It is just as historical as Genesis 12–50 and Exodus through 2 Kings, from the perspective of the text. There is no primary distinction between myth, legend, and history here.[32]

It is no surprise that Van Seters comes back to the Greeks when explaining the overall genealogical shape and much of the substance of Genesis.[33]

---

32. See Averbeck 1994: 98-100 and the literature cited there. See also Van Seters 1992: 330-31.

33. One of the major methodological defects in Van Seters' discussion, in my opinion, is his insistence that, although there is much in Gen. 1–11 that owes its origin to 'eastern' (i.e. ancient Near Eastern) traditions, the genealogical framework must be due to the influence of the early Greek (i.e. 'western') antiquarian tradition (Van Seters 1992: 78-99). He argues similarly regarding Gen. 12–50, 'Although there is little in the patriarchal stories that corresponds to any eastern antiquarian traditions, in spite of Abraham's association with Mesopotamia in the tradition, the parallels with the western traditions are extensive and have been neglected for too long' (Van Seters 1992: 213).

The fact of the matter is that many scholars find a great deal of material in the patriarchal accounts that has significant parallels in the so-called 'eastern' tradition.

His earlier work on the Deuteronomistic History already set this as his agenda based on supposed correspondences between it and Herodotus (see above). However, the level of true correspondence between them has been seriously challenged.[34] Furthermore, his attempt at discrediting the work of others who have argued that the kinds of genealogies and genealogical structure for narrative that we find in Genesis is most characteristic of primitive tribal societies is, in the end, unconvincing (Van Seters 1992: 197-98). Genealogy is an important feature of ancient Near Eastern history and culture from very early (Chavalas 1994). Even the shift from before the flood to after in a genealogical framework is attested, for example, in the Sumerian King List.

The tradition of 'history writing' that begins with the Presargonic inscriptions as witnessed by the Enmetena cone and other such texts is quite sufficient as a literary background for much of what is found in Genesis through 2 Kings without resorting to Herodotus. In this inscription, on the one hand, the deity intervenes on behalf of the ruler and his people and, on the other hand, the ruler also sees himself as acting on behalf of the deity. As Jerrold Cooper puts it:

> This theological rationale of all Mesopotamian imperialism—making war in the name of a god for territory claimed by a god or given to the warring ruler by a god—was thus present at the beginning of recorded Babylonian history. It persisted in royal inscriptions through two millennia and figured prominently in the propaganda of Cyrus the Persian when he justified bringing the last independent Babylonian kingdom to an end (Cooper 1983: 11).[35]

This is certainly integral to the 'history writing' in Genesis through 2 Kings as well.

Admittedly, however, the combination of the overarching scope, extensive development, and literary quality and diversity of Israel's history as presented in Genesis through 2 Kings is truly unprecedented in the ancient Near East.

That brings me back to Genesis 1–11 and the issue of 'theology'. I have already argued that on the level of the larger literary structure of Genesis

The correspondences with the Ugaritic Poems of *Keret* and *Aqhat* leap to mind. See the convenient summary in Parker 1989: 225-32.

Moreover, the association of Abraham with Mesopotamia in the tradition cannot be so easily pushed aside.

34. See, e.g., the extensive remarks in Nicholson 1994: 141-46.

35. See also the quote from Grayson above.

these chapters are presented as 'history'. This does not mean that the Israelites would have seen no distinction between the primeval history in Genesis 1–11 and the patriarchal history in chs. 12–50. On the contrary, they surely would have recognized the difference between the origins of humankind and all the nations from creation to the tower of Babel as opposed to the origins of the nation of Israel from Abraham to Joseph. In light of that, one must ask the question: why was it so important for the author of Israel's earliest history to include the material of Genesis 1–11 in his 'history writing'?

At least part of the answer must be that this section of Genesis sets the agenda for Israel's engagement with the nations roundabout them and, therefore, their national history as reflected in the rest of Genesis through 2 Kings. It is this agenda, not the influence of Herodotus, that led to the distinctiveness of Israel's 'history writing' in its ancient Near Eastern context. The mentality of distinctiveness is pervasive in the Hebrew Scriptures. This is not just a matter of modern conservative concern about the superiority of the Bible (Machinist 1991: 196-212). The difficulty is in defining that distinctiveness in a way that stands up under the scrutiny of careful reading and comparison with other ancient Near Eastern literature.

Perhaps the best way to say it is that the whole perspective on God, his people, and the relationship between the two is different in the Hebrew Bible as opposed to the rest of the ancient Near East (Machinist 1991: 207-12; Arnold 1994: 129-48, esp. 142-48). It is true that there are some instances of what seems to be a sort of 'monotheism' in the ancient Near East outside of Israel, although with Finkelstein I am not convinced that they are of the same kind and quality as that found in the Bible. They certainly did not permanently replace polytheism in their religious cultures.[36] Whatever one concludes on that count, the distinctiveness actually extends beyond monotheism to the relationship between the one true God, his world, and his people Israel.

Genesis 1–11 presents one true God who stands above and outside of the world and history. He created the world from outside of it and still stands in that transcendent position. He is neither bound by nature nor determined or undermined by history. Nevertheless, Genesis 12 through 2 Kings proceeds to narrate why and how this God has committed himself by covenant bond to a particular people, Israel, who stand in a particular

36. See Finkelstein 1958: 431-44, esp. 438-44, as opposed to, e.g., Machinist 1991: 197-200 and Lambert 1975: 191-99.

kind of relationship to the world.[37] It is through *them* (literally, Abraham their father) that 'all the families of earth will be blessed' (Gen. 12.3b). The whole earth belongs to the Lord, but Israel is his 'treasured possession', his 'kingdom of priests', his 'holy nation' (Exod. 19.5-6).

There is a position and a commission here that sets Israel apart from all other nations even as they struggle with their God, who is so far above and beyond them (and yet still present with them), and with the natural and national world that surrounds them. Genesis 12 through 2 Kings only takes us so far with this, but there is enough written there to let us know that more is coming. The comprehensiveness of Israel's history derives from the comprehensive nature of Israel's God, not the historiography of Herodotus or anyone else.

9. *Summary and Implications*

I have argued here that some of the problems in the scholarly discussion of comparative historiography as it relates to biblical history writing may be sorted out and resolved by more careful attention to certain basic principles of research. First and foremost one should take Talmon's third comparative principle seriously. If it can be established that there is history writing in the ancient Near East that served the same sociological *function* as biblical history writing in the respective societies, then there is no good reason to categorize such texts as 'historiographic' as opposed to 'history writing' in the Bible.

A comparison of biblical history writing with Pre-Sargonic history writing is certainly appropriate on the level of the function of the texts, and that is one of the main points of this part of the discussion. This functional principle can be violated either by imposing a comparison where the texts are not comparable from a sociological point of view, or it can be violated by ignoring function and shifting the comparison to the literary level isolated from function. This is not to say that comparison on the literary level is not important, but when something is defined in a functional way (see Huizinga's definition of history) and allowing for several different literary genres to perform that sociological function, then it is important to base the comparison on the functional comparability of the texts. It is not

37. As Machinist puts it: 'Cosmology where it occurs in the Biblical text is *not* identical with national history. Similarly, there is no notion of autochthonous origins—of a primordial connection between the people and a particular territory' (1991: 208, emphasis original).

fair to shift the definition away from the function of history writing in order to avoid the rather significant implications of functional comparability when it is really there.

Second, the fact that 'theology' (or 'mythology', depending on one's point of view, ancient or modern) serves an important *function* within history writing in the ancient Near East does not mean that these ancient history writers were not concerned about what actually happened in their past. On the contrary, by definition, a composition does not belong to the category of history writing at all if it does not present what the writer and the civilization to whom he is writing would consider to be a realistic presentation of their own historical past. To be sure, history, ancient and modern, is always written from a certain perspective, but that does not necessarily falsify it from an historical point of view. By the standards of function as well as the realistic presentation of the historical facts, the Enmetena cone is history writing and so is, for example, Genesis through 2 Kings in the Hebrew Bible.

Finally, what stands out about history writing as it is found in Genesis through 2 Kings is its 'metanarrative' quality. That is, it claims 'to make sense of all other stories and the whole of reality'.[38] It goes much further than any other history writing in the ancient Near East by presenting a history of Israel and the world that is, in turn, a *function* of the nature of Israel's view of their God and how he relates to the world. This was a gigantic leap in the ancient Near Eastern history writing, but it was, in fact, inherent to the way in which ancient Israel rendered 'account to itself of its past' (Huizinga 1963: 9). It was the ancient Israelites' view of their own history and the significance of their history for the history of the entire world.

10. *The Holistic Approach to Texts and Comparisons: Temple Building in Sumer and the Bible*

The main burden of sections 4-9 was to show the importance of comparing not only texts but also the sociological function of texts. If a genre of text had a particular function in the civilization in which it was composed, then it is important that one compare it with the corresponding genre of text from another culture that fulfills the same function there. This functional concern actually matches well with the recent emphasis on language and

---

38. See Vanhoozer 1997: 39 for this definition of the term 'metanarrative'.

texts as acts of communication.[39] I can go no further with that here, except to add that contrast can be just as informative as comparison. If similar kinds of literature actually function differently in different cultures, this too is an important contribution in the comparative analysis of the literature.

Now I need to shift my attention away from this form critical emphasis on *function* to the purely *literary* analysis of compositions used in comparative analysis. One must take the sociological function of a text as it fits into a particular culture seriously, but one also needs to realize that what are being examined in the first place are texts, not cultures or the functions of texts in socio-cultural contexts. Function is not the most immediate reality an ancient text presents to us, the modern readers. In an important article on historiographic texts, Mario Liverani made an essential distinction when he wrote:

> The thing to do should be to view the document not as a 'source of information', but as information in itself; not as an opening on a reality laying beyond, but as an element which makes up that reality… In this type of approach our attention is no more centered on the events, but on how they are narrated (Liverani 1973: 180).

Since 1973 when Liverani made these remarks the literary method has infiltrated biblical and even ancient Near Eastern studies in general at an ever-increasing rate.

Talmon's fourth point of methodological concern in comparative analysis is that 'the "holistic" approach always should be given preference over the "atomistic"' (Talmon 1978: 356 with pp. 327-29). However, as he develops this point he continues to emphasize the sociological function of the compared element within its larger socio-cultural complex. He wants scholars to keep foremost in their minds that they need to compare similar elements in two different cultures under the control of their shared comparable function within their distinctive cultures. The socio-cultural complex within which the cultural element is imbedded is of utmost importance. This helps to make comparative work 'holistic' rather than 'atomistic'.

Liverani rightly suggests that a holistic approach from a functionalist perspective must be complemented and, in fact, should be *preceded* by the *literary* holistic approach where compositions are analyzed from the top down—structure—as well as the bottom up—philology—and from multiple

---

39. See the very helpful summary in Vanhoozer 1997: 31-35.

points of view (Liverani 1973: 180). A rigorous holistic method, therefore, will take an initially *literary* approach to the comparison between texts as distinct from the realities lying behind them. Furthermore, such literary analysis necessarily engages the text first at the word and sentence level and moves progressively toward the paragraph, section, and whole text level with constant interplay along the continuum between the two poles of word and whole text. However, the *comparison* between *already analyzed texts* proceeds in the opposite direction, from the higher level of literary analysis to the lower level in order to avoid the atomistic fallacy rightly emphasized by Talmon and others.

This means that one must emphasize what Liverani calls the 'comprehensive reading' of the single text, biblical or otherwise, standing on its own, as a necessary first step in the comparative study of literary compositions. Approaching ancient Near Eastern literature from the standpoint of interests in the Bible is a legitimate endeavor, but one must avoid running rough shod over the texts in a rush to find biblical parallels. It is only right that the extra-biblical literature receive fair and comprehensive treatment, even if for no other reason than to avoid inadequate or even inaccurate comparisons between individual texts or genres or whole literary traditions and the Bible (Sasson 1982: 217-25, esp. 220 and 224-25). Some of the work done in comparing the biblical temple building accounts and the Gudea Cylinders has been fraught with errors and misunderstandings of immense proportions (see Lundquist 1983). Fortunately, there have also been highly competent treatments of the same subject (Hurowitz 1985; 1992).

The goal in the remainder of this article is to illustrate the importance of the 'holistic literary principle' in comparative research by showing how a comprehensive reading of the Gudea Cylinders improves one's perspective for comparison and contrast with the Bible, especially biblical temple building accounts. The present author has already published on this subject, so the reader can see more thorough discussions of some points in those places (see Averbeck 1997; 2000).

At the outset one must recognize two major problems. First, although the Gudea Cylinders constitute one of the most important ancient Near Eastern temple building compositions, its use in comparative work is hindered by the fact that the Sumerian language is not always easy to understand, and the Gudea Cylinders are particularly difficult. Second, the Gudea Cylinders stand isolated as a separate composition, not imbedded in a literary context as such accounts are in the Bible. For example, the

Solomonic temple building account in 1 Kings 5–9 stands within the ideology and literary flow of the Joshua–Kings narrative account. This informs the reading of 1 Kings 5–9. There is no such literary context for the Gudea Cylinders. Moreover, the basic nature of the accounts is different. One is narrative preserved in a narrative context while the other stands alone as an isolated poetic narrative with hymnic sections and characteristics. This point of contrast, in fact, impacts the overall structural comparability of these compositions, to which we now turn.

11. *Overall Compositional Literary Structure*

In his work, referred to above, on temple building in the Bible in light of Mesopotamian and Northwest Semitic writings, Victor Hurowitz has shown that there is a common fivefold thematic structure in the ancient Near Eastern temple building accounts: (1) the decision to build with an expression of divine sanction (Cyl. A i-xii and 1 Kgs 5.3-5[17-19]); (2) preparations for the building, including materials, workers, and laying foundations (Cyl. A xiii-xx and 1 Kgs 5.6-18[20-32]); (3) description of the construction process, the buildings, and their furnishings (Cyl. A xxi-xxx and 1 Kgs 6–7); (4) dedication prayers and festivities (Cyl. B i-xviii and 1 Kgs 8); and (5) divine promises and blessings for the king (Cyl. B xix-xxiv and 1 Kgs 9.1-9) (Hurowitz 1992: 56, 109-10).[40] On this basis he asserts that:

> the 'building account' may safely be added to the list of traditional literary types or forms recognizable as common to Israelite and neighboring literatures of the ancient Near East in general and in Mesopotamia in particular. The similarities between the biblical 'building account' and the traditional Mesopotamian 'building account' are no less and no different in nature than the recognized, well known similarities between other types of biblical and ancient Near Eastern literary forms, such as treaties and covenants, law corpora, proverb collections and wisdom instructions, letters and the like (Hurowitz 1992: 312).

It is important to notice, however, that Hurowitz includes temple, palace, and city(-wall) building accounts in his comparative sources. Similarly, Jacob Klein sees essentially the same thematic pattern for building a sacred chariot and boat as for a temple.[41] This is not necessarily

---

40. Regarding comparisons with the tabernacle account in Exod. 25–40 see Hurowitz 1985: 21-26; and for Ezekiel's temple vision (Ezek. 40–48) see Sharon 1996: 99-109.

41. In his own investigations of this subject Klein has taken the results of

a problem. In fact, although there are a few distinctions between temple and other accounts, they are relatively minor and do not affect the overall fivefold pattern. But this may suggest that the thematic pattern itself is actually a natural outcome of the necessary pragmatics of undertaking any such building project. That this is in fact the case is suggested by a more synchronic analysis of the structure of the Gudea Cylinders.[42]

Within the main body of the composition there is a relatively frozen formula that recurs five times at major breaks between movements in the narrative: 'The faithful shepherd Gudea had come to know what was important, (so) he proceeded to do it' (Cyl. A vii 9-10, xii 20, xxv 22-23, Cyl. B ii 7-8, and the expanded formula in xiii 11-13). This results in a sevenfold literary structure: (1) the initial dream and its interpretation (Cyl. A i 12-vii 8); (2) incubation of a second dream (Cyl. A vii 9-xii 19); (3) the construction of the new Eninnu (Cyl. A xii 20-xxv 19); (4) furnishing, decorating, supplying, and praising the temple complex (Cyl. A xxv 20-xxx 5); (5) preparations for the induction of Ningirsu and his consort, Baba, into the new Eninnu (Cyl. B i 12-ii 6); (6) induction of Ningirsu and Baba into the new Eninnu (Cyl. B ii 7-xiii 10); and (7) the housewarming celebration of the induction of Ningirsu and Baba into the new Eninnu (Cyl. B xiii 11-xxiv 8). Another formula recurs four times and helps the reader follow the movements in the relatively complicated third section of Cylinder A: 'For the faithful shepherd, Gudea, it was cause for rejoicing' (Cyl. A xiv 5-6, xvii 28, xx 4, and xx 12).[43]

The overall literary structure derived from the recurrence of these formulas does not fit the comparative form critical pattern established by Hurowitz. This does not mean that one analysis is correct and the other is wrong. Instead, they are reflective of different levels of textual analysis, one form critical and the other purely literary. That is the point here. On the one hand, a form critical analysis concentrates on the level of structure

---

Hurowitz's work as part of his foundation for suggesting that the Gudea Cylinders are the literary prototype of all later Sumerian 'building and dedication hymns'. He has discovered three other examples of such hymns. See Klein 1989: 27-67.

42. See the comprehensive remarks on this matter in Averbeck 1997: 59-62.

43. See the more detailed discussion in Averbeck 1997: 65-74; and the translation with notes of major sections of the Cylinders in Averbeck 2000: 418-33 with headings that reflect these formulaic patterns, and esp. n. 18 pp. 421-22 and n. 35 p. 425.

There are also other structural frames and thematic echoes in the Cylinders that overlap with the section by section analysis that derives from these formulaic patterns. See the detailed discussion in Averbeck 1997: 76-89.

in texts that makes them comparable to one another, not their literary distinctiveness. On the other hand, a purely literary analysis focusses on the inherent structural indicators that appear in each individual literary composition.

In the case of the Gudea Cylinders, both structural formulas I have referred to above participate in the ritual nature of the composition as well as the building and dedication processes recounted in it. Both the nature of the formulas themselves and their placement within the composition shows this. The first formula leads from one section to another by announcing that: 'The faithful shepherd Gudea had come to know what was important, (so) he proceeded to do it'. The second formula actually concludes subsections within the third major section of the composition (as established by the major formula) by announcing that what he had accomplished 'was cause for rejoicing for the faithful shepherd Gudea'.

As I observed earlier in this essay, the Gudea Cylinders present the temple building and dedication process as essentially a step by step ritual process. Ritual actions and processes saturate and structure the text. This is not the case in the biblical temple building accounts, and it does not come out in a form critical comparative analysis. It requires a literary focus that pays attention to the peculiarities of this particular temple building text. From the initial call to build the temple, to the preparation of the construction area, the fashioning of the first brick, the design of the temple, the actual laying of the foundation, constructing the superstructure, the calling of Ningirsu (the patron deity of Lagash) and Baba (his consort) to occupy the temple, the staffing and furnishing of the temple on the divine level, the actual induction of Ningirsu and Baba into the temple, and the temple dedication feast of the gods, everything was permeated with ritual procedures. Thus, Gudea had to pry the specific desires and plans for the temple out of the heart of the deity for whom the temple was to be built (i.e. Ningirsu, the patron deity of Lagash). There was no ready revelation as we have it in the Bible (Exod. 25–40).

I do not propose to do the same kind of literary analysis here for the biblical accounts in Exodus 25–40, 1 Kings 5–9; 2 Chronicles 2–7; or Ezekiel 40–48. However, such an investigation would show that all of them have their own peculiarities on the level of overall structure as well as at the lower levels of the text, to which I will now turn. As I proceed it is important to keep in mind that there are important commonalities between the texts, but the differences are just as informative and profound for understanding the texts and the cultural context from which they arose.

12. *Detailed Textual Parallels*

Parallels between the Bible and the Gudea Cylinders also come through in the details of the text. They can be broken down into two main categories. First, there are those that relate directly to the subject of temple building. Second, there are general parallel concepts and expressions that do not relate directly to temple building. It is not my goal to explain all the parallels here, since they are treated in the second *COS* volume to which the reader is referred for further study (Averbeck 2000).[44] Instead, the various parallels will be listed as they occur sequentially through the composition, with only a very brief description so the reader knows what the parallel is about.

The previous discussion of the overall structure and nature of the composition provides the needed contextual background for our understanding of the more detailed parallels I am about to treat. Having looked at the text from that point of view, one is more able to avoid the atomistic comparisons that have often plagued comparative research. This frees one to attempt to screen the text at all levels for comparative concepts, expressions, and other points of interest. This includes even isolated textual items that have nothing to do specifically with temple building.

13. *Temple Building Parallels*

1. The close association between temple building and fertility, abundance, and prosperity in the ancient Near East and the Bible: Cyl. A i 5-9, xi 5-11; *COS*: II, 419 n. 4, 2.423 n. 26; 2 Sam. 7.1-2 (= 1 Chron. 17.1); 1 Kgs 5.1-8[4.20-28], 18[4] (= 2 Chron. 1.14–2.10); Ezek. 47.1-12; Hag. 1.2-11, 2.15-19; Zech. 9.9-13.

2. Royal wisdom in association with temple building: Cyl. A i 12-14; *COS*: II, 419 n. 6; 1 Kgs 3.3-15; 5.9-14[4.29-34] (= 2 Chron. 1.7-13); 1 Chron. 28.6-10.

3. The need for a divine call or at least divine permission to build a temple: Cyl. A i 19; *COS*: II, 419 n. 8; Exod. 20.24; 25.1-9; 2 Sam. 7.1-7, 12-18; 1 Chron. 17.1-16, 11-12; 21.28–22.19; 28.2-3.

---

44. In this final section of the essay I will be referring to and depending on the reader having access to this translation of selected portions of the Gudea Cylinders and notes on parallels between them and the Bible, or at least some other good modern translation. See, e.g., Edzard 1997; and Jacobsen 1987.

4. The importance of constructing the temple according to every detail of a divinely revealed plan: Cyl. A i 20-21, xvii 15-17; *COS*: II, 419-20 n. 9, 426 n. 43, 426 n. 44; Exod. 25.9, 40; 26.30; 27.8; Num. 8.4; Josh. 22.28; 2 Kgs 16.10; 1 Chron. 28.11-19; Ezek. 40–42, 43.10-12.

5. The tireless commitment of the ruler to the temple building project: Cyl. A vi 11-13, xvii 5-9, xix 20-27; *COS*: II, 421 n. 16, 426 n. 42, 427 n. 50; Ps. 132.2-5; 1 Chron. 22.14-19; 28.2–29.5.

6. The levying of laborers and materials for building the temple: Cyl. A xiv 7–xvi 20; *COS*: II, 425-26 nn. 36, 37, 38, 40; Exod. 35.5, 10-19, 22; 36.1-4; 1 Kgs 5.20-32[6-18]; 6.20-22, 30, 35; 2 Chron. 2.1-18 (cf. 1 Chron. 22.2-5; 28.14-18); 3.4-10; 4.19–5.1 (cf. 1 Chron. 22.14-16).

7. The importance of the first brick: Cyl. A xvii 29–xix 15; *COS*: II, 426-27 n. 48; perhaps with some kind of parallel in Zech. 4.7-9.

8. The special significance of laying the foundation of the temple: Cyl. A xx 24-26; *COS*: II, 428 n. 54; Zech. 4.8-10; Ezra 3.8-13.

9. The pronouncement of blessings on the temple: perhaps Cyl. A xx 27–xxi 12; *COS*: II, 428 n. 55; 1 Kgs 8.31-53.

10. The building of a temple (or the residence of a deity) on a mountain or raised platform: Cyl. A xxi 19-23; *COS*: II, 428 n. 56; Exod. 3.1; 15.17; Isa. 2.2-3 (= Mic. 4.1-2); Pss. 2.6; 48.2-4[1-3].

11. Laudatory descriptions of the temple: Cyl. A xxv 24–xxix 12; *COS*: II, 429 n. 59; Exod. 25.10–28.43; 30.1-10; 36.8–38.31; 1 Kgs 6.14-38; 7.13-51.

12. Petitionary announcement of the completion of the temple and the invitation to the deity to occupy it: Cyl. B ii 14–iii 1; *COS*: II, 430 n. 63; 1 Kgs 8.12-13 (= 2 Chron. 6.2).

13. The seven-day temple dedication festival: Cyl. B xvii 18-19; *COS*: II, 432 n. 74; Lev. 8.33; 1 Kgs 8.2, 65-66; 2 Chron. 7.8-9; Ezek. 45.21-25.

14. Social justice, equity, and purity in association with temple building and dedication: Cyl. B xviii 6-11; *COS*: II, 432 n. 75; Ezek. 42.13-14, 20; 43.6-12.

15. The close association of temple building with the blessings and responsibilities of kingship: Cyl. B xxiii 18–xxiv 8; *COS*: II, 433 n. 79; 2 Sam. 7.4-17 (= 1 Chron. 17.3-15); 1 Kgs 8.14-21; 9.1-9 (= 2 Chron 7.11-22); Ps. 78.68-70.

14. *General Parallels*

1. Dreams, dream incubation, and interpretation of dreams: Cyl. A i 17-19, ii 1-3, viii 2–ix 4; *COS*: II, 419 n. 7, 420 n.12, 422 n. 19; Gen.

40.1-23; 41.1-36; 46.1-4 (cf. 26.23-25?); Num. 12.6; 1 Kgs 3.4-5, 2 Chron. 1.6-7; Dan. 2.1-45; 4.4-27.

2. Theophanies, dreams, and visions struck awe in people, even a fear of death: Cyl. A i 22-23; *COS*: II, 420 n. 10; Gen. 41.8; Exod. 33.18-23; Judg. 13.21-22; Isa. 6.5; Dan. 2.1-4, 10-13; 4.5, 19.

3. The ruler described as a 'shepherd': Cyl. A i 26; *COS*: II, 420 n. 11; 2 Sam. 5.2 (= 1 Chron. 11.2); 7.7 (= 1 Chron. 17.6); Ps. 78.70-72; Jer. 3.15; 23.1-4; Ezek. 34.2, 8, 10, 23; Zech. 11.4-17; Mic. 5.3[4]; Psalm 23 and Ezek. 34.11-22 refer to the Lord their God as the ruler-'shepherd' of Israel.

4. Gigantic awe-inspiring images in dreams: Cyl. A v 13-17; *COS*: II, 420-21 n. 14; Dan. 2.31-33.

5. The attention a cow pays to its calf: Cyl. A xix 24; *COS*: II, 427; 1 Sam. 6.10-12.

6. A legitimate king is divinely chosen and commissioned: Cyl. A xxiii 25-29; *COS*: II, 429 n. 57; 1 Sam. 13.14; 16.1-13; 1 Kgs 2.15; 1 Chron. 28.5.

7. Expression of concern for the disadvantaged and helpless in society: Cyl. B xviii 6-11; *COS*: II, 432 n. 75; Exod. 22.21-24; Deut. 24.17-18; Isa. 1.17; Jer. 7.5-6.

15. *Conclusion*

Sumer and the Sumerian language and literature influenced ancient Near Eastern culture in a formative way. This is due in no small part to the fact that they were the originators of many of the cuneiform cultural and scribal traditions that dominated much if not all of the fertile crescent for almost two millennia. The underlying common cultural foundations that developed through this influence penetrated into and persisted in many cultures near and far, both geographically and chronologically, from ancient Sumer. Some reflections of this influence are found also in the Hebrew Bible.

The four major principles of comparative research described and illustrated in this essay are: proximity in time and place, the priority of inner biblical parallels, correspondence of social function, and the holistic approach to texts and comparisons. They are important not only in the proper isolation and explanation of comparisons between Sumerian language and literature and the Bible, but in all such comparative analysis.

BIBLIOGRAPHY

Algaze, G.
1993   *The Uruk World System* (Chicago: University of Chicago Press).
Archi, A.
1987   'More on Ebla and Kish', in C.H. Gordon, G.A. Rendsburg and N.H. Winter
            (eds.), *Eblaitica: Essays on the Ebla Archives and Eblaitic Language*, I
            (Winona Lake, IN: Eisenbrauns): 125-40.
Arnold, B.T.
1994   'The Weidner Chronicle and the Idea of History in Israel and Mesopotamia',
            FTH: 129-48.
Astour, M.C.
1992   'An Outline of the History of Ebla (Part 1)', in C.H. Gordon and G.A.
            Rendsburg (eds.), *Eblaitica: Essays on the Ebla Archives and Eblaitic
            Language*, III (Winona Lake, IN: Eisenbrauns, 1992): 3-82.
Averbeck, R.E.
1994   'The Sumerian Historiographic Tradition and its Implications for Genesis
            1-11', *FTH*: 79-102.
1997   'Ritual Formula, Textual Frame, and Thematic Echo in the Cylinders of
            Gudea', in *Studies Astour*: 37-93.
2000   'The Cylinders of Gudea', *COS*: II, 417-33.
Bodine, W.R.
1994   'Sumerians', in *POTW*: 19-42.
Chavalas, M.W.
1994   'Genealogical History as "Charter": A Study of Old Babylonian Period
            Historiography and the Old Testament', *FTH*: 103-28.
Cooper, J.S.
1973   'Sumerian and Akkadian in Sumer and Akkad', *Or* 42: 239-46.
1983   *Reconstructing History from Ancient Inscriptions: The Lagash-Umma
            Border Conflict* (SANE, 2.1; Malibu: Undena Publications).
1986   *Sumerian and Akkadian Royal Inscriptions*. I. *Presargonic Inscriptions*
            (New Haven: The American Oriental Society).
Dion, P.-E.
1999   'The Tel Dan Stele and its Historical Significance', *Studies Heltzer*: 145-56.
Doty, W.G.
1986   *Mythography: The Study of Myths and Rituals* (Tuscaloosa, AL: The
            University of Alabama Press).
Edzard, D.O.
1997   *RIME* 3.1.
Ellis, R.S.
1968   *Foundation Deposits in Ancient Mesopotamia* (YNER, 2; New Haven: Yale
            University Press).
Finkelstein, J.J.
1958   'Bible and Babel: A Comparative Study of the Hebrew and Babylonian
            Religious Spirit', *Commentary* 26.5: 431-44 (= Greenspahn 1991: 355-80).
Gelb, I.J.
1992   'Mari and the Kish Civilization', *Mari in Retrospect*: 121-202.

Grayson, A.K.
    1980   'Histories and Historians of the Ancient Near East: Assyria and Babylonia',
            Or 49: 140-94.
Greenspahn, F.E. (ed.)
    1991   *Essential Papers on Israel and the Ancient Near East* (New York: New York
            University Press).
Hallo, W.W.
    1957   *Early Mesopotamian Royal Titles* (New Haven: American Oriental Society).
    1988   'Sumerian Literature: Background to the Bible', *BR* 4: 28-38.
    1990   'Compare and Contrast: The Contextual Approach to Biblical Literature',
            SIC 3: 1-30.
    1997   'Introduction: Ancient Near Eastern Texts and Their Relevance for Biblical
            Exegesis', *COS*: I, xxiii-xxviii.
    2000   'Introduction: The Bible and the Monuments', *COS*: II, xxi-xxvi.
Halpern, B.
    1985   'Review of Van Seters, *In Search of History*', *JBL* 104: 506-509.
Huizinga, J.
    1963   'A Definition of the Concept of History', in R. Klibansky and H.J. Paton
            (eds.), *Philosophy and History: Essays Presented to Ernst Cassirer* (New
            York: Harper & Row Publishers; Dutch original 1928): 1-10.
Hurowitz, V.
    1985   'The Priestly Account of Building the Tabernacle', *JAOS* 105: 21-30.
    1992   *I have Built you an Exalted House: Temple Building in the Bible in Light of
            Mesopotamian and Northwest Semitic Writings* (JSOTSup, 115; Sheffield:
            JSOT Press).
Jacobsen, T.
    1987   *The Harps That Once...Sumerian Poetry in Translation* (New Haven: Yale
            University Press).
    1997   'The Eridu Genesis', *COS*: I, 513-15.
Klein, J.
    1989   'Building and Dedication Hymns in Sumerian Literature', *ActSum* 11: 27-67.
    1990   'The "Bane" of Humanity: A Lifespan of One Hundred and Twenty Years',
            ActSum 12: 57-62.
    1997   'Enki and Ninmah', *COS*: I, 516-18.
Kramer, S.N.
    1959   'Sumerian Literature and the Bible', *AnBib* 12: 189-204.
Lambert, W.G.
    1975   'The Historical Development of the Mesopotamian Pantheon: A Study in
            Sophisticated Polytheism', *Unity and Diversity*: 191-99.
    1982   'Interchange of Ideas between Southern Mesopotamia and Syria-Palestine as
            Seen in Literature', in *Mesopotamien und Seine Nachbarn*: 311-16.
Liverani, M.
    1973   'Memorandum on the Approach to Historiographic Texts', *Or* 42: 178-94.
Lundquist, J.M.
    1983   'What is a Temple? A Preliminary Typology', *Studies Mendenhall*: 205-19.
Machinist, P.
    1991   'The Question of Distinctiveness in Ancient Israel: An Essay', *Studies
            Tadmor*: 196-212 (= Greenspahn 1991: 420-42).

Nicholson, E.
 1994 'Story and History in the Old Testament', *Studies Barr*: 135-50.
Parker, S.B.
 1989 *The Pre-Biblical Narrative Tradition: Essays on the Ugaritic Poems Keret and Aqhat* (SBLRBS, 24; Atlanta: Scholars Press).
Roberts, J.J.M.
 1984 'Review of Van Seters, *In Search of History*', *The Princeton Seminary Bulletin* 5.3: 250-51.
Rogerson, J.W.
 1986 'Review of Van Seters, *In Search of History*', *JTS* 37: 451-54.
Sasson, J.M.
 1982 'On Relating "Religious" Texts to the Old Testament', *Maarav* 3.2: 217-25.
Schmandt-Besserat, D.
 1995 'Record Keeping before Writing', *CANE*: IV, 2097-103.
Schniedewind, W.M.
 1996 'Tel Dan Stela: New Light on Aramaic and Jehu's Revolt', *BASOR* 302: 75-90.
Sharon, D.M.
 1996 'A Biblical Parallel to a Sumerian Temple Hymn? Ezekiel 40–48 and Gudea', *JANESCU* 24: 99-109.
Steible, H., and H. Behrens
 1982 *Die Altsumerischen Bau- und Weihinschriften* (FAOS, 5; 2 vols.; Wiesbaden: Franz Steiner Verlag).
Talmon, S.
 1978 'The "Comparative Method" in Biblical Interpretation—Principles and Problems', in J.A. Emerton (ed.), *Congress Volume: Göttingen, 1977* (VTSup, 29; Leiden: E.J. Brill): 320-56 (= Greenspahn 1991: 381-419).
Thompson, T.L.
 1974 *The Historicity of the Patriarchal Narratives* (BZAW, 133; Berlin: W. de Gruyter).
 1999 *The Mythic Past: Biblical Archaeology and the Myth of Israel* (London: Basic Books).
Vanhoozer, K.
 1997 'Introduction: Hermeneutics, Text, and Biblical Theology', *NIDOTE*: 15-50.
Van Seters, J.
 1975 *Abraham in History and Tradition* (New Haven: Yale University Press).
 1983 *In Search of History: Historiography in the Ancient World and the Origins of Biblical History* (New Haven: Yale University Press).
 1992 *Prologue to History: The Yahwist as Historian in Genesis* (Louisville, KY: Westminster/John Knox Press).
 1994 *The Life of Moses: The Yahwist as Historian in Exodus–Numbers* (Louisville, KY: Westminster/John Knox Press).
Vanstiphout, H.
 1995 'Memory and Literacy in Ancient Western Asia', *CANE*: IV, 2181-96.
Walton, J.H.
 1995 'The Mesopotamian Background of the Tower of Babel Account and its Implications', *BBR* 5: 155-75.

Younger, K.L., Jr
1990   *Ancient Conquest Accounts: A Study in Ancient Near Eastern and Biblical History Writing* (JSOTSup, 98; Sheffield: JSOT Press).
1988   'Review of Van Seters, *In Search of History*', *JSOT* 40: 110-17.

SYRIA AND NORTHERN MESOPOTAMIA
TO THE END OF THE THIRD MILLENNIUM BCE

Mark W. Chavalas

1. *Introduction*

Except for Mari and Nineveh, the area of Syria east of the Euphrates River, and Iraq north of the confluence of the Lesser Zab and Tigris Rivers (areas that connote northern Mesopotamia) have not been known as areas that have contributed much to our knowledge of biblical history and culture. However, the writers of the Bible claimed that their ancestors originated in this area from Harran in the Upper Euphrates region. The past generation of archeological research in this region has offered a great deal of background information for furthering knowledge of the greater geographic and chronological background to Old Testament history, religion, and culture. Although research in Iraq was interrupted by the Gulf War, scholars have had the opportunity to stop and synthesize material from the previous years of research in Iraq. In the immediate period before the cessation of archeological fieldwork, there had been a shift in research emphasis in northern Iraq. Because of the impending dam projects in Iraq, the State Antiquities Organization in Iraq mounted a massive campaign of rescue operations in various regions, including the Hamrin basin, the Haditha Dam project, and the Eski Mosul Dam region (now called the Saddam Dam Salvage Project) (see Anonymous 1986; Roaf 1980).

The situation in the Syrian portion of Mesopotamia, however, has been somewhat different. Compared to Iraq, Syria had not been the recipient of much archeological investigation until the past generation. There are now, however, currently over 60 archeological expeditions to Syria, many of which are concerned with periods that shed light on the Old Testament (see Weiss 1991; 1994; 1997). Like Iraq, the last generation of research in Syria has witnessed numerous salvage projects in areas threatened by modern dam construction and other development projects, as well as numerous major projects that have revolutionized our understanding of the region. The Tishreen Dam project has probed many sites, collected environmental information, and chosen some specific sites in which to do salvage operations. As over two dozen sites in the Habur Basin in northern Syria are imperiled by dams, the Syrian government has assembled an international team to study the environmental setting of the Habur plains (Bounni 1990; Fortin 1991). Most recently, the Directorate General of Antiquities and Museums in Syria has sponsored an international colloquium of over 60 archeologists working in Syria east of the Euphrates (1996; see Weiss 1997: 97). This conference provided a forum for scholars to synthesize material and establish some long term goals in the region.

In this study, I will discuss developments in northern Mesopotamia in a rough chronological order, from the early Neolithic (Natufian, Hassuna, and Samarra), Halaf, Ubaid, and Uruk periods, and then give a geographic survey of the region in the Early Bronze Age.

2. *The Early Neolithic Periods (c. 10,000–5200 BCE)*

Archeological research in the past generation has shown that the early Neolithic period in the Near East (before the Halaf period, c. 5200 BCE) was far more widespread than previously thought. Not only did it flourish along coastal Syro-Palestine, but there is now massive evidence from a series of chance discoveries and salvage operations of a widespread and uniform material culture (in terms of ceramics and lithics) from the Mediterranean coast to eastern Syria and northern Iraq.

The Natufian period (c. 10,000–8300 BCE), which may have been centered in coastal Syria and Palestine, is also evidenced along the Middle Euphrates region of Syria at Dibsi Faraj, Nahr el-Homr (Boerma and Roodenberg 1977), Abu Hureya, and Mureybit (Cauvin 1980a). These are not isolated cases, since there have been a large number of international teams in the Eski-Mosul Dam Project region, finding material similar to the Natufian period in the southern Levant.

Our understanding of the Neolithic Hassuna/Samarra periods in Northern Iraq has changed dramatically over the past 30 years (Huot 1987; J. Oates 1973). In 1965, the earliest village known was Jarmo in the hill country of northeastern Iraq (Braidwood and Howe 1960; Braidwood and Braidwood 1983). Since then, a Soviet team has investigated the Sinjar area (about 60 km north of Mosul in northern Iraq), at the mounds of Yarim Tepe I (Merpert and Munchaev 1973; Merpert *et al.* 1981), primarily at the site of Maghzaliyah, finding obsidian blades and other cultural material unlike any found in Iraq (Bader 1989). A number of the newly excavated sites in the Sinjar region in particular and in northern Iraq in general have shown new evidence for the beginning of agriculture and the transition to sedentary life. This has also been evidenced at the sites of Umm Dabagiyah (Kirkbride 1982), Tell es-Sawwan (Breniquet 1991), and Arpachiyah (Mallowan and Cruikshank-Rose 1935; Hijara *et al*. 1980). To this phase of early village culture can be added the substantial houses with rectangular rooms grouped around a courtyard found at Hassuna (Lloyd and Safar 1945), and pottery styles found in graves at Samarra (Herzfeld 1930).

Syria likewise was a significant cultural force in the post-Natufian Neolithic periods with major centers of occupation in Habur and Balih regions (both of which have been systematically surveyed) showing evidence of Neolithic levels at Tell Abu Hureyra (Moore 1975), Tell Mureybit (van Loon 1968; Cauvin 1977; 1980b), Chagar Bazar (Mallowan 1936; 1937), Bouqras (de Contenson *et al*. 1966; Akkermans *et al*. 1983), Tell Assouad (Cauvin and Cauvin 1972), Hammam et-Turkman (Akkermans 1988; van Loon 1988a), a brief sounding at Tell Sinn (Roodenberg 1979–80), and others.[1] The Habur Basin Project in particular has found innovations in agricultural technology from the development of new cereals and livestock to the use of animal drawn plows and new storage techniques.

3. *Halaf (c. 5200–4800 BCE)*

The Halaf period, named after the site of Tell Halaf,[2] has also been better understood because of the last generation of research in northern Mesopotamia. Because of the work at the mounds of Yarim Tepe, we can now observe what appears to be a sudden spread of Halaf material culture into northern Syria, Iraq, and southern Turkey (Yoffee *et al*. 1993). A Halaf sequence from the Habur triangle has been found at Tell Aqab south of the Turkish border (Davidson and Watkins 1981). A recent survey in the upper Balih valley in Syria has exposed a number of small Halaf period sites (but only a few larger permanent settlements, such as Tell Sabi Abyad), which have helped in furthering the understanding of the origins of the Halaf culture (Akkermans 1989). Once thought to have originated in the later Ubaid period, the earliest seals in Syria have been found at Halaf

---

1.   For a general description of the prehistoric period in Syria, see Moore 1988. For a survey of the Neolithic sites in the Balih Valley, see Copeland 1979.

2.   See von Oppenheim 1943–62; and his more general survey 1931.

period levels at Sabi Abyad. A number of small sites (such as Khirbit Garsour) have also been recently studied in the northern Jezira in Iraq (Wilkinson 1990). The Halaf period in northern Iraq is well represented at Arpachiyah; the earliest levels at Tepe Gawra (Tobler 1950), and sites in the Sinjar region.[3] The Halaf cultures must have employed methods of administration and agriculture which did not include many large settlements (Campbell 1992). Theories now abound that the Halaf period was not an intrusion but an integral part of the Near East.

4. *Ubaid (c. 5500–4000 BCE)*

We now know that the Ubaid culture of Southern Iraq was the first to expand into the north and into the Syrian Euphrates region (J. Oates 1984; Thuesen 1989). Various Syrian sites have Ubaid period remains, including Tell Brak,[4] Tell Leilan, Tall Hammam-et Turkman (van Loon 1983; 1988a; 1988a; Akkermans 1988), Zaidan, Carchemish, Samsat (Kohlmeyer 1984: 108), Tell Aqab (Davidson and Watkins 1981: 10), and Tell Mefesh,[5] a number of the mounds on the plain of Antioch (Braidwood and Braidwood 1960: 175-225), and Hama (Fugmann 1958: 14-31). Of special interest are the Ubaid remains at Tell Mashnaqa, just south of the Habur triangle. Over a dozen Ubaid period burials (probably attesting the existence of a cemetery) have been found there, thereby helping to further our knowledge about Ubaid burial practices in general, and in the outlying regions, far removed from southern Mesopotamia (Thuesen 1997). An entire ceramic sequence from the Halaf to Ubaid periods can be seen in Syria from Halula (Molist 1994). In fact, 16 Ubaid sites were identified in a survey of the Balih Valley (Akkermans 1984). The gradual transition from Halaf to Ubaid culture is reflected in the change in pottery styles at Tepe Gawra, Telul eth-Thalathat (Dunham 1983), Grai Resh in the Sinjar region (Lloyd 1940) and Tell Uqair (Lloyd and Safar 1943).

5. *Uruk (c. 4000–3000 BCE)*

Massive urbanization began in the Uruk period in southern Iraq. Recent archeological excavations and surveys in Syria and northern Iraq (and as far away as Turkey) have given us a chance to explore a number of

3. Merpert and Munchaev 1973; 1984; Merpert *et al.* 1981.
4. Tell Brak has an abundance of Ubaid period material; see J. Oates 1990. A prehistoric chronological sequence has been established for Tell Brak; see Fielden 1977.
5. Mallowan 1946: 126, figs. 7.1-4, 8, 8.3-8.

questions about the Uruk expansion and/or colonization into outlying areas (Algaze 1993). As lower Mesopotamia lacked the natural resources to sustain its newly formed complex social system, it has been posited that the inhabitants had to import them from the periphery. Recent excavations show what Algaze calls, 'a loosely integrated supraregional interaction system using an informal mode of imperial domination'. This was accomplished by the establishment of a network of strategically located enclaves and garrisons. The Uruk 'states' appear to have had direct control of the upper Tigris, and intensified trade contacts in other areas. It has also been postulated that there may have been periodic military expeditions against areas resistant to trade (Larsen 1979: 97). In the north only a small number of urban sized enclaves were found, surrounded by a cluster of dependent villages. The presence of urbanized sites with an Uruk assemblage represents not a break in the cultural sequence but a select infringement into the environment of the indigenous material cultures (Sürenhagen 1986). The enclaves are found along the Euphrates, the Habur (e.g. Tell Brak),[6] and Nineveh along the Tigris (Mallowan 1964).

Many of the Uruk settlements were large and heavily fortified. Their locations suggest that the Uruk polities desired to facilitate downstream commerce. There were also smaller stations that existed along the waterways that were linked between large urban enclaves. Although many of the enclaves were fortified, there does not appear to be evidence of an attempt to control the hinterland, but rather a take-over of strategic locations, tapping into pre-existing trade networks, causing some to call this an informal empire (Algaze 1989). This trading relationship came to an abrupt halt in the succeeding Jemdet Nasr period (c. 3000 BCE), but had a profound impact on the socio-political and economic evolution of the indigenous cultures in Syria and northern Mesopotamia in particular. There was evidence of institutional change with the copying of Uruk architecture, artifacts, ceramics, and sealing practices at many sites in the outlying areas. The Uruk expansion may have acted as a catalyst to foster complex growth and independent socio-political systems in northern Iraq and Syria.

In particular, the sites of Tell Kannas (Finet 1975; 1977), Tell Habuba Kabira (Strommenger 1977; 1980), Jebel Aruda,[7] and possibly Tell Hadidi

6.   For the Middle Euphrates sites, see Algaze 1989; Finet 1975; 1977; Strommenger 1977; 1980; van Driel 1980; van Driel and van Driel-Murray 1979; 1983. For Tell Brak, see J. Oates 1985; 1990.

7.   Van Driel 1980; van Driel and van Driel-Murray 1979; 1983. For the tablets at Jebel Aruda, see van Driel 1982. For sealings, see van Driel 1983.

(Dornemann 1988) on the middle Euphrates, attest to this widespread expansion of the larger urban centers in southern Mesopotamia. The central district at Habuba Kabira was a densely settled town with living quarters and workshops and had cult and administrative activities. The site provides the first evidence for town planning in Syria in this period. There is, however, no evidence of any agricultural activities that would have sustained the town. The site itself was occupied for less than two centuries. Moreover, further south on the Euphrates there is evidence of small and relatively isolated sites at Tell Qraya (Simpson 1988) and Tell Ramadi (Geyer and Monchambert 1987: 318, figs. 8, 10), where Uruk-period domestic architecture and artifacts have been found. Surface finds dating to the Uruk period have also been found at Tell Barri (ancient Kahat) in the upper Habur region (Pecorella and Salving 1982).

Tell Brak has been shown to have been of great importance in this period. It had a sequence of Uruk period temples similar to the slightly later Sin temples at Khafaje,[8] in addition to a ring of late Uruk-period settlements surrounding it.[9] The site, however, had a long prehistory and was not an implanted colony like Habuba Kabira (J. Oates 1990: 133-47). Some of the earliest stratified clay sealings in the ancient Near East have been found at Brak (see Mathews 1996). The site was very large in this period, and the large corpus of sealings attests to well developed administrative practices, showing a social and economic complexity previously not known in the Habur region.[10]

The distribution of these sites appears to show a network of settlements along the Balih and Habur River basins, as well as the middle Euphrates region, forming a long chain of towns following the Euphrates river to the north into the Anatolian plateau, apparently consciously placed in strategic locations along lines of communication (Sürenhagen 1986: 15). Sites that show this widespread distribution include, Tell Leilan and surface finds from Hamoukar (Weiss 1986) in northeastern Syria; Tell Hammam et-Turkman (van Loon 1983: fig. 4), Zaidan (Sürenhagen 1986: 15 n. 11), and Jebel Belene (Kohlmeyer 1984: 109) on the Balih River (Akkerman 1984); Carchemish and Samsat in the upper Euphrates Region (Özten 1976-77); and Hama and Judaidah along the Orontes River.[11] However, of

8.   For Tell Brak chronology, see J. Oates 1986.
9.   See D. Oates 1977: 234; Weiss 1983: 42.
10.   For Tell Brak in the Uruk period, see J. Oates 1986: 245-73; Mathews 1995; 1997; Mathews, *et al.* 1994.
11.   Braidwood and Braidwood 1960: I, 226-29, 259-64.

great import is the fact that there do not appear to be many Uruk-period sites away from the major rivers in the outlying regions,[12] although there is some evidence in the Syrian desert (Cauvin and Storder 1985). Few sites were founded upon existing socio-political entities, with the exception of Samsat, Carchemish, and Tell Brak.

The indigenous native settlements in Syria which were distant from the colonies continued to thrive with the traditions of agricultural and craft productions with which they were accustomed. There is evidence at Habuba Kabira that the local population supported the colonists with foodstuffs. It is still not clear as to whether these centers were directly under southern control, or were dominated by local elites.[13] The function of these so-called colonies affirms to the Uruk culture's need for materials which were not present in the south, but only available over great distances. Such commodities may have included copper ores, lapis lazuli, and other semi-precious materials. The nature of the exchanges remains obscure. The Uruk culture was apparently not interested in a broad acquisition of territory or domination of agricultural enterprises (Algaze 1989: 580). The colonies, however, were relatively short-lived, and none were maintained in the succeeding periods. This abandonment may indicate either that other sources for materials were now available, local communities had successfully thwarted the southern domination of trade routes, or that the need for colonists became obsolete due to the emergence of other forms of exchange.

6. Early Bronze (c. 3000–2100 BCE)

In the Early Bronze Age, the indigenous cultures in northern Iraq and Syria became more powerful, and southern Mesopotamian interference did not appear to occur again for at least one half of a millennium. The political and economic organization of this region in the first half of the third millennium BCE, however, is presently unknown, but was probably centered around small towns without any central control (Weiss 1985b: 269). It is not clear whether these newly created walled towns were initiated by the southerners or were autonomous creations (Weiss 1986: 2).

The ceramic remains for this period for Northern Iraq and Syria have

12. Braidwood and Braidwood 1960: I, 17.

13. J. Oates (1985) has postulated that Tell Brak was under direct southern Mesopotamian control during the latter half of the third millennium BCE, while Weiss has argued for local control (Weiss 1985a).

been called Ninevite V after the pottery style found at the prehistoric sounding at Nineveh (Mallowan 1933). The pottery type is found from Assyria to the Habur plains, and is dated 3300–2500 BCE. Ninevite V pottery has specifically been found in the Lower Jagjagh survey (Meijer 1986), around Leilan (Weiss 1986: 67-104), and by H. Kühne on the middle Habur (Kühne 1979: 168-71). It is especially prevalent in northern Iraq at Tepe Gawra (Speiser 1935; Tobler 1950), Tell Billa (Speiser 1933), in the Sinjar region at Telul-eth-Thalathat V (Fukai *et al.* 1974), where there is an extensive granary with a Ninevite V assemblage, and Tell Mohammad Arab in the Eski Mosul Dam region (Roaf 1984). Survey data concerning Ninevite V ware has also been done (Reade 1968; Abu al-Soof 1968).

Whereas the Uruk culture was able to penetrate the northern areas with relative ease, by the mid-third millennium BCE the Sumerian and Sargonic kings were required to exercise force to control local rulers and walled towns (Algaze 1989: 601), as the south was no longer unique in its incipient urbanism (Gelb 1992: 122). A new type of settlement in dry-farming regions began to foster a new relationship with southern Mesopotamia. Both the Habur region (Tell Hamoukar, Tell Leilan, Tell Mozart, Tell Brak, Tell 'Atij,[14] Tell Chuera, and Tell Gudeda[15]) and the plains of Aleppo in coastal Syria (Byblos, Homs, Ebla, and Qatna on the Euphrates) permitted the extensive cultivation of wheat and barley without major irrigation. Instead, farmers employed dry-farming and extensive raising of sheep and goat herds (Weiss 1986: 1-6).

a. *Northern Iraq*

There are extensive urban remains in Northern Iraq in the second half of the second millennium from a number of sites. There is a sequence of rebuilding of an Ištar Temple at Assur (Andrae 1922), as well as remains from nearby Yorghan Tepe,[16] including some Old Akkadian period tablets. A deep sounding at Tell Taya on the Sinjar plain produced occupation levels in the late Early Dynastic III/Sargonic periods (Reade 1968: 234-64; 1982). A deep sounding was also done at Tell al-Rimah (Oates 1970). Akkadian-period remains have been found in the Hamrin Basin at several sites (Hansen 1982), including Akkadian texts that have been located in

14. Fortin 1997a; 1995. The excavators have uncovered a number of monumental buildings at this site (dated to c. 2800–2700 BCE), similar to those found at Tell Leilan.

15. Fortin 1995.

16. Known in the second millennium BCE as Nuzi; see Starr 1937–39.

the Hamrin Basin at Tell Sleima, some of which indicate the site's ancient name was Awal.[17]

b. *Upper/Middle Euphrates/Balih Regions*
Along the Upper Euphrates, the Euphrates Salvage Project has uncovered on the mounds of Tell Banat a series of White Monuments dated to the second half of the third millennium BCE. In fact, the presence of such monumental construction, as well as other public buildings, and a sophisticated ceramic industry suggest a very complex social hierarchy for this region in this period. The excavators have postulated that Tell Banat may have been an autonomous state or functioned as a cultic or mortuary area.[18] Further south near the confluence of the Euphrates and Balih Rivers is Tell Bi'a (ancient Tuttul), which has remains dating to the Early Dynastic Period (c. 2900–2300 BCE).[19] Along with a number of public buildings, the excavators have uncovered four above-ground tombs belonging to rulers of Tuttul. These tombs bear a striking resemblance to the roughly contemporary Royal Tombs at Ur (although they are subterranean). The Tuttul tombs were partially looted in antiquity, but had ceramics, jewelry, and furniture like the Ur tombs. Moreover, the Shakanakku Palace (c. 2100 BCE) is a more modest version of one found at contemporary Mari.

Further north in the middle Euphrates region there is also evidence of occupation in the late third millennium BCE at Selenkahiye (van Loon 1977) and Tell Hadidi (Dornemann 1977; 1988). Selenkahiye appears to have been founded in around 2400 BCE and was possibly a merchant colony of a Sumerian city. Its destruction coincides with the fall of the Ur III dynasty (c. 2000 BCE). The Early Bronze remains at Tell Hadidi have shown it also to have been a new urban center in the latter half of this period. Still further north, the Tishreen Dam Salvage Project just south of Carchemish on the Euphrates near the Turkish border has revealed occupation in that area, showing an increase in the number of settlements in the second half of the third millennium BCE (McClellan *et al.* 1991), including Tell Gudeda and Tell el-Bazey (Fortin 1988a; 1988b). Of note is

---

17. Rashid 1984. More Sumerian literary texts have also been found at Tell Hadad; Cavigneaux and F. al-Rawi 1993.

18. Porter 1995a; 1995b. For a recent general survey of the remains at Tell Banat, see McClellan 1997.

19. Over a dozen preliminary reports of Tuttul have been published (beginning in *MDOG* 109; 1976) by E. Strommenger *et al.*

the site of Tell es-Sweyhat, which had a substantial settlement with an upper and lower town in the late third millennium BCE.[20] A series of salvage operations have been undertaken since 1993 that have revealed a cemetery that may have had over one hundred tombs. Some of these tombs had not been looted. One tomb in particular had at least ten individuals, one of whom was a woman who was associated with two crossed bronze/ copper straight pins, limestone rings, a series of beads at the breast. The arrangement of the beads is reminiscent of those worn by females on contemporary Mari reliefs.

c. *Lower Euphrates Regions*

During the third millennium BCE, Mari (Tell Hariri) on the Euphrates exhibited notable cultural independence from the Sumerian south. Recent excavations have shown that the city may have been founded either at the end of the Early Dynastic I or beginning of the Early Dynastic II period.[21] The excavators may have located a dike in the hills south of the mound, a branching canal which traversed the city, and a number of canal feeders, permitting the production of wheat. The city had a large wall, three re-buildings of the Ištar temple, and a large Sargonic palace. Graves reminiscent of the Ur III period tombs have been uncovered in a small structure of the same period (c. 2100 BCE). Forty Akkadian-period texts have been recently found at Mari (Margueron 1991a: 711). North of Mari on the Euphrates River is the site of Tell Ashara (ancient Terqa) which had a massive defensive system rivaling any other site of this period (Buccellati *et al.* 1979: 42-83). The continuing excavations in this region reveal that this area was of paramount importance in the third millennium BCE.

d. *Habur Region*

Much has also been learned from investigations in the Syrian Habur region about the Hurrians, a major ethnic group firmly rooted in the Mesopotamian tradition (Wilhelm 1989). One of these Hurrian sites was Tell Chuera, which had similarities with the Sumerian south (Orthmann 1986: 69). It showed evidence of the large stone architecture of this period as well as a clearly defined upper and lower citadel, typical of many of the northern Syrian centers. Judging from the absence of Uruk period occupation, it is apparent that this site was founded during this period

---

20. McClellan and Zettler 1994; Zettler, *et al.* 1997.

21. The most recent excavation reports can be found in *MARI* 1-6 (1982–90), and Margueron 1994.

(Moortgat-Correns 1975; Orthmann 1986: 69). Another nearby Hurrian center in the last quarter of the millennium was Tell Barri.[22]

Also in the Habur region is the site of Tell Beydar, which has a major defense system, an upper and lower citadel, and evidence of nearly 150 tablets contemporary with Early Dynastic texts found at Ebla, Abu Salabikh, and Fara.[23] Nearly all of them were found under the original floor of a domestic residence.

Tell 'Atij along the Middle Habur Valley was occupied during the first half of the third millennium BCE.[24] It consists of two small mounds with a 30 m wide river channel in between the two. The most conspicuous buildings on the site are a series of semi-vaulted silos that were used as grain storage facilities. Near the structures were a number of clay tokens, probably used to calculate grain quantities. The site apparently specialized in the storage of agricultural products, and was likely a trading post, possibly having an economic relationship with the site of Mari in the south (Margueron 1991b; 2000). In fact, other small sites have been identified as specializing in agricultural production (Fortin 1997b; 2000). These include Tell al-Raqa'i,[25] Mashnaqa (Beyer 1993), and Ziyada (Buccellati *et al.* 1991). Moreover, defensive systems were found protecting storerooms at Rad Shaqrah (Kolinski 1996), Kerma (Saghié 1991), and Tell Gudeda (Routledge 1998), while a massive wall protected the entire site of Bderi (Monchambert 1986a; 1986b; 1988; 1990). No such wall or storage facilities have yet been found at the large site of Melebiya (Lebeau 1993). Small traces of third millennium BCE material have been found at Mulla Mutar (Sürenhagen 1990). In sum, the Middle Habur Valley was well populated in this period and likely had close connections with southern Mesopotamia (Schwartz 1994a; 1994b).

Another large site excavated in this region is Tell Mozan (ancient Urkesh) (Buccellati and Kelly-Buccellati 1988), which has a city wall and one of the largest bent-axis temple structures in this period which was located on the high mound. The structure has walls 1.6 m wide, in addition to a statue of a lion in a building interpreted as a cella. The first stratified

22. See Pecorella 1990a: 48. For Tell Barri in the second millennium BCE, see Pecorella 1990b.

23. For a preliminary survey of Tell Beydar, see LeBeau 1997.

24. For Tell 'Atij, see Fortin 1998. Five previous preliminary reports have been published by Fortin (1988a; 1988b; 1990; 1994; 1995).

25. Curvers 1987; Curvers and Schwartz 1990; Schwartz and Curvers 1994; 1993–94.

epigraphic remains in the Habur plains of Syria have recently been found at Urkesh (c. 2300–2200 BCE). Two stratified administrative tablets written in Akkadian, but with Sumerian and Hurrian personal names, have been discovered (Milano *et al.* 1991: 1-34). The most recent seasons of excavation have established that Tell Mozan, a Hurrian capital in the third millennium BCE, was indeed Urkesh (Buccellati and Kelly-Buccellati 1997). Seal imprints with the name 'Tupkish, King of Urkesh', have been found, along with the name of Queen Uqnitum and her many retainers. In fact, most of the seal impressions belonged to the queen and her staff. The glyptic style is distinct from both that found in southern Mesopotamia and even from nearby Tell Brak.[26] Of over 1000 seal impressions found, more than 170 were inscribed. It has even been suggested that a Hurrian scribal equivalent to Semitic Ebla may have existed in this region.[27]

Tell Brak (ancient Nagar) had a number of large Akkadian-period buildings and a unique ceramic sequence from the Uruk to Akkadian periods (Oates and Oates 1989; 1991). Hundreds of clay sealings have been uncovered that had scenes which included banquets, chariots, and contests. One trench (HS3) exposed a large hoard of silver objects.

Near the border of Iraq on the Habur plains of Syria is Tell Leilan (Weiss 1985; Weiss *et al.* 1990). There, the lower town shows evidence of third and second millennium BCE settlements where a number of domestic units, drain filled alleys, and planned streets were encountered (Weiss 1990a). The lower town appears to have been built about 2600–2400 BCE, and the excavators have speculated that there was a profound social transformation that occurred soon after, changing Tell Leilan into a class-based society. The excavators have noticed that many walled cities of the type at Tell Leilan were constructed at this time (Weiss 1986: 83). It also has been speculated that these cities were not formed through intimate contact with the southern centralized states (i.e. Sargonic Akkad), but were the result of an indigenous and autonomous process. Probably the urbanization in this area may have caused the southern states to move into the area during the Sargonic period (Weiss 1990b: 163). Many of these walled towns were in fact larger in size than their southern counterparts. A survey in 1995 confirmed the fact that after the period of Akkadian centralization at Leilan, there is no evidence of occupation at the site for a period of about three centuries (c. 2200–1900 BCE) (Weiss 1993; Courty and Weiss

26. For the glyptic art at Urkesh, see Buccellati and Kelly-Buccellati 1996a; 1996b; Kelly-Buccellati 1996.
27. See Wilhelm 1989: 77-79; Buccellati and Kelly-Buccellati 1988: 31.

1997). The town was thus repopulated and became the basis of Shamshi-Adad's state at the end of the nineteenth century BCE (Weiss 1997: 127).

e. *Coastal Syria*

Although somewhat outside the strict boundaries of northern Mesopotamia (since the city was west of the Euphrates River), Tell Mardikh (ancient Ebla) deserves mention, if only to provide perspective for the spectacular discoveries found there.[28] Ebla was one of the few sites west of the Euphrates that showed signs of sophistication equal to any contemporary urban center in the south of Mesopotamia. The city displayed cultural autonomy but historical continuity with Sumer, as the inhabitants employed the cuneiform script. Thousands of cuneiform tablets have been uncovered, predominantly from a major palatial archive, written in a previously unknown Semitic language now called Eblaite.[29] For example, many of the religious texts at Ebla have their counterparts in the southeast; however, incantations written in Eblaite have no counterpart elsewhere (Hallo 1992: 72), and feature geographic and divine names pointing to a native Syrian context. In fact, both Ebla and Mari shared a common writing system, language, and calendar in this period (Gelb 1992: 197-200). Most likely, Ebla borrowed cultural phenomena from the east (Gelb 1977: 15). Recently at Ebla, excavators have uncovered a large palace (called the Archaic Palace) dated to c. 2150 BCE, which was probably the royal palace at Ebla during the Ur III period. After a brief abandonment following the intrusion of Sargon of Akkad, settlement reappeared in the northern region of the town, centered around this palace.[30]

f. *Prospect*

Although it is apparent that our knowledge of northern Mesopotamia in the third millennium BCE is fragmentary and that no complete synthesis can be made, this region provides a rich and diverse context for understanding the socio-cultural and historical context to the world of the Old Testament.

---

28. General works concerning Ebla include Matthiae 1981; Pettinato 1981; 1991.

29. The corpus of Ebla texts has been published in Pettinato *et al.* 1979–; Archi *et al.* 1979–.

30. For the mention of Ebla in the economic texts from the Ur III period (c. 2100–2000 BCE), see Owen 1992: 117-21.

BIBLIOGRAPHY

Abu al-Soof, B.
1968   'Distribution of Uruk, Jamdat Nasr, and Ninevite V Pottery as Revealed by
            Field Survey Work in Iraq', *Iraq* 30: 74-86.
Akkermans, P.
1984   'Archäologisch Geläandbegehung im Balih-Tal', *AfO* 31: 188-90.
1988   'An Updated Chronology for the Northern 2 Ubaid and Late Chalcolithic
            Periods in Syria: New Evidence from Tell Hammam et-Turkman', *Iraq* 50:
            109-46.
1989   *Excavations at Tell Sabi Abyad* (Oxford: British Archaeological Reports).
Akkermans, P., *et al.*
1983   'Bouqras Revisited: Preliminary Reports on a Project in Eastern Syria', *PPS*
            49: 335-72.
Algaze, G.
1989   'The Uruk Expansion: Cross-Cultural Expansion in Early Mesopotamian
            Civilization', *Current Anthropology* 30: 571-608.
1993   *The Uruk World System: The Dynamics of Expansion in Early Meso-
            potamian Civilization* (Chicago: University of Chicago Press).
Andrae, W.
1922   *Die archaischen Ichtar-Tempel in Assur* (Leipzig: J.C. Hinrichs).
Anonymous
1986   *Researches on the Antiquities of Saddam Dam Basin Project and other
            Researches* (Baghdad: State Organization of Antiquities and Heritage).
Archi, A., *et al.*
1979-   *Archivi reali di Ebla: Testi* (Rome: Missione Archeologia Italiana in Siria).
Bader, N.
1989   *Earliest Cultivators in Northern Mesopotamia: The Investigations of Soviet
            Archaeological Expedition in Iraq at Settlements Tell Magzaliya, Tell Sotto,
            Kültepe* (Moscow: Nauka).
Beyer, D.
1993   'Masnaqa 1993: rapport sommaire sur les travaux de la mission archéo-
            logique française', *Orient Express* 1.1: 7-8.
Boerma, J., and J. Roodenberg
1977   'Une deuxème industrie Epipalaéolithic sur le Nahr el-Homr', *Palaeo-
            historica* 19: 8-17.
Bounni, A.
1990   'The Kabur and the Hasseke Dam Projects and the Protection of Threatened
            Antiquities in the Region (A Preliminary Report)', in S. Eichler *et al.* (eds.),
            Tall al-Hamidiya 2: Recent Excavations in the Upper Khabur Region
            (Göttingen: Vandenhoeck & Ruprecht): 19-29.
Braidwood, R.J., and L.S. Braidwood
1960   *Excavations on the Plain of Antioch. I. The Earlier Assemblages Phases A-j*
            (OIP, 61; Chicago: University of Chicago Press).
Braidwood, R.J., and L.S. Braidwood (eds.)
1983   *Prehistoric Archeology along the Zagros Flanks* (Chicago: University of
            Chicago Press).

Braidwood, R., and B. Howe
    1960   *Prehistoric Investigations in Iraqi Kurdestan* (Chicago: University of Chicago Press).
Breniquet, C.
    1991   'Tell es-Sawwan 1988–1989: comte rendu des fouilles menées par la DAFIQ', *Orient Express* 1.2: 7-8.
Buccellati, G., *et al.*
    1979   *Terqa Preliminary Reports 10: Introduction and the Stratigraphic Record* (Malibu: Undena).
    1991   'Tell Ziyada: The First Three Seasons of Excavation (1988–1990)', *BCSMS* 21: 31-61.
Buccellati, G., and M. Kelly-Buccellati
    1988   *Mozan 1: The Soundings of the First Two Seasons* (Malibu: Undena).
    1996a   'The Royal Storehouse of Urkesh: The Glyptic Evidence from the Southwestern Wing', *AfO* 42-3: 1-32.
    1996b   'The Seals of the King of Urkesh: The Glyptic Evidence from the Western Wing of the Royal Storehouse AK', *WZKM* 86: 65-100, Pls. 1-7.
    1997   'Urkesh: The First Hurrian Capital', *BA* 60: 77-96.
Campbell, S.
    1992   'The Halaf Period in Iraq: Old Sites and New', *BA* 55: 182-87.
Cauvin, J.
    1977   'Les Fouilles Mureybit (1971–74) et leur signification pour les origines de la sedéntarisation au Proche-Orient', in D.N. Freedman (ed.), *Archaeological Reports from the Tabqa Dam Project—Euphrates Valley, Syria* (= AASOR 44: 19-48).
    1980a   'Du natoufienne sur l'euphrate?', in J.-Cl. Margueron (ed.), *Le Moyen Euphrate: Zone de contacts et d'échanges, acres du Colloque de Strasbourg, 10–12 mars 1977* (Leiden: E.J. Brill): 11-20.
    1980b   'Le Moyen Euphrate au VIIIe millénaire d'àpres Mureybit et Chiekh Hassan', in J.-Cl. Margueron (ed.), *Le Moyen Euphrate: Zone de contacts et d'échanges, acres du Colloque de Strasbourg, 10–12 mars 1977* (Leiden: E.J. Brill): 21-34.
Cauvin, J., and M.-C. Cauvin
    1972   'Sondage à Tell Assouad', *AAAS* 22: 85-96.
Cauvin, J., and D. Storder
    1985   'Une occupation d'époque Uruk en Palmyrene: Le niveau superieur d'el Kowm 2-Caracol', *Cahiers de l'Euphrate* 4: 191-206.
Cavigneaux, A., and F. al-Rawi
    1993   'New Sumerian Literary Texts from Tell Hadad (Ancient Meturan): A First Survey', *Iraq* 55: 91-106.
Contenson, H. de, *et al.*
    1966   'Première sondage à Bouqras en 1965: Rapport préliminaire', *AAAS* 16: 181-92.
Copeland, L.
    1979   'Observations on the Prehistory of the Balikh Valley, Syria, during the Seventh to Fourth Millennium B.C.', *Paléorient* 5: 251-75.
Courty, M.-A., and H. Weiss
    1997   'The Scenario of Environmental Degradation in the Tell Leilan Region, NE

Syria', in N. Dalfes and H. Weiss (eds.), *Third Millennium Climate Change and Old World Social Collapse* (Berlin: Springer): 107-48.

Curvers, H.
1987   'The Middle Habur Salvage Operation: Excavations at Tell al-Raqa'i, 1986', *Akkadica* 55: 1-29.

Curvers, H., and G. Schwartz
1990   'Excavations at Tell al-Raqa'i, A Small Rural Site of Early Urban Northern Mesopotamia', *AJA* 94: 3-23.

Davidson, T., and T. Watkins
1981   'Two Seasons of Excavation at Tell Aqab in the Jezirah, NE Syria', *Iraq* 43: 10-18.

Directorate General of Antiquities and Museums in Syria
1996   'International Colloquium on the Syrian Jezirah', 22–25 April, 1996 in Deir ez-Zor (with the collaboration of the Free University of Berlin).

Dornemann, R.
1977   'Tell Hadidi: A Millennium of Bronze Age Occupation', *AASOR* 44: 113-51.
1988   'Tell Hadidi: One Bronze Age Site among Many in the Tabqa Dam Salvage Area', *BASOR* 270: 13-42.

Driel, G. van
1980   'The Uruk Settlement on Jebel Aruda: A Preliminary Report', in J.-Cl. Margueron (ed.), *Le Moyen Euphrate: Zone de contacts et d'échanges, acres du Colloque de Strasbourg, 10-12 mars 1977* (Leiden: E.J. Brill): 75-93.
1982   'Tablets from Jebel Aruda', in *Studies Kraus*: 12-25.
1983   'Seals and Sealings from Jebel Az-ada', *Akkadica* 33: 34-62.

Driel, G. van, and C. van Driel-Murray
1979   'Jebel Aruda, 1977–78', *Akkadica* 12: 2-8.
1983   'Jebel Aruda: The 1982 Season of Excavations', *Akkadica* 33: 1-26.

Dunham, S.
1983   'Notes on the Relative Chronology of Early Northern Mesopotamia', *JANESCU* 15: 13-38.

Fielden, K.
1977   'Tell Brak 1976: The Pottery', *Iraq* 39: 245-55.

Finet, A.
1975   'Les temples sumériens du Tell Kannas', *Syria* 52: 157-74.
1977   'Bilan provisoire des fouilles belges du Tell Kannas', *AASOR* 44: 79-95.

Fortin, M.
1988a   'Rapport préliminaire sur la seconde campagne de fouilles à Tell 'Atij et le première à Tell Gudeda (Automne 1987), sur Le Moyen Euphrate', *Syria* 67: 219-56.
1988b   'Rapport préliminaire sur la première campagne des fouilles (printemps 1986) à Tell 'Atij, sur le moyen Khabour (Syrie), *Syria* 65: 139-71.
1990   'Rapport préliminaire sur le 3ème campagne de fouilles à Tell 'Atij et la 2e à Tell Gudeda, sur la Kabour (automne 1988)', *Syria* 67: 535-77.
1991   'Récentes recherches archéologiques dans le moyenne vallée du Khabour (Syrie)', *BCSMS* 21: 5-15.
1994   'Rapport préliminaire sur la quatrième campagne à Tell 'Atij et la troisième à Tell Gudeda (printemps 1992)', *Syria* 71: 361-96.

1995   'Rapport préliminaire sur la cinquième campagne à Tell 'Atij et la quartrième à Tell Gudeda (Printemps 1993)', *Syria* 72: 23-53.

1997a   *AJA* 101: 104-106.

1997b   'Urbanisation et redistribution des surplus agricoles en Mésopotamie septentrionale (3000-2500 av. J.-C.)', in W. Aufrecht, *et al.* (eds.), *Aspects of Urbanism in Antiquity: From Mesopotamia to Crete* (Sheffield: Sheffield Academic Press): 50-81.

1998   'New Horizons in Ancient Syria: The View from 'Atij', *NEA* 61: 15-24.

2000   'Economie at société dans le moyenne vallée du Khabour durant la période de Ninive 5', in O. Rouault and M. Wäfler (eds.), *La Djazira et l'euphrate syriens: Tendances dans l'interprétation historique des donées nouvelles de la protohisoire à la fin du second millénaire av. J.-C.* (Paris: Recherches sur les Civilisations).

Fugmann, E.
1958   *Hama: Fouilles et recherches 1931–38*, II (Copenhagen: National Museet).

Fukai, S., *et al.*
1974   *Telul eth-Thalathat: The Excavations of Tell V: The Fourth Season, 1965* (Tokyo: Yokohama).

Gelb, I.
1977   'Thoughts about Ibla: A Preliminary Evaluation', *Syro-Mesopotamian Studies* 1.1: 3-30.

1992   'Mari and the Kish Civilization', in *Mari in Retrospect*: 121-202.

Geyer, B., and J.-Y. Monchambert
1987   'Prospection de la moyenne vallée de l'Euphrate: rapport préliminaire: 1982–1985', *MARI* 5: 318, Figs. 8,10.

Hallo, W.W.
1992   'The Syrian Contribution to Cuneiform Literature', *NHSAS*: 69-88.

Hansen, D.
1982   'A Reevaluation of the Akkad Period in the Diyala Region on the Basis of Excavations from Nippur and in the Hamrin', *AJA* 86: 531-38.

Herzfeld, E.
1930   *Die Vorgeschichtlichen Töpfieren von Samarra* (Berlin: D. Reimer).

Hijara, I., *et al.*
1980   'Arpachiyah', *Iraq* 42: 131-54.

Huot, J., *et al.* (eds.)
1987   *Préhistoire de la Mésopotamie: La Mésopotamie préhistorique et l'exploration recente du Djebel Hamrin* (Paris: Editions Recherche sur les Civilsations).

Kelly-Buccellati, M.
1996   'Nuzi Viewed from Urkesh: Urkesh Viewed from Nuzi: Stock Elements and Framing Devices in Northern Syro-Mesopotamia', *Studies on the Civilization and Culture of Nuzi and the Hurrians* 8: 247-68.

Kirkbride, D.
1982   'Umm Dabagiyah', in J. Curtis (ed.), *Fifty Years of Mesopotamian Discovery* (London: The British School of Archaeology in Iraq): 11-21.

Kohlmeyer, K.
1984   'Euphrat-Survey: Die mit Mitteln der Gerda Henkel Stiftung durchgeführte archäologische Geländebegehung im syrischen Euphrattal', *MDOG* 116: 108.

Kolinski, R.
1996 'Tell Rad Shaqrah 1991–1995', *Orient Express* 3: 67-69.
Kühne, H.
1979 'Zur historischen Geographie am unteren Habur', *AfO* 25: 168-71.
Larsen, M.
1979 'The Tradition of Empire in Mesopotamia', in *Power and Propaganda*: 75-103.
Lebeau, M.
1993 *Tell Melebiya: Cinq campagnes de recherches sur le Moyen-Kabour (1984–1988)* (Louvain: Peeters).
1997 'Beydar', *AJA* 101: 111-12.
Lloyd, S.
1940 'Iraq Government Soundings at Sinjar', *Iraq* 7: 13-21.
Lloyd, S., and F. Safar
1943 'Tell Uqair', *JNES* 2: 131-55.
1945 'Tell Hassuna: Excavations by the Iraq Government Directorate General of Antiquities in 1943 and 1944', *JNES* 4: 255-89.
Loon, M. van
1968 'The Oriental Institute Excavations at Mureybit, Syria', *JNES* 27: 265-92.
1977 '1974 and 1975 Preliminary Reports of the Excavations at Selenkahiye near Meskene, Syria', *AASOR* 44: 97-113.
1983 'Hammam et-Turkman on the Balih: First Results of the University of Amsterdam's 1982 Excavation', *Akkadica* 35: 1-23.
1988a *Hammam et-Turkman I* (Leiden: Nederlands Historisch-Archeologisch Institutte Istanbul).
1988b 'New Evidence for North Syrian Chronology from Hammam et-Turkman', *AJA* 92: 582-87.
Mallowan, M.
1933 'Prehistoric Sondage of Nineveh, 1931–1932', *AAA* 20: 131-55.
1936 'Excavations at Tell Chagar Bazar and an Archaeological Survey of the Habur Region of North Syria', *Iraq* 3: 1-86.
1937 'The Excavations at Tell Chagar Bazar and an Archaeological Survey of the Habur Region: Second Campaign', *Iraq* 4: 91-177.
1946 'Excavations in the Balikh Valley, 1938', *Iraq* 9: 126, figs. 7.1-4,8, 8.3-8.
1964 'Ninevite 5', in K. Bittel (ed.), *Vorderasiatische Archäologie Studien und Aufstätze, Festschrift Moortgat* (Berlin: Gebr Mann, 1964): 142-54.
Mallowan, M., and J. Cruikshank-Rose
1935 'Excavations at Tell ArphachiYah', *Iraq* 2: 1-178.
Margueron, J.-Cl.
1991a 'Tell Hariri/Mari', *AJA* 95: 711.
1991b 'Mari, l'Euphrate, et le Khabur au milieu du IIème millénaire', *BCSMS* 21: 79-100.
1994 'Tell Hariri/Mari', *AJA* 98: 130-31.
2000 'Mari et le Khabur', in O. Rouault and M. Wäfler (eds.), *La Djazira et l'euphrate syriens. Tendances dans l'interprétation historique des donées nouvelles de la protohisoire à la fin du second millénaire av. J.-C.* (Brepol: Turnhout): 151-65.

Mathews, D.
1995   'Excavations at Tell Brak, 1995', *Iraq* 57: 87-111.
1996   *The Early Glyptic of Tell Brak: Cylinder Seals of Third Millennium Syria* (OBO, 15; Freiburg: University Press).
1997   'Brak', *AJA* 101: 116-17.
Mathews, D., *et al.*
1994   'Excavations at Tell Brak, 1994', *Iraq* 56: 177-94.
Matthiae, P.
1981   *Ebla: An Empire Rediscovered* (Garden City, NY: Doubleday).
McClellan, T.
1997   'Banat', *AJA* 101: 106-108.
McClellan, T., *et al.*
1991   'Tell es-Sweyhat', *AJA* 95: 700-707.
McClellan, T., and R. Zettler
1994   'Tell es-Sweyhat', *AJA* 98: 139-42.
Meijer, D.
1986   *A Survey in Northeastern Syria* (Leiden: Nederlands Historisch-Archeologisch Instituut te Istanbul).
Merpert, N., *et al.*
1981   'Investigations of the Soviet Expedition in Northern Iraq, 1976', *Sumer* 37: 22-54.
Merpert, N., and R. Munchaev
1973   'Early Agricultural Settlements in the Sinjar Plain, Northern Iraq', *Iraq* 35: 93-113.
1984   'Soviet Expedition's Research at Yarim Tepe III Settlement in Northwestern Iraq, 1978-79', *Sumer* 43: 54-68.
Milano, L., *et al.*
1991   *Mozan 2: The Epigraphic Finds of the Sixth Season* (Malibu: Undena).
Molist, M.
1994   'Archaeology of Syria', *AJA* 98: 105-106.
Monchambert, J.-Y.
1986a   'A Short Account of the Excavation in Tell Bderi 1985', *AAAS* 36-37: 276-88.
1986b   'The Excavations at Tell Bderi 1986', *AAAS* 36-37: 292-303.
1988   'Tell Bderi 1985: Bericht über die erste Kampagne', *Damaszener Mitteilungen* 3: 223-386.
1990   'Tell Bderi—the Development of a Bronze Age Town', in S. Kerner (ed.), *The Near East in Antiquity*, I (Amman: Goethe Institute): 63-79.
Moore, A.
1988   'The Prehistory of Syria', *BASOR* 270: 3-12.
Moore, A.T.
1975   'The Excavation of Tell Abu Hureyra in Syria: A Preliminary Report', *PPS* 41: 50-77.
Moortgat-Correns, U.
1975   'Huera, Tell', *RlA* 4: 480-87.
Oates, D.
1970   'The Excavations at Tell al-Rimah, 1968', *Iraq* 32: 1-26.
1977   'The Excavations at Tell Brak: 1976', *Iraq* 39: 234.

Oates, J.
1973 'The Background and Development of Early Farming Communitites in Mesopotamia and the Zagros', *PPS* 39: 147-81.
1984 'Ubaid Mesopotamia Reconsidered', in *Studies Braidwood*: 251-81.
1985 'Tell Brak: Uruk Pottery from the 1984 Season', *Iraq* 47: 175-86.
1986 'Tell Brak: The Uruk/Early Dynastic Sequence', in U. Finkbeiner and W. Röllig (eds.), *Gemdet Nasr: Period or Regional Style?* (Wiesbaden: Dr. Ludwig Reichert Verlag): 245-73.
1990 'Tell Brak in the Fourth and Third Millennia: From Uruk to Ur III', in S. Eichler, *et al.* (eds.), *Tall al-Hamidiya 2: Recent Excavations in the Upper Khabur Region* (Göttingen: Vandenhoeck & Ruprecht): 133-47.

Oates, D., and J. Oates
1989 'Akkadian Buildings at Tell Brak', *Iraq* 51: 193-211.
1991 'Excavations at Tell Brak, 1990-1991', *Iraq* 53: 127-46.

Oppenheim, B. von
1943–62 *Tell Halaf*, I-IV (Berlin: W. de Gruyter).
1931 *Der Tell Halaf: Eine neue Kultur im ältesten Mesopotamien* (Leipzig: F.A. Brockhaus).

Orthmann, W.
1986 'The Origin of Tell Chuera', in H. Weiss (ed.), *The Origins of Cities in Dry-Farming Syria and Mesopotamia in the Third Millennium B.C.* (Guildford: Four Quarters Publishing Co.): 61-70.

Owen, D.
1992 'Syrians in Sumerian Sources from the Ur III Period', in *NHSAS*: 117-21.

Özten, A.
1976–77 'Two Pots Recovered in the Excavations at Samsat belonging to the Late Chalcolithic Period', *Anadolu* 20: 267-71.

Pecorella, P.E.
1990a 'The Italian Excavations at Tell Barri (Kahat)', in S. Eichler, *et al.* (eds.), *Tall al-Hamidiya 2: Recent Excavations in the Upper Khabur Region* (Göttingen: Vandenhoeck & Ruprecht): 47-66.
1990b 'Tell Barri/Kahat durante il II millennio', in *Studies Bounni*: 259-75.

Pecorella, P., and M. Salving
1982 *Tell Barri/Kahat 1: Relazione preliminare sulle campagne 1980 e 1981 a Tell Barri/Kahat, nel bacino del Habur* (Rome: Istituto per gli studi Micenei ed Egeo-Anatolici).

Pettinato, G.
1981 *The Archives of Ebla: An Empire Rediscovered in Clay* (Garden City, NY: Doubleday).
1991 *Ebla: A New Look at History* (Baltimore: The Johns Hopkins University Press).

Pettinato, G., *et al.*
1979– *Materiali epigrafici di Ebla* (Naples: Istituto Universitario Orientalie di Napoli).

Porter, A.
1995a 'Tell Banat-Tomb I', *Damazener Mitteilungen* 8: 1-50.
1995b 'The Third Millennium at the Tell Banat Settlement Complex', *Damazener Mitteilungen* 8: 125-63.

Rashid, F.
1984   'Akkadian Texts from Tell Sleima', *Sumer* 40: 55-56.
Reade, J.
1968   'Tell Taya (1967): Summary Report', *Iraq* 30: 235-36.
1982   'Tell Taya', in J. Curtis (ed.), *Fifty Years of Mesopotamian Archaeology* (London: British School of Archaeology in Iraq): 72-78.
Roaf, M.
1980   'A Report on the Work of the British Archaeological Expedition in the Eski Mosul Dam Salvage Project', *Sumer* 39: 68-87.
1984   'Excavations at Tell Mohammed Arab in the Eski Mosul Dam Region', *Iraq* 47: 141-56.
Roodenberg, J.
1979–80   'Sondages de niveaux néolithiques de Tell Sinn, Syria', *Anatolica* 7: 21-33.
Routledge, B.
1998   'Making Nature Human: Small-Scale Production and Specialization at Tell Gudeda in the Middle Habur Valley', in M. Fortin and A. Aurenche (eds.), *Espace natural, espace habité en Syrie du Nord: 10ème–2ème millénaires av. J.-C.* (Quebec-Lyon: La Société canadienne des études mésopotamiennes-Maison de l'Orient Méditerranéen): 243-56.
Saghié, M.
1991   'The Lebanese University Recent Excavations at Tell Kerma: A Salvage Operation on the Middle Khabur, NE Syria', in *Mésopotamië et Elam* (RAI, 35; Ghent: University of Ghent): 171-84.
Schwartz, G.
1994a   'Before Ebla: Models of Pre-State Political Organization in Syria and Northern Mesopotamia', in G. Stein and M. Rothman (eds.), *Chiefdoms and Early States in the Near East: The Organizational Dynamics of Complexity* (Madison: Prehistory Press): 153-74.
1994b   'Rural Economic Specialization and Early Urbanization in the Khabur Valley, Syria', in G. Schwartz and S. Falconer (eds.), *Archeological Views from the Countryside: Village Communities in Early Complex Societies* (Washington: The Smithsonian Institution Press): 19-36.
Schwartz, G., and H. Curvers
1994   'Tell al-Raqa'i 1989 and 1990: Further Investigations at a Small Rural Site of Early Urban Northern Mesopotamia', *AJA* 96: 397-419.
1993–94   'Tell al-Raqa'i: Excavations and Analyses: A Progress Report', *AfO* 40-41: 246-57.
Simpson, K.
1988   *Qraya Modular Reports 1: The Early Soundings* (Malibu: Undena).
Smith, C.C.
1968   'The Impact of Assyriology on Old Testament Study, with Special Reference to the Publications of Leonard William King (doctoral dissertation, University of Chicago).
Speiser, E.
1933   'The Pottery of Tell Billa', *Museum Journal* 23: 249-83.
1935   *Excavations at Tepe Gawra, Level I-VIII*, I (Philadelphia: University of Pennsylvania Press).

Starr, R.
1937–39   *Nuzi: Report on the Excavations at Yorghan Tepe Near Kirkuk, Iraq* (Cambridge, MA: Harvard University Press).

Strommenger, E.
1977   'Ausgrabungen der Deutschen Orient-Gesellschaft in Habuba-Kabira', *Annual of the American School of Oriental Research* 44: 62-78.
1980   *Habuba Kabira: Eine Stadt vor 5000 Jahren* (Mainz am Rhein: Verlag Philipp von Zabern).

Sürenhagen, D.
1986   'The Dry Farming Belt: The Uruk Period and Subsequent Developments', in H. Weiss (ed.), *The Origins of Cities in Dry-Farming Syria and Mesopotamia in the Third Millennium B.C.* (Guildford: Four Quarters Publishing Co.): 7-44.
1990   'Ausgrabungen in Tall Mulla Matar 1989', *MDOG* 22: 125-52.

Thuesen, I.
1989   'Diffusion of Ubaid Pottery into Western Asia', in E. Henrickson and I. Thuesen (eds.), *Upon This Foundation: The Ubaid Reconsidered* (Copenhagen: Museum Tusculanum Press): 419-40.
1997   'Mashnaqa', *AJA* 101: 131-32.

Tobler, A.
1950   *Excavations at Tepe Gawra, Levels IX-XX*, 2 (Philadelphia: University of Pennsylvania Press).

Weiss, H.
1983   'Excavations at Tell Leilan and the Origins of North Mesopotamian Cities in the Third Millennium B.C.', *Paléorient* 9: 42.
1985a   'Review of J. Curtis (ed.), *Fifty Years of Mesopotamian Archaeology* (London: British School of Archaeology in Iraq, 1982)', *JAOS* 105: 327-30.
1985b   'Tell Leilan and Shubat Enlil', *MARI* 4: 269.
1985c   'Tell Leilan on the Habur Plains of Syria', *BA* 48: 5-35.
1986   'The Origins of Tell Leilan and the Conquest of Space in Third Millennium Mesopotamia', in H. Weiss (ed.), *The Origins of Cities in Dry-Farming Syria and Mesopotamia in the Third Millennium B.C.* (Guildford: Four Quarters Publishing Co.): 67-104.
1990a   'Tell Leilan 1989: New Data for Mid-Third Millennium Urbanization and State Formation', *MDOG* 122: 193-218.
1990b   'Third Millennium Urbanization: A Perspective from Tell Leilan', S. Eichler, *et al.* (eds.), *Tall al-Hamidiya 2: Recent Excavations in the Upper Khabur Region* (Göttingen: Vandenhoeck & Ruprecht): 159-66.
1991   'Archaeology in Syria', *AJA* 95: 683-740.
1993   'The Genesis and Collapse of Third Millennium North Mesopotamian Civilization', *Science* 261: 995-1004.
1994   'Archaeology in Syria', *AJA* 98: 101-58.
1997   'Archaeology in Syria', *AJA* 101: 97-149.

Weiss, H., *et al.*
1990   '1985 Excavations at Tell Leilan, Syria', *AJA* 94: 529-82.

Wilhelm, G.
1989   *The Hurrians* (trans. J. Barnes; Warminster: Aris & Phillips).

Wilkinson, T.
  1990   'The Development of Settlement in North Jezira between the 7th and 1st
                  Millennia B.C.', *Iraq* 52: 49-62.
Yoffee, N., *et al.* (eds.)
  1993   *Early Stages of the Evolution of Mesopotamian Civilization: Soviet Exca-
                  vations in Northern Iraq* (Tucson: University of Arizona Press).
Zettler, R., *et al.*
  1997   'Tell es-Sweyhat', *AJA* 101: 141-44.

Syro-Mesopotamia:
The Old Babylonian Period

Ronald A. Veenker

1. *The End of the Third Dynasty at Ur*

The Old Babylonian period of Mesopotamian history extends from the end
of the Third Dynasty of Ur until 1594 BCE when the Hittite monarch
Muršili attacked and decimated the city of Babylon. The decline of the Ur
III period was brought about by an increasingly independent spirit among
the Babylonian cities, an influx of semitic nomads or Amorites and an
unstable relationship between Elam and Babylon itself. Information gleaned
from date formulae (years 3–7) indicate Eshnunna, Susa, Lagash, Umma
and Nippur were all falling away from the old empire.[1] Then, in 2017 BCE,
Išbi-Erra of Mari established his dynasty at Isin. After blackmailing Ibbi-
Sin into appointing him commandant of Isin, Išbi-Erra seized Nippur and
with it the spiritual foundation of the Ur empire. His was now the title
'favorite of Enlil', legitimate suzerain of Sumer and Akkad. Ibbi-Sin's rule
came to an end at the hand of the Elamites with the assistance of the
Simaški and was taken captive to Elam. Six years later, Išbi-Erra moved
into the city of Ur.

2. *The Old Babylonian Successor States*

Isin, the royal residence of the new kingdom, was the cult center of the
deities Nin-Isina and Dagan. Išbi-Erra took over the administrative system,
which had been skillfully crafted by the kings of the Ur III empire, by
currying favor with the *ensi*'s ('governors') appointed by Ibbi-Sin. Note
that Išbi-Erra's administrative texts followed the Ur forms exactly. From
Isin, his shining new capital, he constructed fortresses to keep the Amorites

---

1. For recent editions of the royal inscriptions utilized in this paper see: *RIME* 2;
RIME 3/1; *RIME* 3/2; *RIME* 4.

at bay and jousted on occasion with Elam to the south.

Larsa and Eshnunna were probably independent of Išbi-Erra in the early years of the Isin dynasty,[2] but the latter was not really a force to be reckoned with in either case. Der, an independent state when Ibbi-Sin lost the empire, eventually fell to Isin as well. Assyria took advantage of the brief power vacuum which marked the confusion of the period to separate itself completely from Babylonian rule.

The first three monarchs of the dynasty at Isin suffered few if any threats from outside city states. Damage inflicted on Ur by the Elamites was repaired, the statue of Nannar was recovered and literature flourished, most notably, the famous composition *Lamentation over the Destruction of Sumer and Ur* (Klein 1997) as well as the law code of Lipit-Eštar.[3] Royal hymns were written alluding to peace in the land.

Then, under Išme-Dagan, the fourth monarch, trouble developed between Isin and Kish. The Amorites were once again attacking the settled areas of the region, Nippur in particular. During the reign of Lipit-Eštar, Gungunum of Larsa captured Ur and Isin lost the south forever.

At the beginning of the nineteenth century, there were essentially three competing local dynasties: Isin, Larsa and Babylon (occasionally, Eshnunna and Uruk were forces to be reckoned with as well). By the beginning of the eighteenth century, we see the movement to form larger states culminating in the empire of Hammurabi of Babylon (1792–50), the most impressive political result of the Amorite migration, equal in significance to the empire of Agade achieved in the Akkadian expansion. For the history of the 300 years from Lipit-Eštar to the end of the first dynasty of Babylon, there was an excellent expansion of sources. In contrast to the so-called temple-state of Sumer, we witness the expansion of the economy in the private sector. Temples are limited to function as cult centers while the middle class rises in prominence. In contrast to earlier Mesopotamian royalty, the Amorites did not envision a divinized monarch. Although, for example, there was a royal hymn to Samsu-iluna, it was a throwback to the poetry of Sumer, an attempt to archaize the new regime and identify with the glory of the past.

2. For some of the royal inscriptions of the Isin dynasty, see Frayne 2000a: 246-48.

3. Babylon was located quite near Kish where one copy of the Laws of Eshnunna (Roth 2000c) were found. Both the earlier codes of Ur-Nammu (Roth 2000a) and the Lipit-Eštar code (Roth 2000b) have a prologue, rules, and epilogue, the same form as the Code of Hammurabi.

'Old Babylonian' is a linguistic as well as a political term. It is the classical stage of development of the Akkadian dialects. Old Babylonian literature is the crowning achievement of a flowering *belles-lettres* tradition which began at the end of the Isin Dynasty and culminated at the beginning of the sixteenth century. The chronology of the period is based upon the king lists from Isin, Larsa and Babylon. Isin (1923–1794) had 12 kings beginning with Lipit-Eštar; Larsa flourished from 2025–1763. The First Dynasty of Babylon began with Sumu-abum (1894–1881) and came to an end with Samsu-Ditana (1625–1594). Two very significant dates for early period chronology are: (1) 'King Rim-Sin of Larsa broke the power of Isin' (1793) and (2) 'Hammurabi took control of Larsa' (1762).

3. *Nomads in the Old Babylonian Period*

All nomads mentioned in the literature of the period are simply referred to by the Sumerogram MAR.TU. The corresponding Akkadian term is *Amurrum*. These two terms are in use consistently throughout all periods in many venues. As a consequence, the term refers to a great variety of 'nomadic' peoples in the Old Babylonian period.

Shar-kali-sharri of Akkad fought against Amurrum and the nomads that brought down the third dynasty at Ur, all of whom were called MAR.TU. Note that the names of some of the new dynastic rulers are 'non-Akkadian Semites': Naplanum of Larsa; Sumuabum of Babylon; Ashduniarim of Kish; Yazir-el of Kazallu. Ammisaduqa of Babylon refers to his population as 'Akkadians and Amurrum'.

Who are these Amurrum or 'Amorites'? Are they related, even linguistically, to the Canaanites? Historically and linguistically it would probably be more prudent to simply call them Amurrum/Amorites. More significant than seasonal pastoral migration were the larger movements of people into sedentary occupation which would eventually become permanent. Their migratory patterns into Mesopotamia from the western steppes are seen in two regions, the mid-Euphrates and further south to about Sippar. Their northern route led to the upper regions of the Ḫabur river. Then, fording the Tigris and Euphrates at Sippar, they would arrive in the east Tigris and south of Diyala in a territory called Yamutbal. Raiding and looting the sedentary settlements was the economic goal of most nomads. One may see similar patterns in the biblical book of Judges. Working the land was not an easy life, so mercenary activity was immediately more attractive—hunger probably drove some to join the sedentary labor forces.

Old Babylonian texts even provide individual tribal names. For example, at Mari, an important Amorite tribal name is 'Amnanum'. Even king Sin-kashid of Uruk uses Amnanum as a royal title.[4] Amnanum, Yaḫ-rurum and Ubrabum were branches of the Maru/Binu-Yamina, literally 'sons of the south', that is Southerners. Note the similarity in the biblical tribe Benjamin which carries the same meaning. Ḫanu, in the Mari tablets, refers to nomadic mercenaries in the service of a particular king while Amurrum refers to nomads in general. By the end of the second millennium, the assimilation was complete. Amorites used the Akkadian language and were part of the mainstream culture.

4. *The Nineteenth Century*

Gungunum (1932–1906), mentioned above, the first shaker and mover of the Larsa dynasty (see Frayne 2000a: 248-54), took Ur, the strategic seaport, from Lipit-Eštar of Isin. Nevertheless, he normalized relations with Isin very quickly thereafter. For another 100 years, the kings of Isin maintained the fiction that Ur was still part of their state. But the reality is that Lipit-Eštar was the last ruler at Isin to function as a successor to the Ur III empire.

Gungunum, on the other hand, left more of a mark on history. He moved against Anshan continuing the tradition of Babylonian expansion in the Elamite east and, at home, he established an admirable improvement and expansion of the famous Larsa canals.

By the eighth year of Abišare of Larsa (1898), hostilities had broken out with Isin over control of Ur. Under Sumu'el (1894–1866) Larsa expanded its territory northward and continued to fight with Isin for control of Nippur. While Larsa was an important power it should not be considered truly imperial. From 1894 BCE on, Babylon was an emerging independent power that quickly annexed Sippar to its north. Very soon thereafter, Sumula'el (1880–1845) annexed Kish nine miles northeast.

Other independent states were Kazallu, Marad, Malgium, and Kisurra, among others. Eshnunna dominated the Diyala region with the single exception of Tutub (Khafaji D). The political situation in nineteenth century Babylonia soon reached the point where an individual state could do no more than raid its neighbors. Larger enterprises called for coalition. About 1860, Uruk seceded from Isin and joined the consortium of

4.   It has only recently been pointed out by scholars that there are two Sippars, one of which was known as Sippar-Amnanum. See van Lerberghe 1991: I, xi.

Babylonian states, but, in 1803, fell to Larsa. Uruk, a relatively small city, nevertheless enjoyed enough importance to have a firm alliance with Babylon throughout the entire period.

There is no clear evidence of a canal system in the mid-nineteenth century. There was a violent flood c. 1860–1850 which caused the Tigris to shift its bed. The Tigris and the Euphrates deposit tons of sediment annually causing major shifts in the flow even in modern times.

A generation prior to Sin-Kashid at Uruk, an Amorite dynasty established itself in Babylon. While Babylon's tradition regards Sumula'el as the founder, it is now known that the dynasty was headed by Sumuabum.

Practically nothing is known about the tribal or geographic origins of Sumu'abum and no more is known of Babylon between Ibbi-Sin's time and his own. Until the third dynasty at Ur, Babylon had its own *ensi* ('governor'). And then, following the collapse of Ur, it became part of Isin's burgeoning kingdom. The First Dynasty of Babylon retained Amorite throne names longer than most. Of the 11 kings, only Apil-Sin and Sin-muballit took Akkadian names. It was difficult for the early Babylonian kings to establish independence. After all, Babylon, like Isin and Larsa, had no great political and literary traditions in their past. Only after more than two decades of Hammurabi's rule could Babylon move apart from traditional alliances with other north Babylonian states.

On the Middle Euphrates and in Syria, there were many small kingdoms in the nineteenth century. For Mari, there are sources only from the end of the period. Yadun-Lim's son Zimri-Lim drove out the Assyrian king's son Yasmah-Adad and regained control of his father's dynasty. Both Mariotes and the Assyrians were of Amorite origin.

At the end of the nineteenth century major kingdoms began to develop after the chaotic political scenes of the immediate past. A balance of power was maintained among Larsa, Eshnunna and Assur for about 50 years. The unification of Babylonia did not occur until the twelfth year of Hammurabi, that is, 1763 BCE. Though the empire formed by the First Dynasty of Babylon was not of great duration its importance for all subsequent Mesopotamian culture was enormous. The city of Babylon was *the* city so that the entire country took on its name, Babylonia. Outsiders even referred to the Akkadian language as 'Babylonian'.

The struggles between Isin and Larsa, earlier defined by the alternating possession of Nippur, was in 1835 taken by the Amorites of Yamutbal, Kudur-mabuk. His two sons, Warad-Sin (1834–1823) and Rim-Sin (1822–1863), were his designated kings of Larsa (Frayne 2000a: 251-54). This

72-year rule resulted in stability as well as great literary productivity. As well there was economic stability that led to vast canal and irrigation projects. In 1793 Rim-Sin conquered Isin, eliminating Larsa's only real competition in central Babylonia. For the following 30 years Rim-Sin named those years: 'Year X; Isin conquered'. This victory marked the end of Isin as an independent state forever.

In the Diyala territory, Ipiq-Adad of Eshnunna took Rapiqum on the Euphrates cutting off the possibility of northward expansion for Babylon. His son Naram-Sin moved beyond Assur in the upper Ḫabur region. Namra-Sin's brother Dadusha continued the dynasty until 1790. Incidentally, it was likely during Dadusha's reign that the *Code of Eshnunna* was drawn together. Eshununna remained an important power under Dadusha's successor Ibalpi'el II.

According to the *Assyrian King List*, Shamshi-Adad was actually an exile from Terqa. Basing himself in Ekallatum, he forced out the last king of the dynasty, Puzur-Assur, and took the throne there. A contemporary of Dadusha, reigning from 1815–1782, he established a second capital in Shubat-Enlil in the upper Ḫabur region. Shamishi-Adad resembled in many ways his younger contemporary Hammurabi. He was the first ruler in northern Mesopotamia to take the title 'king of the universe' (*šar kiššatim*), and was a talented, successful administrator as well as a skillful politician. By today's standard he would be called a 'micro-manager'! His letters are an excellent source for reconstructing the political history of the day. His power and influence reached as far south as Babylonian Sippar where a document survives in which the oath is sworn by 'brother Hammurabi and Shamshi-Adad'. However, these expansive actions did not result in a highly organized empire reminiscent of the third dynasty at Ur. Although his influence died with him, his son Ishme-Dagan made his own power felt beyond the borders of Assyria.

5. *The Rise of Babylon*

Hammurabi's year date formulas found in contracts and government documents again tell the story of Babylon's rise to power under the notorious king: fortification of several cities in the north from 1776–1768 BCE; victory over a coalition of Elam, Assur, the 'Gutians', Eshnunna and Malgium in 1764 BCE. Just exactly whom is indicated by the term 'Gutians' is difficult to say. After a siege of several months, Larsa was taken in 1763. At that same time, Hammurabi took possession of 'the banks of the Tigris into Subartu', meaning Assur and probably Ekallatum. Mari and Malgium were overtaken in 1759 while two more skirmishes with Assur were recorded in 1757 and 1755. Left to these sources alone, one would think Hammurabi a most successful and triumphant military leader (Frayne 2000b: 256-58). But Babylon did not stand alone against the remainder of Mesopotamia and the date formula do not mention his allies. Hammurabi's success was more diplomatic in putting together alliances than it was pure military force. In a letter of Zimri-Lim of Mari we are told that 10 to 15 kings marched in coalition with Hammurabi and that nearly as many were in league with Rim-Sin of Larsa and Ibal-pi'el of Eshnunna. Another letter suggests that Hammurabi had to negotiate carefully with Eshnunna before attacking Larsa. In his thirtieth year, his date formulae suggests finally and for the first time he 'established the foundations' of Sumer and Akkad, that is, he ruled all of Babylonia. In the prologue to his famous law code, Hammurabi names the great cities under his rule during the last years of his kingship. In Babylon: Eridu, Ur, Lagash, Girsu, Zabalam, Larsa, Uruk, Adab, Isin, Nippur, Keshi, Dilbat, Borsippa, Babylon, Kish, Malgium, Mashkanshapir, Kutha, and Sippar. In the Diyala region: Eshnunna; mid-Euphrates: Mari and Tuttul; mid-Tigris: Assur and Nineveh. Excepting Elam, Hammurabi's empire was identical to that of the third dynasty at Ur. However, it did not endure nearly so long as the latter. Assur and Nineveh were held for a very few years. Then there was always internal dissension from particular interest from the past. By the second decade of Samsu-iluna (Frayne 2000b: 258), Hammurabi's son and successor, the whole southern region of Babylonia had broken away from the First Dynasty.

6. *Mari*

The palace archive covers the period from 1810 to 1760 BCE.[5] Besides the invaluable correspondence of Zimri-Lim and Yasmay-Adad, the archive contains more than 100 legal texts and nearly 1000 administrative documents. Mari was strategically located on the trade routes between Syria and Babylonia. It was the main link between the Mediterranean Sea and the Persian Gulf for both river traffic and overland caravans. While its territory was not vast, it controlled the Euphrates valley from the mouth of the Balih river to the modern town of Hit. There was a voluminous correspondence between Zimri-Lim and Kibri-Dagan, his governor at

---

5.   For some of the royal inscriptions, see Frayne 2000b: 260-61.

Terqa. Thirty-six miles upriver from Mari, Terqa had earlier been inde-pendently ruled by Ilakabkabuhu, Shamshi-Adad's father.

Commercial revenue had made the rulers of Mari very wealthy so that they were able to endow their city with many temples. But the greatest monument to their success was the Old Babylonian period palace, the largest of its time. It contained 260 courts and chambers and covered an area of two and a half acres. The diplomatic correspondence indicates that it was a well-known attraction for royal visitations. The splendid frescoes are known to all who peruse ancient Near East art books.

The magnificent archive records civilization from Crete to Asia Minor, Susa to the east and Larsa and Dilmun to the southeast, not to mention Hazor in the Levant. The language of the Mari letters is Old Babylonian once again. Letters from Hurrian outposts while rather barbaric in gram-matical form are clear enough to be understood. Thus, Old Babylonian or Akkadian was the diplomatic tongue of the period. The correspondence covers a wide range of topics from international political affairs at Mari, that is, relations with nomadic peoples, agriculture, irrigation, palace administration, legal problems, to international politics. The itineraries of ambassadors, foreign and domestic, are regularly noted.

7. *Syria*

Syria in the eighteenth century, typical of nineteenth-century Meso-potamia, was filled with independent kingdoms and their vassal states. Yamhad was the most powerful of these kingdoms; its capital was Halab (modern Aleppo). Alalah was its vassal state. To the northeast on the Euphrates was Carchemish, a thriving city on the caravan route leading to the Anatolian plateau. Its king, Aplahanda, was vassal to Shamshi-Adad, while his son, Yatar-ammi, was an ally of Zimri-Lim of Mari. To the north were several Hurrian states. Ugarit on the Mediterranean, Qatna on the Orontes plain and Byblos on the coast were all three Semitic states. Qatna had political relations with major Mesopotamian rulers as well as Susa and Arrapha near Kirkuk. Syria was a major player in international affairs in all of western Asia at the time.

From the end of the Mari archival sources to the beginning of the fifteenth century BCE we have very few sources which pertain to Syria and northern Mesopotamia west of Assyria. The Hittite monarch Hattušili I destroyed both Yamhad and Alalah. The sources are silent until after the middle of the second millennium when we see the Empire of the Mitanni dominating from the Mediterranean east to Nuzi.

8. *Hammurabi's Babylon*

Long before this most famous Mesopotamian monarch held sway, his city had a political history. During the Dynasty of Agade, Shar-kali-sharri built a temple in Babylon and the kings of the Third Dynasty of Ur appointed several leaders to the position of *ensi*, 'governor', there as well. What remains of this ancient civilization is now found on a number of tells lying beneath the remains of the first millennium city of the same name. The Old Babylonian city has been one of the great archeological disappointments of the ancient Near East. The rising water table managed to eradicate nearly all of the physical remains of the period. What is known today about Hammurabi's Babylon is from correspondence and inscriptions taken from other Old Babylonian sites. His most famous legacy, the notorious *Code of Hammurabi*,[6] was found by French archeologists in 1902 at the Elamite capital of Susa where it had been taken by raiders in the twelfth century.

While I have suggested above that the kings of the First Dynasty who preceded Hammurabi never achieved the level and status of the most famous monarch, they did leave him with a considerable legacy upon which to build. Although archeology cannot reconstruct Old Babylon, it is known Hammurabi's city already contained a palace and several temples. Without mentioning the many temples that were patronized in other cities under Babylonian control, it becomes clear that Hammurabi took over an empire that had the impressive resources required for the building and maintaining of so many cult centers.

Scholars learn about Hammurabi's rule and his view of himself from inscriptions, economic/legal/administrative documents, and personal correspondence that he exchanged with other kings and political leaders. In his royal inscriptions, as one would expect, there are recurring themes upon which the king expounds. Like all monarchs, Hammurabi was fond of listing great numbers of deities who had conferred in antiquity and decreed that he would be the greatest king of all. In addition however, there is a theme not found in the inscriptions of other kings, namely, Hammurabi's intense focus upon his establishing justice in the land. In

6.   See the recent translations of Roth 1995/97; 2000d; and Richardson 2000. See also Roth 1995; 1998.

fact, he used his *Code* to impress the nation and the gods with his devotion to justice. In his first regnal year he claims to have 'established justice in his land'. Former kings of the first dynasty had upon occasion proclaimed a *mīšarum*, that is, an edict to effect economic reform by forgiving citizens who were in arrears in their taxes as well as canceling debts between private parties. Not only did he announce a *mīšarum* in his first year, but he did the same after taking control of Larsa.

The *Code*, which was probably executed around his fortieth year, is, of course, his most prestigious and infamous inscription. This magnificent stela is grand testimony to Hammurabi's dedication to establishing justice for all his citizens. All were invited to stand before his stela and have it read to them that they might understand their legal standing and feel comforted by the king's devotion to justice for all.

Whether to call this collection of law a 'code' in the traditional legal sense has been called into question. While the collection covers a great many facets of the law in Old Babylonian society, it falls short of covering them all. For example, there are no sections of the code which deal with surety, antichretic pledges that paid off interest but no principal, temple prebends, property easements, theft of cattle, abduction of slaves, nor arson. As well, Hammurabi's *Code* does not contain many cases which are found in the contemporaneous collection of the Laws of Eshnunna. Many of the laws found in Hammurabi and Eshnunna are also found in the older collections of earlier kings. This reinforces the fact that Hammurabi wished to publicly convey his strong commitment to justice in the land.

It is interesting to observe differences in various collections of laws in the ancient Near East. For example, in contrast to lighter punishments found in other Akkadian and Sumerian legal collections, the *Code of Hammurabi* (CH) advocates corporal punishment for theft:

> If a citizen made a breach in a house, they shall put him to death in front of that breach and wall him in (CH §21).

Compare with this the *Covenant Code* of the Hebrew Bible:

> If a thief is found breaking in and is struck so that he dies, there shall be no bloodguilt for him (Exod. 22.2).

Note that in old Babylon breaking and entering was considered a capital crime. In the Hebrew Bible we see that the Israelites regarded it a serious crime so as to justify manslaughter on the part of the victim, but probably not a capital crime *per se*. What follows is a selection of cases from the *Code of Hammurabi* with a parallel section from the Hebrew Bible for comparison:

Perjury

> If a man has come forward in a case to bear witness to a felony and then has not proved the statement that he has made, if it is a capital case, that man shall be put to death (CH §3).

> If a malicious witness rises against any man to accuse him of wrongdoing, then both parties to the dispute shall appear before the LORD, before the priests and the judges...(who) shall inquire diligently, and if the witness is a false witness and has accused his brother falsely, then you shall do to him as he had meant to do to his brother... (Deut. 19.16-19).

Indentured Servitude

> If a man has become liable to arrest under a bond and has sold his wife his son or his daughter or gives them into servitude, for 3 years they shall do work in the house of him who has bought them or taken them in servitude; in the fourth year their release shall be granted (CH §117).

> When you buy a Hebrew slave, he shall serve six years, and in the seventh he shall go out free, for nothing. If he comes in single, he shall go out single; if he comes in married, then his wife shall go out with him. If his master gives him a wife and she bears him sons or daughters, the wife and her children shall be her master's and he shall go out alone (Exod. 21.2-4).

Adultery

> If a married woman is caught lying with another man, they shall bind them and cast them into the water; if her husband wishes to let his wife live, then the king shall let the other man live (CH §129).

> If a man is found lying with the wife of another man, both of them shall die, the man who lay with the woman, and the woman; so you shall purge the evil from Israel (Deut. 22.22).

Marriage/Divorce

> If the wife of a citizen leaves the house of her husband on her own business, and if she neglects the house and shames her husband, then her husband may either divorce her without paying a fine, or may marry another woman while his former wife is to live in the house as a slave (CH §141).

> When a man takes a wife and marries her, if then she finds no favor in his eyes because he has found some indecency in her, and he writes her a bill of divorce and puts it in her hand and sends her out of his house and she departs out of his house, and if she goes and becomes another man's wife, and the latter husband dislikes her and writes her a bill of divorce and puts it in her hand and sends her out of his house, or if the latter husband

dies...then her former husband...may not take her again to be his wife, after she has been defiled (Exod. 24.1-4).

Personal Injury

If a citizen strikes his father, then his hand is to be cut off (CH §195).

Whoever strikes his father or his mother shall be put to death (Exod. 21.15).

Manslaughter

If a citizen accidentally hits another citizen and causes injury, then that citizen must swear: 'I did not strike this citizen deliberately', and must pay for the cost of a physician. If the victim dies from the blow, then the citizen must swear the same oath, but if the citizen is a member of a royal household, then the fine paid to the household of the victim is one-half mina silver (CH §§206-207).

When men quarrel and one strikes the other with a stone or with his fist and the man does not die but keeps his bed, then if the man rises again and walks abroad with his staff, he that struck him shall be clear; only he shall pay for the loss of his time, and shall have him thoroughly healed (Exod. 21.18-19).

Rental

If a citizen rents an ox and a member of the divine assembly (i.e. a god) strikes it with lightning and it dies, then the citizen who had rented the ox must swear in the name of a member of the divine assembly that the death of the ox was an act of God, and then there is no fine (CH §249).

If a man borrows anything of his neighbor, and it is hurt or dies, the owner not being with it, he shall make full restitution. If the owner was with it, he shall not make restitution; if it was hired, it came for its hire (Exod 22.14-15).

The Goring Ox

If the ox of a citizen, who has neither tethered, nor blunted the horns of the animal, even after the city assembly has put the owner on notice that it was dangerous, gores a state official, then the fine is one-half mina silver (CH §251).

When an ox gores a man or a woman to death, the ox shall be stoned and its flesh shall not be eaten; but the owner of the ox shall be clear. But if the ox has been accustomed to gore in the past, and its owner has been warned but has not kept it in, and it kills a man or a woman, the ox shall be stoned, and its owner also shall be put to death (Exod 21.28-29).

We also learn a good deal about Hammurabi as king from his large corpus of personal correspondence with his two administrative officers, Sin-iddinam and Shamash-ḥazir. These two were assigned to the city of Larsa after it was 'annexed' into Hammurabi's growing empire. These two officers found themselves in the difficult situation of having to arbitrate local matters in a local situation that was not known by them. With regard to Hammurabi's administrative style, their correspondence shows the king to be involved in the most trivial legal cases which one would think barely worthy for the scrutiny of Shamash-ḥazir himself. Here are three excerpts from separate letters the king sent to his representation Shamash-ḥazir:

> Let Ea-kima-iliya, the musician, keep control of his field as he did of old. Don't take a single square foot from him!

> Qishtum and Awil-ili wrote to me, '30 *bur* of land assigned to us was taken from us and given to Shamash-shatakalim. He did not farm what they gave him, but handed it over to farmers who did'. This is what they wrote me.
> You and Shamash-mushallim must stand by. Qishtum, Awili-ili and Shamash-shatakalim should be summoned before you. Look into their grievance and come up with a final judgment for them. Then send me a report on that final judgment.

> The provincial leaders of Emutbal have not yet brought into Babylon their barley tax. Put pressure and check on them so that they bring their barley tax into Babylon promptly. You will be punished for their failure.

For a man of such influence and diverse responsibilities, it is surprising to find Hammurabi micro-managing affairs of such insignificant detail during the final ten years of his rule.

9. The Last Old Babylonian Kings and the Coming of the Kassites

During the reign of Samsu-iluna (1749–1712), Hammurabi's carefully constructed empire was in significant peril. Not only did central and southern Babylon rebel, but the Kassites began a massive invasion of the eastern border territories. Rim-Sin II, an interloper who borrowed the name of Larsa's last king, led a rebellious but short-lived state at Larsa and Ur. Samsu-iluna's eleventh and fourteenth year dates tell us that he probably had to put down rebellions at Ur, Uruk and Isin. Toward the end of his reign, documents from Nippur are dated under the name of a king Ili-man. This may be evidence of a southern dynasty later called the 'Sealand Dynasty' by the *Babylonian Chronicle*. Most ominous by far was the nineteenth year date of Samsu-iluna: 'Army of the Kassites'. This phrase implies Babylonian victory over the invaders, however. The king built a fortress 'Dur-Samsu-iluna' in the Diyala's confluence with the Tigris. Thus he held back the Kassite attack and, until the reign of Samsu-ditana, the only mention of Kassites in Old Babylonian texts reveals denoument between the parties.

Little is known about migrants from the east and the Kassites are certainly no exception. They probably came from Iran, from the modern region of Khuzistan which may be traced to the ancient term 'Kassite'. Since no Kassite names appear in Ur III messenger texts we may assume that they did not arrive at the Iranian–Mesopotamian border until the second millennium.

Next to nothing is known about the Kassite language since it bears no affinites with any of the regional language groups such as Sumerian, Elamite or Ḫurrian. Their records are written in Akkadian and they made no attempt ever to write their native Kassite language in cuneiform.

Defensive strategies of Samsu-iluna and Abiešuḫ held the Kassites back for a time in the northwestern regions. They settled then in the upper Euphrates valley at Ḫana. Texts from Terqa mention a king Kaštiliašu, which is clearly Kassite. An Old Babylonian letter mentions 'the houses of Agum', perhaps military encampments. Agum and Kaštiliašu are names given to the second and third Kassite rulers in the *Babylonian King List* (see Millard 2000) as well as the *Synchronistic Chronicle.*

The Kassites rose to power in Babylonia as a result of the raid of Muršili on the city of Babylon itself. While the raid was inconsequential, it is intriguing to ask why Muršili was not attacked by the Kassites in Ḫana as he came down the Euphrates. As tempting as it might be to suggest collusion between the Kassites and the Hittites, the whole affair remains quite unclear. Nevertheless, it appears that the Hittite attack opened the door for the eventual takeover of the Kassites in 1595.

Of the last kings in the dynasty, Abiešuḫ (1711–1648), Ammiditana (1683–1647), Ammi-ṣaduqa (1646–1624) and Samsu-ditana (1625–1595) there is no small amount of political and economic data. None of these rulers was really outstanding; they fought rebellions, repaired canals and fortresses. Ammi-ṣaduqa left behind a *mīšarum* document (*The Edict of Ammi-ṣaduqa*[7]) issued in his first year. The king proclaims the remission of private debts and arrears in taxes, a reduction of rents for certain royal officials working land belonging to the crown, redemption of debtor's

---

7.   See now Hallo 2000.

family members left under the control of creditors, and the like. The purpose of the edict, it would appear, was to prevent the collapse of the economy because of the great amount of private indebtedness and to prevent excessive accumulation of wealth in the hands of a few individuals. The edict also informs us that near its end the First Dynasty of Babylon still controlled Babylon, Borsippa, Larsa, Uruk, Isin, Kisurra and Malgium. The date formulae in the last century indicate little military action hinting at peace and prosperity. Threats from the Kassites or the 'Sealand Dynasty' are not mentioned. But, since all the documents come from Sippar, this picture is no doubt incomplete.

10. *Literature in the Old Babylonian Period*

The scribes of the Old Babylonian period were very zealous copyists and went to great lengths to preserve the literature that came down to them from the past, especially the archives of the Third Dynasty at Ur. There were as well, however, many marvelous and original works put together by these Akkadian scribes themselves. Although the version of the Gilgamesh Epic most well known in the West is the eleven tablet neo-Assyrian recension from Aššurbanipal's library referred to as the 'standard' version, its history is quite complex. There were several short stories or 'epics' about the hero Gilgamesh written in Sumerian. Then sometime between 1800–1600 an Old Babylonian scholar wove a new tapestry producing the first Old Babylonian story which would be known as the Epic of Gilgamesh (see Foster 1996; George 1999). Although the existence of a complete and integrated Old Babylonian epic is not without its detractors, there are two tablets (*Gilg.P* [Pennsylvania] and *Gilg.Y* [Yale]) which appear to come from the same series suggesting an Old Babylonian edition of at least four tablets. The first is not extant, the second deals with the advent of Enkidu, the third includes preparations for the journey to the Cedar Mountains. The third tablet implies at least one more dealing with the journey itself.

The episodes of the Old Babylonian version are, for the most part, arranged in the same order as those of the later standard Assyrian version. The opening phrase of the Old Babylonian version (*šūtur eli*) is the same as that of the later version. Since Enkidu is an established character in Old Babylonian tablet two, then he must have been introduced in tablet one as in the late version. The meeting of Enkidu and Gilgamesh takes place in tablet two in both versions as well. The journey of Gilgamesh and Enkidu to the Cedar Mountain (found in four separate Old Babylonian tablets) obviously took place after their meeting just as the later version has recorded it. The Old Babylonian version of Gilgamesh's journey to Utnapishtim mentions Enkidu's death which presupposes the same. This again reflects the story line of the later version. Again, in the Old Babylonian tablets, Gilgamesh meets the Barmaid Siduri and Utnapishtim's boatman Puzur-Amurri in the same manner as the later version again.

As well, the Old Babylonian version of the epic agrees with the later version in stressing the futility of Gilgamesh's hope for literal immortality. Even though it comes to us in a fragmentary state, there is much to suggest that the later Assyrian version of the epic is based upon a rather complete Old Babylonian version.

Another very important Old Babylonian story is the *Epic of Atra-ḫasis* (see Foster 1997a). Although the main tablets and very many fragments had been in the British Museum since 1889, the complete epic and the correct sequence were not put together until the Danish scholar J. Laessøe produced the entire story in 1956. The standard version of Atra-ḫasis was copied/edited during the reign of Ammi-ṣaduqa by Ku-Aya the 'junior scribe', complete in three tablets. Of course, it was known to the scribes of Mesopotamia as 'When the gods like man...' (*inuma ilu awilum*), the first three words of the opening line.

The story begins when gods alone inhabited the universe and of necessity had to produce food stuffs by their own labor. The three senior gods Anu (sky), Enlil (middle earth) and Enki (subterranean fresh waters) administered their respective realms. Enlil assigned the digging of canals (an agricultural task) to the junior gods. After 40 years of hard labor, the worker-gods rebelled, burned their tools and surrounded Enlil's house in an angry mob. After some consultation, Enki, who is, after all, the god of wisdom, suggested that a new kind of being be created to do this unpleasant agricultural work. A mother goddess, Mami, was called in to assist Enki whose skill was superior to hers. After a very complicated and lengthy process, man is created. But the humans multiplied and their noise kept Enlil from sleeping. The grouchy god commisioned a plague to reduce the number of humans and, thereby, the decibel level. Without fanfare, Atra-ḫasis, king of humankind, is abruptly introduced as the one who goes to plead their case with Enki, who hears none of the noise far beneath the earth. Special instructions for averting the plague were given to the people. So, the story continued on tablet one. At the beginning of tablet two, humankind had multiplied once again and Enlil was losing more sleep. Having failed with his plague, Enlil tried famine this time. Again Atra-ḥasis went to Enki, who advised him in a similar manner. Enki then discreetly watered the earth and the famine was put off. Although the tablets are very fragmentary from this point onward, it appears that a third time Enlil lost sleep and was suspicious that some god was working against him. He renewed his drought plan with vigor and with guards posted to maintain a high level of security. Then Enki thwarted the program by causing a great water spout to proceed out of the fresh water abyss, his home beneath the earth, laden with fishes to feed humankind. At the end of tablet two, it was decreed that because Enki had used water to rescue the noisy earthlings, there would be a great flood to wipe them out completely.

Tablet three contains the flood story which became the sources for the standard Assyrian version of the flood in *Gilgamesh* Tablet XI (Foster 1997b). The flood story, although somewhat fragmentary, follows closely the well-known outline complete with the speeches of the great goddess, her jeweled fly necklace, and so on. So humankind was saved by the gods who rallied to Enki's side in the assembly. Enlil, however, won a drastic reduction in the population and, as a result, a quiet earth. Safeguards against inappropriate future overpopulation were introduced by the creation of three new classes of beings: barren women, a demon that snatches babies' breath away, and three classes of cloistered women who take vows not to have sexual relations.

We see in *Atra-ḥasis* similar themes to those of early Genesis, namely, the creation of humans, the early history of society and its problems, and then, the flood with its attendant policies to avoid problems from the past, the three classes of beings just mentioned; in the Bible, God gives humans several laws to help them live a better life than did the wicked antediluvians. The outline of the *Gilgamesh Epic* does not reflect the thematic concerns of the Bible so closely as does *Atra-ḥasis*, but the theme of the 'ascent of knowledge' played out in the Seduction of Enkidu in *Gilgamesh* I is certainly echoed in the narratives of Genesis 3–4. Enkidu represents primal or original man much like Adam in the Bible. He roams the rural grassy plains with a herd of gazelle. The literary signs of his primal state is that animals accept him as one of them and he, having the stamina of a gazelle, runs with them. A trapper sets him up to be seduced by a prostitute and, immediately after his first sexual experience, the animals reject him and his strength is reduced. But, he is learning about himself as a human being. The prostitute clothes him and takes him to the city where he is introduced to human culture. Similarly, Adam lived alone with animals until God presented him a woman. The biblical text describes the first pair as 'naked and unashamed', that is, lacking any sense of themselves as sexual beings. The next narrative event is their 'eating fruit', immediately after which they know they are naked and seek clothing. They, like Enkidu, lose their former life of innocence in the garden. God gives them clothing and they leave to establish human culture, building cities and establishing arts and crafts.

While having little to do with the literature of the Hebrew Bible, one of the really magnificent achievements of the Old Babylonian literati was the Sumerian-Akkadian word lists. These bilingual lists, a product of the scribal schools, have given us moderns much more understanding of the literary texts, Sumerian and Akkadian, than could ever have been hoped for without them.

A literary innovation of the period were the omen texts. One of the larger of these was the list *šumma izbu*, 'If a fetus...' (Leichty 1970). Human and animal birth anomalies were noted and extraordinary events that occurred soon after the monstrous births were recorded to see whether there might be a causal relationship. Hymns, proverbs, didactic literature of other kinds were produced as well. Mathematics were well developed and attested in writing.

So with the end of Samsu-ditana's reign, little is known for the next century or so. Then, when texts again appear telling us about Babylon, profound changes have taken place; new peoples have entered the land and have brought with them a new culture.

BIBLIOGRAPHY

Bottéro, J.
1992   *Mesopotamia: Writing, Reasoning, and the Gods* (trans. Z. Bahrani and M. Van de Mieroop; Chicago: University of Chicago Press).
Dalley, S.
1989   *Myths from Mesopotamia: Creation, the Flood, Gilgamesh, and Others* (Oxford: Oxford University Press).
Edzard, D.O.
1957   *Die Zweite Zwischenzeit Babyloniens* (Wiesbaden: Otto Harrassowitz).
Foster, B.R.
1987   'Gilgamesh: Sex, Love and the Ascent of Knowledge', *Studies Pope*: 21-42.
1996   *Before the Muses* (2 vols.; Bethesda, MD: CDL Press, 2nd edn).
1997a   'Atra-asis', *COS*: I, 450-53.

1997b	'Gilgamesh', *COS*: I, 458-60.

Frayne, D.
2000a	'Early Old Babylonian Inscriptions', *COS*: II, 246-55.
2000b	'Late Old Babylonian Inscriptions', *COS*: II, 256-61.

Gadd, C.J.
1973	'Hammurabi and the End of His Dynasty', in I.E.S. Edwards *et al.* (eds.), *The Cambridge Ancient History*, II.1 (Cambridge: Cambridge University Press, 3rd edn).

George, A.R.
1999	*The Epic of Gilgamesh: A New Translation* (New York: Barnes & Noble).

Greengus, S.
1995	'Legal and Social Institutions of Ancient Mesopotamia', *CANE*: I, 469-84.

Hallo, W.W.
2000	'The Edicts of Samsu-iluna and his Successors', *COS*: II, 362-64.

Klein, J.
1997	'Lamentation over the Destruction of Sumer and Ur', *COS*: I, 535-39.

Knapp, A.B.
1988	*The History and Culture of Ancient Western Asia and Egypt* (Belmont, CA: Wadsworth Press).

Kovacs, M.G.
1989	*The Epic of Gilgamesh* (Stanford: Stanford University Press).

Lambert, W.G., and A.R. Millard
1969	*Atra-ḫasis: The Babylonian Story of the Flood* (Oxford: Clarendon Press).

Leichty, E.V.
1970	*The Omen Series Šumma Izbu* (Glückstadt: Augustin).

Lerberghe, K. van
1991	*Sippar-Amnānum: The Ur-utu Archive* (Ghent: University of Ghent).

Millard, A.R.
2000	'The Babylonian King Lists', *COS*: I, 461-63.

Richardson, M.E.J.
2000	*Hammurabi's Laws: Text, Translation and Glossary* (The Biblical Seminar, 73; Semitic Texts and Studies, 2; Sheffield: Sheffield Academic Press).

Roth, M.T.
1995	'Mesopotamian Legal Traditions and the Laws of Hammurabi', *Chicago-Kent Law Review* 71.1: 13-39.
1995/97	*Law Collections from Mesopotamia and Asia Minor* (SBLWAW, 6; Atlanta: Scholars Press, 2nd edn 1997).
1998	'The Priestess and the Tavern: LH §110', *Studies Borger*: 445-64.
2000a	'The Laws of Ur-Namma (Ur-Nammu)', *COS*: II, 408-10.
2000b	'The Laws of Lipit-Ishtar', *COS*: II, 410-14.
2000c	'The Laws of Eshnuna', *COS*: II, 332-35.
2000d	'The Laws of Hammurabi', *COS*: II, 335-53.

Sasson, J.M.
1995	'King Hammurabi of Babylon', *CANE*: II, 901-15.

Tigay, J.H.
1982	*The Evolution of the Gilgamesh Epic* (Philadelphia: University of Pennsylvania Press).

SYRIA TO THE EARLY SECOND MILLENNIUM

Victor H. Matthews

At its height, the territory controlled by the kingdom of Mari extended over '600 kilometers along the Euphrates, from present day Hitt northward toward Raqqa...appreciably larger than the size of Judah and Israel combined' (Sasson 1985: 438). In the period from c. 1830–1750 BCE, this area of northern Syria saw the emergence of territorial monarchies, which strove to control as much of the area as possible and eventually lost their independence to the empire-building ambitions of Hammurabi of Babylon. The fact that Mari seems to be the most important of these small kingdoms attests to the strength of its army and the administrative acumen of two men, Shamshi-Adad and Zimri-Lim. Each engaged in skillful diplomatic maneuvers with individual city states and coalitions, added to their domain, and dealt effectively with the disruptive forces represented by the tribal groups that occupied much of their western territories.

The body of letters found at Mari (modern Tel Hariri) and sites within its sphere of influence (Terqa, Tell Leilan, Tell el-Rimah, Tell Brak)[1] document the activities of the various kings of that region. They include the administrative, military, and diplomatic correspondence of these dynasts, as well as internal palace memoranda, personal letters sent by the royal family, and a few prophetic texts.[2] Unfortunately, the official archives of the government were ransacked in antiquity by the Babylonians when they captured the city in about 1760 BCE (Guichard 1997: 420; Sasson 1972: 55). At that time they destroyed or took away many of the records pertaining to Babylon—an interesting means of insuring that their version of history would become the official one. What remains, however, has

---

1. Oates 1985: 585-94, for discussion of the excavation and identification of these cities.

2. While it is outside the scope of this article, recent studies of the Mari prophetic texts include: Parker 1993: 50-68; and Barstad 1993: 39-60. The texts themselves have been collected in Durand 1988: 377-412.

proven extremely useful in tracing the relationship between the monarch and his regional governors and neighboring kingdoms. In particular, the manner in which they dealt with the tribal groups that inhabited the steppe area in the Ḥabur triangle and the region west of the Euphrates has been instructive in determining their bureaucratic style and the strategies employed in administering a non-traditional population in a rural and pastoral district. It will be the task of this article to examine the style of management employed by the Mari kings to administer their nation and its various political and economic units. In the process, some attention will also be given to analogous situations and practices in the biblical text.

1. *Administrative Policies*

There seems to have been an insatiable appetite for information by the Mari dynasts. Their correspondence includes news from all levels of their society that might in some way infringe upon or affect their rule. As a result, descriptions come in about the dreams of prophets and ordinary citizens along with critical diplomatic dispatches, and the rather tedious and formulaic reports of bureaucrats in charge of agricultural production and garment manufacture. Such concern for current events was necessitated by the often fragile relationships with other city states with whom Mari competed—creating an intricate web of negotiated alliances and a general sense of regional instability.[3]

The need for a management style combining flexibility and the shrewd assessment of deteriorating situations was made even more difficult by changes in the ruling dynasty of Mari three times in 60 years. This necessitated a high level of visibility on the part of the king or his surrogates (high ranking officials or members of the royal family—especially Zimri-Lim's queen Shibtu[4]). There was a system of royal itineraries which took them throughout the kingdom, dedicating new temples or statues of the gods or participating in important religious festivals, inspecting

3. Dossin 1938: 117-18, contains the famous assessment of the political situation of the time: 'There is no king who, of himself is the strongest. Ten or fifteen kings follow Hammurabi of Babylon, the same number follow Rim-Sin of Larsa, the same number follow Ibal-pi-El of Eshnunna, the same number follow Amut-pi-il of Qatanum, twenty kings follow Yarim-Lim of Yamhad.'

4. Zimri-Lim's queen Shibtu also helped her husband by receiving delegations from other kingdoms in his name. See *ARM* X 121 and the description of her role in Daly 1984: 97-99; Batto 1974: 18.

military installations or the construction of public works.[5]

In the case of Shamshi-Adad's ruling style, he chose, once he had established himself in his new capital at Shubat-Enlil (Tell Leilan in the eastern Ḥabur region), to appoint his two sons as co-regents at different points in his kingdom. In this way he was able to divide the region from the Tigris to the lower Ḥabur, which he had captured from Mari's king Yaḫdun-Lim (c. 1798), into manageable administrative districts and give his sons valuable experience prior to their accession to his throne. Unfortunately, one son, Yasmaḫ-Addu, whose seat of power was in Mari, proved to be a weak ruler. In his frustration, Shamshi-Adad shames his son, accusing him of immaturity (*ARM* I 61 and 73) and saying he was no match for his brother Išme-Dagan (*ARM* IV 11.21-23), who ruled at Ekallatum.[6]

Any system of administration as complex as that which ruled the Mari kingdom would have had to also include numerous management units and levels of authority. There was in fact an interconnecting network of royal governors, military officials, district inspectors, and local tribal chiefs who were required to report to the king through channels or directly.[7] As a result, a voluminous correspondence kept a staff of messengers busy carrying news back and forth throughout the kingdom and to neighboring realms.[8]

With so many hands turned to the business of government, it is not surprising to find evidence of mismanagement and corruption or at least charges of these practices. For example in *ARM* VI 39 the regional governor, Baḫdi-Lim, wrote to the king in an effort to cut through a wall of red tape and end a supply problem plaguing his area:

---

5.   Anbar (1975: 1-17) describes these itinerary routes. See Matthews (1978b: 153-54) for a discussion of *ARM* XIV 55.19-23, which provides a good example of the advance work that went into such a royal visit: 'When my lord goes up to Yamḫad, he shall take charge of the matter of the sacrifice in (any) village (which) he may enter. Before the elders of the town...50 soldiers will enter with you...'

6.   See the more complete summary of this period of Shamshi-Adad's reign in Villard 1995: 873-83.

7.   For descriptions of these various governmental units and their administrators, see two studies by Marzal 1971; 1972; as well as Safren 1979. For a study of military officials, see Matthews 1979.

8.   See Meier (1988) for a general discussion of communication practices in the ancient Near East. On the Mari staff of messengers, see Matthews 1996; Fisher 1992.

I checked on the members of the (royal) household; of 400 members only 100 men are provided with garments while 300 are without garments. I questioned Bali-Erah and Mukannishum on account of the men without garments, and Mukannishum answered me as follows: 'This is not my duty, Bali-Erah has to give them garments.' And, Bali-Erah answered me as follows: 'I provided garments for 100, the balance Mukannishum has to provide with garments.' This is what they answered me.

It so happens that Sidqu-epuh[9] is now in the presence of my lord. My lord should instruct Sidqu-epuh (what to do) and he should give me the necessary orders to provide the members of the household with garments.

What is apparently at the heart of this dispute is Mukannishum's desire to monopolize the distribution of garments. He had charge of the female weavers (see *ARMT* XIII 1.xiv.65) who produced the garments and thus could only be required to end this exercise in 'finger-pointing' by a higher authority or perhaps through bribes or 'gifts'. The fact that Baḫdi-Lim does not take direct action himself, but simply reports the problem to the king, suggests he is either proposing to serve as a mediator between the two rival bureaucrats or that it was common practice for the king to be informed of potential problem areas. It would be unusual for the monarch to take a personal interest in such small details as the distribution of garments, but it may be that there was a much larger issue involved that is not made clear by the text.

On other occasions the texts suggest that matters involving mismanagement or corruption did require more personal attention and skillful handling of a delicate situation. Thus, in *ARM* X 90[10] a high ranking administrator named Idin-Sin is charged with embezzlement. However, rather than lose the services of an official who could not easily be replaced[11] he was given the option of paying a fine equal to double the amount of the missing silver.[12] Despite his faults, he was more valuable in office, where, presumably he could be watched for any future discrepancies.

9. See Batto 1974: 32 n. 41, for information on this official's position.

10. This case is also discussed in Dossin 1970: 41, A. 12.

11. The assumption here is that the amount of time required to train a scribe, coupled with the years of experience necessary to rise to a position of high authority, made dismissal or imprisonment an option only taken in the most scandalous of cases. Sasson (1972: 62-63) notes that there was a limited number of literate government officials and scribes. In a later article (Sasson 1982: 341), he hints at the possibility that a scribe might regularly 'cover his tracks' in filing a 'corrected' copy of a text listing expenditures or outlay of government property.

12. Compare the fines assessed for theft or fraudulent dealings in Hammurabi's Code §§93, 101, 124, and 126.

With all this information, however, there are obviously still gaps. To this point, in addition to missing a portion of the royal archive, we lack formal diplomatic documents such as treaties or the royal annals so common in later periods. This makes it very difficult to establish or reconstruct motivation for some actions described in the royal correspondence (see Sasson 1990). As a result, the data from all of these letters must be dealt with carefully. The degree of staged formality required of bureaucrats which prevents them in many cases from being completely candid—their jobs and their lives may depend on being circumspect—may be the basis for some of the difficulties. Thus the scholar must not over-estimate the importance of the Mari texts or, for that matter, eliminate any piece of information as unimportant to the puzzle of historical reconstruction.

2. *Mari and the Ancestral Narratives*

One area of study that has been explored fairly extensively in recent years is the possible comparisons that could be made between the ancestral narratives of Genesis and the Mari texts that describe the interaction between the government and pastoral nomadic tribal groups. While it is impossible, given the current level of physical and literary evidence, to characterize the ancestral narratives as historical, there is sufficient information provided in the Genesis account to reconstruct some aspects of pastoralism and the rural landscape of ancient Palestine.[13]

The most helpful approach to this study seems to be through the use of analogous anthropological data. Those most intimately involved in the anthropological study of Near Eastern texts include the seminal work on Mari tribal groups by J.-R. Kupper (1957), dissertations on the interaction between the state and the tribes by J.T. Luke (1965) and V.H. Matthews (1978b), and a series of articles by H. Klengel (1958; 1959; 1960; 1962; 1966; 1968; 1977) and M.B. Rowton (1967a; 1967b; 1969a; 1969b; 1973a; 1973b; 1974; 1976a; 1976b; 1976c; 1977; 1980) dealing with the concept of 'enclosed nomadism' and the effect of a multi-faceted economic and social structure on the inhabitants of the Mari kingdom.

Archeological data has also been matched with the anthropological theories to aid in the recreation of ancient societies in the Near East. However, the limitations inherent to archeological reconstruction are

13. For examples of this process of reconstruction, see Matthews 1981; 1986; Matthews and Benjamin 1993: 52-66. Selman (1980: 91-139) is also useful in examining this process.

well known and therefore researchers must be careful not to overstep the reasonable boundaries of speculation (Hopkins 1996: 122; Brandfon 1987). For instance, there is evidence in the Early Bronze–Middle Bronze era (c. 2350–1900 BCE) of a retribalization and general deterioration of the Early Bronze urban culture (Prag 1974; 1985: 82). In no way, however, can this activity be ascribed to the incursion or interference of any particular migratory group, such as the biblical ancestors. Surveys have uncovered evidence of seasonal camps and villages in this period (Cohen and Dever 1978). They demonstrate the temporary character of the architecture and the oft told tale of abandonment when the environment or the political situation dictated. No written record remains (unlike in Mesopotamia), however, to further elucidate the picture of semi-nomadic and mixed village economy of that time.

The relatively new field of ethnoarcheology provides some further aid in reconstructing ancient societies by combining the study of artifactual remains with comparative ethnographic data (Watson 1980; Hole 1979; Lees 1979). Zooarcheology also promises some additional insight into pastoral activity and herd management as well as one more set of data upon which to base historical reconstruction (Chang and Koster 1986; Zarins 1992). These complementary disciplines may eventually develop new techniques or methodologies that will further enhance our understanding of ancient tribal peoples and village settlements. However, at this point they have recovered only superficial cultural findings as compared to modern ethnographic research. Most of our interpretations will still have to come from an examination of ancient Near Eastern texts, the Hebrew Bible, and the anthropological analogies that can be made with more recent tribal groups.

a. *Cautions in the Study of Nomadic Pastoralism*
As noted above, whenever new or innovative techniques are developed, certain cautions must be sounded. In his examination of the early history of Israel, Niels Lemche touched on the difficulties involved in the use of anthropology in the study of the Old Testament (Lemche 1985: 161). Among them is the tendency to establish a preconceived paradigm, using analogous material from recent anthropological field work or theory. This can lead to a shaping of interpretations and a stretching of the biblical and other ancient texts far beyond their original intent. J.W. Rogerson voices a similar concern, stating that scholars must be cautious of labeling cultures as semi-nomadic and nomadic, based upon the sketchy information in the

text (Rogerson 1984: 43). Modern researchers can at least gain first hand information through field work with the peoples being studied.

Thus the pessimistic attitude, as Rogerson notes, of the modern anthropological researcher N. Dyson-Hudson seems quite appropriate as research is begun. Dyson-Hudson, in a general introduction to the study of modern pastoral nomadic groups, despairs of ever truly possessing 'adequate knowledge of even a single nomadic society—let alone "nomadism" as some more general form of human experience' (Dyson-Hudson 1972: 26). Therefore, in this study, where definitions or models are presented and analogous modern and ancient materials are used, the proviso of caution noted by Lemche and others will provide a constant check on interpretation.

There is in fact a bewildering number of pastoral types, with subcategories of each and exceptions found to every cultural rule. The wide range of ecological environs, types of animals herded, and political and social factors involved in particular regions has led to individualized studies of herd composition (Rubel 1969), ecology (Kohler-Rollefson 1992; Barth 1961), and political environment (Irons 1974). This can be a shortsighted approach. Only by taking into account all available variables can the researcher truly claim to be establishing a workable ethnographic model (Tapper 1979).

With these cautions in mind, it can still be asserted that the Mari texts are extremely rich ground for anthropological investigation. They contain information on the use of pastures, both near settled areas and in outlying districts, basic animal husbandry, mixed farming and herding practices by tribesmen, and the adjustments both the sedentary and the nomadic peoples make when they interact with each other.

Much can be learned here and much can be ascertained by comparison with similar tribal systems. In particular, the economic activities of these people can be examined with respect to similar pastoral nomadic groups in the Near East and portions of Africa and central Asia. This is not to say that there are no significant differences between ancient and modern pastoral cultures (Gilbert 1975). Religion, social custom, and technology do to some extent set them apart, as do modern political pressures. However, by a close reading of the cuneiform texts and a judicial use of analogous material, in conjunction with anthropological theory, real progress can be made in establishing a better understanding of the Mari Kingdom and the peoples that inhabited it.

b. *Basic Pastoral Economy*

There are certain basic essentials in any pastoral economy. These are grazing, water, and proper herd management. The difficulty that arises in the Near East is that grazing land is often unavailable year round in any one region, and water, in this mainly arid zone, is a precious commodity which is jealously protected and often fought over (Musil 1928: 359; Pastner 1971: 286; Matthews 1986: 120; Cornelius 1984: 53-61). Herd management thus becomes the skill of juggling these two realities, along with the hiring of sufficient help, proper harvesting of wool, milk, and meat, judicial use of markets, and the protection of the herd from animals, raiders, and the designs of local rulers.[14]

A.M. Khazanov (1984: 19-25), best known for his work with the pastoralists of Central Asia, has taken these variables and created a set of eight categories by which to describe the various types of pastoral activity.[15] First among these categories is 'pure nomads'. He notes that they are characterized by constant mobility and 'by absence of agriculture, even in a supplementary capacity'. However, they occur only in a few regions (North Eurasia, High Inner Asia, the Eurasian steppes, Arabia, and the Sahara), and they generally 'co-exist…with other forms of pastoralism'.

By far the most common form of migratory pastoralism is what Khazanov terms 'semi-nomadic pastoralism'. This is 'characterized by extensive pastoralism and the periodic changing of pastures during the course of the entire, or the greater part of the year'. Agriculture and other types of economic activity are also used to supplement their diet and livelihood. This brings the tribes into more intimate contact with the settled community and also directs their migratory routes into areas that allow for seasonal agricultural activity. They thus become identified with and 'enclosed' within the political confines of that region (Rowton 1973b).

Categories, of course, do not tell the whole story of a people, especially one as large as 'semi-nomad'. Khazanov notes several variants within this category, the two most important of which are: (1) when the same groups in a given society (or sub-society) are occupied with both agriculture and pastoralism; (2) when within the framework of a given society (sub-society) there are groups which devote themselves primarily, or even exclusively, to pastoralism, alongside groups which are primarily occupied with agriculture' (Khazanov 1984: 20).

14. See the discussion in LaBianca 1990: 37-38.

15. Note the helpful synthesis of Khazanov's work and that of other anthropologists in Marx 1992.

These variants may reflect the physical and/or political environment which they inhabit or may be a reflection of the transition from a single to a multi-faceted tribal economy. Single faceted tribal economies were almost unknown in the Mari kingdom or elsewhere in ancient northern Syria. Herding activity by the tribes was generally combined with seasonal agriculture, participation as mercenary or conscripted soldiers and laborers, and a sort of 'carrying trade' as they passed from one region of the kingdom to another (Klengel 1977: 163-64).

Other categories of pastoralism as identified by Khazanov include 'herdsman husbandry', in which

> the majority of the population leads a sedentary life and is occupied for the most part with agriculture, while the livestock or more often, some of it, is maintained all year round on pastures, sometimes quite far from the settlement, and tended by herdsmen especially assigned to this task (Khazanov 1984: 22).

These herdsmen thus function as a complementary group to the village agriculturalists. They may be a permanent part of the area's population, or they may act as migratory workers, moving from one herding situation to another (Alon and Levy 1983: 107; Matthews 1979: 132).

A somewhat similar form of pastoralism is 'yaylag pastoralism'. This corresponds fairly closely to what anthropologists call transhumance. While the agricultural base is maintained by the majority of the people, 'during part of the year the livestock is kept in mountain pastures and during the other parts is driven to lower zones' (Khazanov 1984: 23). This has been confused with seasonal pastoralism or vertical pastoralism by some researchers. It is possible to stretch the definition somewhat, and in the Middle East it is to be associated with sheep and goat production. However, is should be understood that this type of economic activity, originally based on specific forms researched in the Spanish and French Pyrenees (Sorre 1950: 647; cf. LaBianca 1990: 36), is designed to deal with particular environmental conditions. It cannot be indiscriminately applied to every seemingly similar situation.

The remainder of Khazanov's categories involve village pastoralism. 'Sedentary animal husbandry' is generally a supplementary activity to the agricultural pursuits of the settlement. Sub-division within this category is dependent on the use of 'stockpiled fodder in maintaining livestock' (Khazanov 1984: 24). Stock-breeding, the establishment of feed lots and free grazing within fairly close proximity or the use of enclosures are other variants in this category.

W. Dever's suggestion that some of Khazanov's categories could be collapsed into a 'ruralism' model has much in its favor (Dever 1992). As he notes, it takes into account the lack of 'pure' nomadism in most of the Middle East and provides a broader use of Rowton's 'enclosed nomadism' model and 'dimorphic society' in the Early Bronze IV period of Palestine. In this way, the virtual impossibility of an economy based solely on pastoralism is replaced by village sites that provide both markets for pastoralists as well as stages in the process of sedentarization.[16]

3. *Nomadic Pastoralism in the Mari Kingdom*

Pastoral nomadic activity, such as that described in the Mari texts and in the ancestral narratives of Genesis,[17] appears to include aspects of both 'semi-nomadic pastoralism' and 'herdsman husbandry'. A basic sketch of the differences between these two categories include: the size and mix of herds, timing of migratory activity, areas of pasturage, and percentage of the group involved in pastoral activity. The fact that the herds of semi-nomadic tribes may be larger and consist of a different mix of breeding stock (generally sheep and goats in ancient times) is based on the route of travel, markets to be visited, and available pasturage. Since they are not always tied to the grazing and water restrictions of their immediate area, a greater flexibility is therefore to be found in their herd management decisions (Salzman 1971; Spooner 1973).

Semi-nomadic pastoralists also tend to develop predatory or at least trickster-like attitudes toward all groups other than their own.[18] As a result, relations between the villagers and pastoral nomads, and governments and pastoral nomads were often strained at best.[19] And this could be exacerbated by changes in environmental conditions that increased competition

16. See Haiman (1992: 93-94) for discussion of archaeological evidence of sedentarization.

17. See the discussion on 'The Herder' in Matthews and Benjamin 1993: 58-63. In particular (pp. 58-63) the interaction between the ancestors and local administrators in Canaan are reconstructed based on the model of pastoral nomadism found in more modern anthropological studies.

18. See the discussion of this protective mechanism in Matthews and Mims 1985. Marx (1992: 256-57) suggests that the higher price attached to meat products as opposed to grain may be one basis for the suggestion that pastoralists considered themselves 'superior to settled agriculturalists'. See Hobbs (1989: 30) on this attitude.

19. Irons 1965; Amiran and Ben-Arieh 1963: 162; and Anbar 1985: 22.

for markets and resources.[20] For example, here are texts which report a variety of problems the Mari dynasts had with the tribal groups:

Raiding practices:[21]

> *Benj.* 988.a: 'Three hundred Yaminites have gone to raid the encampment on the bank of the Euphrates.'

> *Tell el Rimah* Tx. 9.13: '...an encampment raided by some Haneans...'

Revolt from authority:

> *ARM* III 12.16-20: 'Shortly before my lord went on campaign, all of the Yaminites revolted. They went to their villages in the Upper Country and they have not returned.'

Cautious Dealings:

> *ARM* I 6: 13-21: 'Under no circumstances shall you census them.[22] Give them a strong talking to as follows: "The king is going on campaign. Let every man and boy assemble. Any *sugāgum* who fails to assemble his allotment of troops or who allows even one man to remain behind will be in violation of the interdict of the king." Give them this ultimatum, but, whatever you do, do not census them!'

On the other hand, the semi-nomadic pastoral groups also have to operate within the political and economic spheres of various regions and states. They are just as 'enclosed' as their sedentary neighbors, and it may contribute to cautious dealings by both nomadic and sedentary peoples (Rowton 1976b; 1980). In fact, if Charpin and Durand are correct, it was out of one of these tribal groups, the Simalites (a branch of the Haneans), that the Lim dynasty originated and eventually rose to rule the Mari kingdom (Charpin and Durand 1986). That suggests a political fluidity and volatility existent in this region that makes the interchanges between the government and the tribal groups even more significant.

---

20. Herzog (1994: 144-45) points to the climatic changes in the Beer-Sheba Valley as the cause of strains which are 'reflected in the conflicts between King Saul and the Amalekites and in the raid of King David on the Geshurites and Amalekites (1 Sam 27.8)'.

21. Benj. = G. Dossin, 'Benjaminites dans les textes du Mari', *Mélanges Syriens offerts à M. René Dussaud*, II (Paris: P. Geuthner, 1939), pp. 981-96.

22. Sasson (1985: 444) notes in XIV 62 that six steps and a series of administrative levels (king, governor, *sugāgum*, an officer, 10 witnesses) were involved in taking a census. With such a long paper trail and such a cumbersome procedure it is no wonder that it would be avoided in delicate or volatile political situations.

Another difference between sedentary and semi-nomadic pastoralists involves basic group dynamics. The semi-nomadic clansmen rely on their own judgment in determining route of march, division of herds to take maximum advantage of grazing zones, and parceling out of water rights. These rights were often based on kinship ties as well as formal tribal alliances.[23] In contrast, those pastoralists associated with a village culture are not as free in their movements and are often restricted in what they do by higher authorities. For instance, in *ARM* II 102.9-16 a report is sent to the provincial governor, Yaqim-Addu, that a group of herdsmen had, on their own initiative, taken their flocks to new pasturage in the 'Upper Country' because of the scarcity of grazing in the vicinity of Saggaratum.

Such freedom of movement was not always acceptable to the government. One study, by Anbar (Anbar 1985: 17-24), provides a geographical distribution of the Yaminites as described in the official reports of the provincial officials. These texts and others indicate that whenever possible the government tried to restrict, or at least keep track of, the movements of these nomadic and village pastoralists:

Careful records of their movements:

> *ARM* V 27.25-27, 36-37: '…with regard to the Yaminites, who were planning to cross over into the land of Bisir…I arrived late and they had already moved into that area.'

> *ARM* II 90.7-11: 'The camps of the Yaminites have crossed from the far side of the Euphrates to the near side. Their flocks are grazing with the sheep of the Ḥaneans. There have been no losses.'

Strategic cautioning by a governor to the king:

> *ARM* III 15.10-15: 'If the flocks of the Ḥaneans graze on the east bank of the river, the enemy will make a retaliatory attack and there will be trouble.'

These same authorities tried to manage the activities and movements of the semi-nomadic groups for the benefit of the state or local agricultural needs, but this sometimes led to conflict and it was certainly not always a successful policy. This can be seen in numerous texts from ancient Mari:

Regarding the need for agricultural laborers:

> *ARM* III 38.15-26: 'I wrote to the villages of the Yaminites (and) the *sugāgum* of Dumteti answered me in this manner: "Let the enemy come and

---

23. See Malamat 1967: 136-37; and 1989: 41-43, on the tribal unit, the *ummatum*.

carry us off from our villages!" ...Likewise, no one from the villages of the Yaminites helped with the reaping.'

To the *sugāgum* in charge of recruiting laborers and soldiers:

> *ARM* II 92.14-18: 'Whoever does not seize any man from your villages, who leaves for the Upper Country, and does not bring him to me will most assuredly be executed!'

Aid might also be given to pastoralists in crossing rivers or reaching pasturage for political reasons. For example, in *ARM* IV 6.5-28 orders were sent by the king Shamsi-Addu to the governor of Tuttul, Yašub-El, to provide boats for the Rabbean tribesmen so that they could cross the Euphrates: 'The Rabbeans who live in the land of Yamḫad wrote to me saying, "We have decided to cross the river, but there are no boats to make the crossing" ...Write to Yašub-El telling him to send boats upstream so that there will be no delays in their crossing.' Not only would the king be aiding these tribesmen in their movements, but he could also embarrass other dynasts who had failed to act so expeditiously (Sasson 1966: 89-90).

When natural resources were scare and might be exhausted—thereby depriving village pastoralists of their livelihood—with no significant return in taxes or labor service for these losses[24]—the government often stepped in to deal with the problem:

Shifting of herds due to water shortages:

> *ARM* XIV 86.31-40: 'I had portents taken in Dur-Yaḫdun-Lim to determine the suitability of the water. These proved unfavorable and thus I have sent word that the sheep which were pasturing in the river valley should be driven onto the plain. Now, let my lord advise me on whether to have the sheep taken across to the opposite shore.'

Aid extended to maintain order:

> *ARM* I 43.10'-12': 'Tell the Yaminites that I have been up to the pasture lands to guarantee free movement there.'

Direct action taken by the government:

> *Benj.* 989.c: 'You ordered me to force the camps and pens of the Ḫanean Yaminites to cross the Baliḫ...'

---

24. Matthews (1986: 123-24), describes this process when Abraham and Isaac are portrayed as pastoralists who bargain with the local authority, Abimelech of Gerar, for water rights.

4. *Village Pastoralism in the Mari Texts*

It is evident from the texts that the tribal groups that inhabited the Mari kingdom were not all solely engaged in nomadic pastoralism. Many tribesmen lived part or all of the year in permanent encampments or villages. In the village environment they could find a firm regimen of life for the efficient extraction of plant and animal resources (Sherratt 1981), although not one that would allow them the freedom they had as pastoral nomads. Using Khazanov's categories, these village tribesmen would have engaged in either 'yaylag pastoralism' or 'herdsman husbandry', or using Dever's model, they were part of a socio-economic characterized by 'ruralism'. Only a portion of the population would be engaged in pastoral activity while the rest put their efforts into agricultural and cottage industrial pursuits.

This situation, marked by varied social and economic activities, was the result of several factors. The environment played a significant role. With limited fertile lands to farm it would have been impossible for the entire population to support itself simply through agricultural activity. Plus, the need for raw materials and the possibilities for trade and travel opened up by the Tigris–Euphrates river system and some well-marked overland routes made a mixed economy a likely reality. This was also aided by the imperial, political pursuits of the kings of Mari, Babylon, Elam, and Yamḫad during this period. Each was engaged in a power struggle designed to weaken its neighbors both militarily and economically. Thus, a marked effort was made by each political entity to make full use of the material and human resources in their kingdom. If they could extend their hegemony over those elements of their region that were the least politically-affiliated, then they could use them to aid in economic development, military endeavors, and as political pawns in dealing with their political rivals (Asad 1973).

One means to create political homogenization was the continual struggle by the government to either settle the nomadic pastoralists into villages or to control the resources of their area and channel the activity of the semi-nomadic group's young men, who did not always have enough to do in every season.[25] Sedentarization meant broader political control, thereby effectualizing the reality of an 'enclosed' kingdom for all its subjects. This

25. Awad (1959: 25-56), and Bailey (1969) describe modern efforts to deal with nomadic populations.

policy was only marginally successful, however, since for most nomadic tribesmen the decision to permanently settle into village life was one which came only because of economic necessity or political coercion.[26]

A similar policy in ancient Israel is described by I. Finkelstein,[27] who notes the struggle by Israel's kings to control their southern border by building a series of fortresses and forcing the desert tribes (Amalekites, etc.) into submission and a sedentarized existence. However, they eventually were too weakened by foreign invaders (Assyrian, Egyptians, Babylonians) to maintain this policy and the tribes simply reverted back to pastoral nomadic activity. Similarly, the surest sign of weakened conditions within the Mari hierarchy was its inability to check the movements or activities of the tribal groups (see *ARM* II 48; III 38; XIV 86).

Still there is abundant evidence that a certain degree of sedentarization did take place among the tribes. This can not be fully analyzed from a few letters, but some suggestions may be made about the ways in which the settled portions of the tribes interacted with other tribal groups and with the Mari government:

Surplus, seasonal labor was siphoned from the tribal villages to help with building projects, military campaigns, and were controlled through hearding contracts:

> *ARM* XIV 22.23-25: 'the cattle shall graze the pasturage and the replacements and unattached men shall raise up the dams.'

> *ARM* III 6.5-9: 'I have gathered working men of the district and the men of Terqa for labor on the canal of Mari. Among the men of the villages...half have not come.'

> *CBS* 727.3-11: '(...) have been given into the care of Ištar-kû-anāku, the herdsman. For each 100 head he will breed 80 sheep... He will pluck two minas of wool. It will be his responsibility to replace those sheep which are lost or crippled.'[28]

Sedentarization was achieved through an exchange of labor and through the granting of plots of lands (Matthews 1978b: 88-89, 94).

---

26. Swidler 1980. See also LaBianca's comparison of forces leading to sedentarization, including political allegiance and coercion (1990: 41-49).

27. Finkelstein (1984: 201-202).

28. Compare the herding contract between Jacob and Laban in Gen. 30.31-32. See also Stol (1985: 273-75), which also sets forth the number of animals, expected death rates, and a penalty clause.

ARM XIV 80.5-6: 'In exchange for the use of a team of oxen, the Ḫaneans are to remain in the villages.'

Benj. 984.b: 'If it pleases my lord, allow the Ḫaneans to go down to the bank of the Euphrates and give them one of the (former) Yaminite villages.'

Members of the tribal elite were coerced or corrupted into compliance with desires of the government (Matthews 1977; Talon 1985).

ARM XIV 75: 7-14: 'I sent stern orders to the *bazaḫātum* and each town governed by a *sugāgum* and *laputtum*: "All the Yamḫadeans and Zalma-queans, who have fled north, are to be quickly returned to me".'

Tell el-Rimah Tx 100.16: 'I have written to Aqba-hammu and the *sugāgum* regarding the NIG.BAR cloth which is to be given to your sister in Andariq.'

ARM V 16-24: 'Now I am sending Kali-Ilima to my lord so that my lord may appoint him as *sugāgum* of Tizrah, accepting from his hand a mina of silver.'

Agricultural activities are also mentioned among the tribesmen. These may reflect the mixed character of the tribes (partially nomadic and partially settled) or they may be part of the government's program of sedentarization. It is certainly not unusual for tribesmen to spend a season planting a quick growing or non-labor intensive crop while a portion of their men take the herds to pastures elsewhere.[29] Examples of agriculture among the tribes are found in *Benj*. 989.b, where mention is made of Yaminite fields near the banks of the Euphrates, and *ARM* XIII 39, which describes the plowing of Yaminite fields using government supplied teams of oxen (Matthews 1978b: 87-88). Such efforts both increased their economic viability and also made them vunerable to government manipulation since they required longer periods of remaining settled and brought them within the political sphere of the kingdoms of the Mari region.

5. *Summary*

This brief examination of the activities of the tribal groups in the Mari kingdom has attempted to demonstrate the complexities of administration faced by the rulers of that area during the Old Babylonian period. Both Shamshi-Adad and Zimri-Lim discovered that they needed to control the

---

29. Salzman 1972: 63-66. Finkelstein (1992: 136) notes how pastoral groups made use of the various ecologic niches available to them in the highlands, including pasturage and dry-farming.

pastoral nomadic tribal groups in order to maintain peace and best exploit their economic resources. The tribes also proved useful as political pawns in the diplomatic manuvering of the kings—as military personnel, spies, and potentially disruptive forces in the border areas.

The usefulness of anthropological research in conjunction with this study has also been argued here. Particular forms of pastoralism may be identified, shifts in economic endeavor noted, and the effect of the transition from semi-nomadic to village pastoralism and back have been briefly discussed. The 'enclosed' nature of tribal activities within the political realm of the Mari kingdom has been noted and could be used as data for future study.

This same research also may be applied, with due caution, to the ancestral narratives of Genesis and other examples of pastoral nomadic activity elsewhere in the biblical text. For instance, the difficulties faced by Abraham and Isaac in dealing with Abimelech of Gerar (Gen. 20 and 26) provide one of the best comparisons to the administrative texts from Mari. Negotiation of water rights and the problems associated with transient populations are quite clear irregardless of the issue of historicity of these narratives (Matthews 1986: 119-24; Marx 1992: 257-58).

It will probably never be possible to completely reconstruct the social and economic world of the ancient Near East. However, the use of anthropological and ethnographic methodologies can be an aid to developing a fuller understanding of that period than would otherwise be possible. This study can serve as one model for future research into various aspects of the lives of the tribal peoples mentioned in the letters from the royal archive at Mari and elsewhere in the ancient world and the manner in which they interacted with each other and local political entities.

BIBLIOGRAPHY

Alon, D., and T.E. Levy
    1983   'Chalcolithic Settlement Patterns in the Northern Negev Desert', *Current Anthropology* 24: 105-107.
Amiran, D.H.K., and Y. Ben-Arieh
    1963   'Sedentarization of Beduin in Israel', *IEJ* 13: 162.
Anbar, M.
    1975   'La region au sud du district de Mari', *IOS* 5: 1-17.
    1985   'La distribution geographique des Bini-Yamina d'apres les Archives Royales de Mari', in *Studies Birot*: 17-24.

Asad, T.
1973 'The Bedouin as a Military Force: Notes on Some Aspects of Power Relations between Nomads and Sedentaries in Historical Perspective', in C. Nelson (ed.), *The Desert and the Sown* (Berkeley, CA: University of California Institute of International Studies): 61-73.

Awad, M.
1959 'Settlement of Nomadic and Semi-Nomadic Tribal Groups in the Middle East', *International Labor Review* 79: 25-56.

Bailey, F.G.
1969 *Stratagems and Spoils: A Social Anthropology of Politics* (Oxford: Oxford University Press).

Barstad, H.M.
1993 'No Prophets? Recent Developments in Biblical Prophetic Research and Ancient Near Eastern Prophecy', *JSOT* 57: 39-60.

Barth, F.
1961 *Nomads of South Persia: The Basseri Tribe of the Khamseh Confederacy* (New York: Little Brown).

Batto, B.F.
1974 *Studies on Women at Mari* (Baltimore: The Johns Hopkins University Press).

Brandfon, F.R.
1987 'The Limits of Evidence: Archaeology and Objectivity', *MAARAV* 4: 5-43.

Chang C., and H.A. Koster
1986 'Beyond Bones: Toward an Archeology of Pastoralism', in M.B. Schiffer (ed.), *Advances in Archeological Method and Theory* 9 (Orlando: Academic Press): 97-147.

Charpin, D., and J.-M. Durand
1986 '"Files de Sim'al": Les origines tribales des rois de Mari', *RA* 80: 141-83.

Cohen R., and W.G. Dever
1978 'Preliminary Report of the Pilot Season of the "Central Negev Highlands Project"', *BASOR* 232: 29-45.

Cornelius, I.
1984 'Genesis XXVI and Mari: The Dispute over Water and the Socio-Economic Way of Life of the Patriarchs', *JNSL* 12: 53-61.

Daly, S.
1984 *Mari and Karana: Two Old Babylonian Cities* (London: Longman).

Dever, W.G.
1992 'Pastoralism and the End of the Urban Early Bronze Age in Palestine', in *PLAMAP*: 88-90.

Dossin, G.
1938 'Les archives epistolaires du palais de Mari', *Syria* 19: 117-18.
1970 'Archives de Sumu-Iamam, Roi de Mari', *RA* 64: 41.

Durand, J.-M.
1988 *Archives epistolaires de Mari.* I/1. *ARM* 26/1 (Paris: Editions Recherche sur les Civilisations).

Dyson-Hudson, N.
1972 'The Study of Nomads', in W. Irons and N. Dyson-Hudson (eds.), *Perspectives on Nomadism* (Leiden: E.J. Brill): 2-27.

Finkelstein, I.
  1984   'The Iron Age "Fortresses" of the Negev Highlands: Sedentarization of the
              Nomads', *Tel Aviv* 11: 201-202.
  1992   'Pastoralism in the Highlands of Canaan in the Third and Second Millennia
              B.C.E.', in *PLAMAP*: 133-42.
Fisher, R.F.
  1992   'The *Mubassiru* Messenger at Mari', *Mari in Retrospect*: 113-20.
Gilbert, A.S.
  1975   'Modern Nomads and Prehistoric Pastoralists: the Limits of Analogy',
              JANESCU 7: 53-71.
Guichard, M.
  1997   'Mari Texts', in *OEANE*: III, 420.
Haiman, M.
  1992   'Sedentarization and Pastoralism in the Negev Highlands in the Early Bronze
              Age: Results of the Western Negev Highlands Emergency Survey',
              PLAMAP: 93-94.
Herzog, Z.
  1994   'The Beer-Sheba Valley: From Nomadism to Monarchy', in I. Finkelstein
              and N. Na'aman (eds.), *From Nomadism to Monarchy: Archaeological and
              Historical Aspects of Early Israel* (Jerusalem: Israel Exploration Society):
              122-49.
Hobbs, J.J.
  1989   *Bedouin Life in the Egyptian Wilderness* (Austin: University of Texas Press).
Hole, F.
  1979   'Rediscovering the Past in the Present: Ethnoarcheology in Luristan, Iran', in
              Kramer (ed.), 1979: 192-218.
Hopkins, D.
  1996   'Bare Bones: Putting Flesh on the Economics of Ancient Israel', in V. Fritz
              and P.R. Davies (eds.), *The Origins of the Ancient Israelite States*
              (JSOTSup, 228; Sheffield: Sheffield Academic Press): 121-39.
Irons, W.G.
  1965   'Livestock Raiding among Pastoralists: An Adaptive Interpretation', *Papers
              of the Michigan Academy of Science, Arts, and Letters* 50: 396-97.
  1974   'Nomadism as a Political Adaptation: The Case of the Yomut Turkmen',
              American Ethnologist 1: 635-58.
Khazanov, A.M.
  1984   *Nomads and the Outside World* (Cambridge: Cambridge University Press).
Klengel, H.
  1958   'Benjaminiten und Hanaer', *WZHB* 8: 211-27.
  1959   'Halbnomaden am mittleren Euphrat', *Das Altertum* 5: 195-205.
  1960   'Zu den *sibutum* in altbabylonischer Zeit', *Or* 29: 357-75.
  1962   'Zu einigen Problemen des altvorderasiatischen Nomadentums', *ArOr* 30:
              585-96.
  1966   'Sesshafte und Nomaden in der alten Geschichte Mesopotamiens', *Saeculum*
              17: 205-22.
  1968   'Halbnomadischer im Konigreich von Mari', *Akademie der Wissenschaften,
              Berlin* 69: 75-81.
  1977   'Nomaden und Handel', *Iraq* 39: 163-69.

Kohler-Rollefson, I.
1992   'A Model for the Development of Nomadic Pastoralism on the Trans-
            jordanian Plateau', in *PLAMAP*: 11-18.
Kupper, J.-R.
1957   *Les nomades en Mesopotamie au temps des rois de Mari* (Paris: Societe
            d'Edition 'Les Belles Lettres').
Kramer, C. (ed.),
1979   *Ethnoarcheology: Implications of Ethnography for Archeology* (New York:
            Columbia University Press).
LaBianca, O.S.
1990   *Sedentarization and Nomadization* (Hesban, 1; Berrien Springs, MI:
            Andrews University Press).
Lees, S.H.
1979   'Ethnoarchaeology and the Interpretation of Community Organization',
            Kramer (ed.), 1979: 265-76.
Lemche, N.P.
1985   *Early Israel* (Leiden: E.J. Brill).
Luke, J.T.
1965   'Pastoralism and Politics in the Mari Period' (PhD dissertation, University of
            Michigan).
Malamat, A.
1967   'Aspects of Tribal Societies in Mari and Israel', in J.-R. Kupper (ed.), *La
            civilisation de Mari* (RAI, 15: Paris): 129-38.
1989   *Mari and the Early Israelite Experience* (The Schweich Lectures, 1984;
            Oxford: Oxford University Press).
Marx, E.
1992   'Are there Pastoral Nomads in the Middle East?', *PLAMAP*: 255-60.
Marzal, A.
1971   'The Provincial Governor at Mari: His Title and Appointment', *JNES* 30:
            186-217.
1972   'Two Officials Assisting the Provincial Governor at Mari', *Or* 41: 359-77.
Matthews, V.H.
1977   'The *raison d'etre* of the *sugagum* in Mari', *Or* 46: 122-26.
1978a   'Government Involvement in the Religion of the Mari Kingdom', *RA* 72:
            153-54.
1978b   *Pastoral Nomadism in the Mari Kingdom (ca. 1830-1760 B.C.)* (ASORDS,
            3; Cambridge, MA: American Schools of Oriental Research).
1979   'The Role of the *Rabi Amurrim* in the Mari Kingdom', *JNES* 38: 129-133.
1981   'Pastoralists and Patriarchs', *BA* 44: 215-18.
1986   'The Wells of Gerar', *BA* 49: 118-26.
1996   'Messengers and the Transmission of Information in the Mari Kingdom',
            Studies Young: 267-74.
Matthews, V.H., and D.C. Benjamin
1993   *Social World of Ancient Israel* (Peabody, MA: Hendrickson Publishers): 52-
            66.
Matthews, V.H., and F. Mims
1985   'Jacob the Trickster and Heir of the Covenant: A Literary Interpretation',
            PRS 12: 185-95.

Meier, S.M.
    1988   *The Messenger in the Ancient Semitic World* (HSM, 45; Atlanta: Scholars Press).

Musil, A.
    1928   *Manners and Customs of the Rwala Bedouins* (New York: AMS Press).

Oates, D.
    1985   'Walled Cities in Northern Mesopotamia in the Mari Period', *MARI* 4: 585-94.

Parker, S.B.
    1993   'Official Attitudes toward Prophecy at Mari and in Israel', *VT* 43: 50-68.

Pastner, S.L.
    1971   'Camels, Sheep, and Nomad Social Organization: A Comment on Rubel's Model', *Man* 6: 285-88.

Prag, K.
    1974   'The Intermediate Early Bronze-Middle Bronze Age: An Interpretation of the Evidence from Transjordan, Syria and Lebanon', *Levant* 6: 69-116.
    1985   'Ancient and Modern Pastoral Migration in the Levant', *Levant* 17: 82.

Rogerson, J.W.
    1984   *Anthropology and the Old Testament* (The Biblical Seminar, 1; Sheffield: JSOT Press).

Rowton, M.B.
    1967a   'The Topological Factor in the Hapiru Problem', *Studies Landsberger*: 375-87.
    1967b   'The Physical Environment and the Problem of the Nomads', *La Civilisation de Mari* (RAI, 15; Paris): 109-22.
    1969a   'The Abu Amurrim', *Iraq* 31: 68-73.
    1969b   'The Role of the Watercourses in the Growth of Mesopotamian Civilization', in *Lišan mitḫurti: Festschrift W.F. von Soden* (AOAT, 1; Berlin: Verlag Butzon & Bercher Kevelaer): 307-16.
    1973a   'Urban Autonomy in the Nomadic Environment', *JNES* 32: 201-15.
    1973b   'Autonomy and Nomadism in Western Asia', *Or* 42: 247-58.
    1974   'Enclosed Nomadism', *JESHO* 17: 1-30.
    1976a   'Dimorphic Structure and the Problem of the "Apiru-" Ibrim', *JNES* 35: 13-20.
    1976b   'Dimorphic Structure and Topology', *OA* 15: 17-31.
    1976c   'Dimorphic Structure and the Tribal Elite', *Studia Instituti Anthropos* 28: 219-57.
    1977   'Dimorphic Structure and the Parasocial Element', *JNES* 36: 181-98.
    1980   'Pastoralism and the Periphery in Evolutionary Perspective', *Colloques internationaux du C.N.R.S.* 580: 291-301.

Rubel, P.
    1969   'Herd Composition and Social Structure: On Building Models of Nomadic Pastoral Societies', *Man* 4: 268-73.

Safren, J.D.
    1979   'New Evidence for the Title of the Provincial Governor at Mari', *HUCA* 50: 1-15.

Salzman, P.C.

1971 'Movement and Resource Extraction Among Pastoral Nomads: the Case of the Shah Nawazi Baluch', *AQ* 44: 185-97.

1972 'Multi-Resource Nomadism in Iranian Baluchistan', in W.G. Irons and N. Dyson-Hudson (eds.), *Perspectives on Nomadism* (Leiden: E.J. Brill): 63-66.

Sasson, J.M.

1966 *The Military Establishment at Mari* (Studia Pohl, 3; Rome: Pontifical Biblical Institute).

1972 'Some Comments on Archive Keeping at Mari', *Iraq* 34: 62-63.

1982 'Accounting Discrepancies in the Mari NI.GUB [NIG.DU] Texts', in *Studies Kraus*: 341.

1985 'Year: "Zimri-Lim Offered a Great Throne to Shamash of Mahanum" An Overview of one year in Mari, Part I: The Presence of the King', *MARI* 4: 438-44.

1990 'Mari Historiography and the Yakhdun-Lim Disc Inscription', in *Studies Moran*: 439-41.

Selman, M.J.

1980 'Comparative Customs and the Patriachal Age', in A.R. Millard and D.J. Wiseman (eds.), *Essays on the Patriachal Narratives* (Winona Lake, IN: Eisenbrauns): 91-139.

Sherratt, A.

1981 'Plough and Pastoralism: Aspects of the Secondary Products Revolution', in Ian Hodder *et al.* (eds.), *Pattern of the Past: Studies in Honour of David Clarke* (Cambridge: Cambridge University Press): 261-305.

Sorre, M.

1950 *Les fondements de la Geographie Humaine* (Paris: A. Colin).

Spooner, B.

1973 *The Cultural Ecology of Pastoral Nomads* (Reading, MA: Addison-Wesley.).

Stol, M.

1985 'Fragment of a Herding Contract', in *Studies Birot*: 273-75.

Swidler, N.

1980 'Sedentarization and Modes of Economic Integration in the Middle East', in P.C. Salzman (ed.), *When Nomads Settle: Processes of Sedentarization as Adaptation and Response* (New York: Praeger Scientific): 21-33.

Talon, P.

1979 'La taxe *sugagutum* a Mari', *RA* 73.143-51.

1985 'Quelques reflexions sur les clans Haneens', in *Studies Birot*: 277-84.

Tapper, R.L.

1979 'The Organization of Nomadic Communities in Pastoral Societies of the Middle East', in L'Equipe ecologie et anthropologie des societes pastorales (ed.), *Pastoral Production and Society* (Cambridge: Cambridge University Press, 1979): 43-65.

Villard, P.

1995 'Shamshi-Adad and Sons: The Rise and Fall of an Upper Mesopotamian Empire', in *CANE*: II, 873-83.

Watson, P.J.
    1980   'The Theory and Practice of Ethnoarchaeology with Special Reference to the
                Near East', *Paleorient* 6: 55-64.
Zarins, J.
    1992   'Pastoral Nomadism in Arabia: Ethnoarchaeology and the Archaeological
                Record', in *PLAMAP*: 219-40.

APPREHENDING KIDNAPPERS BY CORRESPONDENCE
AT PROVINCIAL ARRAPḪA

David C. Deuel

1. *Background for Correspondence Analysis*

The fifteenth century BCE introduced the breakup of several ancient Near Eastern empires and the extending of others: Egypt maintained supremacy unrivaled in the southwest; Babylonia in the southeast had come under Kassite control with connections to the east; and a loose federation of Mittanian states dominated the northeast. The weakening Mittanian empire, which once spanned the northern region from the Zagros Mountains to the Mediterranean Sea, would soon give way to its northeastern neighbors, the Hittites. This, in turn, would permit the Assyrians in the northeast to reclaim the eastern regions (Larsen 1979: 82) thereby contributing to the collapse of the Mittanian confederacy. With widespread political upheaval, social and economic transition was already in progress. This was the historical context for an administrative correspondence sequence treating a case of kidnapping at provincial Arrapḫa, one of the Mittanian outposts.

a. *Administrative Correspondence*
Administrative correspondence describes several document types officials used to accomplish administrative activity over distance and through the agency of other officials.[1] Correspondence was a tool administrators used to communicate,[2] but particularly to authorize other officials to perform

1. Letters to the Gods and other pseudo-epistolary documents are the exceptions. Esarhaddon's 'Letter to Assur' appears to be a protocol for succession. See Leichty 1991: 52. For a description of this unique subclass of letter see Lambert 1960: 12; Oppenheim 1977: 280. It seems probable that these documents were liturgical in nature. See Kutscher 1975: 5.
2. In addition to other ways of communicating such as sending fire signals. See Sasson 1969: 10; Millard 1999.

administrative activity.[3] Other administrative correspondence document types[4] achieved similar functions.[5] Letters also interacted reflexively with orders or decrees and reports, to the extent that these occasionally appear embedded in letters.[6]

The collection of texts under investigation illustrates the manner in which several different kinds of documents functioned within the correspondence system. All are administrative in nature. The decree or order (*ṭēmu*),[7] the report (*šunku*),[8] and especially the letter (*šipru*),[9] each served a variety of functions within the regional inner and inter city administration. All three are dispatched texts that required a courier to carry information between a sender and a recipient.[10] Because each text initiates another reflexively, they form a sequence. As a correspondence sequence,[11] these

---

3. Mullen (1980: 168) argues that the messenger, divine or human, 'had the same authority' as the individual who dispatched him. This is an over generalization for at Nuzi, most letters provided the messenger with authorization to perform only one administrative task or to communicate a single authoritative message on behalf of the sender. Handy has demonstrated that messenger gods at Ugarit operated at the lowest level of administrative status and that the messenger exercised 'no independent authority beyond that conferred upon it by it superiors'. See Handy 1994: 150-51.

4. For example, letters provide instructions for exchange procedures and interact with exchange documents. See Andrews 1994: 53-54.

5. Letters may be sub classified based on function: (1) Letters to God(s); (2) Edicts and Proclamations; (3) Historical Letters; (4) Military Correspondence; (5) Administrative Correspondence; (6) Scholarly Letters, Divination Reports, Astrological Observations, etc.; (7) Letter Prayers; (8) Letters to the Dead; (9) Business Letters; (10) Feminine Correspondence. See White 1981: 5; Millard 2000.

6. Embedding occurs when a letter sender includes another text type, for example a decree, within his message to the recipient.

7. This term applies to several document types: At Nuzi it is used to represent an order to mayors of cities (HSS 15 1); a decree to be read publicly by a herald (HSS 9 6); and a work detail for laborers (HSS 5 104). In a letter to an Egyptian Pharaoh it refers to an alliance between two rulers. See Wouters 1989: 227-28.

8. An unusual type of spoken (*qabû*) correspondence, recorded in one letter (HSS 13 49).

9. The high frequency term for letter, however, other texts were dispatched (e.g. decrees (*ṭēmu*), and edicts (*šūdūtu*). Embedded letters served non-epistolary functions germane to the embedded document type.

10. According to one study, relay messengers were capable of traveling on foot over 30 kilometers in one day. See Crown 1974: 264-65.

11. A sequence of administrative correspondence from one site is unusual because most administrative correspondence, particularly letters, was destroyed when the administrative action commanded in the tablet was completed. The 'royal correspon-

disparate document types illustrate the use of correspondence to engage the Arraphian administration.

2. *A Correspondence Sequence from Arrapḫa*

In the ancient Near East correspondence played an important role in the transmission of information.[12] Officials administered their areas of responsibility,[13] and established[14] and maintained diplomatic relations[15] with other regions[16] by dispatching oral and written missives. Messengers played critical roles in correspondence systems. The correspondence that informs the present study comes from Nuzi, a city in provincial Arrapḫa.

a. *The Messenger*

Officials from Nuzi bear the title *mār šipri* ('messenger') in apposition to their names.[17] This suggests that they performed messenger activity regularly, although not exclusively as an occupation. The vizier, scribe, and other titled officials also served as candidates for message delivery. An individual was qualified to deliver a message for the simple reason that

dence' of the Ur III period which was copied and passed down for centuries would be one exception to this pattern. See Kramer 1963: 36.

12. A strictly informative administrative correspondence document without any prescriptive or manipulative force would be unexpected, for the fundamental purpose of administrative correspondence is to engage the will of the administration. Assurbanipal's message to the Babylonians (*ABL* 301) sounds like a friendly message of concern for the reputation of the Babylonian people, but concludes with a veiled threat of retribution from the gods should they not comply with the will of Assurbanipal. See Moran 1991: 320-31.

13. Correspondence helped to maintain a close interaction between tribal groups and the state and local government at Mari. See Matthews 1978: 1.

14. M. Cogan cites as an account in which an Egyptian king dispatched messengers to Tarqu, king of Ethiopia to establish friendly relations (Cogan 1974: 43 n. 6).

15. The Mari letters illustrate the strategic use of diplomacy initiated and maintained through correspondence (Matthews 1996: 267-74). The role of letters in maintaining diplomatic relations is seen in many letters from Mari officials and contemporary rulers. See Munn-Rankin 1956: 68.

16. Already in the Early Dynastic III period. The alliances and coalitions that appear in Old Babylonian texts reflect the elaborate system of ambassadors and diplomatic missions that was already in place in the Presargonic period. See Cooper 1983: 10.

17. For a discussion of the named *māri šipri* at Nuzi see Mayer 1978: 161-64.

he was available and best suited to the need (Meier 1988: 22). For example, a merchant might travel to or beyond a letter's intended destination; thus, he became an excellent candidate to deliver a message (*AbB* 7 15.34-36).

Messengers operated in conjunction with the Arrapḫian bureaucracy,[18] particularly in matters pertaining to distant cities.[19] If the occasion demanded, they escorted litigants to court (HSS 5 102) and service people, such as temple personnel, to their work sites (HSS 9 3). The administrative texts from the Nuzi corpus differ from most other letter corpora in that they are primarily inner- as opposed to inter-regional (Meier 1988: 6). Consequently, Nuzi messengers add detail to the broader picture of letter and messenger studies.[20] In contrast to his diplomatic international counterpart (Dalley 1984: 171-75), the Nuzi messenger is 'an *ad hoc* errand runner' (Maidman 1981: 238-39 n. 20) involved in local activity such as the transport and delivery of goods (Zaccagnini 1977: 171), or the transfer of real estate (Negri Scaffa 1995: 64). The role of the messenger within the provincial Arrapḫian administration is best understood in relation to the roles of the officials who dispatched him as well as those who received the correspondence. The identities of the messengers who delivered the texts in this study are not given in the documents.

b. *The Officials*

Messengers interacted fluidly[21] within the administrative structure of the Arrapḫian bureaucracy. Titled Nuzi officials using correspondence performed a variety of overlapping functions outside the administrative correspondence; however, their use of missives tends to follow restricted patterns. The administrators' roles[22] visible in the texts for this study

18. Demonstrated in titles, for example, 'the messenger of the king' *mār šipri ša šarri* (HSS 13 363), and in administrative relationships such as the 'governor' (*šākin māti*), Wantiya claiming his own messenger (HSS 13 175).

19. Some forms of administrative correspondence met the demands of the judiciary, which was led by the king and moved from one city to another.

20. Regarding Neo-Babylonian missives in particular, Brinkman concludes that letters help fill out the details missing from historical reconstructions based on other types of data. See Brinkman 1984: 11.

21. Illustrated humorously in the irony of *The Poor Man of Nippur* when the poor man, having been abused by the mayor, disguised himself as an emissary of the king and returned abuse on the unsuspecting official. See Cooper 1975: 168.

22. W. Moran emphasizes the importance of roles, titles, and status for interpreting an administrator's position in the Amarna letters: 'In short, running through the

illustrate several of those patterns.[23] All of the officials are active in the last period at Nuzi.[24] In the following discussion, the officials are ordered as their names appear in the correspondence sequence and their contributions to the case of kidnapping are explained.

(i) *Šeḫal-Tešup*. In a letter (HSS 14 22) Šeḫal-Tešup is appointed 'canal inspector' (*gugallu*) (Mayer 1978: I, 129). He is supervisor[25] over several retainers (*nīš bīti*) in the correspondence related to this case of kidnapping.[26] When the retainers do not return after fieldwork, Šeḫal-Tešup discovers that they are missing. Acting as their supervising official, he initiates administrative action by engaging the services of an official named Tatip-Tešup.

(ii) *Tatip-Tešup*. A high-ranking official, Tatip-Tešup, initiates administrative action for Šeḫal-Tešup by sending a letter to another official named Šeḫram-mušni. Although Tatip-Tešup's title is not recorded in the letter, he wields considerable authority, particularly in this case of kidnapping. In the final lines of the first letter (HSS 14 20), he orders another official to apprehend the perpetrators and then escort them before the king. In the last letter (HSS 14 30), he reissues this order. The fact that he does not affix his title suggests that the recipients, Šeḫram-mušni and Aqaya respectively, work with him, perhaps as routine practice.

Tatip-Tešup's profile is characteristic of a vizier[27] (*sukkallu*) as seen in

correspondence like a theme is a concern for origins of authority, title, and status that is without parallel in the letters of other vassals, and it requires explanation' (Moran 1975: 156).

23. Four of the five administrative correspondence messages in this study lack any identification by patronymic, title or seal for the letter senders. Archival connections and role interactions are the only ways an administrator can be distinguished from another individual bearing the same name.

24. Šeḫal-Tešup, initiator of the correspondence sequence, is among the final generation of officials. See Morrison 1993: 59.

25. The relationship between his appointment to the titled role, 'canal inspector' (*gugallu*) and his supervision of retainers (*nīš bīti*) is a matter of speculation. Šeal-Tešup and the workers may be paid staff. It is plausible that the labor and supervision for upkeep of canals and the broader irrigation system was supported by some form of taxation at Nuzi as it was in the Old Babylonian period (Ellis 1974: 247).

26. Fadhil treats all three letters in which Šeḫal-Tešup is involved. See Fadhil 1983: 87-88.

27. *CAD* S 354.

several other texts in which individuals bear this title and their roles are similar to his. Authorized by the king,[28] viziers commissioned services (HSS 9 3) and commodities (HSS 15 89), delivered litigants to court (HSS 5 102), and oversaw work groups (HSS 14 9). Some moved with the king's entourage as he traveled from city to city in order to administrate the region.[29] While journeying with the king, the *sukkallu* received rations and dispatched correspondence for him as his 'superintendent of envoys' (Negri Scaffa 1995: 61). In the correspondence, the *sukkallu* is the only official to speak directly to the king and the king speaks only and directly to them. The king gives orders to other officials through the *sukkallu*, and all other administrators must address the king through him. In short, the *sukkallu* is a conduit for communication between the king and his administration. As such, the *sukkallu* functions in both political and judicial spheres of activity at Arrapḫa.

(iii) *Šeḫram-mušni*. Based on the activity he performs, Šeḫram-mušni appears to be an official in the king's court, probably a vizier[30] (*sukkallu*). In the Nuzi corpus he is named only in the two letters dealing with kidnapped retainers.[31] In one other letter to which he affixes his seal (HSS 5 102), Ḫeltip-Tešup is the letter sender.[32] This letter summons a litigant to appear before Ḫeltip-Tešup, Šeḫram-mušni or both. In one of the letters in the correspondence sequence (HSS 14 21), Šeḫram-mušni orders another official to bring the kidnappers before himself rather than the king.[33]

28. Already in pre-Sargonic Lagaš the *sukkalmaḫḫum* is second in command (Hallo 1957: 112-13).

29. Judicial responsibilities, involvement in religious festivals, and limited resources partially account for the king's travel from one palace to another (Wilhelm 1989: 45). In Suruppak and the adjacent areas, the uru-Du officials were personnel who traveled on behalf of the administration and who guaranteed a communication system, which served as the connective tissue of the Hexapolis (Visicato 1995: 92).

30. There is a close relationship between the roles of the *sukkallu* and the messenger. A messenger accompanied a *sukkallu* in a Hittite letter (*KUB* 3 66.14).

31. He is the recipient of a letter of unknown provenience (BM 24017). Morrison (1993: 60) argues that Šeḫram-mušni is Šeḫal-Tešup's major-domo. In a letter (HSS 14 21) he plans to bring a report to the king and he orders officials to bring kidnappers before himself rather than before the king. His position is high ranking and in close proximity to the king.

32. In four letters (JEN 5 494; HSS 5 10; 9 2, 3) another official affixes his seal instead of the sender. The sealer may have been the assisting official or the scribe who wrote the letter.

33. Common procedure at Nuzi and elsewhere. For example, as the highest legal

(iv) *Akip-tašenni*. Akip-tašenni is a high-ranking official loosely identified as 'governor'[34] (*šākin māti*). Unlike the vizier who works in the 'central government'[35] as superintendent of envoys, he oversees a region. His responsibilities include settling territorial differences, representing the king in court, and overseeing grain distribution. He is clearly among the highest officials in provincial Arrapḫa.

Akip-tašenni takes part in a decree dispatch (HSS 13 36) from the king to guard (*naṣāru*) and to return (*târu*) unnamed men under the supervision of an individual named Ḥašimaru. Two texts (HSS 16 387, 398) treat a specific instance where six women are returned to Akip-tašenni for oversight. His jurisdiction over a district seen in another decree (HSS 15 1) makes him responsible for any wrongdoing that may occur there. The king held the district (*dimtu*)[36] official accountable for murder, theft, and presumably kidnapping. He could loose his position as administrator over the *dimtu* should he fail to maintain order in these matters (HSS 15 1). The decree states that it was the responsibility of the governor (*šākin māti*) to take away the *dimtu* and replace the official should any such activity occur.

Šeram-mušni wrote to Akip-tašenni because, as *šākin māti*, he was responsible to ensure the protection of peoples such as Šeḫal-Tešup's field workers. The official relationship[37] of the *sukkallu* and *šākin māti* required that they collaborate in the judicial process (Mayer 1978: I, 124), although much is uncertain about their respective roles.[38]

(v) *Aqaya*. Aqaya is an official ordered to escort a group of people from one city to another and to bring them before the king. The text in which he is commissioned by Tatip-Tešup is quite damaged (HSS 14 30). What is clear is that the group, and probably Aqaya, is at a city other than Arrapḫa. From there, they required an escort to Arrapḫa either because they needed

---

authority in ancient Egypt, the king had the right to make legal decisions personally or to 'delegate this right to a lower authority' (Shupak 1992: 5).

34. *CAD* Š/I: 160.

35. Here understood to include 'those officials and underlings who worked in close proximity to the king, without intervening regional authority in their chain of command' (Zimansky 1985: 77).

36. A type of settlement. See Al-Khaiesi 1977: 95; Zaccagnini 1979: 47-52.

37. The governor (*šākin māti*) and the vizier (*sukkallu*) work closely together in the Middle Assyrian administrative correspondence (see Machinist 1982: 21).

38. Wilhelm comments on the significant but uncertain roles of the *sukkallu* and *šākin māti*, both a kind of minister with unknown responsibilities (Wilhelm 1989: 46).

to be protected or perhaps because they had resisted and needed to be brought before the king by force. The letter authorizes Aqaya, an official of unknown status, to perform this administrative task.

c. *The Administrative Correspondence Documents*

Three of the administrative correspondence documents in this study are letters (HSS 14 20, 21, 30). Letters[39] are introduced by formulae[40] that mark them as written communication (Pfeiffer 1923).[41] The letter address ('to PN_1, from PN_2, thus [speak]'), may have provided instructions for the scribe who read the document.[42] In the address formulae administrators often affixed their titles to personal names so that the recipient could easily identify the sender.

Letters vary in length. Those which contain embedded genre for example, court-related missives (38 lines—JEN 4 325),[43] tend to be considerably longer than simple orders for commodities (seven lines—HSS 14 439; six lines—*EN* 9/1 137). The three letters under consideration are of medium length.[44]

(i) *Letter 1 (HSS 14 20)*. Tatip-Tešup sends a letter (HSS 14 20) to Šeḫram-mušni on behalf of Šeḫal-Tešup whose retainers were kidnapped[45]

---

39. Restricted in this study to non-literary letters. Grayson's (1983: 143) distinction between literary letters and epistles is based on the following criteria: literary letters are characterized by composition in elaborate style, content which often concerns matters of state importance, and storage in libraries and schools. It should be noted that this distinction between letters and epistles could not be maintained for Greek letter studies where A. Diessmann first propounded it. See Stowers 1986: 17-19.

40. Decrees and reports are distinguished from letters by form.

41. Some variation in formulae did occur. For example, in the later stages of Mesopotamian letter writing, when the address was directed immediately to the recipient and not to the scribe, about 90 per cent of the Neo Babylonian letters wrote the sender's name before the recipient's (White 1981: 7).

42. The cuneiform letter is believed to be a descendant of the oral correspondence message (Knutson 1981: 16). At Arrapḫa the number of the verb in the command to the scribe 'speak' (*qibīma*), remains singular regardless of the number of senders suggesting that the formula had become fixed. The lack of grammatical concord may indicate that the formula no longer served as instructions for the recipient's scribe.

43. Some of the letters 'gave instruction for definite legal action' (Hayden 1962: 179). Other letters served as 'summons' to appear before the royal tribunal (Liebesny 1943: 132).

44. In order, they are 16 lines (HSS 14 20), 23 lines (HSS 14 21), and 13 lines (HSS 14 30).

45. Several studies concluded that the retainers stole grain and fled; consequently,

while doing fieldwork, perhaps gleaning, in the merchant district.[46] He orders Šeḫram-mušni to act by seizing and bringing (*ṣabātu...wabālu*) the abductors before the king (*ina muḫḫi šarri*).

> Say to Šeḫram-mušni: Thus says Tatip-Tešup: 'People of Šeḫal-Tešup's house went to buy barley in the merchant district and were kidnapped. Whoever their kidnappers are, let Šeḫal-Tešup identify, apprehend, and bring them before the king.'

(ii) *Letter 2 (HSS 14 21)*. Responding to the first missive, Šeḫram-mušni dispatches a letter (HSS 14 21) to inform another official, Akip-tašenni about Šeḫal-Tešup's missing retainers. The official adds that they were abducted[47] and taken to the land of Lullu, a reputed slave trade center,[48] where they had been sold.

Apparently Šeḫram-mušni had received information regarding the whereabouts of the missing retainers. As an official who gave oversight to

no kidnapping was involved: Regarding the situation, Speiser said, 'The sense of this terse message is plainly that the servants, who had come ostensibly to glean, appropriated grain to which they were not entitled' (Pfeiffer and Speiser 1936: 121). Friedmann argues that the retainers had fled. The intention of the letters was to apprehend them (Friedmann 1982: 197). Based on the first letter (HSS 14 20) M. Morrison also concludes that they stole grain. But in her discussion of the second letter (HSS 14 21), she argues that the retainers had 'been stolen and...sold in the land of Lullu' (Morrison 1993: 59-60). Taken together as an administrative correspondence sequence, the two letters are best understood as a case of kidnapping. Also, the translation of *šarāqu* commonly translated 'to steal' may be rendered 'to kidnap' (stealing people) as is attested in a memorandum unrelated to this incident (HSS 5 35). Trafficking in slaves was a common practice of this region, particularly in Lullu where the victims and their abductors described in these two letters had gone. Additionally, although theft and flight did occur at times, this course of action typified slaves who wanted to escape rather than grain thieves permitted to glean. For a discussion of runaways (see Zaccagnini 1995: 93).

46. The 'merchant district' may have been a residential and operative center (possibly a village) where merchants conducted business, their own and perhaps that of the palace (Zaccagnini 1977: 174). The term for merchant (DAM.GAR) was used during the UR III period to describe a class of persons, many of whom were not engaged in mercantile activity (Snell 1982: 238).

47. For a discussion of the potential confusion of subject and object, and number for the verb *šarāqu*, see Wilhelm 1970: 64-70.

48. The land of Lullu was 'the principal foreign source of slaves' (Wilhelm 1989: 48). Both private and temple slaves may be found as early as c. 2700 BCE (see Diakonoff 1974: 9; Müller 1999: 84).

the those traveling to Lullu, Akip-tašenni is ordered in the second letter to inform Šeḫal-Tešup that he may go to Lullu to identify his retainers, presumably held there. In an attempt to apprehend the perpetrators, Šeḫram-mušni orders Akip-tašenni to seize (*ṣabātu*) anyone traveling to Lullu who is not able to produce tablet and seal identification,[49] and to bring (*wabālu*) that person(s) before Šeḫram-mušni.

> Say to Akip-tašenni: Thus says Šeḫram-mušni: 'Now people of Šeḫal-Tešup's house were kidnapped and sold in the land of the Lulluites. Now as for Šeḫal-Tešup, authorize him to look for/identify (those people). But as for you, anyone who comes from the land of Nuzi to the land of the Lulluites and does not carry tablet and seal, seize them and bring them before me (not the king). The king did not issue a decree. When these people who are missing are found, I will speak a report to the king.'

(iii) *Decree (HSS 14 21)*. In the same letter, Šeḫram-mušni also reminds Akip-tašenni that the king did not issue an order or decree[50] (*ṭēmu*) regarding the kidnapping. This statement implies that when no decree had been issued, the party did not go before the king, but rather before a lower administrative official such as himself. One decree found at Nuzi states that any official who refused to comply with the king's orders could lose his district (HSS 15 1). In another decree, officials could lose their heads should they fail to guard a group of people (HSS 14 14). These two documents and the letter dealing with kidnapping (HSS 14 21) illustrate the serious nature of decree-related matters.

In a third decree (HSS 13 36) issued by the king through Akip-tašenni, *šakin māti*, the governor is ordered to guard and escort three men. The details of this text correspond closely with the case of kidnapping cited in the first two letters (HSS 14 20, 21): the decree/order is dispatched to Akip-tašenni, *šakin māti*, the recipient of Šeḫram-mušni's letter (HSS 14 21); it is issued by the king, the same official, Šeram-mušni claimed had not issued an order; the command is to guard and return the three men involved, the same activity required for the occasion; the rendezvous point

---

49. The combination of tablet and seal as a means of identification is attested elsewhere at Nuzi (JEN 5 554).

50. Morrison translates the line, 'The king will not pronounce judgment' (Morrison 1993: 60). If one takes this letter (HSS 14 21) as a response to the first letter (HSS 14 20) from Tatip-Tešup, Šeḫram-mušni seems to be challenging the command to bring the perpetrators before the king. The line might better be rendered, 'The king did not issue a decree/order'.

in which Akip-tašenni will meet the group is Lullu, the very region suspected as the location for the kidnapping victims; and once the group arrives in Lullu, Akip-tašenni will guard and return them. He is the same official addressed in both documents.

(iv) *Report (HSS 14 21)*. In addition to the two letters and the decree, a third form of administrative correspondence is introduced. Because Šeḫram-mušni believed that the king had not issued a decree or an order, the official states that he will personally deliver a report (*šunku*) to the king. 'The king did not issue a decree. When these people who are missing are found, I will speak a report to the king.'

Reports (*šunku*)[51] were messages spoken or written to the king or other officials regarding specific administrative action. In this particular case, the official intended to inform the king of what had transpired in the kidnapping incident.[52] Whether by report from Šeḫram-mušni or by the kidnappers' responses to the interrogation by the king, the king would receive the crucial information regarding the kidnapping.[53]

(v) *Letter 3 (HSS 14 30)*. At this point in the case of kidnapping it is not clear what transpired. A third letter may be related to this correspondence sequence. Tatip-Tešup, sender of the first letter (HSS 14 20), dispatched another letter (HSS 14 30) to Aqaya ordering him to bring (*wabālu*) five persons before the king (*ina muḫḫi šarri*). Because the text is damaged, the names are difficult to read. The name of the city to which Aqaya must escort the men is also damaged, but the phrase 'into the presence of the king' (*ina muḫḫi šarri*) may indicate that it is Arrapḫa, the king's regional base of operation. The crucial issue is that this letter is an abbreviated restatement of the original command issued in the first correspondence (HSS 14 20).

---

51. HSS 13 149, a letter, contains an embedded *šunku* report.

52. On at least three other occasions the king did issue decrees. One decree (*ṭēmu*) embedded in a letter (HSS 14 14) orders officials to guard a group of people. The other decree addresses the mayors of a region (HSS 15 1) warning them against permitting illegal activity in their districts. A third decree (HSS 9 6) embedded in a letter summons a man into the king's presence.

53. Kidnapping may not have been the king's only concern. A memorandum (JEN 2 195) recording a decree of the king states that the price a merchant must pay for a native of Arrapḫa purchased as a slave in Lullu may have been different than the price for a foreigner.

Speak to Aqaya: Thus says Tatip-Tešup: '[five lines with personal names severely damaged] Let these five men come up to the City of [?]. Bring [them], and let them come before the king'. [The rest destroyed].

Several factors support the connection of this letter with the other two: The information found in this letter, particularly the name of the sending official and the approximate number of people, as well as the archive in which this third letter was found, all are consistent with the details of the kidnapping incident in the first two letters; no other Nuzi letter orders individuals to be brought before the king in a manner that clearly assumes previous correspondence. Perhaps most importantly, Tatip-Tešup appears only in these two letters at Nuzi and issues the same command, 'to bring' (*wabālu*) or escort people before the king, in both of them. This third letter also helps to tie the decree to the first two letters and adds significant details to the administrative action taken.

The fact that Tatip-Tešup ordered the kidnapping victims, and possibly the perpetrators, to be brought into the presence of the king implies that Šeḥram-mušni was wrong when he argued that the king had not issued a decree. The king had dispatched a decree or an order. Although one cannot say for certain, it is tempting to make HSS 13 36 the decree which Šeḥram-mušni denied had been commissioned. If so, it also became the documentary authorization which cancelled Šeḥram-mušni's order to bring the kidnappers before himself rather than the king (HSS 14 21). The existence of a decree document of which he was unaware[54] foiled his administrative letter-order.

d. *The Archival Relationships*

The archives in which the three letters are found connect them and the decree. The first two letters (HSS 14 20, 21) come from S113, an archive maintained by Šeḥal-Tešup. Šeḥram-mušni, Šeḥal-Tešup's assisting official was the recipient and the sender of the two letters respectively. The decree (HSS 13 36) and the third letter (HSS 14 30) were both found in area 4, the center of administration for the provincial militia. Akip-tašenni, recipient of the second letter (HSS 14 21) and the decree, is attested in chariot consignments within this area. Tatip-Tešup, sender of the first and third letters (HSS 14 20, 31) held two accounting records (HSS 14 151, 152) and two disbursements (HSS 14 159; 16 31), all of his other documents in the same archive.

---

54. It is also possible, but less likely, that the decree was issued subsequent to the first or second letter.

The personal, contextual, and archival evidence indicates that the third letter (HSS 14 30) details the final action taken after the retainers and possibly their kidnappers were found. Only if a decree did exist could one explain the change of direction from Šeḫram-mušni's order to bring the kidnapping victims before him back to the original directive (to bring them before the king). The sequence of administrative activity ordered in the correspondence also supports this connection.

e. *The Administrative Activity*
The repetition and progression of the commands given in each of the texts also support identifying them as a sequence of administrative action. The commands were the primary impetus for the correspondence. The sequence of primary commands reveals their relationships. In order of dispatch they are as follows:

HSS 14 20	*abātu...wabālu*	'seize...bring'	(letter 1)
HSS 14 21	*abātu...wabālu*	'seize...bring'	(letter 2)
HSS 13 36	*naṣāru...târu*	'guard...return (transitive)'	(decree)
HSS 14 30	*wabālu*	'bring' (*abātu* ['seize'] had occurred)	(letter 3)

The list does not include the report, which Šeḫram-mušni only planned to deliver orally to the king. The progression of activity seen in the commands reflects the administrative strategy and procedure employed to find the kidnapped individuals.[55]

3. *Conclusion*

The five administrative missives, when interpreted in the light of the roles of the messengers and named officials, their archival relationships and administrative activity ordered therein, offer one example of how officials used correspondence at provincial Arrapḫa. Rather than a group of unrelated texts, these administrative documents comprise a single case of kidnapping, the only of its kind found at Arrapḫa thus far. As such, they provide a unique window through which to view the regional administration.

Based on the proposed reconstruction, this sequence of administrative correspondence demonstrates how certain documents, for example, letters

55. Reminiscent of the letters found at Mari used to formulate and carry out a plan to achieve military victory (see Sasson 1969: 3). In the Neo-Babylonian resurgence, news of the Assyrian army's mobilization led Nabopolassar to reposition his troops at Takrit and, as a result, gain military victory (see Wiseman 1956: 13).

engaged (or were engaged by) other types of documents such as decrees and oral reports. As evidence of administrative authorization, these texts were held in archives until their administrative life had ended, in this case, until the kidnappers were seized, guarded, returned, and brought into the presence of the king.[56] It is possible that documents of this nature were retained after the administrative activity required was completed. The absence of any other correspondence sequence at Nuzi would suggest that when a text's administrative 'life' was over, it was destroyed.[57]

BIBLIOGRAPHY

Al-Khaiesi, Y.M.
1977   'Tell al-Fakhar (Kurru anni), a *dimtu*-Settlement: Excavation Report', *Assur*
           1.6: 95.
Andrews, S.J.
1994   'The *Šupe'ultu* "Exchange" Transaction at Nuzi', Part 2 (PhD dissertation,
           Hebrew Union College).
Brinkman, J.A.
1984   *Prelude to Empire: Babylonian Society and Politics, 747–626 B.C.* (Occa-
           sional Publications of the Babylonian Fund, 7; Philadelphia, PA: University
           Museum).
Cogan, M.
1974   *Imperialism and Religion: Assyria, Judah and Israel in the Eight and
           Seventh Centuries B.C.E.* (SBLMS, 19; Missoula, MT: Scholars Press).
Cooper, J.S.
1975   'Structure, Humor, and Satire in the Poor Man of Nippur', *JCS* 27: 163-74.

56. The precise nature of the crime and resulting punishment are not recorded in the texts. It is difficult to determine whether the officials in this sequence of correspondence show a concern for the kidnapped victims primarily as supervised labor for Šeḥal-Tešup or as private citizens whose rights have been violated. For a general perspective on the welfare of individuals in relation to the state see Jacobsen 1946: 185. Weinfeld has argued that the proclamations at Nuzi which released land and established freedom for people from enslavement are evidence of such interests (Weinfeld 1995: 158). Zaccagnini underscores the significance of the proclamations of release for understanding the impact of state intervention into the family sector of household economies, but also warns that our understanding of these remains incomplete. See Zaccagnini 1999: 95.

57. Regarding the 'life' of a letter, Morrison has said, 'Administrative archives are composed of texts that document the inflow and outflow of goods, services, personnel, and equipment from a central agency such as the palace or a large estate. Among such are letters. By nature these texts have a more limited life span' (Morrison 1987). Veenhof explores the metaphor of text life (Veenhof 1987).

1983   *Reconstructing History from Ancient Inscriptions: The Lagash-Umma Border Conflict* (SANE, 2.1; Malibu: Undena Publications).

Crown, A.D.
1974   'Tidings and Instructions: How News Traveled in the Ancient Near East', *JESHO* 17: 264-65.

Dalley, S.
1984   *Mari and Karana* (London: Longman).

Diakonoff, I.M.
1974   *Structure of Society and State in Early Dynastic Sumer* (MANE, 1.3; Malibu: Undena Publications).

Ellis, M. de Jong
1974   'Taxation in Ancient Mesopotamia: The History of the Term *miksu*', *JCS* 26: 211-50.

Fadhil, A.
1983   *Studien zur Topographie und Prosopographie der Provinzstädte des Königreichs Arrapḫe* (Baghdader Forschungen, 6; Mainz am Rhein: Verlag Philipp von Zabern).

Friedmann, A.
1982   'Economic Geography and Administration at Nuzi' (PhD dissertation, Hebrew Union College).

Grayson, A.K.
1983   'Literary Letters from Deities and Diviners: More Fragments', *JAOS* 103: 143-48.

Hallo, W.W.
1957   *Early Mesopotamian Royal Titles: A Philological and Historical Analysis* (AOS, 43; New Haven, CT: The American Oriental Society).

Handy, L.K.
1994   *Among the Host of Heaven: The Syro-Palestinian Pantheon as Bureaucracy* (Winona Lake, IN: Eisenbrauns).

Hayden, R.E.
1962   'Court Procedure at Nuzu' (PhD dissertation, Brandeis University).

Jacobsen, T.
1946   'Mesopotamia', in H. Frankfort *et al.* (eds.), *The Intellectual Adventure of Modern Man: An Essay on Speculative Thought in the Ancient Near East* (Chicago: University of Chicago Press): 125-222.

Knutson, F.B.
1981   'Cuneiform Letters and Social Conventions', *Semeia* 22: 15-23.

Kramer, S.N.
1963   *The Sumerians: Their History, Culture, and Character* (Chicago, IL: University of Chicago Press).

Kutscher, R.
1975   *Oh Angry Sea (a-ab-ba hu-luh-ha): The History of a Sumerian Congregational Lament* (YNER, 6; New Haven, CT: Yale University Press).

Lambert, W.G.
1960   *Babylonian Wisdom Literature* (Oxford: Clarendon Press).

Larsen, M.T.
1979   'The Tradition of Empire in Mesopotamia', in *Power and Propaganda*: 75-103.

Leichty, E.
1991 'Esarhaddon's "Letter to the Gods"', in *Studies Tadmor*: 52-57.
Liebesny, H.
1943 'The Administration of Justice at Nuzi', *JAOS* 63: 128-44.
Machinist, P.
1982 'Provincial Governance in Middle Assyria and Some New Texts from Yale', *Assur* 3.2: 65-101 (Monographic Journals of the Near East; Malibu: Undena Publications).
Maidman, M.P.
1981 'The Office of *ḫalṣuḫlu* in the Nuzi Texts', in *Studies Lacheman*: 233-46.
Matthews, V.H.
1978 *Pastoral Nomadism in the Mari Kingdom (ca. 1830–1760 B.C.)* (ASORDS, 3; Cambridge, MA: American Schools of Oriental Research).
1996 'Messengers and the Transmission of Information in the Mari Kingdom', in *Studies Young*: 267-74.
Mayer, W.
1978 *Nuzi-Studien*, I (AOAT, 205.1; Neukirchen–Vluyn: Neukirchener Verlag).
Meier, S.M.
1988 *The Messenger in the Ancient Semitic World* (HSM, 45; Atlanta, GA: Scholars Press).
Millard, A.R.
1999 'Oral Proclamation and Written Record: Spreading and Preserving Information in Ancient Israel', *Studies Heltzer*: 237-41.
2000 'Letters', in P. Bienkowski and A.R. Millard (eds.), *Dictionary of the Ancient Near East* (Philadelphia: University of Pennsylvania): 80-81.
Moran, W.M.
1975 'The Syrian Scribe of the Jerusalem Amarna Letters', in *Unity and Diversity*: 146-66.
1991 'Assurbanipal's Message to the Babylonians (*ABL* 301), with an Excursus on Figurative *biltu*', in *Studies Tadmor*: 320-31.
Morrison, M.A.
1987 'The Archives at Nuzi: An Archeological and Philological Retrospective', *ASOR* meetings, Boston, MA.
1993 'The Family of Ar-tura and Šeḫal-Tešup: Texts from Group 17', in M.A. Morrison (ed.), *The Eastern Archives of Nuzi* (SCCNH, 4; Winona Lake, IN: Eisenbrauns): 47-65.
Mullen, E.T.
1980 *The Divine Council in Canaanite and Early Hebrew Literature* (HSM, 24; Chico, CA: Scholars Press).
Müller, G.G.W.
1999 'The Geography of the Nuzi Area', in D.I. Owen and G. Wilhelm (eds.), *Nuzi at Seventy-Five* (SCCNH, 10; Bethesda, MD: CDL Press): 73-88.
Munn-Rankin, J.M.
1956 'Diplomacy in Western Asia in the Early Second Millennium B.C.', *Iraq* 18: 68-110.
Negri Scaffa, P.
1995 'The Scribes of Nuzi and their Activities Relative to Arms According to

Palace Texts', in D.I. Owen (ed.), *General Studies* (SCCNH, 5; Winona Lake, IN: Eisenbrauns): 53-69.

Oppenheim, A.L.
1977   *Ancient Mesopotamia: Portrait of a Dead Civilization* (Chicago, IL: University of Chicago Press).

Pfeiffer, R.H.
1923   'Assyrian Epistolary Formalae (sic)', *JAOS* 43: 26-40.

Pfeiffer, R.H., and E.A. Speiser
1936   *One Hundred New Selected Nuzi Texts* (AASOR, 16; New Haven, CT: American Schools of Oriental Research).

Sasson, J.M.
1969   *The Military Establishments at Mari* (Studia Pohl, 3; Rome: Pontifical Biblical Institute).

Shupak, N.
1992   'A New Source for the Study of the Judiciary and Law of Ancient Egypt: The Tale of the Eloquent Peasant', *JNES* 51: 1-18.

Snell, D.C.
1982   *Ledgers and Prices: Early Mesopotamian Merchant Accounts* (YNER, 8; New Haven, CT: Yale University Press).

Stowers, S.K.
1986   *Letter Writing in Greco-Roman Antiquity* (LEC, 5; Philadelphia, PA: Westminster Press).

Veenhof, K.R.
1987   ' "Dying Tablets" and "Hungry Silver": Elements of Figurative Language in Akkadian Commercial Terminology', in M. Mindlin, M.J. Geller, and J.E. Wansbrough (eds.), *Figurative Language in the Ancient Near East* (London: School of Oriental and African Studies): 50-62.

Visicato, G.
1995   *The Bureaucracy of Šuruppak: Administrative Centers, Central Offices, Intermediate Structures and Hierarchies in the Economic Documentation of Fara* (Münster: Ugarit-Verlag).

Weinfeld, M.
1995   *Social Justice in Ancient Israel and in the Ancient Near East* (Publications of the Perry Foundation for Biblical Research in the Hebrew University of Jerusalem; Jerusalem: Magnes Press; Minneapolis, MN: Fortress Press).

White, J.L.
1981   'The Ancient Epistolary Group in Retrospect', *Semeia* 22: 89-106.

Wilhelm, G.
1970   *Untersuchungen zum Hurro-Akkadischen von Nuzi* (AOAT, 9; Kevelaer: Butzon & Berker, 1970).

1989   *The Hurrians* (trans. J. Barnes; Warminster: Aris & Phillips).

Wiseman, D.J.
1956   *Chronicles of the Chaldaean Kings (626–556 B.C.) in the British Museum* (Aberdeen: Aberdeen University Press).

Wouters, W.
1989   'Urḫi-Tešub and the Ramses-Letters from Boghazköy', *JCS* 41: 227-28.

Zaccagnini, C.
1977   'The Merchant at Nuzi', *Iraq* 39: 171-89.

1979 *The Rural Landscape of the Land of Arraphe* (Quaderni di Geografia Storica, 1; Rome: University of Rome).

1995 'War and Famine at Emar', *Or* 64: 92-109.

1999 'Features of the Economy and Society of Nuzi', in D.I. Owen and G. Wilhelm (eds.), *Nuzi at Seventy-Five* (SCCNH, 10; Bethesda, MD: CDL Press): 89-101.

Zimansky, P.E.

1985 *Ecology and Empire: The Structure of the Urartian State* (SAOC, 41; Chicago, IL: Oriental Institute).

The Bible and Alalakh

Richard S. Hess

Previous study of the relationship between Alalakh and the Bible (Hess 1994b) concluded that comparisons must be evaluated on a case by case basis. The evidence is again reviewed here and updated with recent discussions of the Alalakh texts. It is suggested that neither the study of the Alalakh texts themselves nor their application to the world of the Hebrew Bible have been exhausted.

Tell Atchana, the site of Alalakh, lies on the heavily populated and fertile Amq plain beside the Orontes River. It is east of modern Antakya in Turkey. Passing through Alalakh, trade routes ran from the east, toward Aleppo and on to the Euphrates Valley, and from the west, toward the sea coast and the eastern Mediterranean commercial world (Woolley 1953: 19-20). The city also lay on important ways north to the land of the Hittites and south to Damascus and the Jordan Valley. Thus Sir Leonard Woolley chose it for excavation in order to examine these cultural influences. The 17 levels unearthed at the site date from c. 3100 BCE until c. 1200 BCE. Levels seven and four excited the most interest because these yielded hundreds of cuneiform texts whose study has served to reconstruct the society (von Dassow 1997).

At level seven Woolley found a palace, a temple, and a city gate. The period covered the reigns of three kings who lived sometime about the end of the eighteenth century. Frescos decorated the palace rooms. Most of the tablets that can be dated come from the reign of Yarimlim. Some were found in rooms of the palace (Woolley 1955: 91-106). Others were uncovered on the floor of the temple archive room (Woolley 1955: 59-65). Yarimlim's rule probably saw the expansion of the buildings and the fortifications. A fire destroyed the city, that was known to its inhabitants as Alalakh.

A second cuneiform archive was discovered in level four of Woolley's excavation, dated one or two centuries after that of level seven. More

Mesopotamia and the Bible

tablets than those of level seven were found here in the royal palace (Woolley 1955: 110-31; Hess 1996a). The personal and place names, as well as the names of objects and social groups, reveal a society primarily influenced by Hurrian culture but also populated by West Semitic peoples (though less so than at neighbouring Ugarit; Hess 1999).

An important inscription was found on a broken statue of Idrimi, which had been buried in a room in the annex of a temple from the latest level of Alalakh, destroyed c. 1200 BCE. The inscription identifies the figure as Idrimi and relates his life. It is an adventure story about a prince who flees the kingdom when his father is murdered. He lives in Emar and then in Ammia in Canaan for seven years. Upon his return, Idrimi re-establishes his rule and extends it with an expedition into Hittite territory. He records his building activities in Alalakh, including a palace that can be identified with the structure of 33 rooms found on the site. Idrimi reigns 30 years before causing the inscription to be written and passing rulership to his son.

Wiseman catalogued and published many of more than 450 cuneiform texts excavated from Tell Atchana (Wiseman 1953). His continued publication of the texts was supplemented by the work of other scholars, especially Dietrich and Loretz (Dietrich and Loretz 1969a; 1969b; 1969c; see the publication history and bibliography, Hess 1988; 1992). The statue of Idrimi has been studied in separate publications and treatments (Smith 1949; Greenstein and Marcus 1976; Dietrich and Loretz 1981; Mayer 1995). The relevance of these texts for the study of the Hebrew Bible has been observed in numerous studies. The following summary will consider some of the chief comparisons book by book through the Old Testament.

1. *Genesis*

Among the many personal names occurring in the Alalakh texts, several have roots that may be similar to those occurring in the personal names of Genesis 1–11: Jared, Eber, and Haran (Hess 1993: 69, 81, 93). The *qnh* root, that in Gen. 4.1 is made to play on the name of Cain, also occurs in an Alalakh personal name (Hess 1993: 26, 112-13). In addition, a form of the personal name Adam may appear on a level 4 text.

Although Alalakh lies outside the region of Canaan, as is clear from the Idrimi inscription, individuals from Canaan are mentioned several times in the texts. In every case they are associated with military activities (Hess 1998a). Most of the Canaanites bear West Semitic names but one has a northern name, perhaps Anatolian (Hess 1998b). This same mixture of linguistic backgound for personal and group names of Canaanites is found in the Bible's naming of Canaanites, for example in the non-Israelites in the book of Joshua (Hess 1996c: 27-30; 1996d).

At Ugarit, Nuzi, and Alalakh, the special inheritance of the first born son could be legally transferred to someone else (AT 92.15-19; Mendelsohn 1941; 1959), as with Abraham's adoption of Eliezer (Gen. 15.2-3) and Jacob's choices of Joseph instead of Reuben (Gen. 48.22; 49.3-4) and of Ephraim instead of Manasseh (Gen. 48.13-14). A betrothal gift for the father-in-law (*nidnu*; Hebrew *mattān*) allowed the bridegroom to marry (AT 17.4-6; Gen. 34.12; Finkelstein 1969: 546). If a wife remained barren for seven years, a husband could marry again (AT 93 and 94, though 94 is fragmentary). Jacob also served seven additional years before his marriage to Rachel (Gen. 29.18, 27). Barrenness and remarriage in order to produce an heir are also found in the Patriarchal Narratives (Gen. 16.1-4). Some of these parallels to patriarchal customs can be found elsewhere in the ancient Near East. Significant for Gen. 12–50 is the cluster of parallels in second millennium BCE West Semitic societies such as Alalakh.

The term 'Ḥapiru' occurs throughout the second millennium BCE Levant (Bottéro 1954; Greenberg 1955; Loretz 1984; Lemche 1992). It is of interest because it has been related to the biblical 'Hebrew'. Although similar in sound, the two terms are not unlikely to be related to one another linguistically (Rainey 1989: 571) even though at times they exhibit sociological similarities (Na'aman 1986). In the fourteenth-century Amarna correspondence the Ḥapiru are enemies of the established order and of all who are loyal to the pharaoh (Moran 1987). This characteristic has sometimes been likened to the Hebrews of Gen. 14.13; 39.14, 17, and of Exod. 21.1-9. At Alalakh, however, the Ḥapiru play a different role. They first appear in the Idrimi inscription (1.27), notwithstanding attempts to find them in earlier level seven texts (see the discussion in Hess 1994b: 206-207; and the readings of Dietrich and Loretz 1969b: 119 n. 29; Kienast 1980: 58). Idrimi flees to the land of the Ḥapiru (written as LÚ SA.GAZ) and finds protection there. Perhaps for this reason the level four texts show examples of Ḥapiru well integrated into Alalakh society (Redford 1992: 195). They hold a variety of occupations: priest, LÚ.SANGA *iš*]-[*ḫa-ra*] (AT 180.20); diviner, LÚ *bá-a-ru* (AT 182.16); mayor, LÚ *ḫa-za-an-nu* (AT 182.13); and slave, ÌR (AT 182.14). Ḥapiru can serve as soldiers and carry weapons (AT 180.1). They can also have land or property, (É-AT 183.5; 198.48).

Following Wiseman (1958), Weinfeld (1970; 1972: 74-75, 102) identifies both level seven AT 456 and Genesis 15 as land grants because in both: (1) the overlord is obligated to the servant; (2) the giver of land takes an oath; and (3) animal carcasses are divided as part of an accompanying sacrifice (see AT 54). McCarthy (1978: 86-97) finds in the cutting of the sheep's throat the background for the Hebrew expression, 'to cut (*krt*) a covenant'. Although Van Seters (1975: 100-103; but not mentioned in 1992: 248-51) denies this comparison, his arguments are not compelling and at times rest on confusion of the data (Hess 1994d). Along with Jer. 34.17-20, later Aramaic (Fitzmyer 1967: 14-15) and Akkadian treaties (Parpola and Watanabe 1988: 9, 58) also describe dismemberment of an animal, although usually as part of the curses for those who violate the treaty. The second millennium parallels relate more to the life of the treaty makers than to an actual form of death envisaged for its violation.

The Joseph story is an account with similaritites of content when compared with the story of Idrimi's rise to power (Albright 1950: 20; cf. also Oppenheim 1955). For example, there are seven-year periods, practices of divination, and the reconciliation of brothers in both.

2. *Exodus*

Alalakh's goddess claimed the king as her *sikiltu* ('special possession') (AT 2 seal *et passim*; Reiner 1969: 531-32), related to *sĕgullâ* a word describing God's relationship to Israel (e.g. Exod. 19.5). This expression, used of a deity to describe a special relation with a mortal, occurs frequently and almost exclusively at Alalakh (Seux 1967: 261-62). It has been used this way in two other occurrences (*CAD*: XV, 245), that are both Middle Babylonian. Thus all the evidence suggests that this expression is characteristic of the second millennium BCE.

At Alalakh *ḫupšu* (AT 186, 187, 202, 211; Dietrich and Loretz 1969b: 97-99, 104-106; Dietrich and Loretz 1969c: 43-45) owned houses or lived as tenants (Mendelsohn 1955), like the Hebrew *ḥopšî*, free-born individuals exempt from certain royal taxes (Exod. 21.5; 1 Sam. 17.25; Wright 1990: 256-57). Although the legal texts (Exod. 21.2-6, 26-27; Lev. 19.20; Deut. 15.12-13, 18; Jer. 34.9-16) attest a usage that describes the freedom of a slave, and although this is supported by occurrences elsewhere (Job 3.19, and possibly Isa. 58.6), the usage is different in other passages. Psalm 88.6 relates *ḥopšî* to the dead and their grave, whether in terms of liberation from it (Loretz 1977: 255-57) or otherwise (Lohfink 1986: 116).

In 1 Sam. 17.25 Saul promises 'freedom' (from taxation) for anyone who will engage in battle with Goliath. The residence of a leper king, a *bêt haḥopšît* in 2 Kgs 15.5 (= 2 Chron. 26.21), has been related to Hebrew *ḥopšî* and to Ugaritic *bt ḥptt* (Wright 1987: 144 n. 25). It may be translated as 'house of freedom', whether literally (Loretz 1976: 131) or euphemistically (de Moor 1987: 66 n. 304), but this rendering is not certain (Cogan and Tadmor 1988: 165-67). Lemche's critique of Gottwald's study (Lemche 1976; 1985: 167, 193-94; Gottwald 1979: 480-84) understood *ḥupšu* as clients, bound by specific contractual terms to work the land. Like Byblos, Ugarit, and elsewhere, Alalakh *ḥupšu* held a variety of occupations, but none with political power.

3. *Leviticus*

The release of prisoners is discussed in Alalakh level seven using the terms *darārum* (AT 29.11; 30.9; 31.9; 38.10; 42.6) and *andurārum* (AT 65.6-7). The biblical concept of *dʳrôr*, 'release', during the year of Jubilee, as suggested in Lev. 25.10-15, is a related term in Hebrew. Whether the Jubilee and its release of debt slaves is pre-Monarchic (Lewy 1958: 29*-30*; Weinfeld 1972: 153) or postexilic (Lemche 1979; Westbrook 1991: 44-55), the use of *dʳrôr* in this context and in the prophets (Isa. 61.1; Jer. 34.8, 15, 17; Ezek. 46.17) is different from the usage of its cognate at Alalakh. There it describes an unchangeable debt: *ú-ul uš-a-ab ú-ul id-dá-ra-ar*, 'it cannot increase (through interest) nor can it decrease' (thus forbidding the charging of interest, Zeeb 1991a: 426-27; 1995: 651), and a person who cannot go free (AT 65.6-7): *i-na an-da-ra-ri-im ú-ul i-na-an-da-ar*, 'At a general release, she may not be released'. In Leviticus 25 (and Jeremiah and Ezekiel) *dʳrôr* describes the return of the land to its original owners (vv. 10-15) and the return of those sold into debt servitude to their freedom (vv. 39-42; cf. Wright 1990: 123-28, 249-58). Isaiah 61.1 describes the release of prisoners (North 1978). The Alalakh uses, common in other periods of Akkadian, may account for the Levitical law. It was designed to guarantee that no citizen of Israel should be able to bind themselves or their families to permanent servitude.

4. *Deuteronomy*

The term, *mištannu*, 'equivalent', in AT 3 has been used to translate *mišneh* in Deut. 15.18 (and Jer. 16.18; see Tsevat 1958: 125-26; Wiseman

1982: 24). However, the Alalakh word is now understood as originally Indo-Aryan (Mayrhofer 1965) and unrelated to the biblical expression. Although Lindenberger argues for the meaning 'double' in the Hebrew Bible (Lindenberger 1991), Tsevat (1994) has reaffirmed his understanding of the biblical term, though no longer related to Alalakh *mištannu*.

Compare Deut. 23.15-16 with AT 2, where fugitives were extradited by elders of the city (Wiseman 1982: 23).

5. *Joshua*

Several personal names also occur at Alalakh that contain Semitic roots or Hurrian elements resembling those in the narratives of Joshua: Achan (Hess 1994a: 91), Talmai, and Ahiman (Hess 1996d: 211-13). These Hurrian names (Achan and Talmai) are especially significant, if the parallels are legitimate, because they are found almost exclusively in the second millennium BCE.

The tribal allotments of Joshua 13–21 contain many examples of border descriptions and town lists. Both of these have parallels at Alalakh and Ugarit (Hess 1996c: 53-60). The boundary between Alalakh and Ugarit, its southern neighbor, is described on several treaty documents and resembles the tribal boundaries of Joshua in several ways: (1) formally both documents include town lists and brief narrative comments in the middle of the boundary descriptions; (2) both have summaries and introductions describing the lands concerned; (3) both repeat the same boundaries with minor variations of selection, organization, and spelling; and (4) both boundary descriptions occur as part of larger documents that are either treaties or covenants (Josh. 8.30-35; 24; Hess 1994c).

Many of the town lists in Joshua 13–21 resemble lists of place names found on administrative documents from Alalakh and Ugarit in terms of introductions, summary statements and general organization of the lists (Hess 1996b: 163-67). Those in Joshua 13, 20, and 21 resemble place name lists found in land grants such as AT 56 and AT 456. Both AT 456 and Joshua 13 use town lists for historical recollections at the beginning of texts that go on to describe further grants (Josh. 13.17-20, 27). Both AT 56 and Joshua 21 use a similar expression describing the towns 'with their districts' (AT 56.4) and 'with its surrounding pasture land' (Josh. 21; Hess 1996b: 162-63). In fact, the whole book of Joshua resembles a land grant. In particular its form parallels many aspects of the grant of Alalakh in AT 456. For example, both of these texts begin with a history of the events involved in obtaining the towns and territory (Josh. 1–12), details of the towns given (Josh. 13–21), and a concluding description of a treaty/ covenant event between the giver and the recipient. (See further Hess 2000; forthcoming.)

6. *Judges; 1 and 2 Samuel*

Oppenheim (1955) and others have seen in Idrimi's account of his acquisition of his kingdom a narrative not unlike David's rise to kingship (Oppenheim 1955; Buccellati 1962). The narrative style (Wiseman 1967: 122) including the hiding with maternal relatives (1 Sam. 22.3-4; cf. Absalom, 2 Sam. 13.37), divine requests to regain rulership (2 Sam. 2.1-4; 5.1, 3), and the use of spoils of war to build a temple are examples of similarities. Although the story of the Idrimi inscription has most often been compared with David, Greenstein and Marcus (1976: 76-77) also mention the story of Jephthah in Judges 11. In addition to the flight, they suggest that all three narratives include the recognition by kinsmen, the act of others joining the exiled hero, and the recognition of the hero as their leader. In fact, this theme of gaining rightful rulership occurs elsewhere in the ancient Near East. The *Apology of Hattusili* may be compared with Idrimi (Dietrich and Loretz 1981: 255) and with the story of David's rise to kingship (Wolf 1967). Here is a narrative tradition common to the Levantine world: the outcast hero gains his place as leader of a people and then succeeds in battle. On the basis of present evidence, this style of literature, which becomes so popular in Semitic and Western cultures, makes its first appearance at Alalakh.

If grabbing the hem of a garment was an act of submission (AT 456.45-57) (cf. 1 Sam. 15.27-28), David's cutting the hem of Saul's garment (1 Sam. 24.3-4) may have implied the opposite.

7. *1 and 2 Kings*

David's public proclamation of Solomon as his heir (1 Kgs 1.17, 20, 30-36) resembles Yarimlim's attempt to reduce sibling rivalry for his power by publicly naming his heir (AT 6). Solomon gave 20 towns to Hiram of Tyre (1 Kgs 11.11; cf. Fensham 1960). At level seven of Alalakh, an international treaty (AT 1; cf. Na'aman 1980), and other texts (AT 52-58; cf. Kienast 1980) record the exchange of a city or towns and villages. As already noted, the extradition of fugitives, common enough in ancient

Near Eastern treaties and mentioned in level four treaties at Alalakh (AT 2 and 3; cf. Reiner 1969: 531-32), is comparable to the diplomacy that lay behind Shimei's search for fugitive slaves in Philistine territory (1 Kgs 2.39-40).

As with the place name lists of Joshua 13–21, the administrative list of Solomon's districts in 1 Kings 4 resembles those lists found at Alalakh and Ugarit in formal details such as a list associating a personal name and a place name (Hess 1997).

A king could confiscate the property of an executed criminal (1 Kgs 21; AT 17; cf. Finkelstein 1969: 546; Westbrook 1991: 123).

8. *Psalms*

Psalms mention dwelling in the house of the king (Pss. 23.6; 27.4). At Alalakh, 'stand-ins' or pledges (*manzazānūtu* and *mazzazānu*) owed the king money and rendered service to the palace as a means of paying interest on a loan (AT 18-28, 36, 41, 43, 44, 47, 49; cf. Klengel 1963; Eichler 1973: 63-78; Zeeb 1991a: 428-29).

9. *Amos*

Although much evidence exists from the administrative archives for the reconstruction of the social world of ancient Alalakh, no simple correlation between it and the biblical world can be assumed. Noting this, Zeeb is careful to qualify his study of the economic realities of Israel during the time of Amos and of the Alalakh level seven economic texts. His own research and publication of the latter (Zeeb 1991a; 1991b; 1992; 1993) is developed and applied to theories of 'rent capitalism' to examine the critique of the prophet, and especially Amos 2.6-8. Noting that the Alalakh texts suggest an economy in which people could serve a form of debt servitude under specific conditions and until the debt was repaid, Zeeb (1995) reads these verses as though the victims are just such pledges who undergo unjust treatment at the hands of their creditors. Forbidden to sell these pledges to others in slavery, the creditors do just that (v. 6) and use the profits to purchase luxurious garments and drink (v. 8). Forbidden sexual liberties with women in such conditions, the creditors nevertheless take them (v. 7) and thus treat fellow Israelites as chattel.

10. *Conclusion*

Some of the comparisons that have been made here are of the sort that could be found elsewhere in the ancient Near East, especially in texts from Nuzi and Ugarit. This especially concerns matters of names, social customs, and boundary descriptions. However, it is not so much the presence of a single comparison, for which individual examples abound in various ancient Near Eastern and other literary sources. Instead, it is the cumulative weight of many biblical comparisons from second millennium sources such as Alalakh that argues for a similar milieu for much of the biblical material from the books of the Pentateuch, Joshua, Judges, Samuel, and the first part of 1 Kings. Other comparisons, such as those derived from the wealth of economic and administrative documents, are unique to Alalakh, or rare elsewhere in the West Semitic world. This is due to the distinctive nature of the Alalakh archive. As is clear when this review is compared with earlier ones (Wiseman 1967; 1982; Hess 1994b), research in the relationship between the Bible and Alalakh continues to generate important and useful insights.

BIBLIOGRAPHY

Albright, W.F.
 1950   'Some Important Recent Discoveries: Alphabetic Origins and the Idrimi Statue', *BASOR* 118: 11-20.

Bottéro, J.
 1954   *Le problème des Ḫabiru à la 4ᵉ rencontre assyriologique internationale* (Cahiers de la Société asiatique, 12; Paris: Imprimerie Nationale).

Buccellati, G.
 1962   'La "carriera" di David e quella di Idrimi, re di Alalae', *BeO* 4: 95-99.

Cogan, M., and H. Tadmor
 1988   *II Kings: A New Translation and Commentary* (AB, 11; Garden City, NY: Doubleday).

Dietrich, M., and O. Loretz
 1969a   'Die soziale Struktur von Alalaḫ und Ugarit (II): Die sozialen Gruppen *ḫupše-namê*, *ḫaniaḫḫe-ekû*, *eḫele-šūzubu* und *marjanne* nach Texten aus Alalaḫ IV', *WO* 5: 57-93.

 1969b   'Die soziale Struktur von Alalaḫ und Ugarit (IV): Die É=*bîtu*-Listen aus Alalaḫ IV als Quelle für die Erforschung der gesellschaftlichen Schichtung von Alalaḫ im 15. Jh. v. Chr.', *ZA* 60: 88-123.

 1969c   'Die soziale Struktur von Alalaḫ und Ugarit (V): Die Weingärten des Gebietes von Alalaḫ im 15. Jahrhundert', *UF* 1: 37-64.

 1981   'Die Inschrift der Statue des Königs Idrimi von Alalaḫ', *UF* 13: 201-68 (plus Addendum).

Draffkorn, A.
  1959   'Was King Abba-AN of Yamad a Vizier for the King of Ḫattuša?', *JCS* 13:
              94-97.
Eichler, B.L.
  1973   *Indenture at Nuzi: The Personal Tidennūtu Contract and its Mesopotamian
              Analogues* (New Haven: Yale University Press).
Fensham, F.C.
  1960   'The Treaty between Solomon and Hiram and the Alalakh Tablets', *JBL* 79:
              59-60.
Finkelstein, J.J.
  1969   'Documents from the Practice of Law', *ANET*: 542-47.
Fitzmyer, J.A.
  1967   *The Aramaic Inscriptions of Sefire* (Biblica Orientalia, 19; Rome: Pontifical
              Biblical Institute).
Gottwald, N.K.
  1979   *The Tribes of Yahweh: A Sociology of the Religion of Liberated Israel,
              1250–1050 B.C.E.* (Maryknoll, NY: Orbis Books).
Greenberg, M.
  1955   *The Ḫab/piru* (AOS, 39; New Haven: American Oriental Society).
Greenstein, E.L., and D. Marcus
  1976   'The Akkadian Inscription of Idrimi', *JANESCU* 8: 59-96.
Hess, R.S.
  1988   'A Preliminary List of the Published Alalakh Texts', *UF* 20: 69-87.
  1992   'Observations on Some Unpublished Alalakh Texts, Probably from Level
              IV', *UF* 24: 113-15.
  1993   *Studies in the Personal Names of Genesis 1–11* (AOAT, 234; Kevelaer:
              Butzon & Bercker; Neukirchen–Vluyn: Neukirchener Verlag).
  1994a   'Achan and Achor: Names and Wordplay in Joshua 7', *HAR* 14: 89-98.
  1994b   'Alalakh and the Bible: Obstacle or Contribution?', *Studies King*: 199-215.
  1994c   'Late Bronze Age and Biblical Boundary Descriptions of the West Semitic
              World', in *UB*: 123-38.
  1994d   'The Slaughter of the Animals in Genesis 15: 18-21 and its Ancient Near
              Eastern Context', in R.S. Hess, P.E. Satterthwaite, and G.J. Wenham (eds.),
              He Swore an Oath: Biblical Themes from Genesis 12–50 (Cambridge:
              Tyndale House, 1993; 2nd edn; Carlisle: Paternoster; Grand Rapids: Baker
              Book House): 55-65.
  1996a   'A Comparison of the Ugarit, Emar and Alalakh Archives', in *Studies
              Gibson*: 75-83.
  1996b   'A Typology of West Semitic Place Name Lists with Special Reference to
              Joshua 13–21', *BA* 59.3: 160-70.
  1996c   *Joshua: An Introduction and Commentary* (Tyndale Old Testament Com-
              mentaries; Leicester: IVP).
  1996d   'Non-Israelite Personal Names in the Book of Joshua', *CBQ* 58: 205-14.
  1997   'The Form and Structure of the Solomonic District List in 1 Kings 4.7-19',
              in *Studies Astour*: 279-92.
  1998a   'Occurrences of Canaan in Late Bronze Age Archives of the West Semitic
              World', in Sh. Izre'el, I. Singer and R. Zadok (eds.), *Past Links: Studies in
              the Languages and Cultures of the Ancient Near East* (IOS, 18; Winona

Lake, IN: Eisenbrauns): 365-72.

1998b   'The Late Bronze Age Alalakh Texts at the Australian Institute of Archaeology', *Buried History* 34.1: 4-9.

1999   'The Onomastics of Ugarit', in W.G.E. Watson and N. Wyatt (eds.), *Handbook of Ugaritic Studies* (Handbook of Oriental Studies; First Part: The Near and Middle East, Band 39; Leiden: E.J. Brill): 499-528.

2000   '5. Royal Grants: Will of Ammitaku Leader of Alalakh (AT 6); Land Grant (AT 456*), *COS*: II, 368-70.

forthcoming   'The Books of Joshua as a Land Grant'.

Kienast, B.
1980   'Die altbabylonischen Kaufurkunden aus Alalaḫ', *WO* 11: 35-63.

Klengel, H.
1963   'Zur Sklaverei in Alalaḫ', *Acta Antiqua* 11: 1-15.

Lemche, N.P.
1976   'The Manumission of Slaves—The Fallow Year—The Sabbatical Year—The Jobel Year', *VT* 26: 38-59.

1979   '*Andurārum* and *Mišarum*: Comments on the Problem of Social Edicts and their Application in the Ancient Near East', *JNES* 38: 11-22.

1985   *Early Israel: Anthropological and Historical Studies on the Israelite Society before the Monarchy* (VTSup, 37; Leiden: E.J. Brill).

1992   'Ḫabiru, Ḫapiru', in *ABD*: III, 6-10.

Lewy, J.
1958   'The Biblical Institution of *dᵉrôr* in the Light of Akkadian Documents', *EI* 5: 21*-31*.

Lindenberger, J.M.
1991   'How Much for a Hebrew Slave? The Meaning of *Mišneh* in Deut 15.18', *JBL* 110: 479-82.

Lohfink, N.
1986   '*ḥopšî*', in *TDOT*: V, 114-18.

Loretz, O.
1976   'Ugaritisch—Hebräisch *ḪB/PṮ, BT ḪPṮṮ—ḪPŠJ, BJT ḪḪPŠJ/WT*', *UF* 8: 129-31.

1977   'Die Hebräischen Termini *ḪPŠJ* "Freigelassen, Freigelassener" und *ḪPŠH* "Freilassung"', *UF* 9: 163-67.

1984   *Habiru-Hebräer: Eine sozio-linguistische Studie über die Herkunft des Gentiliziums* 'ibrî *vom Appellativum* ḫabiru (BZAW, 160; Berlin: W. de Gruyter).

McCarter, P.K., Jr
1980   *I Samuel: A New Translation with Introduction and Commentary* (AB, 8; Garden City, NY: Doubleday).

McCarthy, D.J.
1978   *Treaty and Covenant* (AnBib, 21A; Rome: Pontifical Biblical Institute).

Mayer, W.
1995   'Die historische Einordung der "Autobiographie" des Idrimi von Alala', *UF* 27: 333-50.

Mayrhofer, M.
1965   'Ein arisch-ḫurritischer Rechtsausdruck in Alalaḫ?', *Or* 34: 336-37.

Mendelsohn, I.
1941   'The Canaanite Term for "Free Proletarian"', *BASOR* 83: 36-39.
1955   'New Light on the Ḫupšu', *BASOR* 139: 9-11.
1959   'On the Preferential Status of the Eldest Son', *BASOR* 156: 38-40.

Moor, J. de
1987   *An Anthology of Religious Texts from Ugarit* (Nisaba, 16; Leiden: E.J. Brill).

Moran, W.L.
1987   'Join the 'Apiru or Become One?', in *Studies Lambdin*: 209-12.

Na'aman, N.
1980   'The Ishtar Temple at Alalakh', *JNES* 39: 209-14.
1986   'Ḫabiru and Hebrews: The Transfer of a Social Term to the Literary Sphere', *JNES* 45: 271-88.

North, R.
1978   '*dᵉrôr*', in *TDOT*: III, 265-69.

Oppenheim, A.L.
1955   'Review of S. Smith, *The Statue of Idri-mi*', *JNES* 14: 199-200.

Parpola, S., and K. Watanabe
1988   *Neo-Assyrian Treaties and Loyalty Oaths* (SAA, 2; Helsinki: University of Helsinki Press).

Rainey, A.F.
1975   'Chapter III. Institutions: Family, Civil, and Military', in L.R. Fisher (ed.), *Ras Shamra Parallels: The Texts from Ugarit and the Hebrew Bible Volume*, II (Rome: Pontifical Biblical Institute): 69-107.
1989   'Review of W. Moran, *Les lettres d-el-Amarna: Correspondance diplomatique du pharaon*', *Bib* 70: 566-72.

Redford, D.B.
1992   *Egypt, Canaan, and Israel in Ancient Times* (Princeton: Princeton University Press).

Reiner, E.
1969   'Akkadian Treaties from Syria and Assyria', in *ANET*: 531-41.

Seux, M.-J.
1967   *Épithètes royales Akkadiennes et Sumériennes* (Paris: Letouzey et Ané).

Smith, S.
1949   *The Statue of Idri-mi* (Occasional Publications of the British Institute of Archaeology at Ankara, 1; London: British Institute of Archaeology at Ankara).

Tsevat, M.
1958   'Alalaḫiana', *HUCA* 29: 109-43.
1994   'The Hebrew Slave according to Deuteronomy 15.12-18: His Lot and the Value of his Work, with Special Attention to the Meaning of *mišneh*', *JBL* 113: 587-95.

Van Seters, J.
1975   *Abraham in History and Tradition* (New Haven: Yale University Press).
1992   *Prologue to History: The Yahwist as Historian in Genesis* (Louisville, KY: Westminster/John Knox Press).

Von Dassow, E.
1997   'Social Stratification of Alalah Under the Mitanni Empire' (doctoral dissertation, New York University).

Weinfeld, M.
1970   'The Covenant of Grant in the Old Testament and in the Ancient Near East',
            JAOS 90: 184-203.
1972   *Deuteronomy and the Deuteronomic School* (Oxford: Clarendon Press).
Westbrook, R.
1991   *Property and Family in Biblical Law* (JSOTSup, 113; Sheffield: JSOT
            Press).
Wiseman, D.J.
1953   *The Alalakh Tablets* (Occasional Publications of the British Institute of
            Archaeology at Ankara, 2; London: British Institute of Archaeology at
            Ankara).
1958   'Abban and Alalaḫ', *JCS* 12: 124-29.
1967   'Alalakh', in *AOTS*: 118-35.
1982   'Alalah', in *NBD*: 23-24.
Wiseman, D.J., and R.S. Hess
1994   'Alalakh Text 457', *UF*: 26, 501-508.
Wolf, H.M.
1967   'The Apology of Ḫattušiliš Compared with other Political Self-Justifications
            of the Ancient Near East' (PhD dissertation, Brandeis University).
Woolley, C.L.
1953   *A Forgotten Kingdom: Being a Record of the Results Obtained from the
            Excavation of Two Mounds, Atchana and Al Mina, in the Turkish Hatay*
            (Harmondsworth: Penguin Books).
1955   *Alalakh: An Account of the Excavations at Tell Atchana in the Hatay, 1937–
            1949* (Reports of the Research Committee of the Society of Antiquaries of
            London, 18; London: Society of Antiquaries).
Wright, C.J.H.
1990   *God's People in God's Land: Family, Land, and Property in the Old Testa-
            ment* (Grand Rapids: Eerdmans).
Wright, D.P.
1987   *The Disposal of Impurity: Elimination Rites in the Bible and in Hittite and
            Mesopotamian Literature* (SBLDS, 101; Atlanta: Scholars Press).
Zeeb, F.
1991a   'Studien zu den altbabylonischen Texten aus Alalaḫ I: Schuldscheine', *UF*
            23: 405-38.
1991b   'Tell Leilan und die Gründung des altbabylonischen Alalaḫ', *UF* 23: 401-
            404.
1992   'Studien zu den altbabylonischen Texten aus Alalaḫ. II: Pfandurkunden', *UF*
            24: 447-80.
1993   'Studien zu den altbabylonischen Texten aus Alalaḫ. III: Schuldabtretung-
            surkunden', *UF* 25: 461-72.
1995   'Alalaḫ VII und das Amosbuch', *UF* 27: 641-56.

EMAR: ON THE ROAD FROM HARRAN TO HEBRON

Daniel E. Fleming

Ancient Emar was situated on the wide bend of the Euphrates River
that the Bible occasionally treats as the northern bound of Israel's
sphere of interest.[1] By the thirteenth and twelfth centuries BCE, the
date of the cuneiform archives recently discovered there, Emar was
already an ancient town. Over 1000 years earlier, the town was already
known to the royal court at Ebla (Archi 1990). While the influential
archives from Mari, Ugarit, and El-Amarna have been known for
decades, and biblical scholars have considered their usefulness at
length, the texts from Emar were only published in the mid-1980s.
The Emar texts offer important new illumination for various biblical
concerns, but they also give us a chance to try the task of comparison
afresh, perhaps with some wisdom gained from past applications
drawn from similar sources.[2]

A generation ago, it was common to read confident discussions of
the historical setting for the patriarchal narratives in Genesis. Biblical
scholars made frequent reference to cuneiform texts from northern
Syria and Mesopotamia of the second millennium: Mari, Ugarit, Nuzi,
and Alalakh, along with the Amarna letters from Syria and Palestine.[3]

1. See Gen. 15.18, 'I have given your offspring this land, from the river of
Egypt up to the great river, the Euphrates River'; 1 Kgs 5.1 (4.21), 'Solomon was
sovereign over all the kingdoms from the (Euphrates) River (to) the land of the
Philistines, up to the border of Egypt'.
2. For a general introduction in English to the finds from Emar, and a somewhat different overview of biblical applications, see Margueron 1995; Fleming
1995.
3. This has been particularly common among American and Israeli scholars.
Compare Albright 1946: ch. 4, 'When Israel Was a Child', for 1600–1200 BCE;
Bright 1981: 77-87 on 'The Historical Setting of the Patriarchs'; Cross 1973: chs.
1–3 on religious origins, with heavy use of Ugarit; Malamat 1989: 29-34, and the
premise of the whole book; and Speiser 1964: xl-lii in the introduction, and

Similarities between personal names and social custom in Genesis and the cuneiform texts were understood to confirm a second-millennium setting for the biblical tales, even if these were recorded at much later dates. These comparisons have been criticized on two main grounds; that they neglect as good or better first-millennium parallels, and that distances of date, geography, and culture have been underestimated.[4]

While such critique has forced a healthy re-evaluation of the whole framework for comparison, cuneiform texts from the second millennium still offer an invaluable backdrop for the Bible. The Bible as we have it is the trove of first millennium communities in the two kingdoms of Israel and Judah, and in early Judaism after the dissolution of these states. Naturally, then, the first millennium offers the immediate setting for the Bible, and independent evidence from this period is essential for understanding both what is said and what is left unsaid. Unfortunately, the written remains from the first millennium in Syria-Palestine are meager, because the alphabet was only occasionally inscribed on durable materials.

This is where earlier Syria makes a contribution that will not be superceded by new archeological finds from the first millennium. Cuneiform writing was most often inscribed with a reed stylus on clay, a material that can survive thousands of years in the dirt debris of cities, even when unbaked. Moreover, we know from the tablets actually found that this system had spread from Mesopotamia across northern Syria by the middle of the third millennium, and 1000 years later enjoyed varying degrees of use in ancient Iran to the east, Anatolia to the north, and Palestine and even Egypt to the south.[5]

During this period, cuneiform scribes produced letters, administrative and legal documents, and other texts for practical use outside their own circle, as well as a wealth of manuals and literature that specially served to develop and pass on scribal knowledge. They worked for palaces and temples in various bureaucratic roles, and private citizens

throughout. Cross and Malamat are still active, but still represent this earlier generation and approach. Of course, this list is only a small sample.

4.   The two classic English language critiques are those of Van Seters 1975: part I, 'Abraham in History'; and Thompson 1974, especially the detailed analysis of chs. 1–4. In Germany, there was never the same confidence, though there has been a similar trend in recent years.

5.   For an overview of cuneiform use, see Black and Tait 1995: IV, 2197-2209 (2205).

could hire a scribe if they could afford it. This description over-simplifies drastically, but it should be clear that such a system would leave those who could decipher it in ages to come mountains of detailed data regarding life in the ancient Near East.

It would be nice if such written evidence were available from the immediate neighborhood of Israel during the first millennium, but it is not. At the end of the Bronze Age, shortly after 1200, there came a devastating disruption of the old societies that also paved the way for Israel's rise. The old powers were weakened or removed. Use of cuneiform virtually disappeared in the regions west of Mesopotamia proper. By the time the Assyrians could realistically expand their power in the west, the alphabet was firmly entrenched, never to be replaced. The older system had never been based on political authority, and the Assyrians would never have imagined imposing a cuneiform written culture on its provinces and vassals.

Writing from second-millennium Syria is particularly important because this region displays a closer cultural kinship with the neighborhood of Israel than does the Mesopotamian home of cuneiform. The peoples who lived between the Mediterranean and the Arabian desert shared much in common, and though the Syrian use of cuneiform was concentrated at the northern end of this band, it can still show us shared cultural features that do not pertain to Mesopotamia. Even sites further east in the Syro-Mesopotamian segment of the 'Fertile Crescent' can show similar traits more at home toward the Mediterranean.

It used to be argued that the patriarchal stories could be proven appropriate to a second-millennium setting by the mere observation of comparable notions or names in Syrian documents of the period. This reasoning fails when equally close comparisons can be found in the first millennium, or when on the biblical side the material under consideration is not unique to Genesis.[6] The early Syrian writing rather shows how people in this ancient neighborhood organized their world with words, an aspect of life that other archeological artifacts do not illuminate. This perspective should obviously be relevant to the Bible, as a written remembrance of Israel.

---

6. That is, the biblical citations are drawn from other books, showing that the features are not unique to an ancient period on this side of the comparison. See Sasson 1998. Sasson's essay was part of 'Actes de la table ronde "les traditions amorrites et la Bible"' published in *RA* 92.1.2 (1998) and 93.1 (1999).

These texts contain no references to Israel, never mind the patriarchs, and the focus of debate about Israelite origins will probably remain the evidence from archeological excavations and surveys. Nevertheless, there remain abiding questions about the larger cultural affiliations of biblical lore, questions that do have a chronological component. Does the Bible reflect in no way the culture of the second millennium? Is the biblical context in general so late (after dissolution of the two states) that it has little memory of the Israelite past? The answers to these questions will be found not simply by shifting the ground of comparison to the first millennium. Rather, we must continue to build a nuanced picture of Bronze Age (so, third- and second-millennium) cultural patterns as a baseline for evaluating the Israelite peoples and states of the Iron Age (roughly 1200–600 BCE).

Surely the largest contributor to this baseline of knowledge about western Syria in the Late Bronze Age has been Ugarit, on the Mediterranean coast. The cuneiform scribes at Ugarit used extensively an alphabetic adaptation with their native dialect, especially in recording various expressions of local religion, with an assortment of narrative and ritual elements. These texts alone, with their West Semitic language and pantheon of El, Asherah, and Baal, renovated our understanding of early Hebrew language and Israelite religion.

Although it lacks Ugarit's invaluable West Semitic texts, Emar's Akkadian documents hold added interest because of the inland location of the site. The Bible occasionally lays claim to coastal territory for Israel, but generally it denies close affinity with that region in favor of relations east and north. This preference is expressed most vividly in the ancestry claimed from Harran or Aram.

In 1964 William Hallo published an itinerary for early second-millennium travel across Mesopotamia and Syria under the title, *The Road to Emar* (Hallo 1964). The last stage of the journey reached Emar from Harran, further north in the valley of the Balikh River, a tributary of the Euphrates. Further business could have led the traveler overland west to Aleppo or south to Tadmor and on to Damascus, Hazor, and beyond. Abraham's journey from Harran to his home in Hebron assumes some such inland route, as do the return visits of his servant in search of a wife for Isaac and his grandson Jacob in flight from Esau. The tradition that placed Israel's ancestors in Harran puts Abraham on a road to Hebron that follows an ancient north–south passage. In a way not true for Ugarit, Emar belongs to that road.

1. *The Biblical Idea of Syrian Kinship*

The Bible proclaims repeatedly that Israel was rescued from the land of Egypt, but behind that notion lie two prior assertions about Israelite origins. First, Israel was not a nation of Egyptian immigrants. They were in some sense returning home to Canaan. Second, a close ethnic relationship is asserted between Israel and its immediate eastern neighbors, Edom, Moab, Ammon, and Ishmael of Arabia, all associated in turn with inland northern Syria. These peoples are sharply separated from Egypt, Philistia, and Canaan, especially as presented in the world map of Genesis 10.[7]

The book of Genesis provides a stage for traditions of Israelite origins behind the dominant escape from Egypt. Israel is accounted for in two principal identities, Abraham and Jacob, both of which assume a single core ethnicity. Northern and southern groups are bound together in a national kinship as sons of one father, Jacob, the closest ethnic connection. Genesis also sketches, however, a broader regional ethnicity in Abraham, which defines relations at increasing distances with a brother in Edom, an uncle in Arabia, and distant cousins in Moab and Ammon. One can consider explanations for the specific conflicts described in the mid-first millennium antagonisms found in the prophetic oracles against these neighbors.[8] Nevertheless, this approach risks a fragmented view that misses entirely the larger and deeper pattern that distinguishes family squabbles from struggles with outsiders.

---

7.   This tradition represents a provocative idea of Israelite identity at any date. Regardless of how old terms such as Canaan, Akkad, Hittite, etc., are applied in a later geographical sketch, in this context they belong to a coherent idea of world regions. The choice of affiliations is clear, just as in the larger narrative. Oded (1986) proposes that the distinctions between Shem, Ham, and Japhet are based on way of life, like Gen. 4.19-22. Shem would represent mobile populations, in their enmity to the settled peoples of Ham, with Japhet identified especially with those who earn their livelihood by the sea. It is not clear to me that all of Shem would have been identified by biblical authors as 'nomads', but there may be a link in the contact with the desert fringe.

8.   For instance, during the middle and later part of the first millennium, Edom encroached considerably on the land once held by the kingdom of Judah, and one early episode of this struggle is reflected in the prophecy of Obadiah (cf. Jer. 49.7-22).

Both of Israel's primary identities are provided links to northern Syria that are expressed in two distinct traditions. Abraham's family comes from Mesopotamian Ur, but they settle in Harran, in the northern part of the Euphrates basin.[9] Jacob flees to Laban at Harran, and spends years there with his mother's family.[10] He acquires two wives there, with their servants as concubines. Eleven sons are born in Syria, excepting only Benjamin.[11] Unlike his brother Esau, Jacob acquires his wealth in Syria and has to bring it back to Palestine. The region may be called Aram of the Two Rivers or Paddan (The District of) Aram,[12] and their relatives may be called Arameans.[13]

With these designations for Syria, the text reveals a first-millennium setting for the telling, without requiring an Aramean ethnic identity in the narrow sense. These contacts with Syria are attributed directly only to Abraham and Jacob, the two figures who dominate this account of Israelite ethnic identity. Isaac has no direct connection.

Genesis accounts for Israel's origins not by movement of masses, as conceived in the exodus and conquest, but by kinship. The book defines Israelite ethnicity in relation to its neighbors. The travels of Abraham and his family have been interpreted to reflect nomadic or tribal migrations, but the accounts of the patriarchs may be more useful for their provocative definition of ethnic relationships.[14] In particular, they explain the peoples who live on either side of the Jordan Valley as kin from a north Syrian stock.

The same ethnic identity with Syria appears in biblical traditions outside Genesis. Most famous is the liturgical pronouncement of Deut. 26.5, which begins *'arāmî 'ōbēd 'ābî*, a phrase that reflects a displaced and unstable condition but does not itself indicate a nomadic way of life.[15] Israel's covenant renewal at Shechem in Josh. 24.2-3 is

9. Ur is mentioned in Gen. 11.31 and 15.7; Harran in Gen. 11.31-32 and 12.4-5.

10. Gen. 27.43; 28.10; 29.4.

11. Gen. 35.18.

12. Aram Naharaim, Gen. 24.10; Paddan Aram, Gen. 25.20; 28.2, 5, 6, 7; 31.18; 33.18; 46.15; 48.7.

13. Gen. 25.20; 28.5; 31.20, 24. This identification recalls also the notion of ancestry among displaced Arameans, according to Deut. 26.5.

14. The classic study is that of Alt 1953: 126-75. Finkelstein (1988: 353) endorses Alt's model, while consciously setting aside the biblical narrative in favor of a purely archeological analysis.

15. Janzen (1994) argues convincingly that this statement emphasizes the

introduced by quotation of Yahweh: 'Your fathers lived on the other side of the river...'[16] Hosea 12.13 recalls instead the Syrian sojourn of Jacob, with focus on the fact that he married Syrian women.[17] All of these texts draw the connection with Syria by means of patriarchal kinship.

Whether in Genesis or elsewhere, whenever the Bible defines Israel by ancestry, it is given a Syrian origin.[18] From the perspective of biblical scholars hungry for illumination by outside evidence, cuneiform texts from second-millennium Syria demand comparison in many individual cases by their very similarities. The tradition of Syrian ancestry, however, should provoke the same comparison apart from specific points of contact. Uncertainty dogs the search for Israelite origins in artifacts and texts outside the Bible, but even if the whole Hebrew scriptures were created during the first millennium, it is difficult to avoid a starting point in the second. Assyrian, Aramean, and Moabite texts identify an Israelite kingdom by the ninth century, and Egypt's Merenptah stela mentions some Israelite population in the area near 1200 BCE.[19]

hunger experienced by the ancestors invoked, as a contrast to the plenty now appreciated (so, v. 10), and he translates, 'a starving Aramean was my father'. The common translation with 'wandering' is advocated by Otzen in the popular *TDOT* (Otzen 1974: 20).

16. There is no agreement about the date of this passage, in an argument that generally follows its attribution or not to Deuteronomistic writing. A recent argument for an eighth-century date and separate origin may be found in Sperling 1987.

17. In this case, most scholars tend to attribute this text to the prophet himself, so the eighth century; see, for example, Yee 1987: 229; Wolff 1990: 268; Diedrich 1977: 489.

18. This reads the Ur tradition of Gen. 11.28 and 15.7 according to the first text, which treats Ur as the ultimate background of a north Syrian family. Westermann (1985: 136) proposes that even if Ur must be understood as the Mesopotamian city ('of the Chaldeans'), it 'represents the pagan world from which Terah departed for Canaan', not in strict geographical terms, but as the ancestor of Babylon.

19. These fixed points are acknowledged even in a more skeptical history, as that of Ahlström 1993: 282-88 (Merneptah), 573-74 (Assyrian identification of Israel with Omri/Ḫumri), and 579-81 (the Mesha stela of Moab). The ninth-century stela from Tel Dan was discovered after Ahlström's volume was published, and has already provoked a voluminous bibliography. A small

It is interesting at this point to remember that early inscriptions also show connections between Israel and the lands east of the Jordan River and Dead Sea. The victory stela of King Mesha of Moab, dated to the middle of the ninth century, proclaims a new era of Moabite supremacy over lands east of the Jordan. Israel had controlled territory in this region during the preceding period.[20] At the beginning of the eighth century, several inscriptions from Kuntillet Ajrud in the southern desert voice travelers' devotion to Yahweh of Samaria and Yahweh of Teman.[21] These texts have attracted lavish attention because of the accompanying Asherah, and the reference to Teman has been taken to sustain the notion that Israel's national deity may have originated in the southern deserts toward Arabia and Sinai.[22] When the text is read by itself, the striking feature is the continuity between the worship of Yahweh at the capital of Israel, the northern kingdom, and a south-eastern inland city associated with the kingdom of Edom.[23]

The Bible refers repeatedly to Israelite populations in the east, including Makir, Reuben, and Gilead in the song of Deborah.[24] This poem addresses the time before states with kings, with a rendition of tribal identities that is independent of the well-known lists of 12.[25] I have only sketched the evidence, but the early identification of Israel

selection with bias toward English includes, Biran and Naveh 1993; Biran 1995; Cryer 1996; Halpern 1994; Sasson 1995; Schniedewind 1996.

20. Lines 4-8 refer to previous oppression of Moab by King Omri and his son, who had taken Mehadaba and occupied it for 40 years. The text goes on to celebrate the sites retaken from Israel: Aṭarot (lines 10-11), Nebo (14), and Yahaṣ (18-20). For the text and translation of the stela, with historical comment, see Jackson and Dearman 1989; Jackson 1989; Dearman 1989.

21. The texts are listed together in Davies 1991: 78-82, 8.016 and 8.021 for Teman, 8.017 for Samaria. For discussion of the texts, see McCarter 1987; Müller 1992.

22. See, e.g., van der Toorn 1996: 284-85.

23. On Edom, see Ahlström 1993: 656-64; Bartlett 1989; and Edelman 1995.

24. Judg. 5.14-17; Makir is associated with Manasseh in Josh. 13.31, and Gilead with both Manasseh and Gad in the same text (13.25, 31). Of these, only Makir is given credit for assisting Israel (notice that Manasseh is Ephraim's brother from Joseph), and the others apparently do not consider the threat relevant to their regions.

25. It is interesting that the primary differences relate to the land across the Jordan, in particular. The southern tribes of Judah and Simeon appear to have stood beyond the range of accountability, and their omission from this version of Israel is important.

with regions across the river gives credibility to the Genesis idea that
even the competing peoples there were close kin. With such a strong
orientation away from the sea, Israel may be suspected to have
affinities with peoples inland, as well as with the Canaanites nearer to
the Mediterranean.

According to the stories of ancestry in Abraham and Jacob,
northern Syria, across the Euphrates, is the cultural and ethnic source
for the Israelite and Transjordanian populations. Although this con-
ception serves a later Israelite view, it is not easily explained by first-
millennium circumstances.[26] Syria of the Euphrates basin was never
directly involved in Israelite affairs, unlike Damascus or even Hamath.
Northern Syria has no symbolic value evident for the first millennium,
as suggested for Ur of the Chaldeans.[27] Harran was a last refuge of the
Neo-Assyrian dynasty and held personal interest for the Babylonian
King Nabonidus during the late-seventh and sixth centuries, as
pointed out by Van Seters, but this prominence offers a geographical
tag at best, even if the accounts are from this period.[28] It is not clear
how by its own lights Harran explains the idea of an ethnic link with
the southern peoples. The biblical traditions that give us Harran display no association with the moon god who so preoccupied Nabonidus.

2. *Emar in Syria*

Ugarit has proved its primary importance for biblical studies many
times over, but this coastal city stands outside the inland region that
the Bible itself offers as the location of Israel's Syrian connection.
Emar, on the other hand, is situated directly in its path. Moreover,
Emar in the thirteenth century was dominated by a Semitic-speaking
population that had preserved a cultural heritage from ages long

26. For a similar evaluation of attitudes toward the 'Arameans', as encountered in Deut. 26.5, see Daniels 1990: 240. Daniels focusses on the hostile relations throughout the first millennium, though the same might be said of relations
with Moab and Edom. It is not clear that an idea of kinship depends on current
amity.

27. See Westermann 1985: 135-41. Ur can only have suggested a little-known
world of ancient Mesopotamia, without any specific contemporary significance,
by contrast with Assyria or Babylon.

28. See Van Seters 1975: 24-25, who proposes that Ur and Harran are linked
as moon god centers for a king who also spent time in the Arabian desert.

before.[29] Whereas the finds from Ugarit and Mari have palace archives as centerpieces, no proper palace was excavated at Emar, and most of the Emar texts derive from institutions independent of the king.[30] Biblical tradition insists that kingship came late to Israel, and little of the Bible was produced directly by palace functionaries. Even the histories of the monarchic period in Samuel, Kings, and Chronicles take a critical stance toward their subject. Emar's view of an old Syrian town from outside the palace provides an appropriate vantage point for comparison with Israel as the Bible knows it.

The most striking points of contact between Emar and the Bible are religious, which should not be surprising when the latter is so dominated by religious concerns. At Emar, the overwhelming majority of texts come from a building occupied by an official who identifies himself as 'the diviner of the gods of Emar'.[31] Indeed, a collection of traditional Mesopotamian manuals confirms his interest in divination, but rituals and records show an administrator responsible for religious affairs completely unrelated to the prestigious foreign specialty.[32] In a system that distinguishes palace from 'city' financial commitments,[33]

29. This continuity is visible in the fact that Emar was well-known to the archives of early second-millennium Mari and even third-millennium Ebla, rendered as Imar. See Durand 1990; Archi 1990. Personal names reflect the dominant languages spoken locally, even when naming customs do not always reflect the primary language used in a given home.

30. The texts from the excavations were published by Daniel Arnaud 1985–87. J.-Cl. Margueron, the excavator, has consistently identified the public building on the northwestern promontory of the tell as the palace; see Margueron 1979; 1995. The 22 texts found there reflect the interest of the royal family, but only one involves directly the business of the king (Emar [6.3] no. 17; texts from the excavations will be abbreviated hereafter as Emar 17, etc.).

31. This title is found in the colophons to lexical and divination texts copied from Mesopotamian custom, and gathered by Arnaud as Emar 604 (see nos. 1, 4, and 6). Margueron identifies the structure as a temple, though the form is ambiguous, with three smaller rooms along the eastern side of a long hall. A prominent entry into the long hall follows the main axis, as often found in temples. For interpretation as a house, see Werner 1994: 108-109. There is no doubt that the proprietor is a religious official, so the main question is whether offerings were made there.

32. See the administrative texts nos. 274-368, and the ritual texts 369-535, from the diviner's archive. My book on Emar calendar rituals (Fleming 2000) discusses the nature of the diviner and his archive at length in Chapter 2.

33. This distinction is perhaps clearest in the parallel provision for the *zukru*

the diviner of the gods represents the city in all its religious activities.[34] At the center stand a set of festivals celebrated by the citizens of Emar, evidently old Syrian rites for long-standing Syrian gods.[35] None of these events is known from adjacent religious traditions in Mesopotamia, Anatolia, or Ugarit, and the texts themselves have no duplicates from other sites. While the diviner primarily served the separate interests of 'city' institutions not administered by the palace, his work touched the religious life of a wider circle. Ritual texts from the diviner's archive include one royal procession and Hittite rites for imperial officials or foreign residents.[36] The rituals do reflect the political dominance of the local king and the Hittite overlords, but the administrative texts from the archive show that the diviner was employed by neither.[37]

Emar's diviner of the gods singled out only a small number of rituals for outline on one separate tablet, and these include some of the longest texts. Only such texts are found in multiple copies, and most of these are designated as 'festivals' with the Mesopotamian marker. The three longest texts with the largest ritual tablets are the only festivals said to be celebrated by the 'sons' or citizenry of Emar: the *zukru*, and the installations of priestesses for the storm god and the goddess Ashtartu.[38] Another set of festivals is celebrated by the

festival (Emar 373), which separates supply by palace and king from that by 'city' and *bīt ilī* ('house of the gods'?).

34. The association of the diviner with 'city' ritual is seen best in a text that traces six months of activities under the rubric, 'the rites of the city' (Emar 446.1). The diviner has the chief interest in portions given from offerings (see ll. 28, 39, 26*, 44, 51, 53, 64, 65, 82, 95, 102, 116).

35. For further discussion, see Fleming 1992a: 201-63; 1996.

36. The *imištu* (procession) of the king is Emar 392, with only the beginning of the text preserved. For this reading, see Fleming 1992b: 62-63. The Hittite rites are numbers 471-490, and are discussed in Arnaud 1987; Laroche 1988; Lebrun 1988.

37. Emar 274-368 include inventories, memoranda, and various other records that reflect a broad administration of religious shrines and activities. They show little or no interest in sites identified by the palace or Hittite gods, and no indication of a single employer. The letters found in the diviner's archive (nos. 258-273) indicate close contacts with Hittite officials who are recognized as superior in a general sense, but the diviner does not appear to serve any larger institution.

38. These are texts 373, 369, and 370. I discuss the *zukru* at length in Fleming 2000, and the next in Fleming 1992a.

citizens of a nearby village called Shatappi as *kissu* rites, perhaps for the 'throne' of individual deities.[39]

Rather than describe all the major ritual texts and categories from the diviner's archive, examination of biblical comparisons can be pursued in a more focussed manner from one Emar rite, the *zukru*.[40] Emar's *zukru* occurs in two very distinct versions, each presented in a separate text. The longest ritual text at Emar, originally between 260 and 280 lines, celebrates the *zukru* as a seven-day festival every seven years. In this unusual calendar, the *zukru* begins at the full moon of a month called SAG.MU, 'the head of the year'. By this definition, the festival marks the turn of the year counted by moons, observed at full light rather than at the initial appearance of the lunar crescent, so that the *zukru* deserves consideration in discussion of ancient 'new year'.

The full schedule of the long *zukru* festival is understood best as a series of expansions from a single ritual event. On the first day of the *zukru*, the full moon of the month SAG.MU in the seventh year, all the gods of Emar are brought outside the city to a shrine of upright stones called *sikkānu*, a Syrian term known already at Ugarit and Mari.[41] The stones are prepared by anointing with oil and blood, before Dagan, the head of Emar's pantheon, is transported in a cart between them. This procession, which honors the chief god in the presence of his human and divine company, initiates a grand return to the city.[42]

Although no precise development can be defined, it is nevertheless evident that the *zukru* festival is celebrated by several calendrical expansions of this one rite, and that none of the elaboration is intrinsic to the *zukru* itself. The ritual schedule of the *zukru* has as its core the first full moon of the year. This moment is then extended into a seven-day feast and framed by a seven-year interval. The seven-day feast carries with it special attention to the final day, which therefore

39. Texts 385-388. The reading as 'throne' would reflect a western Semitic vocalization without marking of the final vowel; see Fleming 1992a: 258-59.

40. See Fleming 1997 and esp. pp. 431-36.

41. See Dietrich, Loretz, and Mayer 1989; Durand 1985. Durand (1998) also discusses the related phenomena, the *ḫumūsum* and the *rāmum*. For a general treatment of the phenomenon with focus on Israel, see Mettinger 1995.

42. Dagan has long been known to be the head of the pantheon along the Syrian portion of the Euphrates River, and at Emar he is dominant in ritual, in curses from legal documents, and in theophoric personal names (with references to deities). See Fleming 1992a: 240-47.

repeats the visit to the stones. With expansion beyond the cycle of seasons, two more primary occasions are added: departure from annual routine at the first full moon of the sixth year and 40 days later a consecration of the coming seventh year. They repeat the same celebration of Dagan at the *sikkānu* stones on both of these days. Beyond the primary framework of the festival which is built around the rites at the shrine of stones, additional days are set apart for sacrifice and offerings to the gods in their own temples. These include the days that fill out the festival week of the *zukru* proper, a preparatory day before the full moon, and days both one month and one day before consecration of the year.

Expansion of the time devoted to *zukru* celebration repeatedly draws attention to the anticipated event without producing the *zukru* itself, so that its value is increased with the waiting. This value is calculated also by the expense of the party, which in this case far outstrips any other event, thanks to joint sponsorship by city and king, with the larger bill going to the monarch.[43]

The essential *zukru* celebration, however, lies in departure from the city to the upright stones and subsequent return. In a tradition common to Syria-Palestine and Anatolia, the stones represent assembled gods and derive from sacred places in open air, before enclosure within city walls and temples.[44] When Emar brings Dagan and the images of all the pantheon out to the shrine of upright stones, new goes out to meet old. Worship of Dagan as father of gods and humans is recognized as prior to construction of the city, while the secure walls and grand temples of the city are celebrated as a benefit to all.[45]

---

43. A line added to the edge of the tablet observes that 50 calves and 700 lambs are slaughtered throughout the festival, amounts that indicate a scale comparable even to the larger Hittite events. Haas 1994: 649 and n. 89, observes among the largest numbers given, 1000 sheep in a ritual from Ḫattušili III and 1000 sheep and 50 oxen for the festival for Telipinu in Kašḫa and Ḫanḫana. On the latter, see Haas and Jakob-Rost 1984.

44. At Emar, the identification of *sikkānu* stone and deity is explicit in the identification of two individual examples by name, as 'the *sikkānu* of Ḫebat' (Emar 369.34-35A; 373.158-59) and 'the *sikkānu* of dNIN.URTA' (Emar 375.16). In one case, the stone is even marked with the sign for deity: dSi-ka-ni ša dḪé-bat (373.159).

45. This interpretation is elaborated in Fleming 2000. As a celebration of both the city and the priority of the gods to the city, the *zukru* resembles both the ancient Mesopotamian á-ki-ti (*akītu*) and many Anatolian rites preserved in Hittite

The diviner's archive preserves a second, much shorter version of the *zukru* in four fragmented copies, not called a festival.[46] This *zukru* takes place every year at the full moon of a month named Zarati, most simply understood to be the same time of year as the full moon in the long text.[47] While this annual *zukru* also extends to a seventh day, the text does not mention the expensive feast that fills the intervening week in the other. The short text presents a more modest calendar and outlay, without contribution from the king, but procession of Dagan between the upright stones again stands at center.[48]

Emar's *zukru* practice provides the solution to an old riddle from Mari, where a famous letter regarding king Zimri-Lim's debt to neighboring Aleppo begins with repeated mention of some *zukrum*.[49] A Mari official reports that negotiations with a man named Alpan have been concluded, with witnessed statements by all parties, so that Zimri-Lim should now act. Alpan turns out to be a sheikh from the tribal Yaminite people, a group which Zimri-Lim had battled in the first years of his reign. The Yaminite chief requires that Zimri-Lim give a *zukrum* to the storm god Adad, a condition that the Mari king is ready to grant only when Alpan has sworn before witnesses that he

tradition. See Cohen (1993: 401-406) for the first, and Carter (1962), for the texts involved in the second.

46. Emar 375, including both sides of the tablet, against the original publication by Arnaud. In this case, my reading of the set is so different from the published version that readers should consult the new edition in the Mesopotamian Civilizations volume for even a basic notion of the text.

47. The month appears to coincide with one of those in the text for six months, when the diviner scatters seed and there is an offering to Dagan as 'Lord of the Seed' (Emar 446.50-53). The name Zarati could be explained as 'Sowing' (root *zrʿ*). Emar evidence suggests at least two other matched names in parallel calendars: Abi (text 452) and Marzaḫāni (text 446), (Ḫiyaru, cf. text 463) and Ḫalma (446). Niqali (text 373, etc.) and ᵈNIN.KUR (446) also may hold equivalent positions in independent local calendars.

48. It is interesting to find that the main supplier of sacrificial animals is 'the city', so far as the broken text allows a conclusion. As in the major festival, the city has much more modest means than the palace, and the event reflects these limitations.

49. The tablet consists of two fragments, A.1121 + A.2731, now joined in Lafont 1984. The top piece was published by Dossin and Lods 1950. Malamat (1980: 73) had already suggested that the two fragments were related. Sasson (1994) discusses the relationship of this letter to two others sent by the same writer, Nur-Sin.

ĺwill not revolt. This statement has now been obtained.[50]

The letter presents the *zukrum* as a ritual component of treaty confirmation, unique among the diverse treaty elements now known from Mari.[51] Since Alpan requests it, the *zukrum* appears to belong to Yaminite rather than Mari custom, and Adad appears to be the god of Alpan, who lives in the vicinity of Aleppo. When the sheikh promises peace, Mari's king gives the Yaminite god a ritual acknowledgment that must correspond in some essential way to the *zukru* given to Dagan at Emar, though without any evident calendar setting.

Two homonymous roots could account for the word itself, *zkr* as 'male' or 'to speak, mention, invoke', Akkadian *zikaru* and *zakāru*, both with Hebrew cognates. Emar's ritual texts show no sign of any 'male' animal sacrificed as the center of that event, so that the verb for speech represents the more promising alternative. The *zukru* should be the spoken complement to the concrete obligation and worship expressed in offering. Emar makes this address to Dagan the center-piece of its ritual calendar, when the town pays respects to its chief god.

What is the specific intent of the *zukru* speech? At both Emar and Mari, the verb *zakāru* is used for swearing oaths by gods, and finali-zation of treaties is represented as 'swearing the oath' (*nīš ilī zakārum*).[52] Zimri-Lim agrees to confirm his treaty with Alpan by giving this word to the god of his new partner. The Mari *zukrum*

---

50. Lines 6-12: 'About giving the *zukrum* to Addu: Alpan said to me in the presence of Zū-Ḫatnim, Abī-šadî, and (a third person), "Give the *zukrum* (with?) the...and the cattle". In the presence of the...-men, my lord has told me to give the *zukrum*, (saying) "He must not oppose me at any future time". I have provided witnesses for him. My lord should be aware.'

51. Newly published documents from Mari have vastly extended our knowledge of procedures for establishing political bonds, focussed on oath-taking (*nīš ilim zakārum*) in the major cities and on slaughtering an ass (*ḫayāram qaṭālum*) among so-called 'Amorite' populations, especially in the west. See Durand 1991 with accompanying articles by D. Charpin, F. Joannès, J.-R. Kupper, and J. Eidem; Durand (1988: 119-22) on the *ḫiyārum* rite as 'ass' sacrifice; Charpin 1988: 143-44, on treaty terminology and procedure; also Villard 1990–91; Finet 1993. B. Lafont (1999) gathers the most recent evidence.

52. One probable Emar text, not from the documented excavations, involves an oath that is sworn by witnesses regarding a private financial crisis: 'The kinsmen have assembled and sworn an oath (*ni-iš* DINGIR^{meš} *iz$^{!}$-ku-ru*) concerning his (financial) distress' (RE 96.22-24, in Beckman 1996: 119).

appears to be an oath ceremony. Several centuries later, Emar has removed the second human party and political negotiation and applied the *zukru* directly to relations with their god Dagan. If the *zukru* is an oath, it is not simply by the god but to the god, under the same divine authority that bound the parties to a treaty.

3. *The* zukru *and the Bible*

Even this summary of the Emar *zukru* should suggest various similarities to concepts and practices found in the Bible. Comparisons may be drawn at several levels. The first and most striking is the essential act as illuminated by the Mari and Emar evidence together. In spite of ubiquitous citation of the treaty context as inspiration for the biblical covenants with Yahweh, it has been difficult to find treaty-like arrangements with the god him or herself.[53] Emar supplies an important example with substantial ritual context when it applies the *zukru* treaty commitment to divine instead of foreign relations.

This idea of a treaty-like bond between a people and their god has long been considered the unique feature of the biblical covenant with Yahweh. Past scholarship treated this as an early Israelite patent,[54] and some now treat the covenant with God as the creation of postexilic Judaism.[55] There is nothing about Israelite or Jewish religion that should make the treaty with God unique to this one group, any more than the approach to deity with temples, altars, priests, and sacrifices. The trends toward exclusion of other gods and of divine images offer no special explanation for covenant. Other Near Eastern examples are therefore to be expected.[56]

Placement of the *zukru* outside the city at a shrine of upright stones immediately recalls the various biblical references to *maṣṣēbôt* and

---

53. The initial comparisons included Mendenhall 1954; Hillers 1969; Baltzer 1971; McCarthy 1978; Kalluveettil 1982. Early dissent was expressed in Germany by Perlitt 1969; Kutsch 1973.

54. For instance, M. Noth proposed that during a period before monarchy, Israel was united as an amphyctiony by common worship of Yahweh under such a covenant; see Noth 1954: part I, 'Israel als Zwölfstämmebund'.

55. This analysis owes much to the work of Perlitt (1969), and now represents a highly influential view. See, for example, the general works on the Pentateuch by Blenkinsopp 1992: 21, etc.; Blum 1990: 202-203, etc.

56. The five cases argued by T.J. Lewis would not then be surprising; see Lewis 1996.

similar stones, especially those approved for Israelite use.[57] Anointing
of stones in the *zukru* and in one of the Emar installations resembles
Jacob's procedure at Bethel, and when the installation applies the
identical practice to a priestess, the whole biblical tradition of anointing priests comes in view.[58] The Emar *zukru* is said to be given by the
citizenry of Emar, and the dominant participants are the gathered
populace. Neither the king, who supplies so much of the materials for
the seventh-year event, nor the diviner, who records the text, has any
designated role. The Israelite festivals similarly treat the assembled
people as the essential participants, in a ritual tradition that is
ambivalent about the religious centrality of kings.[59]

One more cluster of comparisons is associated with the timing of
the *zukru*, particularly interesting because the new evidence relates to
biblical definitions most fully elaborated in the priestly law that is
often understood to portray only postexilic religion.[60] Emar reaffirms
its relationship to its chief god every year at the autumn equinox for
seven days at the full moon of what one text identifies as the turn of
the year.[61] The seven-day interval, the special attention to the first and
last days, and the calendar setting resemble the feasts of Unleavened
Bread and Booths, especially in Leviticus and Numbers (Lev. 23.5-8;
34-36, 39, 41; Num. 28.16-25; 29.12-35). In its seven-year cycle, the
timing of the *zukru* matches exactly the covenant renewal at the feast
of Booths prescribed for Israel in Deuteronomy 31.[62]

57. See, for example, the witness stones at Sinai (Exod. 24.4), Mt Ebal (Deut.
27.2-4, 8), the Jordan River (Josh. 4.3-9, 21), and Shechem (Josh. 24.26-27).

58. See 373.34, 61, 167; 375.14 (*zukru*); 369.4, 20-21 (installation, anointing
of priestess), cf. 35A (anointing of stone by priestess). The installation rite
involves pouring oil on the top or head, like Jacob at Bethel (Gen. 28.18; 35.14),
and like the ordained high priest in the priestly law (Exod. 29.7; Lev. 8.12). It
should not be necessary to consider the biblical tradition of anointing priests an
exilic adaptation from the earlier anointing of kings; see Fleming 1998a.

59. The principal descriptions are found in Exod. 23.14-17; 34.18, 22-23; Lev.
23; Num. 28-29; Deut. 16.1-17.

60. The classic statement is found in Wellhausen 1885: 83-120 (Chapter 3 on
'The Sacred Feasts').

61. That is, the festival calls the month SAG.MU, 'the head of the year'. In later
Mesopotamian lore, the SAG.MU is not a month and marks both spring and fall
(see Cohen 1993: 7 and n. 1), but as a month-name, this head could only occur
once a year.

62. Deut. 31.10-11: 'At the end of seven years, at the time of the year of
release, during the feast of Booths, when all Israel comes to appear in the

Emar's premier calendar rite and the two major events of the religious year in the Bible share important features, but they are far from equivalent, even setting aside their different names. Above all, the *zukru* leaves the confines of Emar in order to celebrate the city with return, much like the Mesopotamian *akītu* festival. The shrine of stones is preserved from the religious landscape of Emar before city and temples, not derived from the city focus. The Israelite festivals preserved in the biblical law claim origin in an identity not defined by a city center and are not concerned with city and temple.

This distinction of the urban setting needs to be pursued across the whole constellation of comparisons suggested above. The Jerusalem temple represents the clearest expression of an urban religious perspective in the Bible. References to Yahweh's temple and city as the center of his presence in Israel (Ps. 127.1; Jer. 26.6; etc.) echo an old Sumerian and Babylonian notion that is inextricably bound to the urban framework for religion. While the ritual law of the Bible may be understood to be filtered through a fixed Jerusalem sanctuary from before or after the exile, the tradition of three annual festivals does not originate in this city context. These festivals are not defined by the functions of either sanctuary or priests, unlike Yom Kippur in Leviticus 16, with atoning sacrifice by the high priest at its core, performed in the sanctuary's holiest place.

None of the comparisons between the *zukru* and biblical rites derives from a clearly urban setting, and several point to religious traditions in both sources preserved from other, presumably earlier, settings. Both the diviner's archive and the Bible suggest a long interaction of city centers with smaller towns and villages, along with more mobile populations. Fortified cities with enclosed temples represent a long-term innovation, though traits from other milieux coexist with temples in city religious life.

One of these is the shrine of stones outside city walls. At Emar, this location stands out first of all by its open space. Temples enclose the deity and the point of ritual encounter, and by enclosure restrict access to both. Such stone shrines are found in both archeological and literary contexts from Palestine through Syria and Anatolia, though they are not characteristic of Mesopotamian religion.[63] As mentioned

presence of Yahweh your God at the place he chooses, you shall recite this instruction in front of all Israel, in their hearing.'

63. See the discussion and bibliography in Fleming 1992a: 76-78. In early

already, the Bible describes shrines with multiple stones at Sinai (Exod. 24.4), on Mt Ebal above Shechem (Deut. 27.2-4), and at the Jordan River (Josh. 4.2, 9, 20). These are not conceived as temples, nor are the sites with single stones set up by Jacob and Joshua at Bethel and Shechem (Gen. 28.18; 35.14; Josh. 24.26).

Throughout the ancient Near East, organization of populations into large cities was accompanied by various mechanisms for centralizing government. In Mesopotamia, this phenomenon led to the prominence of both rulers and temples in city leadership.[64] As such urban institutions gather power and resources, they also dominate the religious center. When public religious rites for a city population leave out the kings and temples that dominate city life, or leave them at the margins, these rites remember an older society.

The situation in the Bible is complicated because the period of royal government was followed by a permanent loss of sovereignty, after Babylon ended the line of kings in Judah. The spring and fall festivals of Moses' law share this combination of popular assembly and absence of kings. In every version, their celebration is defined not by professional priests or any leadership but by the gathered people. It is important, then, to observe the absence of a high priest as much as the absence of kings, since the priests in Jerusalem rose to new political prominence in the Persian province.[65]

It is true that the mention of the supervising priests is sporadic, often assumed, but the descriptions of Leviticus often specify their role. The priest stands front and center in the long description of the Day of Atonement in Leviticus 16, though he is omitted from the calendar of ch. 23.[66] When ch. 23 introduces a full calendar of annual

---

Palestine, the best example may be a row of ten upright stones at Middle Bronze Gezer; see Dever 1973. The phenomenon is nearly ubiquitous across the region through the Bronze and Iron Ages, however, as shown by the evidence assembled in Mettinger 1995: 143-91.

64. In southern Mesopotamia, the early cities were characterized by temple leadership, with kings ascendant as the third millennium progressed; see Postgate 1992, and Foster 1993. In regions further north and west, power was focused mainly in kingship; see Steinkeller 1993; Archi 1982.

65. See Meyers (1987: 547) who states: 'Throughout the entire Persian period one may observe a shifting pattern in the relationship between ecclesiastical and secular control of Yehud'. The ambitions of the high priests find an apex in Zech. 6.9-11, where Joshua is to be given a ruling crown.

66. Perhaps this shorter treatment does assume the earlier rendition.

rites, the presence of the priest is required explicitly for the offering of first fruits and for the feast of Weeks, but not for Passover, Unleavened Bread, and Booths, the events attached to the two axes of the year.[67]

Deuteronomy expects the presence of kings who sit under the authority of a law held by Levite-priests, but the whole ritual calendar of ch. 16 gives neither a defining role. Exodus 23 and 34 spend little space on the festivals, but are independent of the other traditions and difficult to explain as postexilic.[68] Whatever their date, these Exodus traditions care little about the institutions that governed the region at any period; neither the ten commandments nor the variety of religious and community law that follows (20.1–23.19), nor the renewed commands of Exod. 34.10-28.

At Emar, the real wealth and power of the king is shown in the amount he spends on the seventh-year *zukru*, but he has no active ritual role in this or any of the other events designated as festivals. A king reigns, but these particular religious traditions do not appear to have their origin in the state under royal rule, even where they do assume a town setting. Likewise, there is clearly a temple of Dagan at Emar, with permanent personnel to staff it, and we need not imagine that the many sacrifices of the *zukru* festival were executed without such ritual professionals. What is significant is that no individuals or groups of specialists play a role that is prominent or indispensible enough to merit mention in the recorded event.

The same is true of the biblical events whose calendar compares most closely to the *zukru*. The spring and fall festivals of Moses' law share this combination of popular assembly and absence of kings. In every version, their celebration is defined not by professional priests or any leadership but by the gathered people. This characteristic of the texts does not mean that priests and kings did not participate, or in certain periods even claim essential roles, but the events at the core do not seem to derive from service of palace, temple, or governing institutions that centralize power in large urban settings.

It is more difficult to account for Emar's unusual application of

67. See Lev. 23.10 for the first fruits: 'you must bring to the priest a sheaf from the first fruits of your harvest' for him to wave as an offering (v. 11); v. 20 for the feast of Weeks, 'the priest must wave them (two lambs) over the bread of the first fruits as a wave offering before Yahweh…'

68. This is the argument of Van Seters 1996.

treaty rites to relations with Dagan himself. The *zukrum* in the Mari letter belongs to Yaminite custom, not to the city-state or kingdom, but Emar's use of the *zukru* is found in city ritual, though not identified with centralizing institutions. At least, the commitment to the local god does not display any obvious urban motivation, and does not require the celebration of the city which is joined to it. The scheduling parallels are even harder to account for and do not require a source either within or outside urban frameworks. Evidently, the priestly law preserves calendar traditions that need not be explained by adaptation of the Babylonian calendar, and that stand in long continuity with custom shared across at least the inland band of western Syria-Palestine.[69]

4. *Conclusion*

This comparison of the Emar *zukru* ritual with biblical religious practice cannot produce specific attributes characteristic of inland Syria and Palestine but excluding the coast. Speculation would be foolhardy because of limited evidence, first of all. Nevertheless, the similarities can be accounted for in part by the regional culture shared north and south along the route between Harran and Hebron. Evaluation of relationships between northern Syria and southern Syria-Palestine too often neglects the distinction of coastal and inland areas.

It is increasingly popular to identify the first Israelites as Canaanites based on continuities of material culture, but the peculiar biblical idea of kinship along an inland track suggests that definitions must be more carefully drawn.[70] During the Late Bronze Age 'Canaan' referred to a region along the coast of the Mediterranean from the Sinai north just past Byblos, apparently including Damascus but not the Transjordan.[71]

---

69. For adoption of the Babylonian calendar in the sixth century, see de Vaux 1960: I, 281-82; after Auerbach 1952.

70. On this identification of Israel with Canaan in the realm of religion, see Smith 1990: xxii-xxiii, referring to material culture. Van der Toorn 1996: 187, allows that the ethnic makeup of earliest Israel was not homogeneous, but the majority 'did not differ from the Canaanites, apart from the fact that they were socially uprooted and in pursuit of a new social environment'.

71. This is the definition of Rainey (1996) who writes specifically to rebut Lemche 1991: 31, 39-40, and 50-51. It still remains unclear how universal and uniform was the use of the term 'Canaan' for any specific site and with any specific set of bounds.

This regional identification was not based on a political entity or perceived kinship, and was most often applied by those outside, namely the Egyptian empire. We do not know whether the inhabitants of individual old cities like Shechem and Jerusalem would have identified themselves as Canaanites, or whether they identified more with the peoples of the coast or with inland groups.[72] The hill country of Palestine had links to two distinct cultural zones, which the name Canaan does not circumscribe.

Emar also yields significant biblical comparisons because it is a smaller town that preserves many ancient social and religious institutions side by side with adaptations to local monarchy and distant empire. These features survive especially because most of the Emar texts come from outside royal circles. In this respect also, Emar may stand closer to ancient Israel than does Ugarit.

Texts from second-millennium Syria will continue to be one of the most valuable resources for research on Israelite origins. The undeniable similarities are founded on an overlapping regional culture that is reflected in the range of the West Semitic language group. At the same time, the nature of the comparisons will turn out to be more diverse than first assumed, as more evidence becomes available. This diversity will reflect contrasting Syrian regions, especially coastal and inland, and will follow different social and political frameworks. Ugarit and Emar display both contrasts.

Ugarit has allowed tremendous progress toward explaining the context for Israelite religion, particularly in the roles of El and Baal. These divine names do reflect the Canaanite world, but Yahweh seems in all traditions to come from inland.[73] For van der Toorn, Yahweh is the contribution of a minority population with inland roots, and a Canaanite identity dominates both Israelite culture and religion (van der Toorn 1996: 187). It may not be possible at present to

---

72. The Amarna letters from and relating to these cities do not provide the evidence to resolve this question one way or another.

73. Yahweh is first of all associated with Sinai/Horeb in the southern desert, and he seems to have enjoyed some special recognition in the southern Transjordan (Deut. 33.2, Sinai/Seir/Paran; Judg. 5.4-5, Seir/Edom/Sinai/Israel; Hab. 3.3, Teman/Paran). Indeed, these have long been identified as southern, but we must recall also that they are separated from the Mediterranean littoral. Notice also that according to Genesis, Israel's closest kin is Edom, his very brother, again in the south.

determine the true size and influence of such a 'minority' in Iron I Age Israel. Yahweh's established popularity among the common people by the later monarchy in both north and south suggests more than the recent application of political power by those who rule. The biblical notion of kinship with the peoples of inland Syria-Palestine, including the desert fringe, perhaps comes from the same non-Canaanite element.

Emar's *zukru* commitment to Dagan, celebrated by the gathered populace at a shrine of stones outside city and temple, may likewise belong to specifically inland religious traditions from the peoples who line the fringes of the great Arabian desert. So far as Emar provides an early precedent for Israel's treaty *with* their God, the comparison may suggest that this Israelite concept, so central to biblical religion, derives from the same setting as the name Yahweh, both foreign to Canaan and the coast. Perhaps new texts from Syria will provide the answers.

Appendix: The Calendar of the Grand Emar Zukru Festival

1. Last standard annual celebration.
   6th year, first month (SAG.MU = Head of the Year), 15th day (full moon)
   —go out to stones

2. Consecration of the year before the grand *zukru*.
   6th year, first month, 25th day
   6th year, second month (Niqali), 24th-25th days
   —go out to stones on 25th

3. Grand *zukru* festival itself
   7th year, first month, 14th day as preparation
   7th year, first month, 15th day, start of *zukru* proper
   —go out to stones
   7th year, first month, festival week of seven days starting on the 15th
   7th year, first month, seventh day of festival week
   —go out to stones

BIBLIOGRAPHY

Ahlström, G.W.
1993   *The History of Ancient Palestine* (JSOTSup, 146; Sheffield: JSOT
            Press).
Albright, W. F.
1946   *From the Stone Age to Christianity* (Baltimore: The Johns Hopkins
            University Press).
Alt, A.
1953   'Erwägungen über die Landnahme der Israeliten in Palästina', in *Kleine
            Schriften zur Geschichte des Volkes Israel* (Munich: C.H. Beck): 126-
            75.
Archi, A.
1982   'About the Organization of the Eblaite State', *Studi Eblaiti* 5: 201-20.
1990   'Imâr au IIIᵉ millénaire d'après les archives d'Ebla', *MARI* 6: 21-38.
Arnaud, D.
1985–87   *Recherches au pays d'Aštata, Emar VI.1-4* (Paris: Editions Recherche
            sur les Civilisations).
1987   'Les hittites sur le moyen-Euphrate: protecteurs et indigènes',
            in *Hethitica VIII: Festschrift E. Laroche* (Louvain-la-neuve: Peeters):
            9-27.
Auerbach, E.
1952   'Die babylonische Datierung im Pentateuch und das Alter des Priester-
            Kodex', *VT* 2: 334-42.
Baltzer, K.
1971   *The Covenant Formulary in Old Testament, Jewish, and Early
            Christian Writings* (Oxford: Basil Blackwell).
Bartlett, J.R.
1989   *Edom and the Edomites* (JSOTSup, 77; Sheffield: JSOT Press).
Beckman, G.
1996   *Texts from the Vicinity of Emar* (Padova: Sargon srl).
Biran, A.
1995   'The Tel Dan Inscription: A New Fragment', *IEJ* 45: 3-18.
Biran, A., and J. Naveh
1993   'An Aramaic Stele Fragment from Tel Dan', *IEJ* 43: 81-88.
Black, J.A., and W.J. Tait
1995   'Archives and Libraries in the Ancient Near East', *CANE*: IV, 2197-
            2209.
Blenkinsopp, J.
1992   *The Pentateuch* (New York: Doubleday).
Blum, E.
1990   *Studien zur Komposition des Pentateuch* (Berlin: W. de Gruyter).
Bright, J.
1981   *A History of Israel* (Philadelphia: Westminster Press, 2nd edn).
Carter, C.W.
1962   'Hittite Cult Inventories' (PhD dissertation, University of Chicago).

Charpin, D.
1988   *Archives épistolaires de Mari*, I/2 (Paris: Editions Recherche sur les Civilisations): 143-44.

Cohen, M.E.
1993   *The Cultic Calendars of the Ancient Near East* (Bethesda, MD: CDL Press).

Cross, F. M.
1973   *Canaanite Myth and Hebrew Epic* (Cambridge, MA: Harvard University Press).

Cryer, F.
1996   'Of Epistemology, Northwest Semitic Epigraphy and Irony: The "*bytdwd*/House of David" Inscription Revisited', *JSOT* 69: 3-17.

Daniels, D.R.
1990   'The Creed of Deuteronomy 26 Revisited', in J.A. Emerton (ed.), *Studies in the Pentateuch* (Leiden: E.J. Brill): 231-42.

Davies, G.I.
1991   *AHI*.

Dearman, J.A.
1989   'Historical Reconstruction and the Mesha Inscription', in *SMIM*: 155-210.

Dever, W.G.
1973   'The Gezer Fortifications and the "High Place": An Illustration of Stratigraphic Methods and Problems', *PEQ* 105: 68-70.

Diedrich, F.
1977   *Die Anspielungen auf die Jakob-Tradition in Hosea 12,1–13,3* (Würzburg: Echter Verlag).

Dietrich, M., O. Loretz and W. Mayer
1989   '*Sikkanum* "Betyle"', *UF* 21: 133-39.

Dossin, G., and Ad. Lods
1950   'Une tablette inédite de Mari, intéressante pour l'histoire du prophétisme Sémitique', in H.H. Rowley (ed.), *Studies in Old Testament Prophecy* (Edinburgh: T. & T. Clark): 104-106.

Durand, J.-M.
1985   'Le culte des bétyles en Syrie', in *Studies Birot*: 79-84.
1988   *Archives épistolaires de Mari*, I/1 (Paris: Editions Recherche sur les Civilisations): 119-22.
1990   'La cité-état d'Imâr à l'époque des rois de Mari', *MARI* 6: 39-92.
1991   'Précurseurs syriens aux protocoles néo-assyriens: considérations sur la vie politique aux Bords-de-l'Euphrate', in *Studies Garelli*: 13-72.
1998   'Réalités amorrites et traditions bibliques', *RA* 92: 3-39.

Edelman, D.V. (ed.)
1995   *You Shall Not Abhor an Edomite for He is Your Brother* (Atlanta: Scholars Press).

Finet, A.
1993   'Le sacrifice de l'âne en Mésopotamie', in J. Quaegebeur (ed.), *Ritual and Sacrifice in the Ancient Near East* (Leuven: Peeters): 135-42.

Finkelstein, I.
1988   *The Archaeology of the Israelite Settlement* (Jerusalem: Israel Exploration Society).

Fleming, D.
1992a   *The Installation of Baal's High Priestess at Emar* (Atlanta: Scholars Press).
1992b   'A Limited Kingship: Late Bronze Emar in Ancient Syria', *UF* 24: 62-63.
— 1995   'More Help from Syria: Introducing Emar to Biblical Studies', *BA* 58: 139-47.
1996   'The Emar Festivals: City Unity and Syrian Identity under Hittite Hegemony', *Emar*: 81-121.
— 1997   'Rituals from Emar', *COS*: I, 427-43.
1998a   'The Biblical Tradition of Anointing Priests', *JBL* 117: 401-14.
1998b   'Mari and the Possibilities of Biblical Memory', *RA* 92: 41-78.
— 2000   *Time at Emar: The Cultic Calendar and the Rituals from the Diviner's Archive* (Mesopotamian Civilizations, 11; Winona Lake, IN: Eisenbrauns).

Foster, B.
1993   'Management and Administration in the Sargonic Period', in M. Liverani (ed.), *Akkad: The First World Empire* (Padua: Sargon srl): 25-40.

Haas, V., and L. Jakob-Rost
1984   'Das Festritual des Gottes Telipinu in Ḫanḫana und in Kašḫa: ein Beitrag zum hethitischen Festkalendar', *AoF* 11: 10-91, 204-36.

Haas, V.
1994   *Geschichte der hethitischen Religion* (Leiden: E.J. Brill).

Hallo, W.W.
1964   'The Road to Emar', *JCS* 18: 57-88.

Halpern, B.
1994   'The Stela from Dan: Epigraphic and Historical Considerations', *BASOR* 296: 63-80.

Hillers, D.R.
1969   *Covenant: The History of a Biblical Idea* (Baltimore: The Johns Hopkins University Press).

Jackson, K.P.
1989   'The Language of the Mesha' Inscription', *SMIM*: 96-130.

Jackson, K.P., and J.A. Dearman
1989   'The Text of the Mesha' Inscription', *SMIM*: 93-95.

Janzen J.G.
— 1994   'The "Wandering Aramean" Reconsidered', *VT* 44: 359-75.

Kalluveettil, P.
- 1982   *Declaration and Covenant: A Comprehensive Review of Covenant Formulae from the Old Testament and the Ancient Near East* (Rome: Pontifical Biblical Institute).

Kutsch, E.
1973   *Verheissung und Gesetz. Untersuchungen zum sogenannten 'Bund' im Alten Testament* (Berlin: W. de Gruyter).

Lafont, B.
1984   'Le roi de Mari et les prophètes du dieu Adad', *RA* 78: 7-18.
— 1999   'Sacrifices et rituels à Mari et dans la Bible', *RA* 93: 57-77.
Lafont, S.
1998   'Le roi, le juge et l'étranger à Mari et dans la Bible', *RA* 92: 161-81.
Laroche, E.
1988   'Observations sur le rituel anatolien provenant de Meskéné-Emar', in
            F. Imparati (ed.), *Studi di storia e di filologia anatolica dedicati a
            Giovanni Pugliese Carratelli* (Florence: Edizioni librarie italiane
            estere): 111-17.
Lebrun, R.
— 1988   'Divinités louvites et hourrites des rituels anatoliens en langue
            akkadienne provenant de Meskéné', in *Hethitica IX* (Louvain-la-neuve:
            Peeters): 147-55.
Lemche, N.P.
1991   *The Canaanites and their Land* (JSOTSup, 110; Sheffield: JSOT
            Press).
Lewis, T.J.
1996   'The Identity and Function of El/Baal Berith', *JBL* 115: 401-23.
Malamat, A.
1980   'A Mari Prophecy and Nathan's Dynastic Oracle', in J.A. Emerton
            (ed.), *Prophecy: Festschrift Georg Fohrer* (Berlin: W. de Gruyter): 68-
            82 (73).
— 1989   *Mari and the Early Israelite Experience* (Oxford: Oxford University
            Press).
Margueron, J.-Cl.
1979   'Un «ḫilani» à Emar', *AASOR* 44: 153-76.
— 1995   'Emar, Capital of Aštata in the Fourteenth Century BCE', *BA* 58: 126-
            38.
McCarter, P.K. Jr
1987   'Aspects of the Religion of the Israelite Monarchy: Biblical and
            Epigraphic Data', in *Studies Cross*: 137-55.
McCarthy, D.J.
1978   *Treaty and Covenant* (Rome: Pontifical Biblical Institute).
Mendenhall, G.
1954   'Covenant Forms in Israelite Tradition', *BA* 17: 50-76.
Mettinger, T.N.D.
1995   *No Graven Image? Israelite Aniconism in its Ancient Near Eastern
            Context* (Stockholm: Almqvist and Wiksell).
Meyers, E.M.
1987   'The Persian Period and the Judean Restoration: From Zerubbabel to
            Nehemiah', in *Studies Cross*: 509-21.
Müller, H.-P.
1992   'Kolloquialsprache und Volksreligion in den Inschriften von Kuntillet
            'Aǧrūd und Ḫirbet el-Qōm', *ZAH* 5: 15-51.
Noth, M.
1954   *Geschichte Israels* (Göttingen: Vandenhoeck & Ruprecht).

Oded, B.
1986   'The Table of Nations (Genesis 10): A Socio-Cultural Approach', *ZAW*
            98: 14-31.

Otzen, B.
1974   ''*ābhadh*', *TDOT*: I, 19-23.

Perlitt, L.
1969   *Bundestheologie im Alten Testament* (Neukirchen–Vluyn: Neukirchener
            Verlag).

Postgate, J.N.
1992   *Early Mesopotamia: Society and Economy at the Dawn of History*
            (New York: Routledge).

Rainey, A.F.
1996   'Who is a Canaanite? A Review of the Textual Evidence', *BASOR* 304:
            1-15.

Sasson, J.
1994   'The Posting of Letters With Divine Messages', in D. Charpin and J.-
            M. Durand (eds.), *Florilegium Marianum*, II (Paris: SEPOA): 314-16.
1998   'About "Mari and the Bible"', *RA* 92: 97-123.

Sasson, V.
1995   'The Old Aramaic Inscription from Tell Dan: Philological, Literary,
            and Historical Aspects', *JSS* 40: 11-30.

Schniedewind, W.M.
1996   'Tel Dan Stela: New Light on Aramaic and Jehu's Revolt', *BASOR*
            302: 75-90.

Smith, M.S.
1990   *The Early History of God* (San Francisco: Harper & Row).

Speiser, E.A.
1964   *Genesis* (AB; Garden City, NY: Doubleday).

Sperling, S.D.
1987   'Joshua 24 Re-examined', *HUCA* 58: 119-36.

Steinkeller, P.
1993   'Early Political Development in Mesopotamia', in M. Liverani (ed.),
            Akkad: The First World Empire (Padua: Sargon srl): 107-30.

Thompson, T.L.
1974   *The Historicity of the Patriarchal Narratives* (BZAW, 133; Berlin: W.
            de Gruyter).

Toorn, K. van der
1996   *Family Religion in Babylonia, Syria and Israel* (Leiden: E.J. Brill).

Van Seters, J.
1975   *Abraham in History and Tradition* (New Haven: Yale University
            Press).
1996   'Cultic Laws in the Covenant Code and their Relationship to Studies in
            the Book of Exodus', in M. Vervenne (ed.), *Studies in the Book of
            Exodus* (Leuven: Peeters): 319-45.

Vaux, R. de
1960   *Les institutions de l'Ancien Testament* (2 vols.; Paris: Editions du Cerf,
            1960).

Villard, P.
      1990–91   'Le rituel-ḫiyârum devant le dieu de l'orage', *NABU*, I, 32: 25.
Wellhausen, J.
      1885   *Prolegomena to the History of Israel* (Edinburgh: T. & T. Clark).
Werner, P.
      1994   *Die Entwicklung der Sakralarchitektur in Nordsyrien und Südost-kleinasien* (Munich: Profil Verlag).
Westermann, C.
      1985   *Genesis 12–36* (Minneapolis: Augsburg).
Wolff, H.W.
      1990   *Hosea* (BK; Neukirchen–Vluyn: Neukirchener Verlag).
Yee, G.A.
      1987   *Composition and Tradition in the Book of Hosea: A Redaction Critical Investigation* (Atlanta: Scholars Press).

VOICES FROM THE DUST:
THE TABLETS FROM UGARIT AND THE BIBLE

Wayne T. Pitard

As the twentieth century ended, the mass media put out their lists of the most influential people, the most important events, the greatest scientific discoveries, the wealthiest people, the most notorious people, the best films, TV shows, plays, books, records, and so on, of the century. While such an enterprise can be (and often is) relatively trivial and distorting, it can be nonetheless an intellectual and historical exercise that can help place things into their historical context. It is not surprising, then, that conversations among scholars of the Hebrew Bible turned to the question of what might be considered the most important and influential discoveries and scholarly achievements in the field over the past 100 years.[1]

What extraordinary developments occurred during the twentieth century! A hundred years ago, the study of the biblical text was still in its infancy. Literary criticism, under the impetus of Wellhausen's work in the last quarter of the century, was in the full flush of its youthful vigor. But form criticism was just beginning its infiltration into biblical studies.[2] In terms of the Near Eastern cultural background of Israel and its religion, scholars at the turn of the century had already done considerable comparative work with the Mesopotamian myths, epics and rituals, which had been found in the archives of several ancient cities, including, most notably, Nineveh.[3]

---

1. The first 'top ten' list related to biblical studies of which I am aware is found in Coogan 1995. Here, Michael Coogan judiciously chose representative finds to illustrate the various types of archeological discoveries that have changed our understanding of the Bible. This particular list was not restricted to the twentieth century.

2. It is instructive to read through some of the major works on biblical studies from the turn of the century. See, for example, S.R. Driver's excellent and long-lived *Introduction to the Literature of the Old Testament* (1891), updated in 1897, which provides an excellent view of the state of literary research at the turn of the century.

3. Perhaps the most notable example is Gunkel 1895.

The first full-scale edition of the Amarna Letters had been published in 1896, creating a major sensation. But the archives of Nuzi, Ugarit, Mari and Alalakh, which would play such significant roles in the study of the biblical world, were still securely under ground.

Archeology in Palestine was in its barest infancy at the turn of the century, with Sir Flinders Petrie's 1890 excavation at Tell el-Hesi marking the true birth of scientific archeology in the land. The large-scale recovery of ancient Israelite material culture and that of its predecessors did not really begin until the first decade of the new century.[4]

Through this century we have seen the proliferation of methodologies for the study of the biblical text and the emergence and flourishing of archeological technologies that have opened avenues toward the reconstruction of ancient Israel that could not have been imagined in 1900. The recovery of textual material, including the tablet finds mentioned above, along with Ebla and Emar in more recent times, as well as the great manuscript discoveries, such as the Elephantine papyri, the Dead Sea Scrolls and the Wadi ed-Daliyeh papyri, have revolutionized our understanding of virtually every aspect of biblical studies.

Of the many great discoveries over this past century that have illuminated our understanding of Israelite religion and culture, I think that a good case can be made that the Ugaritic tablets have had the most profound effect of all. To say this is not to minimize the important contributions of so many other discoveries, but it is to recognize the extraordinarily wide range of fundamental contributions the Ugaritic texts have made to the study of biblical Israel. The tablets are the foundation of our understanding of West Semitic religion in the second millennium BCE, providing us with the only preserved original mythological texts from the Levant. They have also illuminated in extraordinary ways the close relationship between Israelite religion and the religious milieu of Canaanite culture. The language of the Ugaritic texts is closely related to Hebrew and has provided an extraordinary amount of insight into the latter's grammatical structure and lexicon. And the recovery of large amounts of Ugaritic poetry has impacted the study of Hebrew poetry in a number of important ways.

---

4.   On the archeology of the late nineteenth and early twentieth centuries, see King 1983: 1-26; Silberman 1982: 147-79. When Père Hugo Vincent published his study of Prehellenistic Palestinian archeology in 1914, he had access to substantial publications about excavations at only nine sites! See Vincent 1914: 3-4.

1. *The Relationship between the Ugaritic Texts and Canaanite Culture*

Before I look at how Ugarit has shaped our understanding of the Bible, the question of how these texts relate to the Canaanite culture of Palestine in the Late Bronze Age must be addressed. After all, they were discovered in northern Syria, far from the land where Israel emerged.

The question whether the Ugaritic texts should be considered exemplars of Canaanite literature, that is, literature from the same cultural milieu as found in the southern Levant, has been debated off and on for decades. The majority of scholars working with the texts have no problem making such an identification. But some have expressed uneasiness about the assumption that the Ugaritic tablets reflect the religion of the Canaanites of southern Palestine. They have cautioned against making a simple equation between the Ugaritic texts and the Canaanites of the Bible (see the recent studies, Hillers 1985; Grabbe 1994). What is one to make of this issue?

Part of the problem has to do with the difficulty in defining the terms, 'Canaan/Canaanite'.[5] What was the extent of Canaanite culture, and how does one define such boundaries? Should it be delimited along the lines of the apparent political entity that was known as Canaan in the second millennium? It seems that the ancients recognized much of the area of Palestine and the Lebanese coast as the land of Canaan. But there is also good evidence that the people of Ugarit did not consider themselves part of this land.[6] So if one limits the label 'Canaanite' to the boundaries of the land of Canaan, the term should not be applied to the Ugaritic material. In this case, the texts might be defined more appropriately as something like 'Coastal North Syrian' literature.

On the other hand, there can be no doubt that a cultural continuum can extend far beyond the borders of particular political entities. In order to define whether or not Ugaritic literature belongs to the Canaanite cultural sphere, one must examine the other sources of information about Canaanite religion and determine whether there is substantial continuity between it and the Ugaritic texts. I would argue that such a continuity is very much in evidence, and that there is no reason to avoid using the

5.   Considerable discussion has occurred on this issue in response to N.P. Lemche's argument that there was not actually a real 'Land of Canaan' identifiable in ancient Palestine. See Lemche 1991. Lemche's arguments are, in the final analysis, unconvincing. See Rainey 1996; Na'aman 1994.

6.   On Ugarit and Canaan see, most recently, Rainey 1996: 4-6.

adjective 'Canaanite' as a designation for the Ugaritic literature.

At the same time, to say that there is a cultural continuity between Ugarit and the southern Levant does not mean that Ugarit's religion was identical with the contemporary religious thought and practice farther south. In fact, there may have been considerable contrasts between the two. Canaanite religion was not a monolithic system, with carefully controlled dogma and liturgy. In the same way that the land of Canaan was not a political or social unity, so there are indications that the major centers of the Levant developed their own religious systems that combined a substantial stratum of shared belief and practice with local elements that made each area's religion unique. We should not expect Ugaritic religion to be identical with Tyrian religion, or Byblian, or with that in Late Bronze Jerusalem or Megiddo or Shechem. Cities worshipped different patron deities, and this surely created variant forms of myths and theologies, cultic practices and liturgies.[7]

Not only should one expect differences between the various geographic regions of Canaan, but one should also expect to find diachronic development of the religions attested in the area. No religions are static, and the rise and decline in popularity of various deities over a period of centuries can easily be seen in various cultures, including Mesopotamia and Egypt. It is also identifiable in Canaan. By the first millennium BCE, a number of gods not prominent in the second millennium became leading deities in several important cities of the Levant: Melqart at Tyre, Eshmun at Sidon, and so on.

So, although some would argue against identifying the Ugaritic religion as Canaanite on the grounds that there are differences between it and what is known of southern Canaanite religion of the second and first millennia BCE, I believe that this fact should not obscure the essential continuity that relates the Ugaritic material to Canaanite culture. Most of the gods that were important at Ugarit are also known to have played a major role in the religion of southern Canaan as well, even though the exact status of some of the deities may have varied in the different regions.

Once the close relationship between the Ugaritic texts and general Canaanite culture is recognized, it should not be surprising that there are also clear continuities between Ugarit and the Hebrew Bible, since Israel emerged in southern Canaan at the end of the Late Bronze Age. But that

---

7.   Cf. Grabbe (1994: 113-22) emphasizes the differences between Ugarit and the rest of Canaan. Also see Day 1994: 35-52, who accentuates the continuities between Ugaritic and general Canaanite religions.

relationship between them is complex. Some scholars have tended to overinflate the connections, while others have tried to downplay any similarities between the two systems of thought and practice. There is, however, a happy medium in which one can acknowledge the distinct-nesses of Israelite religion while recognizing the substantial debt it owed to the cultural background out of which it developed. It is valuable to recognize the connections between the two cultures, but it is also impor-tant to be very careful not to overstate these connections. One cannot pre-suppose that a religious/cultural element found in the Ugaritic tablets will necessarily have existed in Israel. One can argue for parallels only when there is clear evidence of a belief or practice in both cultures.

2. The Ugaritic Mythological and Epic Texts: Their Impact on Biblical Studies

a. *Canaanite Mythology*.[8]

Before the discovery of the Ugaritic tablets very little was known about the Canaanite gods, their characteristics, their mythologies, their functions in the worldview of the Canaanites. The Bible and the fragments of the *Phoenician History* of Philo of Byblos, preserved primarily in the Christian author Eusebius, were the two primary literary sources available. The Bible showed a decidedly negative attitude toward the Canaanite deities. Philo of Byblos, while preserving some elements of Canaanite religion in his writings, had painted it on a strongly Hellenistic canvas. Both exhibited clear distortions of Canaanite thought, but there was often little way to be certain what reflected the realities of first-millennium Canaanite religion and what did not.[9] But now the Ugaritic literary texts have provided us with primary Late Bronze Age information concerning the mythology of the gods of Canaan. This knowledge has revolutionized our understanding of the Canaanite background of Israelite religion. In the

---

8.   The Ugaritic texts are designated in this article according to their number in the edition of *KTU*[2]. This is the second edition of *KTU* which appeared in 1976. The authors have kept the initials *KTU* in their designations of the tablets, in spite of the change from German to English in the title of the second edition.

There are only a few translations of the major Ugaritic texts currently available in English. The most recent one, Parker 1997, is also the best one. But also see Coogan 1978; de Moor 1987 and Wyatt. See also Pardee 1997.

9.   On Philo of Byblos and the accuracy of his reporting, see especially Baumgarten 1981: 261-68; Attridge and Oden 1981: 1-9.

first place we have a much clearer sense of the characteristics of the major Canaanite deities and their roles in the pantheon.

It is from the Ugaritic texts that we now know that the head of the pantheon in Canaan was El (Ilu). He was the creator god, called 'the father of the gods', 'the father of humanity', 'the creator of creatures'. He is portrayed as a patriarchal figure, 'the bull', 'the kind one, the compassionate god', who rules over the divine council, wise, with a gray beard. In this context he is also referred to as 'the father of years'.[10] He lives on a mountain, from the foot of which flow the sources of the fresh water of the world. At this location he dwells not in a temple, but in a tent,[11] and it is at this location that the council of the gods meets. He is the god who grants offspring to humans, and thus he plays the primary role in the continuation of the family line.

While El rules over the council of the gods, the myths (particularly *KTU* 1.1-6) depict the rise of Baal/Haddu to prominence among the younger gods as their active leader, a position perhaps somewhat grudgingly granted at first by El. Baal is the god of the storm and thus of the fertility of the earth. The stories preserved about him are clearly designed to delineate his place in the divine order. In the narrative poem about his conflict with Yamm (the Sea), the dominant position among the gods is contested between the two, with El initially supporting Yamm. However, in a mighty confrontation Baal defeats Yamm and assumes control (*KTU* 1.1-2). This story is followed by the account of the contruction of Baal's palace/temple as a sign of his new status (*KTU* 1.3-4). But once he is settled in his new position, he is confronted by Mot, 'Death', who swallows him up and kills him. He returns to life, however, bringing fertility to the earth once again after his sister Anat confronts and kills Mot himself. He is called, 'the mighty Baal', 'the rider on the clouds', and 'the prince, the lord of the earth'. These epithets emphasize his strength and position among the gods. His voice is the thunder, and he hurls lightning bolts as his spears (e.g. *KTU* 1.4.v.8-9; vii.28-37).[12] He lives on Mt Zaphon, apparently Mt Cassius, the highest peak in Syria, which is located only some 40 km north of Ugarit, and easily visible from the city on clear days.

---

10. On the epithets of El and their significance, see Cross 1973: 13-24.

11. On the tent dwelling of El, see Clifford 1972: 48-54.

12. A stele found near the temple of Baal at Ugarit shows Baal with a club in his right hand and what is probably a stylized lightning bolt in his left. Several bronze figurines of Baal with his right hand raised as if holding a javelin have also been recovered at Ugarit. See Caquot and Sznycer 1980.

The goddess Asherah, known vaguely from other sources, also comes into greater focus in the Ugaritic texts. She is the consort of El, whose counsel he willingly takes (*KTU* 1.4.iv.20–v.1). She is the mother of 70 of the gods (*KTU* 1.4.vi.46). In the Kirta Epic (*KTU* 1.14-16), King Kirta fails to fulfill a vow he made to Asherah, and she smites him with a deadly disease, in spite of the fact that El is the god who has supported Kirta until now. Only El can undo Asherah's potent curse upon Kirta (*KTU* 1.16.v.9-28). She is called 'the great lady, Athirat of the sea', 'the creatress of the gods' (*KTU* 1.4.i.21-22 ; iii.25-30). Although she supports Baal's building of a palace, there appears to be occasional tension between Baal and Asherah. When Anat announces to El and Asherah that Baal has died, she prefaces her remarks with, 'Let now Asherah and her sons rejoice,/ the goddess and her pride of lions,/ for mighty Baal is dead' (*KTU* 1.6.i.39-42). Upon hearing this news, Asherah immediately prepares to place her son Athtar on Baal's throne.[13]

Another important deity is the goddess Anat, closely linked with Baal, often identified by scholars as his consort, but most likely his sister.[14] She appears to be a warrior and hunting goddess and is portrayed as a tempestuous, violent deity. She plays a active role in the narratives concerning Baal. She asks El (in a very intimidating way) to allow a palace to be built for Baal after the latter's battle with Yamm. In spite of her threats, El refuses her request. (Later Asherah is able to change El's mind.) She plays a more pivotal role in the story of Baal's encounter with Mot, 'Death'. When Mot kills Baal, it is Anat who takes Baal's body and buries it. But she does not stop there. She goes in search of Mot, finds him and takes vengeance upon him by attacking and killing him in a field. After she has done this, Baal returns to life, bringing fertility back to the earth. In the Aqhat Epic, she plays a somewhat different role. Aqhat is the son of the righteous judge/king, Daniel. At a celebration honoring Aqhat's birth, the

13. Asherah has been the subject of considerable research in the last few years, much of this inspired by the increasing recognition that Asherah was probably thought to be Yahweh's consort in many pre-exilic Israelite circles. Most recently, see Maier 1986; Wiggins 1993; Binger 1997. Wiggins' book is the most comprehensive, examining the sources across the Near East.

14. Until recently it has been common to describe Anat as both consort and sister of Baal. But Day (1992) and Walls (1992) have argued convincingly that there is no clear evidence that Anat and Baal engaged in sexual relations (the passages interpreted as such by others actually rely on the assumption that Anat has turned herself into a cow). See also the fine discussion by Day 1995.

craftsman of the gods, Kothar-wa-Hasis, gives Aqhat a wonderful bow and arrow set. Anat covets the bow, and when Aqhat grows to be a youth who enters the forests to hunt, Anat meets him and offers him silver, gold and even immortality for the bow. When he refuses, she has him killed. Her violent streak is emphasized even more fully in a passage whose exact purpose within the Baal Epic remains unclear (KTU 1.3.ii). Here Anat attacks the population of two towns and wipes them out in a furious battle.

Besides these top members of the pantheon, other gods and goddesses appear in the texts, providing a much more nuanced picture of the mythic universe of Ugaritic thought than previously possible. All of this has illuminated not just the cultural milieu out of which Israel emerged, but also many aspects of the Canaanite culture that Israel attempted to distinguish from itself. We can gain a much clearer sense of how the Israelite polemics against Canaanite religion sometimes reflect and sometimes distort the realities of the period.

But the value of these texts is not restricted to their illumination of the religion that was opposed by the authors of the Bible. They have also provided us with extraordinary evidence for a startlingly close continuity between Israel's earliest religious traditions and those of the Canaanites themselves.

The most significant aspect of this continuity is seen in the relationship between Canaanite El and the God of Israel. The Ugaritic tablets showed for the first time that the head of the Canaanite pantheon was a god with the personal name El. This is extremely significant because Israel's God is often referred to with the identical name and is, in certain parts of the biblical text, portrayed in ways that are startlingly reminiscent of the portrait of El in the Ugaritic texts.

The close relationship between Canaanite El and Israel's God is particularly noticeable in the stories of Israel's ancestors preserved in Genesis 12–36. The name El surfaces numerous times as the name of the deity worshiped by the ancestors. Abram is connected to the worship of El Elyon ('El the Highest One'), 'creator of heaven and earth', in Gen. 14.18-24, and of El Olam ('El, the Ancient One') in Gen. 21.33. Jacob (Gen. 28.10-22) has a dream that he is at the foot of a staircase to heaven and names the shrine he sets up at that spot, Beth-El ('House of El'). Later, Jacob buys some land near the town of Shechem and builds an altar on the land, which he names El-elohe-Yisrael, 'El is the God of Israel' (Gen. 33.18-20). The Priestly Source of the Pentateuch explicitly argues that the ancestors did not worship Yahweh under that name. In Exod. 6.2-3,

Yahweh tells Moses, 'I am Yahweh. I appeared to Abraham, Isaac and Jacob as El Shadday. But by my name, Yahweh, I did not make myself known to them'. The name El Shadday appears a number of times in Genesis (in the P source material); its meaning remains uncertain, but it is most probably to be rendered, 'El, the Mountain One'.

The relationship goes beyond the significant appearance of the name of El in the ancestral stories. The character of God in these stories and even the major themes of the ancestral narratives in Genesis are closely related to the depiction of El in the Ugaritic texts. Unlike the portrayal of Yahweh in the rest of the Pentateuch (and elsewhere), the deity of the ancestral narratives is not depicted with storm-god imagery, nor is he described in terms of the warrior god. In these stories the theme centers around the getting of an heir for the continuation of the family line. Abraham and Sarah, long past the age of bearing children, are granted a son in their old age, in fulfillment of a promise God made many years before. Rebekah, Isaac's wife, proves to be barren as well, but God listens to Isaac's prayer and grants her children (Gen. 25.21). When Yahweh sees that Jacob does not love his first wife, Leah, he grants her children, leaving Rachel, Jacob's beloved wife, barren for a while (Gen. 29.31). But eventually he takes pity on Rachel, and, answering her prayer, he opens her womb (Gen. 30.22). This theme, so important for each of the ancestral cycles, also proves to be the primary theme of both epic poems found at Ugarit, the Aqhat and Kirta Epics. In the Aqhat Epic, Daniel, a righteous judge (probably king), earnestly seeks help from the gods to obtain an heir. His patron deity, Baal, comes before the council of the gods, with El presiding, and urges El to grant Daniel and his wife a son. El agrees to bless the couple, and they do have a son, Aqhat. In the Kirta Epic, the hero's family has been wiped out at the beginning of the story. The devastated Kirta falls asleep, weeping, on his bed. In his sleep, El appears to him and gives him instructions on how to win the hand of the beautiful Hurraya, daughter of the king of Udm, in marriage. El and the other gods attend the wedding, and El pronounces a blessing upon the couple: Hurraya will bear Kirta seven/eight sons. It is clear in both stories that granting an heir to the hero is strictly the perogative of El. Baal, although intimately involved in the fertility of the earth, cannot provide children to humans.

The clear parallels between the god of the ancestors described in Genesis 12–36 and the Canaanite El are all the more striking when one considers that the depiction of Israel's God in Exodus and following is quite different from that found here. Beginning in Exodus we find that

while many of the characteristics of El are retained, Yahweh is now
portrayed with strong storm god and martial imagery not found in Genesis,
imagery that relates more closely to that used of Baal. This suggests that
the stories in Genesis have preserved genuine traditions of the more
archaic religion of Israel's ancestors, before their patron deity was known
as Yahweh.

The question of how to understand the close relationship between
Canaanite El and Israelite Yahweh has not been fully resolved. Some
scholars argue that Yahweh was a distinct deity, identified with El at an
early date in Israel's existence.[15] Others have proposed that the name
Yahweh was part of an epithet of El (*yahweh ṣᵉbā'ōt*, 'He brings the
armies into existence') and that thus Yahweh and El were in fact the same
deity.[16] Whatever the situation is, it is clear that the ancestral stories
preserve a memory of a time when Israel's God was explicitly recognized
as El, the head of the Canaanite pantheon, whose characteristics were
widely recognized throughout Canaan. In this way, the Ugaritic tablets
have revolutionized our understanding of the Canaanite background of
Israel's God.

A second very significant area in which the Ugaritic tablets have illuminated the continuity between Canaanite and Israelite cultures is in the
realm of creation theology. The existence in early Israel of a myth in
which Yahweh fought a great battle with the Sea, after which he created
the world, had already been recognized in the late nineteenth century.[17]
But until the discovery of the Ugaritic tablets, scholars generally assumed
that the Israelite myth had been adapted from the Mesopotamian creation
stories, such as the *Enuma elish*. The Ugaritic tablets, however, show that
the Israelite accounts are very closely linked to Canaanite antecedents.

As mentioned above, the Baal Epic provides a detailed narrative of the
battle between Baal and Yamm (the Sea) (*KTU* 1.2), who is given the
parallel epithets, 'Prince Sea' and 'Judge River'. Baal's victory over
Yamm allows him to take his position as effective ruler of the gods.

Besides this primary account of the conflict between Baal and Yamm,
there is a reference to a similar battle in *KTU* 1.5.i.1-8. In this passage,
however, the opponent is described as a dragon-like creature, with seven

15. E.g. Smith 1990: 1-12; Albertz 1994: I, 76-79.
16. The classic discussion is Cross 1973: 60-75.
17. Gunkel 1895. It seems likely that this combat myth was the primary creation
story in Israel until it was replaced by Gen. 1, probably in the exilic period. Recent
discussions of this mythic theme include Day 1985; Wakeman 1973; Kloos 1986.

heads. In the context, the god Mot speaks of the battle as a previous triumph of Baal:

> When you killed Lotan, the fleeing serpent,
> finished off the writhing serpent,
> Shalyat ('Ruler'), the seven-headed one...

In addition, the Baal Epic has a reference to a similar conflict, but with the goddess Anat as the protagonist. As she sees a messenger from Baal approaching her home, Anat says to herself (*KTU* 1.3.iii.38-46):

> Did I not smite El's beloved, Yamm?
> Did I not bring Nahar ('River'), the great god, to an end?
> Did I not muzzle Tannin ('Dragon'), destroy him?
> I smote the writhing serpent,
> Shalyat, the seven-headed one.

There is no doubt that this kind of tale was popular in ancient Canaan. But a very similar story about a conflict between Yahweh and the Sea/dragon was also told in Israel. References to it occur in several biblical passages, the most complete of which is Ps. 74.12-17:

> But God my king is from of old,
>   working salvation in the midst of the earth.
> It was you who divided Yam ('Sea') with your might!
>   You shattered the heads of Tannin[18] upon the waters!
> It was you who crushed the heads of Leviathan (= Lotan)!
>   You gave him as food for the people, the desert ones!
> It was you who cleaved springs and streams!
>   It was you who made ever-flowing rivers dry up!
> To you belong the day and the night!
>   It was you who established all the boundaries of the earth!
>   You are the one who formed summer and winter!

Thus in Psalm 74 we find the use of three names for the opponent of Yahweh—Yam, Tannin and Leviathan—that are paralleled precisely in the Ugaritic material. In the Hebrew passage the three names appear to refer to one and the same being. But there has been considerable controversy as to whether the same is true in the Ugaritic texts. Is Ugaritic Yamm/Nahar the same deity as Tannin/Lotan/Shalyat?

In support of distinguishing Yamm/Nahar from the other three names is

---

18. The Massoretic text has the plural, *tannînîm*, here, but this is a likely example of an enclitic mem on a singular noun being mistaken for a plural ending by later scribes.

the fact that in *KTU* 1.2 Yamm is not explicitly described in dragon-like terms in the story of his battle with Baal. He seems to be depicted in an anthropomorphic way in this passage. For example, he seems to have only one head, which is bashed by Baal's weapon in *KTU* 1.2.iv.21-22, in contrast to the multiple heads of Lotan/Tannin/Shalyat. On the other hand, Anat's description of her conflict strongly suggests an identity between the sets of names. In this case we appear to have a tricolon in which the names Yamm, Nahar and Tannin are parallel to one another.

In fact, the identity of Yamm/Nahar//Tannin is now further supported by a new collation of *KTU* 1.83, another tablet that describes a battle between gods.[19] In this very short text, from which only 12 of its c. 25 lines are preserved, a deity, probably Anat, but perhaps Baal, is described as fighting Tannin, binding him on the heights of Lebanon. At this point, in the newly collated lines, the victorious deity addresses her/his captive:

> Toward the desert shall you be scattered, O Yamm!
> To the multitude of Ḫt, O Nahar!
> You shall not see; lo! you shall foam up!

There can be little doubt here that Yamm/Nahar is being equated with the captured Tannin and is thus being portrayed as a dragon-like figure.

The story of the battle between Yahweh and Yam/Tannin/Leviathan, then, shows extraordinarily close relationships with the Canaanite myth found in the Ugaritic tablets. Not only is there the overlap in the general story line and in the names of the opponent of Yahweh, but other details of the story are paralleled in both: (1) the multiple-headed nature of the monster is found in the two versions; (2) in both Psalm 74 and *KTU* 1.83 the defeated enemy is cast into the desert; (3) in both Psalm 74 and *KTU* 1.83, the casting of the dragon into the desert appears to benefit the people in that region ('the multitude of Ḫt' in *KTU* 1.83, and 'the people, the desert ones' in Ps. 74.14).

The close relationship between the combat myths in these two cultures does not mean, however, that they were identical. There is in fact a striking difference in the larger contexts in which the stories occur. In Psalm 74, the battle with the sea is followed by the creation of the universe, while at Ugarit there does not appear to be a connection between the battle and creation. Baal is not the creator god, and thus his battle with Yamm is portrayed, not as a prelude to creation, but as a struggle for domination in the council of the gods. El, the supreme ruler of the

---

19. The new edition of the text is found in Pitard 1998.

pantheon, is the creator of the universe. So the combat myth has a separate existence in the Ugaritic texts. Baal's victory is succeeded by the story of building Baal's palace. In Israel, on the other hand, Yahweh/El is the creator god, as well as the god of storm. So in Psalm 74 we find the description of the cosmic battle followed by references to God's creation of the world. Many scholars have argued that because there is a clear connection between the combat myth and creation in the biblical text (as well as in the Mesopotamian creation story, the *Enuma elish*), the Baal/Yamm myth must also be cosmogonic in nature.[20] But this is a case where the assumption of parallelism goes too far. Without clear evidence for a connection between the Baal/Yamm myth and creation, there is no reason to assume its existence, just because such a connection occurs elsewhere. Different cultures developed their own understandings of the universe and different roles for their gods. At Ugarit the combat myth was central to the notion of rank among the gods, but since Baal was not the creator god, there was no need to link the myth with creation.

b. *Death and Afterlife at Ugarit and in Israel*

The continuities and dissimilarities just illustrated between the Ugaritic material and the Bible point up the complications and dangers in using the former to illuminate the latter, or vice versa. It is often tempting to reach beyond what is attested as parallel between the two cultures and to make assumptions of continuity where the evidence is less clear or nonexistent. One of the most interesting cases where scholars have used questionable cultural parallels in reconstructing an important aspect of Canaanite and Israelite civilization is the issue of concepts of death and afterlife.

Until the beginning of the 1990s, the study of Ugaritic funerary beliefs and practices was dominated by the opinion that a number of texts and archeological finds from the site directly related to the subject. They seemed to show that the people of Ugarit practiced an elaborate cult of the dead centered on the necessity to care for the dead with regular food and drink offerings. Because the texts were rather obscure, many scholars interpreted them by reference to funerary practices known in Mesopotamia, which were assumed to be similar to those at Ugarit. The Ugaritic texts were interpreted as showing that at least royalty and the upper classes

20. An excellent summary and discussion of this issue can be found in Smith 1994: 75-87. Clifford 1984 redefines 'cosmogony' as the coming into being of the world, usually from chaos into order. With this definition he argues that the Baal narratives are indeed cosmogonic.

were thought to become deified at death, that they were given regular offerings in rituals similar to the *kispu* rituals of Mesopotamia,[21] and that they could grant their descendents blessings and protections from the netherworld. It was further assumed that this view of Ugaritic concepts and practices was basically identical to Canaanite practices in the southern Levant, and that in turn the practices were also generally consonant with early Israelite custom, since the two cultures show such close cultural ties.[22]

This has begun to change over the past few years. While a number of scholars have continued to interpret many Ugaritic texts as related to death and afterlife, several others have expressed considerable skepticism about the amount of material that deals with the subject.[23] It has become increasingly clear that some of the basic interpretations of both the textual and archeological evidence need re-evaluation.

The tombs at Ugarit and at the city's port town, Minet el-Beida, have played an important part in the reconstruction of Ugaritic funerary and mortuary practices. Located under the floors of the houses within the city, and containing the remains of numerous persons, they were clearly family sepulchres. From the beginning of excavations in 1929, Claude Schaeffer, the director of the Mission to Ugarit, identified many items in the vicinity of the tombs as installations for providing food and drink offerings to the dead inside the chambers. There appeared to be vertical tubes for libations, windows and ceiling holes in the tombs for introducing food into the chamber, large jars for offerings by the doorways of the tombs, and so on (Schaeffer 1939: 49-53). It has now become clear, however, that the installations near the tombs have been misinterpreted. When Schaeffer first uncovered the material, he thought he was excavating in a cemetery, unaware that the tombs were built under the houses at Minet el-Beidha and at Ugarit. Thus what he interpreted as funerary installations were actually standard elements of domestic architecture—gutters, drains for dirty water, store jars, and so on. The holes in the ceilings were not intentionally made, but were the work of looters from the time when the city was destroyed. So it turns out that there is no archeological evidence for an extensive practice of cult of the dead at Ugarit (Pitard 1994).

---

21. On the *kispu* ritual, during which food and drink offerings were given to the dead in Mesopotamia, see Tsukimoto 1985; Bayliss 1973.

22. Cf. Schaeffer 1939: 49-56; Ribar 1973: 48-50; Spronk 1986: 142-206; del Olmo Lete 1992: 109-13, 145-70.

23. See, e.g., Lewis 1989: 5-98; Schmidt 1994: 47-131; Pardee 1996: 273-87.

The literary evidence for death and afterlife has also begun to be recognized as much more ambiguous than earlier claimed. A number of ritual texts that have been linked with the funerary cult have been shown to have no relationship with that subject (see especially Pardee 1996: 276-77). An important element in this regard is the institution known as the *marzeah*, attested not just at Ugarit, but across the Levant in Phoenician, Nabataean, and Palmyrene inscriptions, as well as twice in the Hebrew Bible. Scholars often described it as an association whose members held banquets, the function of which was to provide offerings to their deceased ancestors. It was seen as the primary way in which the mortuary cult was perpetuated through the years. But this interpretation has been effectively challenged. None of the evidence for the *marzeah* at Ugarit or elsewhere shows real links with a funerary cult. It rather appears to have been a society whose function was largely social in nature.[24]

Several passages from the tablets have also been used to describe funerary practices at Ugarit, but there have been several problems in their interpretation. Some of them are quite clear. The description of El's mourning over the death of Baal in *KTU* 1.5.vi certainly illustrates (perhaps exaggeratedly) a number of lamentation practices. However, passages interpreted as dealing with cult of the dead have all been much more ambiguous. For example, the Aqhat Epic (in *KTU* 17) presents a list of duties that should be carried out by a loyal son (repeated four times in columns i-ii). Many scholars have argued that several of these duties refer to care that a son should provide for the spirit of his dead father (Pope 1981: 160-62; Spronk 1986: 146-51). But several others have recently challenged this interpretation, pointing out that the surrounding context of those lines strongly suggest that all the duties listed are things that should be provided to the father while he is still alive.[25]

The only ritual text that is universally recognized as illuminating the funerary cult of Ugarit is *KTU* 1.161, which appears to be the liturgy for the funeral of King Niqmaddu III (late-thirteenth century).[26] This text does give us some information about Ugaritic thought on death and afterlife, although there are many obscurities in it. During the ceremony, a number of beings denoted as *rpum*, are summoned from the netherworld to take

---

24. See the discussions in Lewis 1989: 80-94; Schmidt 1994: 62-66.

25. See especially the careful treatment of Lewis 1989: 53-71. See also Schmidt 1994: 59-62.

26. Publications on this tablet have been numerous. See the bibliographies in Bordreuil and Pardee 1991: 151-52; Tsumura 1993: 40-42.

part in the funeral, as are some previous kings of Ugarit. The identity of the *rpum* remains uncertain, although most scholars identify them as deceased royal ancestors.[27] Ambiguity arises from the fact that the *rpum* who are specifically identified as such in *KTU* 1.161 possess names that are not attested as royal names at Ugarit, and in fact, look more like divine names than human ones (e.g. the composite name, *sdn-w-rdn*, and *tr 'llmn)*. On the other hand, two identifiable deceased kings of Ugarit are also summoned during the ritual, but they are not explicitly labeled as *rpum*. Rather, each is designated as a *mlk*, 'king'. Whatever the exact identity of the *rpum*, it is clear that they, the deceased kings and the sun goddess Shapshu are all intimately involved in the process of properly burying Niqmaddu III. There is no clear indication that the funerary ritual included the giving of food and drink offerings to the deceased king.

The preceding underscores the fact that there is very little unambiguous literary or archeological evidence for practices and beliefs concerning the dead at Ugarit. But this problematic material has played a major role in the reconstruction of the poorly-attested funerary concepts of biblical Israel, thereby creating a largely unsubstantiated picture of the entire region!

There are several additional reasons to be reluctant to assume a parallel between Ugarit and Israel concerning death and afterlife without clear evidence of such parallels. For example, Ugarit's burial practices do not even reflect the more general Canaanite practices of the Late Bronze Age in the southern Levant, much less those of Iron Age Israel. At Ugarit, we find corbelled-vaulted, stone-built, family tombs located inside the settlement, under the floors of most of the houses (Salles 1995). To the south, however, intramural burial was rare in the Late Bronze Age and became increasingly uncommon as the period went on. In addition, intramural burial was largely restricted to infants and a few simple adult burials. Almost no stonebuilt tombs like those at Ugarit are known from southern Canaan. For the most part we find two major types of tomb in Canaan during this period—family tombs in caves outside the walls of the settlements, and cemeteries of individual pit burials, also located outside

---

27. On the history of interpretation of the *rpum* and their parallel term in Hebrew, *repha'im*, see L'Heureux 1979: 111-27. Most scholars argue that the *rpum* are deified royal ancestors, pointing to the fact that they are also referred to as *ilnym*, 'godlike ones', and as *ilm*, 'gods', in some passages. See Loretz 1994: 175-224; de Moor 1976: 323-45; Spronk 1986: 161-96. Some scholars have also argued that the term *rpum* in some passages refers to living groups of warriors attached to the royal court of Ugarit. For this idea, see L'Heureux 1979: 201-23; Schmidt 1994: 88-93.

the settlements.[28] This very visible contrast between the two regions again raises questions about assuming a relationship between the Ugaritic material and customs in south Canaan or Israel without clear evidence from the south of such parallels.

A further problem has to do with the way the literary texts from Ugarit are used as a primary source for reconstructing Ugaritic funerary beliefs and practices. Scholars have usually assumed that the depictions within the stories of the Ugaritic narrative poems are a reflection of the practices and beliefs of Ugaritic society. But such a simple equation is far from certain, particularly with regard to epic tales such as the Aqhat and Kirta narratives.[29] In the latter cases, the stories do not appear to be native to Ugarit, neither of them having Ugarit or the region as their setting. In addition, the stories (particularly the Aqhat, where there is more reference to death) carry with them a sense of antiquity, so that the particulars of the story may reflect a view of archaic society intentionally distinguished from the contemporary customs of the author's day. The discontinuity between the Aqhat epic and Ugaritic society is particularly noticeable in the description of the burial of and mourning over Aqhat after his murder. Although some of the elements are not clear, it seems certain that Aqhat is not buried within the confines of his family's house. Rather his tomb is located in the outdoors, and Danel curses any birds who might fly over the tomb and disturb Aqhat's rest (*KTU* 1.19.iii.42-45). If the description of the burial practices in Aqhat are not reliable witnesses to Ugaritic practice, how can we be secure about using the other passages as illustrations of Ugaritic belief, and, beyond that, of southern Canaanite and Israelite belief?

The Ugaritic ritual texts provide us with a more reliable witness, since we can be fairly certain that they were used in local practice. But again,

28. On Late Bronze Age tomb types in Canaan, see Gonen 1992: 9-31. Gonen lists only five structural tombs found in Israel from the MB II and LB that at all parallel the tombs of Ugarit. Three corbelled tombs found at Megiddo are the closest parallels to those at Ugarit. They were built under the floors of palaces. But they are dated to the MB II period and have a different construction technique from those at Ugarit. A structural tomb at Tel Dan was not located within a building, but dug into the slope of the rampart of the site. And a similar tomb at Tel Aphek was located outside the settlement. Thus the rarity of structural tombs in Canaan emphasizes the significant difference in burial customs between the two regions. For her discussion of intramural burials see Gonen 1992: 98-123. For a description of Israelite Iron Age tombs, which are quite different in construction and always located outside the settlements, see Bloch-Smith 1992: 25-62.

29. See the discussion of this issue in Parker 1989: 217-20.

without tangible evidence from southern Canaan or Israel, it is very dangerous to argue for the specific continuity of a ritual practice across the entire Levant through a period of almost a millennium.

3. *Ugaritic Language and Poetics*

One of the great contributions the Ugaritic texts have made to the study of the Hebrew Bible has been in the realm of language. Both in terms of comparative grammar and in lexicography, Ugaritic has significantly helped advance our understanding of Biblical Hebrew.

Some of this is not as simple as one might expect, however. There continues to be a considerable discussion about how closely related the two languages actually are. Over the years a number of scholars have argued that Ugaritic should not be identified as a Canaanite dialect, while others insist that it should. Most recently Josef Tropper has discussed this question and has marshalled a convincing number of parallels between Ugaritic and the Canaanite dialects to show that the former is best understood as a Canaanite language (Tropper 1994: 343-53). Not that they are identical, however. Tropper would classify Ugaritic as the only currently-known representative of 'northern Canaanite'.

This is not the place to go into detail about the contributions of Ugaritic to our understanding of Hebrew grammar,[30] but a few important elements may be mentioned. Ugaritic poetry makes use of the prefix conjugations of the verb to indicate past tense. Here it is done without the use of a *waw* consecutive. This parallels such usages in some Hebrew poetry, and it adds evidence to the argument that the use of prefix forms for narrative past tense in Hebrew derives from an old prefixed preterite form in earlier Canaanite.[31] A second aspect of the Ugaritic verb that has had a significant impact on the study of Hebrew verbs is its use of passive forms of the simple (qal) verbal stem. In biblical Hebrew a number of passive verbs had been identified as either hophal, pual, or niphal, although they had no parallel hiphil or piel forms. Now these forms have been recognized as examples of the qal passive.[32]

Another important contribution has been in the area of particles. For

30. A solid discussion of the major contributions may be found in Emerton 1994: 53-69.

31. Not all scholars agree with this analysis of the prefix conjugation and its use to denote preterite action. See the discussion in Waltke and O'Connor 1990: 496-501.

32. Waltke and O'Connor (1990: 373-77) also discuss this issue very carefully.

example, Ugaritic uses the prepositions *l* and *b* in a number of places where they must be rendered into English as 'from', although *l* also regularly means 'to' and *b* means 'in'. It has become clear that a similar situation also occurred in Hebrew, although not with the frequency that we find in Ugaritic.[33] Another element found frequently in Ugaritic and now recognized in Hebrew is the enclitic mem. This is an *m* placed at the end of a word, presumably for some type of emphasis, although its exact function remains uncertain. There appear to be a number of such enclitic mems in Hebrew as well, many of them mistaken as plural endings by the Masoretes.[34]

Also helpful in the interpretation of both the Hebrew Bible and the Ugaritic tablets is the large number of cognate words found in the two literatures. In many cases, particularly where the Hebrew text attests only a few occurrences of an obscure word, the Ugaritic texts provide new contexts for the word, from which one may determine a clearer meaning. This aspect of the two languages has been responsible for many improvements in the understanding of the texts. On the other hand, a cavalier use of cognates between two languages, even closely related ones, can lead to substantial misunderstandings. Anyone familiar with a language closely related to English (say, either French or German) will be aware of the dangers of assuming that a cognate in the other language must mean the same as in English. There has been much abuse of the Ugaritic cognates in translating Hebrew texts, and this is one of the most important areas where restraint is necessary among scholars.[35]

The discovery of the literary works at Ugarit also inaugurated a new era in the study of Hebrew poetic styles, since it quickly became clear that Hebrew and Ugaritic poetic techniques are very similar to one another. The Ugaritic material has played an important role in the discussion of

33. On this see the discussion of Pardee 1975: 330-37; Aartun 1982: 1-14. Also see Sutcliffe 1955. These scholars make the point that one cannot properly say that *b* and *l* 'mean' one thing or another. Rather, it is better to say that our language requires that these prepositions be rendered 'from' in certain circumstances.

34. See Waltke and O'Connor 1990: 158-60. A few scholars are not convinced that any indisputable example of the enclitic mem exists in the Hebrew Bible. See Emerton 1994: 60.

35. Probably the most outspoken proponent of using Ugaritic vocabulary to interpret Hebrew texts was Mitchell Dahood, whose commentary on Psalms in the Anchor Bible series is a monument to such methodology. Most of his proposals have failed to convince the majority of scholars. For a recent evaluation of Dahood's work, see Curtis 1994.

both Hebrew meter and parallelism. Scholars in this field still remain divided on many issues. Some argue for a metrical basis for both Ugaritic and Hebrew poetry,[36] while others have (I believe more convincingly) suggested that meter, as regularly understood, is absent in the poetry (Pardee 1981; O'Connor 1980: 54-78). Studies of parallelism in the poetry have been greatly enhanced by the ability to compare the two corpora of texts.[37] These studies have moved the analysis of parallelism to a considerably more sophisticated level than before. In addition, the Ugaritic poems have provided us with a considerable bank of common word pairs regularly used together as parallels in the poetic bicola. A considerable number of these paired words also occur in biblical Hebrew poetry, indicating a long-lived tradition concerning the appropriate synonyms to use in parallel.[38]

4. *Conclusion*

This discussion does not exhaust the areas in which the Ugaritic tablets have made a significant impact on the study of the Hebrew Bible. Insights into individual passages of virtually every book of the Bible have resulted from examination of the Ugaritic texts. No doubt there will be more.

As we move into the twenty-first century, it is important that scholars treat the comparative sources such as the Ugaritic tablets with care. The tendency to find more parallels than are actually there and to simplistically

36. See, for example, Stuart 1976: 1-10. Margalit (1975: 289-313) also proposes a system of understanding Ugaritic poetry that is somewhat metrical in nature. Cf. also Geller 1979: 8-10.

37. See, for example, Geller 1979 and Pardee 1988.

38. For the most extensive listing of proposed word pairs, see the collection of Dahood 1975–81. A survey of this material will show that many of the proposals here are highly questionable or impossible. There has been a fair amount of discussion concerning the mode by which these parallel pairs were passed down through the generations. Some, like Dahood (1975–81: I, 74) suggest that there was a very firm set of parallels, from which deviation was rare. Others, however, have argued that the vocabulary choices for parallel terms in Ugaritic, Hebrew, and so on, would naturally tend to produce parallels between the corpora (cf. Craigie 1977). As Pardee (1988: 171-74) has noted, the truth seems to be somewhere in the middle. There can be little doubt that there is a tradition behind many of the word pairs, but it is not necessary to posit (without evidence) a dictionary or thesaurus of such pairs, as suggested by Dahood and others. They were probably passed on through their usage in the living poetry of the culture.

equate aspects of Ugaritic literature and culture with those of ancient Israel has often been unrestrained in Ugaritology, and this must change. An important task for scholars of the new century will be to evaluate carefully just what can and what cannot be used in the Ugaritic texts to illuminate the relationships between Canaanite and Israelite cultures.

The future for Ugaritic studies is bright. New editions of most of the texts are either available or in process from the epigraphic team of the Mission to Ras Shamra.[39] New discoveries of texts continue to be made virtually every excavation season and have been particularly abundant in the past few excavation seasons (1992, 1994, 1996). The ancient mound of Ras Shamra still promises to startle us with new insights into the relationship between the Canaanites and earliest Israel.

BIBLIOGRAPHY

Aartun, K.
    1982   'Präpositionale ausdrücke im Ugaritischen als Ersatz für semitischen *min*', *UF* 14: 1-14.
Albertz, R.
    1994   *A History of Israelite Religion in the Old Testament Period* (Louisville, KY: Westminster/John Knox Press).
Attridge, H.W., and R.A. Oden, Jr
    1981   *Philo of Byblos: The Phoenician History: Introduction, Critical Text, Translation, Notes* (CBQMS, 9; Washington, DC: Catholic Biblical Association).
Baumgarten, A.I.
    1981   *The Phoenician History of Philo of Byblos A Commentary* (Leiden: E.J. Brill).
Bayliss, M.
    1973   'The Cult of Dead Kin in Assyria and Babylonia', *Iraq* 35: 115-25.
Binger, T.
    1997   *Asherah: Goddesses in Ugarit, Israel and the Old Testament* (JSOTSup, 232; Sheffield: Sheffield Academic Press).
Bloch-Smith, E.
    1992   *Judahite Burial Practices and Beliefs about the Dead* (JSOTSup, 123; Sheffield: Sheffield Academic Press).
Bordreuil, P., and D. Pardee
    1991   'Les textes en cunéiformes alphabétiques', in P. Bordreuil (ed.), *Une bibliothèque au sud de la ville* (Ras Shamra-Ougarit, 7; Paris: Editions Recherche sur les Civilisations): 151-52.

39. The new editions are published in the *Ras Shamra-Ougarit* series (Paris: Editions Recherche sur les Civilisations), under the direction of Yves Calvet, director of the Mission archéologique française de Ras Shamra-Ougarit, and Pierre Bordreuil, epigraphist for the Mission.

Caquot, A., and M. Sznycer
— 1980   *Ugaritic Religion* (Iconography of Religions Section, XV, Fascicle 8; Leiden: E.J. Brill).
Clifford, R.
1972   *The Cosmic Mountain in Canaan and the Old Testament* (Cambridge, MA: Harvard University Press).
1984   'Cosmogonies in the Ugaritic Texts and in the Bible', *Or* 53: 183-201.
Coogan, M.D.
1978   *Stories from Ancient Canaan* (Philadelphia: Westminster Press).
1995   '10 Great Finds', *BARev* 21: 36-47.
Craigie, P.
1977   'The Problem of Parallel Word Pairs in Ugaritic and Hebrew Poetry', *Semitics* 5: 48-58.
Cross, F.M.
1973   *Canaanite Myth and Hebrew Epic* (Cambridge, MA: Harvard University Press).
Curtis, A.H.W.
1994   'The Psalms Since Dahood', in *UB*: 1-10.
Dahood, M.
1975–81   in *RSP*: I, 71-382; II, 1-39; III, 1-206.
Day, J.
1985   *God's Conflict with the Dragon and the Sea* (Cambridge: Cambridge University Press).
— 1994   'Ugarit and the Bible: Do They Presuppose the Same Canaanite Mythology and Religion?', in *UB*: 35-52.
Day, P.
1992   'Anat: Ugarit's "Mistress of Animals"', *JNES* 51: 181-90.
1995   'Anat', in *DDD*: 61-77.
Emerton, J.A.
1994   'What Light Has Ugaritic Shed on Hebrew?', *UB*: 53-69.
Geller, S.A.
1979   *Parallelism in Early Biblical Poetry* (HSM, 20; Missoula, MT: Scholars Press).
Gonen, R.
1992   *Burial Patterns and Cultural Diversity in Late Bronze Age Canaan* (ASORDS, 7; Winona Lake, IN: Eisenbrauns).
Grabbe, L.L.
1994   '"Canaanite": Some Methodological Observations in Relation to Biblical Study', in *UB*: 113-22.
Gunkel, H.
1895   *Schöpfung und Chaos in Urzeit und Endzeit* (Göttingen: Vandenhoeck & Ruprecht).
Hillers, D.
1985   'Analyzing the Abominable: Our Understanding of Canaanite Religion', *JQR* 75: 253-69.
King, P.J.
1983   *American Archeology in the Mideast* (Philadelphia: American Schools of Oriental Research).

Kloos, C.
    1986   *Yhwh's Combat with the Sea: A Canaanite Tradition in the Religion of* —
        Ancient Israel (Amsterdam: G.A. van Oorschot; Leiden: E.J. Brill).

L'Heureux, C.
    1979   *Rank among the Canaanite Gods: El, Ba'l, and the Repha'im* (HSM, 21;
        Missoula, MT: Scholars Press).

Lemche, N.P.
    1991   *The Canaanites and their Land: The Tradition of the Canaanites* (JSOTSup,
        110; Sheffield: JSOT Press).

Lewis, T.J.
    1989   *Cults of the Dead in Ancient Israel and Ugarit* (HSM, 39; Atlanta: Scholars
        Press).

Loretz, O.
    1994   '"Ugaritic and Biblical Literature": Das Paradigma des Mythos von den
        rpum—Rephaim', in *UB*: 175-224.

Maier, W.A. III
    1986   *'Ašerah: Extrabiblical Evidence* (HSM, 37; Atlanta: Scholars Press).

Margalit, B.
    1975   'Studia Ugaritica. I. Introduction to Ugaritic Prosody', *UF* 7: 289-313.

de Moor, J.C.
    1976   'Rāpi'uma—Rephaim', *ZAW* 88: 323-45.
    1987   *An Anthology of Religious Texts from Ugarit* (Leiden: E.J. Brill).

Na'aman, N.
    1994   'The Canaanites and their Land, a Rejoinder', *UF* 26: 397-418.

O'Connor, M.
    1980   *Hebrew Verse Structure* (Winona Lake, IN: Eisenbrauns).

Olmo Lete, G. del
    1992   *La religión Cananea según la litúrgia de Ugarit* (AOSup, 3; Barcelona:
        Editorial AUSA).

Pardee, D.
    1975   'The Preposition in Ugaritic, Part I', *UF* 7: 330-37.
    1981   'Ugaritic and Hebrew Metrics', in *Ugarit in Retrospect*: 113-30.
    1988   *Ugaritic and Hebrew Poetic Parallelism: A Trial Cut ('nt I and Proverbs 2)*
        (VTSup, 39; Leiden: E.J. Brill).
    1996   '*Marziḫu, Kispu,* and the Ugaritic Funerary Cult: A Minimalist View', in
        Studies Gibson: 273-87.
    1997   'Ugaritic Myths', 'Ugaritic Epics', *COS*: I, 241-83, 333-56.

Parker, S.B.
    1989   *The Pre-biblical Narrative Tradition* (SBLRBS, 24; Atlanta: Scholars
        Press).

Parker, S.B. (ed.)
    1997   *Ugaritic Narrative Poetry* (SBLWAW, 9; Atlanta: Scholars Press).

Pitard, W.T.
    1994   'The "Libation Installations" of the Tombs at Ugarit', *BA* 57: 20-37.
    1998   '*KTU* 1.83, The Binding of Yamm: A New Edition of the Text', *JNES* 57:
        261-80.

Pope, M.
1981   'The Cult of the Dead at Ugarit', in *Ugarit in Retrospect*: 160-62.
Rainey, A.F.
1996   'Who is a Canaanite? A Review of the Textual Evidence', *BASOR* 304: 1-15.
Ribar, J.W.
1973   'Death Cult Practices in Ancient Palestine' (PhD dissertation, University of Michigan).
Salles, J.-F.
1995   'Rituel mortuaire et rituel social à Ras Shamra/Ougarit', in S. Campbell and A. Green (eds.), *The Archaeology of Death in the Ancient Near East* (Oxford: Oxbow): 171-84.
Schaeffer, C.
1939   *The Cuneiform Texts of Ras Shamra-Ugarit* (Schweich Lectures, 1936; London: Oxford University Press).
Schmidt, B.B.
1994   *Israel's Beneficent Dead* (Tübingen: J.C.B. Mohr).
Silberman, N.A.
1982   *Digging for God and Country: Exploration, Archeology, and the Secret Struggle for the Holy Land, 1799–1917* (New York: Alfred A. Knopf).
Smith, M.S.
1990   *The Early History of God: Yahweh and the other Deities in Ancient Israel* (New York: Harper & Row).
1994   *The Ugaritic Baal Cycle. 1. Introduction with Text, Translation & Commentary of KTU 1.1–1.2* (VTSup, 55; Leiden: E.J. Brill).
Spronk, K.
1986   *Beatific Afterlife in Ancient Israel and in the Ancient Near East* (AOAT, 219; Kevelaer: Butzon & Bercker).
Stuart, D.K.
1976   *Studies in Early Hebrew Meter* (HSM, 13; Missoula, MT: Scholars Press).
Sutcliffe, E.
1955   'A Note on *'al, l*^e, and *from*', *VT* 5 435-39.
Tropper, J.
1994   'Is Ugaritic a Canaanite Language?', *UB*: 343-53.
Tsukimoto, A.
1985   *Untersuchungen zur Totenpflege (kispum) im alten Mesopotamien* (Kevelaer: Butzon & Bercker; Neukirchen–Vluyn: Neukirchener Verlag).
Tsumura, D.T.
1993   'The Interpretation of the Ugaritic Funerary Text *KTU* 1.161', in *OCPR*: 40-42.
Vincent, P.H.
1914   *Canaan d'après l'exploration récente* (Paris: Victor Lecoffre).
Wakeman, M.K.
1973   *God's Battle with the Monster* (Leiden: E.J. Brill).
Walls, N.
1992   *The Goddess Anat in Ugaritic Myth* (SBLDS, 135; Atlanta: Scholars Press).
Waltke, B.K., and M.O'Connor
1990   *An Introduction to Biblical Hebrew Syntax* (Winona Lake, IN: Eisenbrauns).

Wiggins, S.A.
 1993   *A Reassessment of 'Asherah: A Study According to the Textual Sources of the First Two Millennia BCE* (Kevelaer: Butzon & Bercker; Neukirchen–Vluyn: Neukirchener Verlag).

Wyatt, N.
 1998   *Religious Texts from Ugarit: The Words of Ilimilku and his Colleagues* (The Biblical Seminar, 53; Sheffield: Sheffield Academic Press).

THE RISE OF THE ARAMEAN STATES

William M. Schniedewind

The rise of the Aramean states is shrouded in darkness. The deafening silence in our sources continues to make it difficult to penetrate this darkness. The following essay thus comes as an exercise in groping in through the darkness, trying to find a few touch points to guide by, while trying to move carefully so as not to stumble and fall completely.[1] Because of the situation with the sources, we must rely heavily on political geography and social anthropology to provide a framework for reading the sources. The present study will argue that the Aramean states arose from ethnically diverse, semi-nomadic peoples who lived on the periphery of the Fertile Crescent and encroached on the settled lands in the late-second millenium. The initial impetus for the formation of the Aramean states was provided by the great civilizations of the Late Bronze Age for whom the *aḥlamu-*Arameans was a secondary, and dependent, economy. In the wake of the collapse of the Late Bronze kingdoms, these tribes of the Euphrates steppelands—relying on the infrastructure acquired as a secondary economy—filled the vacuum left by the great Late Bronze Age civilizations. In this, they follow a well-established settlement pattern in the Near East.

The Aramean Homeland—the Steppeland of the Middle and Upper Euphrates

The crux of the present study is the sources, or lack thereof. The main source for the early Aramean states is the offhand references in Assyrian annals, although the first mention of the Arameans is found in the topographical list on a funerary temple of Amenophis III at Thebes (Edel 1966: 28-29, 93 [no. 7, right]). In cuneiform literature the Arameans first

---

1. The way through is made somewhat easier by Brinkman 1968: 268-85; and the many studies of Pitard, most importantly, 1987 and 1994. Other important studies include Sader 1987; Dupont-Sommer 1949; Malamat 1973; Schiffer 1911.

appear in the annals of Tiglath-Pileser I (c. 1112 BCE) who refers to battles against 'the *aḥlamû* KUR *armāyya*^MEŠ' (Grayson 1976: §§34, 70), that is, against an entity on the western side of Middle and Upper Euphrates. Tiglath-Pileser's successor, Ashur-bel-kala, claims to have attacked 'a contingent of Arameans (*ḥarrāna ša* KUR *Arimi*)', on several occasions.[2] Tadmor describes a fragmentary part of a Middle Assyrian chronicle which he interprets as a large-scale Aramean invasion during a famine and drought towards the end of Tiglath-Pileser I's reign. Apparently, the invasion ended with the capture of Ninevah and the flight of Tiglath-Pileser I and his troops (Tadmor 1979). There is little evidence for the Arameans before the late-second millennium BCE. Many have pointed out the similarities between Arameans, Gutians, Sutians, and Amorites and argued on this basis for similar origins.[3] Certainly, their geographical ranges are quite similar. Schwartz suggests that 'Aramean' was simply the designation for sheep/goat pastoralists who ranged on the steppelands of the Euphrates (Schwartz 1989: 283). The Amorites were the first attested of these groups; later followed the Sutu, and the Alamu. For these reasons it would be foolish to emphasize any ethnic relationship between these groups.

According to Assyrian sources, the Arameans lived on the desert fringes or, more precisely, the steppeland. Tiglath-Pileser I, for example, recounts

> I took my chariots and warriors (and) set off for the desert (*mudbara*). I marched against the *aḥlamû* Arameans, enemies of the god Ashur, my lord. I plundered from the edge of the land Suhu to the city Carchemish of the land Hatti in a single day (*ARI*: II, 34).

Tiglath-Pileser's campaign ranges along the steppeland of the middle and upper Euphrates. Although Grayson translates the Akkadian term *mudbaru* as 'desert', it would be better translated as 'steppeland'—that is, semi-arid

---

2. Grayson 1976: II, §§235, 236, 239, 240, 241, 242, 244, 245, 247. I follow Grayson's translation for consistency, although I think that *ḥarrāna* might actually be better understood as a 'caravan'. In King's original publication he understoood it as 'an expedition (against the Aramaeans)'; cf. King and Budge 1902: 137 (col. iii, l. 30). King mistakenly attributes the 'Broken Obelisk' to Tiglath-Pileser I; see Grayson 1976: II, §227. *CAD* (*ad. loc.*) gives a number of meanings including '1) highway, road, path 2) trip, journey, travel 3) business trip 4) caravan 5) business venture 6) business capital 7) military campaign, expedition, raid 8) expeditionary force, army 9) corvée work'. See further the discussions of early references to the Arameans in de Vaux 1979.

3. See, e.g., Moran 1961: 57; Albright 1975: 530.

land which will not support dry farming but does support grazing. A similar confusion can be observed in translations of the Hebrew term *midbar* as 'desert' (or sometimes 'wilderness') where the term 'steppe-land' would be more precise (Smith 1966: 439; Hareuveni 1991: 26-31). In Ugaritic we find a helpful opposition between the *mdbr*, 'steppeland', and the *ngr mdr'*, 'sown land',—that is, between the pastoral and the agrarian regions (cf. *Birth of the Twin Gods*, KTU 1.23.65-76 [=UT 52.65-76]) This translation underscores the location of the *aḫlamû* Arameans; namely, they are not nomads but rather semi-nomadic pastoralists who lived on the fringes of and sometimes even in settled areas. This interpretation dovetails nicely with the enigmatic term *aḫlamû* which apparently refers to these 'pastoral nomads'. The curious Akkadian expression *iš-tu tar-ṣi* which Grayson translates 'from the edge', that is, 'from the edge of the land Suhu', should also be understood to reflect the geographical marginality of the Arameans who were on the other side of the Euphrates.[4]

One peculiar aspect of these early cuneiform references is the use of the determinative KUR, that is, *mātu*, 'land, region'. Particularly suggestive are the annals of Ashur-bel-kala who regularly refers to the *ḫarrāna ša* KUR *Arimi* (cf. *ARI* II: §§235, 236, 239, 240, 241, 242, 243, 244, 247). Grayson translates this expression as 'a contingent of Arameans'; however, there is no compelling reason to construe KUR *Arimi* as referring to a people rather than the more obvious meaning of a region, that is, 'the land of Aram'. The determinative KUR (= Assyrian *mātu*) invariably means 'land, country, or region'.[5] To be sure, the annals of Tiglath-pileser I has the curious reading,[6] *a-na* ŠÀ *aḫ-la-mi-i* KUR *ar-ma-a-ya*MEŠ. Grayson paraphrases this as 'against the *aḫlamû* Arameans' (cf. *ARI*: II, §34). King's original publication translated this rather literally as 'into the midst of the Akhlamî, and the men of Aram'. Given the ubiquitous use of parallelism in the literary structure of Tiglath-Pileser I's annals, King's literal translation is closer to the meaning, although perhaps a better translation reflecting the gentilic *aramayya* would be 'into the midst of the *pastoral nomads*, in the land of the Aramaeans'. The very fact that the gentilic *aramayya* is

---

4.   The expression *ana tarṣi* means 'to the other side'; hence, *ištu tarṣi* might be legitimately understood as 'from the other side'.

5.   Cf. von Soden 633-34. *CAD* M: 414-421 gives one possible meaning of *mātu* as 'people'; however, this is clearly a metaphorical meaning and not a possible meaning for the determinative.

6.   Cf. King and Budge 1902: 73 (Cylinder inscription of Tiglath-Pileser I, col. v, l. 46-47).

employed suggests that Aram is first a geographical region which lends its name to the peoples who dwelled there.[7] In this respect, the later designation 'Arameans' should be understood as arising primarily from a geographic term for the steppelands of the Middle and Upper Euphrates. Hélène Sader comes to a similar conclusion in her study of the Aramean states:

> The evidence registered in the Middle Assyrian texts indicates clearly that Aram was a region—a geographic concept extending from the western bank of the Euphrates over to the abur—where the more important part of the population seems to have been formed from nomadic groups that we designate by the term 'Arameans' (editors' translation; Sader 1987: 271).[8]

'Arameans' thus is *not* an ethnic term, but rather comes to refer to diverse tribes living across the Euphrates who had the cultural bond of a way of life, namely, pastoral nomadism.

2. The 'Land' of the Arameans and Socioanthropological Analogy

There are two theories which have been advanced to explain the rise of the Aramean states. The more recent approach has emphasized the symbiotic relationship between pastoral nomadism and sedentary agriculture.[9] The realities of northern Mesopotamian pastoralism and agriculture required a certain interaction. Pastoral nomadism and sedentary agriculture existed along a continuum with a constant give-and-take and movement to-and-fro. Glenn Schwartz emphasizes that 'the nomads, rather than keeping to the fringes of sedentary society, moved well within the borders of the settled zone, where nomad and sedentist existed in a mutually dependent symbiotic relationship' (Schwartz 1989: 281).

---

7.   Note that the gentilic ending *-ajjum* appears first primarily at Mari. This suggests that it may have come into Akkadian through West Semitic influence; cf. von Soden 1969 §§56p-q.

8.   L'évidence livrée par les textes médio-assyriens montre clairement qu'Aram était une région, un concept géographique s'étendant de la rive occidentale de l'Euphrate jusqu'au Ḥabūr où le groupe le plus important de la population semble avoir été formé de groupes nomades que nous désignons par le terme Araméens (Sader 1987: 271).

9.   E.g. Schwartz 1989: 275-91; Pitard 1994: 207-30. Most of the research, however, has focused on the Mari kingdom which has more abundant documentation; see Matthews 1978; Kupper 1957; Luke 1965. More generally see Adams 1974; Briant 1982; Pitard 1996; Oren and Yekutieli 1990; Rowton 1974; Zarins 1990.

The older model saw the origins of the Arameans (as well as other groups like the Amorites) in 'waves' of desert nomads invading and overwhelming the agricultural zones. The collapse of empires were sometimes associated with these invading hordes.[10] Perhaps the most influential supporter of this hypothesis was William F. Albright who proposed that the Arameans were 'camel nomads' whose use of the camel was an integral part of their mercantile and military success.[11] It is apparent now that the camel was not domesticated until the end of the second millennium BCE and does not become an important factor until the eighth century.[12] For example, we do not encounter camels in military annals until the battle of Qarqar (c. 853 BCE) in the days of Shalmaneser III (cf. *ARAB* 1:161). This older model of the desert nomads is undoubtedly too influenced by nineteenth-century notions of the Islamic conquests of the seventh century CE.[13] Although this theory as articulated must be relegated to the dustbin of scholarship, it was not completely misguided. The symbiotic relationship between the desert and the sown begins with an ongoing sedenization from the desert to the sown. However, the 'desert nomads', or more accurately, the sedenization of semi-nomadic pastoralists are not so much the *cause* of the collapse, but rather the *wake* of the collapse of the Late Bronze economies swells the tides of this sedenization process. With the collapse of the primary economy, the secondary economies disappear and the pastoral nomads must either fade back into obscurity or press into the settled areas.

The historical process reflected with the Arameans may be illuminated by socioanthropological analogy. Although a prevalent analogy is with the enigmatic Amorites, it is better to begin with a more well known case. The early history of the Arameans may be compared with the Edomites and the Nabateans in the southern Levant. The Edomites were a semi-nomadic people whose sedentarization was entirely dependent on larger states, namely Judah and Assyria. Edom was a secondary state created in the wake of the Assyrian Empire. Axel Knauf writes:

---

10. See the essays in the volume edited by Yoffee and Cowgill 1988.

11. Albright 1975: 532.

12. See Ripinski 1975; Zarins 1978; Eph'al 1984: 4-5; Schwartz 1989: 282-83.

13. See Donner 1981: 3-4. I would suggest that the Arab conquests actually follow a pattern similar to the Arameans. Namely, the initial cohesiveness of the Arab tribes was created by their relationship to the economy of the Byzantine and Parthian Empires. The disruption of this economy meant either the dissolution of this secondary economy or their advancement into the mainstream economy; cf. Shaban 1971.

Under Assyrian suzerainty Edom experienced the heyday of its political, cultural and economic development. Technicians and techniques from the wider Assyrian empire contributed to its urban culture... The massive increase of agricultural settlements on the Edomite plateau which is attested for the 7th century...presupposes a massive influx of capital into Edom which was provided by the Assyrian-dominated world economy (Knauf 1992: 50; Knauf-Belleri 1995).

The rise of Assyrian and along with it the Judean state supplied the Edomites with the economic impetus to organize and develop a secondary state beginning in the eighth century. With the waning of the Assyrian empire and particularly the Judean kingdom in the late-seventh century, the Edomites expanded their activity in sedentary agriculture and trade, settling in southern Judah (in the biblical Negeb) and the Judean foothills (Beit-Arieh 1995). Ironically, this further encroachment brought them into direct contact with the Babylonians, the heirs of the Assyrian Empire; and ultimately, the Edomites were subjugated and Idumea eventually became a Persian province. Further the Nabateans arise in the Edomites' place to emerge as a secondary state in service of first the Persian Empire and later the Roman Empire. It is worth noting that the Greek geographer Strabo considered the Idumeans (i.e. Edomites) and the Nabateans to be ethnically related suggesting a sense of continuity between the Idumeans and their former homeland. And, this pattern spans the history of the southern Levant. Israel Finkelstein notes,

Looking at the history of the southern desert in the third and second millennia BCE from a '*longue durée*' approach, one notices two interconnected cyclic processes which were strongly influenced by processes in the nearby sedentary lands. The first is the...alternating sedentarization and nomadization, and the second is the emergence and collapse of desert polity (Finkelstein 1995: 155).[14]

In the case of the Edomites, the rise of the Assyrian empire especially in the eighth century alongside the urbanization of the southern Levantine state of Judah furthered the organization of the Edomite polity. The collapse of the Judean state in the wake of the Babylonian invasions brought both further sedentarization as the Edomites migrated north as far as the foothills of Judah and a nomadization of the remaining Edomite population.

The analogy with the Edomites sheds some light on the close relationship between Aramean tribes and the Sutians, semi-nomadic peoples

14. The cyclic processes of civilizations are discussed in volume IV of Arnold Toynbee's classic work (1956). Also see Finkelstein 1994.

whose 'distribution in time and place roughly match the distribution of the contemporary Arameans' (Brinkman 1968: 285). The Sutians are called 'country folk (*ṣābē ṣēri*)' and 'tent-dwellers (*āšibūte kultārē*)' in the later Assyrian annals of Sargon II and Esarhaddon.[15] Brinkman reflects,

> It is a striking coincidence that in the late second and early first millennia, wherever Sutians are mentioned, Arameans are usually in some way connected with the same time and place. It is not inconceivable that reference to Sutians in this period may designate a more mobile type of semi-nomad (especially among Aramean-related groups) rather than a specific ethno-linguistic entity (tribe or tribes) (1968: 286-87).

The Sutians, however, are not mentioned in Assyrian royal inscriptions from Adad-nirari I until Sargon II, that is, from around 1300 until almost 700 BCE. Rather, the Sutians are referred to in Babylonian texts. Brinkman concludes that 'in Babylonian parlance the terms "Sutian" and "Aramean" may not always have designated distinguishable groups' (1968: 285).

The rise of the Aramean states is probably also analogous to the early Israelite states. The silence of the Near Eastern sources for early history of Aram or Edom is not unlike the silence which biblical scholars faced when reconstructing the early history of Israel. For early Edom and Israel, however, the archeological sources have contributed immensely.[16] The archeological spade has provided the historian with a plethora of new evidence even while the Near Eastern literary sources have remained almost completely silent. The Late Bronze Age witnessed a general decline in the population in the Palestinian hill country. It is difficult to ascertain the precise reasons for this decline, but perhaps it may be attributed to the Egyptian domination of the region.[17] At the same time there was a gradual increase in settlement in Transjordan during the Late Bronze Age.[18] Settlement patterns in Palestine also indicate a gradual movement from east to west (Finkelstein 1988). This movement was apparently facilitated by the power vacuum left in Palestine by the waning of the New Kingdom which had began already in the late-thirteenth century BCE.

The appropriateness of the anthropological analogy between Aram and Israel may be first of all justified by the fact that the early Israelites saw

15. Cf. Brinkman 1968: 286; Lie 1929: 266; Borger 1956: 58.15.

16. For recent summaries of the archaeology of the early Iron Age in the southern Levant, see Bienkowski 1992; Finkelstein and Na'aman 1994.

17. See Gonen 1992: 211-57, and the literature cited there.

18. See essays by Bienkowski 1992; 1995; LaBianca and Younker 1995.

themselves as 'Arameans', as we learn from the classic statement of Deuteronomy, *'rmy 'bd 'by* (Deut. 26.5)—usually translated as 'my father was a wandering Aramean' (NRSV). To be sure, this confession is something of an enigma. To begin with, the verb √*'bd* is employed in a rather unusual way. The traditional translation suggesting ancient Israel's nomadic origins, that is, 'wandering Arameans', appears occasionally with reference to animals (e.g. 1 Sam. 9.3, 20; *Sabbath Ostracon*, l. 3). This translation, while based on genuine semantic arguments, seems wrapped up with rather romantic ideas about the origins of early Israel. So, for example, Otzen defends the traditional translation saying that 'it encompasses the entire patriarchal history and in this way emphasizes the relationship of the early Israelite tribes with the Arameans, who lived a nomadic life' (Otzen 1977: I, 20). In point of fact, however, the characterization of the early Arameans as 'nomads' is dubious. Rather, the early Arameans were semi-nomadic pastoralists. Moreover, the verb √*'bd* itself appears more regularly in other northwest Semitic languages and perhaps even in Ugaritic with reference to men (Otzen 1977: I, 19). More generally it means 'to run away' and not 'to roam'—from hence the NJPS translators derive, 'My father was a *fugitive* Aramean'.[19]

It is rather odd that the patriarch of the ancient Israelites should be identified with one of their arch-enemies—the Arameans. If however, we follow the primarily geographic meaning of the term 'Aramean' which is found in the early cuneiform sources, then the confession makes more sense. Certainly, the gentilic nominal formation of 'Aramean (*'rmy*)' allows such an interpretation. It might then reflect the region of Abraham's origin, that is Harran on the Middle Euphrates, as well as the semi-nomadic pastoralist setting that we see in the patriarchal narratives.[20] The confession thus underscores again the fact that the Arameans were not so much an ethnic group as a social group.

The often-posed question of ethnicity of the Arameans must now be dismissed.[21] The fact, for example, that the early rulers of the Bit-Adini

19. Albright 1957: 238. This meaning derives from the Akkadian *abātu* II.

20. This socioanthropological background, unfortunately, does not aid in dating the origins of the Patriarchal narratives since seminomadic pastoralism was and is a staple of these regions even until the present day; cf. Thompson 1974. On the other hand, the use of the term Aramean in Abraham's confession might suggest that the confession, 'My father was a wandering/fugitive Aramean', arose *before* the crystalization of the Araméans states as the arch-enemies of Israel.

21. Some recent studies on ethnicity include Kamp and Yoffee 1980; Lemche 1985: 80-163; Yoffee 1988; Matthews 1978.

state had Hittite personal names and later took Aramean personal names speaks little about ethnicity (Ussishkin 1971). Likewise, the Arameans are often thought to be related with the Amorites.[22] To begin with, the Amorites and Arameans are found occupying a similar geographic range along the Euphrates River. The similarities, however, do not speak to the question of ethnicity (Grosby 1997). And, they point more to the cultural similarities of pastoral nomads than to ethnicity. It is no accident that the so-called Aramean states (Bit-Adini, Bit-Agusi, Guzana, Sam'al, Hamath, Damascus) were never unified in anything more than a loose alliance based on political imperative. The geographic and social bounds were not strong enough to hold the pastoral nomads of the Euphrates steppeland together.

BIBLIOGRAPHY

Adams, R.M.
1974   'The Mesopotamian Social Landscape: A View from the Frontier', in C. Moore (ed.), *Reconstructing Complex Societies* (BASORSup, 20; Baltimore: American Schools of Oriental Research): 1-11.

Albright, W.F.
1957   *From the Stone Age to Christianity* (Garden City, NY: Doubleday, 2nd edn).
1975   'Syria, the Philistines, and Phoenicia', in I.E.S. Edwards *et. al.* (eds.), *The Cambridge Ancient History*, II/2 (Cambridge: Cambridge University Press): 530-32.

Beit-Arieh, I.
1995   'The Edomites in Cisjordan', *Edom and Seir*: 33-40.

Bienkowski, P.
1992   'The Beginning of the Iron Age in Southern Jordan: A Framework', *EEM*: 1-12.
1995   'The Edomites: The Archaeological Evidence from Transjordan', in *Edom and Seir*: 41-92.

Bienkowski, P. (ed.)
1992   *EEM*.

Borger, R.
1956   *Asarh.*

Briant, P.
1982   *Etat et Pasteus au Moyen-Orient* (Cambridge: Cambridge University Press).

Brinkman, J.A.
1968   *PKB*.

22. Buccellati, for example, points out the formal linguistic relationship between MAR.TU (*Ammurrum*) with Aramean Aḫlamu, Aram Ṣoba, and Aram Rehob. He understands these as 'individual tribes of the Amorite group' (Buccellati 1966: 333).

Buccellati, G.
    1966   *The Amorites of the Ur III Period* (Naples: Istituto orientale di Napoli).
Dion, P.-E.
    1997   *Les Araméens à l'àge du Fer: Histoire Politique et Structures Sociales* (Etudes Bibliques, 34; Paris: Gabalda).
Donner, F.
    1981   *The Early Islamic Conquests* (Princeton: Princeton University Press).
Dupont-Sommer, A.
    1949   *Les Araméens* (Paris: A. Maisonneuve).
Edel, E.
    1966   *Die Ortsnamenlisten aus dem Toten Tempel Amenophis III* (Bonn: Peter Hanstein).
Eph'al, I.
    1984   *The Ancient Arabs: Nomads on the Borders of the Fertile Crescent 9th–5th Centuries B.C.* (Jerusalem: Magnes Press).
Finkelstein, I.
    1988   *The Archaeology of the Israelite Settlement* (Jerusalem: Israel Exploration Society).
    1994   'The Emergence of Israel: A Phase in the Cyclic History of Canaan in the Third and Second Millennia BCE', in I. Finkelstein and N. Na'aman (eds.), *From Nomadism to Monarchy: Archaeological and Historical Aspects of Early Israel* (Jerusalem: Israel Exploration Society): 150-78.
    1995   *Living on the Fringe: The Archaeology and History of the Negev, Sinai and Neighboring Regions in the Bronze and Iron Ages* (Monographs in Mediterranean Archaeology, 6; Sheffield: Sheffield Academic Press).
Finkelstein, I., and N. Na'aman (eds.)
    1994   *From Nomadism to Monarchy: Archaeological and Historical Aspects of Early Israel* (Jerusalem: Israel Exploration Society).
Gonen, R.
    1992   'The Late Bronze Age', in A. Ben-Tor (ed.), *The Archeology of Ancient Israel* (New Haven: Yale University Press): 211-57.
Grayson, A.K.
    1976   *ARI*.
Grosby,
    1997   'Borders, Territory and Nationality in the Ancient Near East and Armenia', *JESHO* 40: 1-29.
Hareuveni, N.
    1991   *Desert and Shepherd in our Biblical Heritage* (trans. Helen Frenkley; Tel Aviv: Neot Kidumim).
Kamp, K., and N. Yoffee
    1980   'Ethnicity in Ancient Western Asia during the Early Second Millenium B.C.: Archaeological Assessments and Ethnoarchaeological Prospectives', *BASOR* 237: 85-104.
King, L.W., and E.A. Budge
    1902   *AKA*.
Knauf-Belleri, E.A.
    1995   'Edom: The Social and Economic History', in *Edom and Seir*: 93-118.

Knauf, E.A.
1992   'The Cultural Impact of Secondary State Formation: The Cases of the
            Edomites and Moabites', in *EEM*: 47-54.
Kupper, J.R.
1957   *Les nomades en Mésopotamie au temps des rois de Mari* (Paris: Societé
            d'Edition 'Les Belles Lettres').
LaBianca, O., and R. Younker
1995   'The Kingdoms of Ammon, Moab and Edom: the Archeology of Society in
            Late Bronze/Iron Age Transjordan (ca. 1400–500 BCE)', in T. Levy (ed.),
            The Archeology of Society in the Holy Land (New York: Facts on File): 399-
            415.
Lemche, N.P.
1985   *Early Israel* (VTSup, 27; Leiden: E.J. Brill).
Lie, A.G.
1929   *The Inscriptions of Sargon II, King of Assyria. Part I: The Annals, Trans-
            literated and Translated with Notes* (Paris: Geuthner).
Luke, J.T.
1965   'Pastoralism and Politics in the Mari Period' (PhD dissertation, University of
            Michigan).
Malamat, A.
1973   'The Aramaeans', in D.J. Wiseman (ed.), *Peoples of Old Testament Times*
            (Oxford: Clarendon Press): 134-55.
Matthews, V.H.
1978   *Pastoral Nomadism in the Mari Kingdom (ca. 1830–1760)* (Cambridge, MA:
            American Schools of Oriental Research).
Moran, W.
1961   'The Hebrew Language in its Northwest Semitic Background', in G.E.
            Wright (ed.), *The Bible and the Ancient Near East: Essays in Honor of
            William Foxwell Albright* (New York: Doubleday): 54-72.
Oren, E., and Y. Yekutieli
1990   'North Sinai during the MB I Period—Pastoral Nomadism and Sedentary
            Settlement', *EI* 21: 6-22.
Otzen, B.
1977   ' *'ābhadh*', *TDOT*: I, 19-20.
Pitard, W.
1987   *Ancient Damascus: A Historical Study of the Syrian City-State from Earliest
            Times until Its Fall to the Assyrians in 732 B.C.E.* (Winona Lake, IN:
            Eisenbrauns).
1994   'Arameans', *POTW*: 207-30.
1996   'An Historical Overview of Pastoral Nomadism in the Central Euphrates
            Valley', *Studies Young*: 293-308.
Ripinski, M.
1975   'The Camel in Ancient Arabia', *Antiquity* 49: 295-98.
Rowton, M.
1974   'Enclosed Nomadism', *JESHO* 17: 1-30.
Sader, H.
1987   *Les Etats Araméens de Syrie depuis leur fondation jusqu'à leur trans-
            formation en provinces Assyriennes* (Beirut: Steiner).

Schiffer, S.
1911   *Die Aramäer: Historisch-geographische Untersuchungen* (Leipzig: J.C. Hinrichs).

Schwartz, G.
1989   'The Origins of the Aramaeans in Syria and Northern Mesopotamia: Research Problems and Potential Strategies', in *Studies van Loon*: 275-91.

Shaban, M.
1971   *Islamic History, A.D. 600–750 (A.H. 132): A New Interpretation* (Cambridge: Cambridge University Press).

Smith, G.A.
1966   *Historical Geography of the Holy Land* (Jerusalem: Ariel repr.).

Tadmor, H.
1979   'The Decline of Empires in Western Asia ca. 1200 B.C.E.', in F.M. Cross (ed.), *Symposia Celebrating the Seventy-Fifth Anniversary of the Founding of the American Schools of Oriental Research* (Cambridge, MA: American Schools of Oriental Research): 11-14.

Thompson, T.L.
1974   *The Historicity of the Patriarchal Narratives: The Quest for the Historical Abraham* (Berlin: W. de Gruyter).

Toynbee, A.
1956   *A Study of History* (London: Oxford University Press).

Ussishkin, D.
1971   'Was Bit-Adini a Neo-Hittite or an Aramaean State', *Or* 40: 431-37.

Soden, W. von
1969   *Grundriss der Akkadischen Grammatik* (AnOr, 33; Rome: Pontificium Institutum Biblicum).

Vaux, R. de
1979   *The Early History of Israel* (trans. David Smith; Philadephia: Westminister Press).

Yoffee, N.
1988   'The Collapse of Ancient Mesopotamian States and Civilization', in Yoffee and Cowgill (eds.) 1988: 44-68.

Yoffee, N., and G. Cowgill (eds.)
1988   *The Collapse of Ancient States and Civilizations* (Tucson: University of Arizona Press).

Zarins, J.
1978   'The Camel in Ancient Arabia: A Further Note', *Antiquity* 51: 44-46.
1990   'Early Pastoral Nomadism and the Settlement of Lower Mesopotamia', *BASOR* 280: 31-65.

RECENT STUDY ON SARGON II, KING OF ASSYRIA:
IMPLICATIONS FOR BIBLICAL STUDIES

K. Lawson Younger, Jr

Recent scholarship on the inscriptions, reliefs, and archeological evidence from the reign of Sargon II, king of Assyria, has helped clarify numerous historical issues pertaining to his reign. Sargon campaigned in the southern Levant three times (720, 716/715, 712/711 BCE), imposing Assyrian imperial foreign policy on the region (Grayson 1986: 146-48). While Sargon is explicitly mentioned only once in the Hebrew Bible (Isa. 20.1), his impact is reflected in numerous passages throughout the first part of the book of Isaiah (Machinist 1983), as well as in 2 Kgs 17.1-6, 24, 29-31 and 18.9-12. This essay will look at these three campaigns and some of the ways that they elucidate certain biblical events.

Assyrian relationships with other foreign nations often progressed through three stages: first, *client* or *vassal*;[1] second, *puppet*; and finally, *province*. Sometimes the creation of a client state was achieved by intimidation alone, namely, by the payment of tribute in order to avoid military attacks. But the progression to puppet state and province was almost invariably the result of active measures on the part of the Assyrian army. With the payment of tribute, anti-Assyrian sentiments rose among the people in the vassal state. The Assyrians would violently put down the revolt and sometimes reduce the territory and set up a 'kinglet', though outright annexation of the land could also take place at this point. Any additional uprisings—which often occurred after the death of an Assyrian king—were met with even more comprehensive destructions. The plundering of palaces, temples, and store-houses, the destruction of cities and their

---

1. Some scholars have rightly criticized the use of the term 'vassal' because of its feudalistic connotations. However, the term 'client' is also insufficient since it does not effectively communicate the loyalty oaths and bonds of tribute placed upon the monarchs of these states in relationship to the king of Assyria. I will use the terms interchangeably.

surroundings, the deportation of the royal household, leading families and other members of the population are, of course, common topics in the royal inscriptions. The trio of verbs, 'to raze' (*napālu*), 'to destroy' (*naqāru*), and 'to burn' (*ina išāti šarāpu*), occur repeatedly throughout the royal inscriptions from Aššurnasirpal II to Assurbanipal, and they sum up the utter devastation wrought by the Neo-Assyrian emperors upon conquered cities and their environs. The impression after reading the Assyrian royal annals is that the Assyrians *ruined* before they *ruled* (Russell 1987: 56). The end of this process left the state fully incorporated into the Assyrian bureaucratic system, which maintained strict controls. Thus there were clear distinctions maintained between a province and the status of a vassal or puppet state (Postgate 1992).

In the case of Israel, during the reign of the Assyrian king Tiglath-pileser III (745–727 BCE), the nation went from an initial, voluntary vassalage in the days of Menahem[2] to a puppet state surrounded by Assyrian provinces on its former territory. During the reigns of Shalmaneser V (727–722 BCE) and Sargon II (722–705 BCE), it moved to the status of province within the Assyrian Empire. Sargon's campaigns document the last part of this process for the states of the southern Levant in the last quarter of the eighth century BCE.

1. *The 720 Campaign*

a. *The Fall of Samaria*

Since the fall of Samaria has been recently discussed elsewhere (including the various reconstructive theories, see Younger 1999), a condensed summary will be given here. When Shalmaneser V came to the throne, all the northern kingdom of Israel, except for the rump state in the hill country around Samaria, was part of the Assyrian provincial system. Hoshea, the monarch of this greatly reduced state, was initially loyal, paying his annual tribute (2 Kgs 17.3b-c).[3] However, Hoshea acted treasonously, sending

---

2.   As listed in the Annals and the Iran Stela, e.g., [m]*Me-ni-ḫi-im-me* [uru]*Sa-me-ri-na-a* (Ann. 13.10). See Tadmor 1994: 68-69, 106-107. For translations, see *COS*: II, 284-87.

3.   It seems best to understand the second clause in v. 3 (*wyhy lw hwš' 'bd*) as parenthetical (i.e. as dischronologized narration): 'Now Hoshea had been vassal to him'. This seems to have been the case since Hoshea became an Assyrian vassal paying tribute in the days of Tiglath-pileser III (Summary Inscription 4.16'-19') (Tadmor 1994: 140-41). In fact, the last clause of v. 4 'as (he had done) year by year'

messengers to So', king of Egypt.[4] In response, Shalmaneser V besieged Samaria, conquering the city in 722 BCE.

One of the main sources for this conquest of Samaria is found in the Babylonian Chronicle (i.28) which states: 'He [i.e. Shalmaneser] ruined (*ḫepû*) Samaria'. The Chronicle uses the verb *ḫepû* elsewhere (i.21; i.43-44; ii.25; ii.37-38; iii.10-11) with a semantic range that includes the capture and destruction of cities (including the 'breaking down' of walls).[5] Thus the Chronicle's usage of *ḫepû* may refer to the ruination of Samaria after or as a result of a siege—though this does not necessarily mean a complete and utter destruction. It is a relatively straightforward assertion that Shalmaneser V captured the city of Samaria. One should not make too much of it nor should it be discounted. The evidence of the Babylonian Chronicle is that Shalmaneser V had a significant role in the capture of Samaria, though a firm chronology is lacking. Chronological data are only found in the biblical text where 2 Kgs 17.6 and 18.10 date the fall of Samaria to Hoshea's ninth year (722 BCE).

Sargon II came to power with the death of Shalmaneser V, who apparently died of natural causes (Younger 1999: 468 n. 28). The ensuing internal difficulties indicated in the sources demonstrate that there was a

(i.e. 'annually') stresses the continuity of Hoshea's tribute prior to his conspiracy.

4. The identification of So is still debated. The following are the proposed possibilities:

1. *Śôʾ* = Osorkon IV. The name So' is a hypocoristicon of Osorkon. See Kitchen 1986: 372-76, 551-52; also see his preface to the 2nd revised edition (1996) pp. xxxiv-xxxix; Schipper 1998; 1999: 149-58.
2. *Śôʾ* = Sais. *Śôʾ* is a rendering of 'Sais' or perhaps a *nisbe* derived from the toponym. The monarch would be Tefnakhte I of Sais. See Redford 1992: 346. See also Christensen 1989; Day 1992; Galpaz-Feller 2000.
3. *Śôʾ* = a title. (A) = *tʾ* 'vizier'. See Yeivin 1952. However, Yeivin's solution has been proven wrong. (B) *nśw*—'king'. See Krauss 1978; Donner 1977: 433; Federn 1960: 33; Naʾaman 1990: 216.
4. *Śôʾ* = Pi(hanky). King *Śôʾ* is to be identified with Pi(hanky), the father of Shabako, the founder of the 25th Nubian Dynasty. Green 1993; Kittel 1933: 465. Naʾaman (1990: 216) used the argument of option 3 above and identified the king as Pi(hanky). See also Shea 1992.

5. From the parallels in the royal inscriptions, it becomes clear that the verb denotes the ruination of cities and, perhaps bombastically, to whole countries. The best example comes from a comparison of the Babylonian Chronicle i.21 and Tiglath-pileser III's Summary Inscription 7.23-25. Therefore, the word is not simply a term for the pacification of a region. This is contra Naʾaman 1990: 211, 215-16; Forsberg 1995: 48-49.

significant struggle for the throne in Assyria at this time.[6] The accumulative evidence seems to point to an illegitimate power seizure by Sargon (whose name means 'legitimate king').[7] It was in the midst of this less than smooth transition of power in Assyria in the last years of the 720s that Samaria, the capital of the northern kingdom of Israel, was captured.

Sargon asserts in eight different inscriptions that he conquered Samaria. Two of these (the Great 'Summary' Inscription or *Prunkinschrift* and the Nimrud Prisms) are of primary importance for historical reconstruction.[8] The Great 'Summary' Inscription (*Prunkinschrift*) (Fuchs 1994: 197; *COS*: II, 296) reads:

> I besieged and conquered Samarina. I took as booty 27,290 people who lived there. I gathered 50 chariots from them. And I taught the rest (of the deportees) their skills. I set my eunuch over them, and I imposed upon them the (same) tribute as the previous king (i.e. Shalmaneser V).

The Nimrud Prisms (D & E) (Gadd 1954: 179-80; *COS*: II, 295-96) reads:

> [The inhabitants of Sa]merina, who agreed [and plotted] with a king [hostile to] me, not to endure servitude and not to bring tribute [to Aššur] and who did battle, I fought against them with the power of the great gods, my lords. I counted as spoil 27,280 people, together with their chariots, and gods, in which they trusted. I formed a unit with 200 of [their] chariots for my royal force. I settled the rest of them in the midst of Assyria. I repopulated Samerina more than before. I brought into it people from countries conquered by my hands. I appointed my eunuch as governor over them. And I counted them as Assyrians.

Neither the Great Summary Inscription or the Nimrud Prisms is arranged chronologically.[9] But it is clear from the Aššur Charter, the Borowski Stela, and his Khorsabad Annals and reliefs (room 5),[10] that Sargon's action against Samaria, in every instance, is tied to his campaign in the west in 720 BCE. In that year (Sargon's second year), Yau-bi'di (Ilu-

6.   Note especially the Borowski Stela (ll. 5-12). See Lambert 1981. Lambert's analysis of the stela is particularly important in regard to Sargon's accession.

7.   The Hebrew form of the name in Isa. 20.1 reflects the name accurately as it appeared in the Assyrian dialect of the time, see Millard 1976: 8.

8.   For a discussion of the line restorations, see Younger 1999: 469-71.

9.   N. Na'aman has argued that the Nimrud Prisms are inferior sources for the reconstruction of Sargon's campaigns (1999; 2000). This seems to explain the difference in the number of chariots incorporated into the Assyrian army (50 vs. 200).

10.   Aššur Charter (Saggs 1975: 14-15, l. 20); the Borowski Stela (Lambert 1981: 125, ll. 5-12); Annals (Fuchs 1994: 87-88); Room 5 (Albenda 1986).

bi'di)[11] of Hamath organized a coalition against Sargon including the cities of Arpad, Simirra, Damascus, Hatarikka, and Samaria (Samaria is listed last in all the sources). No doubt the very recent outcome of Sargon's battle with Humbanigash of Elam at Der greatly encouraged the rebels.[12] Sargon defeated this coalition decisively at the battle of Qarqar (the same site where Shalmaneser III had fought a western alliance in 853 BCE). Yaubi'di's public flaying while he was still alive is depicted in realistic detail on one of Sargon's reliefs.[13]

Sometime soon after this battle Sargon besieged and captured Samaria.[14] This would have been a very brief siege and rapid reconquest of the city,[15] since Sargon moved south to subdue Judah, a claim found in Sargon's Nimrud Inscription (Winckler 1889: I, 168-73; Na'aman 1994c; *COS*: II, 298-99). Since this text dates to late-717 or early-716 (Na'aman 1994c: 17-20; Frahm 1997: 231), the reference can only be to Sargon's 720 campaign (see Younger 2002a). It is very possible that Isa. 10.27-32 alludes to this.[16]

In 1974 N. Na'aman demonstrated that a fragment (K 6205) that had been attributed up to that time to Tiglath-pileser III in fact belonged with another fragment (BM 82-3-23, 131) that had been attributed to Sargon II, recovering a document that has come to be known as the 'Azekah Inscription'. With a reference to the Judahite city of Azekah in l. 5' of the text and two occurrences of the name of Hezekiah (at least partially), there is little doubt that the text portrays a military action against Judah. Another city, whose name is not preserved, is described in l. 11' as a 'royal city of

11. This king's name is spelled: Ilu-bi'di or Yau-bi'di. Concerning the theophoric element, see: Zevit 1991; Becking 1992: 35 n. 59 and Younger (forthcoming).

12. Brinkman 1984: 48-49. Sargon seems to admit to a severe defeat at Der according to the Borowski Stela (Lambert 1981: 125, ll. 5-12).

13. Botta and Flandin 1849–50: II, pl. 120; IV: pl. 181, no. 2.

14. For the archeology of Samaria, see Tappy 1996; Avigad 1993; Younger 1999: 473-75.

15. Thus from a purely logistical viewpoint, Sargon's siege of Samaria in the year 720 BCE was very short. Except that Samaria had already undergone a writhing siege with its defenses therefore greatly weakened, it is doubtful that Sargon could have captured the city in such a short time as would be required when the entire campaign and its distance are considered.

16. Sweeney 1994. See his thorough discussion of other options with appropriate bibliography on pp. 457-63. See also Younger 1996. For further analysis of the relationship of Judah to Assyria in the Sargonid period, see N. Na'aman 1994a; 1994b: 235.

the Philistines, which [Hezek]iah had captured and strengthened for himself' (cf. 2 Kgs 18.8). Unfortunately, the text is very fragmentary, making it difficult to date so that scholars have proposed the following dates: 720, 715, 712, 701, 689 BCE.[17] Recently E. Frahm (1997: 229-32) has discussed the text at some length and suggested a date of 720 BCE (see also Fuchs 1994: 314-15). If Frahm is correct, then this has certain implications for biblical chronology, since Hezekiahm, who is apparently mentioned in the inscription, would have been king of Judah at this time. But the evidence, built mainly on an attribution of the inscription to Sargon which is based primarily on literary allusions and negative evidence for other possible dates, is hardly firm.[18] And if Isa. 10.27-32 is describing Sargon's 720 campaign, then it seems less likely that Sargon attacked Judah from both the north and the west.

Continuing his campaign, Sargon captured Gibbethon and Ekron,[19] and then moved further south and defeated the Egyptian army under the command of Rā'û which supported the rebellious Hanunu (Hanno) of Gaza. He also reconquered Gaza (capturing Hanunu and taking him as a prisoner to Assyria), and destroyed the city of Raphia on the Egyptian border (carrying off 9033 captives). Sargon's conquest of Samaria, therefore, occurred in 720 BCE and was only part of a much larger *Blitzkrieg* that subdued virtually all of the Levant in that year. It was a separate action from Shalmaneser V's action against Samaria and the Mesopotamian sources do not conflate the two different events. Sargon appears to have

---

17. The last date is based on the theory of two western campaigns of Sennacherib. See most recently Shea 1997; 1999. The theory misunderstands the reference to Taharqa in 2 Kgs 19 (see Hoffmeier 2002) as well as some questionable understandings of some of the other material. There is no extrabiblical source that even hints at a later campaign (Dion 1989: 12 n. 38, 15-18).

18. The statement in l. 5' also seems problematic: [...] [URU]*A-za-qa-a* É *tuk-la-te-šú šá ina bi-ri*[*t*? *mi-i*]*ṣ-ri-ia u* KUR *Ia-u-di* [...], '[...] the city of Azekah, his stronghold, which is between my [bo]rder and the land of Judah [...]'. Na'aman (1974: 26) restored: *šá ina bi-ri*[*t mi-i*]*ṣ-ri-ia u* KUR *Ia-u-di*, 'which is between my [bo]rder and the land of Judah'. Galil (1992b: 61; 1995: 322) reads: *ina* ⌜*bi-rit*?⌝ [*áš*]-*ri-ia u* KUR.*Ia-u-di*, 'which is located between my [la]nd and the land of Judah'. This reading follows Borger 1979: 134 who reads: ⌜*áš*⌝-*ri-ia*. Frahm rejects the reading of the sign *áš* before *ri*. He suggests [*ki*]- ⌜*ri*⌝ *ṣ-ri-ia*; thus, 'which is between my troop contingent and the land of Judah'.

19. The capture of these cities is only preserved in the palace reliefs, not in the inscriptions. For the most recent assessment, see Russell 1999: 114-23 and the discussion below concerning the 712/711 campaign.

been the Assyrian monarch chiefly responsible for the large deportation of the Samarians to various locations throughout his empire. Samaria never recovered and remained an Assyrian province throughout the remainder of the empire's existence.

b. *The Israelite Deportations*

A surface reading of 2 Kgs 17.6 (and/or 2 Kgs 18.11) might give the impression that the Israelites were only deported after the fall of Samaria, but the fact is Tiglath-pileser III had performed unidirectional deportations from Galilee, and perhaps from Gilead and the Israelite coastal plain, during and after his campaigns of 734–732 BCE.[20] In other words, Tiglath-pileser depleted the Israelite population through slaughter and deportation without replenishing the territory with other peoples. This would be in marked contrast to the more usual bi-directional deportations that Assyrian monarchs normally executed. This is substantiated textually and archeologically.[21]

Like Sargon II later, there is evidence that Tiglath-pileser III incorporated Israelites into the Assyrian army. In Summary Inscription 4.16′, Tiglath-pileser states that he

> carried off [to] Assyria the land of Bīt-Ḫumria (Israel). [...its] 'auxiliary [army',] [...] all of its people.[22]

20. For a fuller discussion, see Younger 1998a: 201-14; Na'aman 1993. Sennacherib's deportation of Judahites in 701 BCE was also an unidirectional deportation.

21. See previous note and Gal 1992: 108-109; 1988–89.

22. Tadmor 1994: 140-41.

23. For the discussion of this term, see Tadmor 1988: 173-75. The last two words of l. 55 (Rassam Cylinder) of Sennacherib's Annals have typically been read *iršû batlati* 'put a stop (to their service)' (see Borger 1979: I, 136; *CAD* B 176). However, in light of Frahm's recent edition of Sennacherib's inscriptions, the preferred reading may be *iršû tillāti*, 'and whom he had acquired as auxiliary troops' (see Frahm 1997: 54). If this is the case, then the term *tillūtu/tillātu* occurs here too. Gallagher concludes: 'This means that there are no allusions to the desertion or failure of Hezekiah's troops, and modern reconstructions of this campaign have no basis for supposing that such an event took place. To be sure Hezekiah lost these troops, but not through a desertion. The troops became part of Sennacherib's booty in the final settlement' (Gallagher 1999: 140). Tadmor writes that *iršû tillāti* was added to Sennacherib's annals because omen literature gave it this undertone of losing the troops. Like the kings in the omens, Hezekiah lost his auxiliary troops; in his case they became part of Sennacherib's booty. See Tadmor 1988: 173-75.

The term translated 'auxiliary troops' is *tillūtu/tillātu*.[23] This word is not found very often in Assyrian royal inscriptions, but used more often in omen literature, particularly the omen series *Šumma Izbu*, where it occurs in the clause *šarru/rubû tillāti irašši*, 'the king/prince will have auxiliary troops'.[24] The omens show that *tillāti* troops could help a king to victory,[25] but they could also be unreliable. Also according to the omens, *tillāti* troops could be lost. Thus, like many of the kings in the omens, Israel lost its auxiliary troops; they became booty and were amalgamated into Tiglath-pileser's army.

One unit of the Assyrian army, at least since the time of Aššurnasirpal II, was comprised solely of deportees (*šaglûte*). It consisted of professional soldiers with equestrian expertise from many of the North Syrian states. It had its own commander, the *rab šaglûte* ('commander of deportees') who was in turn probably subordinate to the chief eunuch (*rab ša rēšē*).[26] Thus it is probable that Tiglath-pileser III added the Israelites to this unit.

While it is possible that there was some sort of deportation connected with Shalmaneser V's actions against Samaria (725–722), his paltry inscriptions contain no information (see Younger 1998a: 214-15).

All this not withstanding, a closer reading of the biblical texts indicates that 2 Kgs 17.6 and 18.11 telescope several deportations of the Israelites into one. There were, from a strict chronological viewpoint, a number of separate deportations. It is also clear that Sargon makes direct assertions that he deported the Israelites. According to his inscriptions, he deported 27,290 (Great Summary Inscription) or 27,280 (Nimrud Prisms) people. This figure probably reflects the number of deportees taken from both the district of Samaria and the city itself,[27] since the city of Samaria, according to my understanding, would have already been reduced by the events in Shalmaneser V's reign.[28]

---

24. Leichty 1970: 112, l. 95'; 116, l. 28'; 117, l. 33'; 118, ll. 43', 49'; etc.

25. Leichty 1970: 118, l. 43': *šarru tillāta iraššima māt nakrišu ušamqat*, 'the king will have auxiliary troops and he will overthrow the land of his enemy'.

26. Dalley and Postgate 1984: 35-41. It was supplied by at least five *mušarkisāni ša* [lú]*šaglûte*.

27. The size of Samaria at the time of its fall has been variously estimated from as little as 75 dunams according to Crowfoot to as much as 640 dunams according to Kenyon. At 40 people per dunam the population of Samaria would be estimated at as little as 3000 to as much as 25,600.

28. See also Na'aman 1993: 106, who understands the figure of 27,290 to reflect

The Israelites deported between 734–716 BCE were apparently of two filtered types: (1) those who received preferred or at least reasonable treatment (a relatively small number); and (2) those who received hardship and bare subsistence (the vast bulk of the deportees). This filtering process was most often determined by the individual deportee's prior status and skills especially as these matched the needs of the Assyrian administration.[29] The personnel necessary to oversee such large scale deportations must have been extensive. Because of the logistical demands on transport of massive groups of people, it is most likely that the filtering process took place in the deportees' homeland (see Younger 2002b).

According to 2 Kgs 17.6 and 18.11, the Israelites were deported to three locations: Halah or Ḫalaḫḫa (Postgate 1972–75: 58), Gozan or Guzāna (modern Tell Ḥalāf), and the cities of the Medes. Extrabiblical material verifies the presence of Israelites at the first two locations, which were—after all—in Assyria Proper.

(i) *Those Deportees who Received Preferred or at Least Reasonable Treament.* The kings of Assyria frequently tried to treat some of the conquered peoples as their own subjects. The phrase 'I counted them as Assyrians' is repeated from the time of Tiglath-pileser I on (Oded 1979: 81-85). Those Israelite deportees who received preferred or at least reasonable treament included military personnel, administrators, priests, some skilled laborers, and some merchants.

(1) *Military Personnel.* Assyria's population was too small to provide an army large enough for the needs of its expanding empire. Conscripts from the conquered countries or vassal states commonly filled the ranks (see Reade 1972: 101-108; Postgate 1989). This practice was particularly widespread during the reigns of Tiglath-pileser III and Sargon II. Consequently, the onomastic evidence shows that 'at least one-fifth' of Sargon's army bore West Semitic names.[30]

Sargon added the Israelite chariot corps after the 720 BCE campaign according to Assyrian administrative documents called the 'Horse Lists' that list a unit of Samarian charioteers.[31] This was a new unit which was

both the city and district, although he has a different interpretation of the events surrounding the fall of Samaria.

29. For more on this process and its impact on the Israelite deportees, see Younger 2002b.

30. Fales 1991: 104. See also the discussion in Becking 1992: 66-93.

31. TFS 99 (Dalley and Postgate 1984: 35-41). See also Dalley 1985: 31-36;

allowed to retain its national identity, and was not amalgamated with the unit of the *šaglûte*-deportees (see earlier discussion above).

(2) *Administrators*. A Samarian deportee named Sama' was highly placed at the Assyrian court, advising Sargon about matters pertaining to his homeland. He is identified in TFS 99.1 as a 'Samarian' who was 'a commander of teams' (*rab urâte* [written LÚ.GAL *ú-rat*.MEŠ]). If he is the same person found in economic and administrative texts from Balawat and Nineveh, he was a man of great significance and influence within the family of the Sargonids. Dalley puts it this way:

> From this evidence it is reasonable to suggest that Sama' the Samarian commander of teams who served Sargon as a reliable, professional soldier in the royal army of Assyria, was a close friend of the king and had access to and perhaps influence over members of the royal family. As such he would have had opportunities to become closely acquainted with Sargon's vizier Nabu-belu-ukin who probably acted as the first commander of the Samarian unit. Whether or not Sama' actually played a part in negotiating preferential treatment for Samaria, the evidence for his career is an indication of the important role played by Samarians in Nimrud and Nineveh in the late eighth and early seventh centuries.[32]

The exciting, recent discovery of a royal tomb hidden under the pavement of room 49 in the domestic wing of the North-West Palace at Kalhu (Tomb II) has revealed three inscribed objects—a golden bowl, a crystal jar, and an electron mirror—that belonged to Atalia, the queen of Assyria, wife of Sargon II. All three inscriptions read: 'Belonging to Atalia, queen of Sargon, king of Assyria'.[33] These objects were discovered in a stone sarcophagus which contained the bodies of two females; one of which can be identified with that of Yabâ, queen and wife of Tiglath-pileser III, the other is presumably Atalia's (Kamil 1999: 13). There were also heirloom-type objects. Two of these belonged to the Assyrian queen, Banitu, the wife of Shalmaneser V.

Damerji (1999: 8) tentatively suggests that the reason that the two women were buried in the same sarcophagus is because Atalia was Iabâ's

---

Becking 1992: 74-77; Younger 1998a; *COS*: II, 295-96.

32.   Dalley 1985: 41. She also notes: 'Nadbi-Yau, *mukil appāti* 'rein-holder' in 709 BCE according to ADD 234 was probably a Samarian; but we cannot be certain he was not a Hamathite' (p. 41 n. 67).

33.   The gold bowl (IM.105695, Kamil 1999: 16-17, no. 5); the crystal jar (IM.124999, Kamil 1999: 16-17, no. 6); the electron mirror (IM.115468, Kamil 1999: 16-17, no. 7).

daughter. Radner (*PNA* I/2: 433) rejects this suggestion, arguing that since Tiglath-pileser III was Sargon II's father, this would have dictated an incestuous marriage, for which practice there is no evidence in the Assyrian royal family. However, it cannot be ruled out that Sargon's claim to be Tiglath-pileser's son may have been nothing more than a propaganda ploy to legitimate his wrongful seizure of the throne.

S. Dalley (1998) has recently suggested that the name Atalia (twice written *ᶠA-ta-li-a* and one *ᶠA-tal-ia-a*) is the cuneiform transcription of the biblical Hebrew name *Athaliah* (*'tlyh*), the daughter of Ahab and Jezebel (2 Kgs 11), and that this Assyrian queen was, in fact, a Judahite princess. While this cannot be completely dismissed, it is far from certain since there is no clear evidence that the Yahwistic theophoric element was ever transcribed into Neo-Assyrian this way (Younger forthcoming a).

(3) *Priests*. A Nimrud Wine list (*TFS* 121.6-11) states that 2 *sūtu*s or 'seahs' (i.e. 20 *qa*s) were given to a *raksūte*-soldier named Adad-būnī[34] and three Samarian lamentation-priests, while only 3½ *qa*s were assigned to three 'Hittite' lamentation-priests, possibly along with a man named Abi-qamu.[35] Since 2 to 3 *qa*s might be considered the average daily ration for the general population (Fales 1990: 30), and since 1 *qa* might be idiomatic for 1 loaf of bread (Fales 1990: 29),[36] the Samarian priests should be counted as part of the elite in the Assyrian daily ration hierarchy: $4^{1}/_{3}$ *qa*s/loaves per Israelite lamentation-priest as compared to the .875 ($^{7}/_{8}$) *qa*s/loaves per Hittite lamentation-priest.

(4) *Skilled Laborers*. One of the locations where some of the Israelites were deported was Halah. This was the district of Ḥalaḫḫa where Sargon was building a new capital, Dūr-Šarrukin. Since the new city was built by enemy captives,[37] there can be no doubt that some of these were Israelites. In fact, a particular letter demonstrates this:

> Concerning what the king, my lord, wrote to me: 'provide all the Samarians in your hands with work in Dūr-Šarrukin', I subsequently sent your word to the sheikhs, saying: 'collect your carpenters and potters; let them come and direct the deportees who are in Dūr-Šarrukin'.[38]

34. For this individual, see *PNA*: I, 24.

35. In this interpretation of this unusual and difficult text, I am following Fales 1990.

36. 1 *qa* = 1 liter = 0.8 kgs of grain.

37. Type 3, 4, 5 (Fuchs 1994: 55-60). Also see the letter in Parpola 1987: letter 259.

38. ABL 1065.1-10. On the building of Dūr-Šarrukin, see Parpola 1995: 47-77.

However, not all the tasks seem to have deserved equal compensation. A fragmentary list of rations (Fales and Postgate 1995: no. 20) divides the laborers into two units: one entitled to a 2-*qa* ration of barley, the other entitled to only a 1-*qa* ration—the absolute minimal daily ration.

(5) *Merchants.* Recently a number of inscriptions from Tīl Barsip (Tel Aḥmar) have been published.[39] Most of the Neo-Assyrian cuneiform documents from the site seem to come from a single archive of a man named Hanni. However, three other tablets (Tablets 13, 18 and 20) attest a possible archive of a certain Ištar-dūri—hardly an Israelite name—but who is further identified as 'the son of Samiraya' ('the Samarian').[40] In Tablet 13 he is a witness and in Tablet 20 he is the sealer and perhaps therefore also the creditor of a loan of silver. The tablets date to the latter days of Assurbanipal's reign and demonstrate two things. First, later generations of deportees adopted non-Israelite, specifically Assyrian, names.[41] Second, some of the deportees could attain reasonably high social positions in their respective communities.

(ii) *Those Deportees who Received Hardship and Bare Subsistence*
(1) *Agricultural Workers.* The Assyrian government organized its agricultural labor force (mostly deportees) into 'cohorts' (*kiṣru*), modelled along military lines (Postgate 1995: 405). This organization provided firm Assyrian control of its deportees.

Gozan[42] or Guzāna (modern Tell Ḥalāf) was the capital of the Assyrian province of Bīt Bahian that was considered part of Assyria's core. The area around Guzāna was vital agriculturally to the Assyrian cities to the

Another Nimrud Wine List (*NWL* 8 = ND 10047) that lists wine allocations to various professions and nationalities mentions 3 KUR.*Sa-me-ri-na-a-a*: '3 Samarians' (R.15'). See most recently, Fales 1994: 373-34; *COS* 3: 246.

39. Dalley 1996–97: 108-17; and Bordreuil 1996–97: 100-107. For the earlier history of Tīl Barsip, see now Ikeda 1999: 271-302. The hieroglyphic Luwian inscriptions indicate that the Luwian name of the city was Masuwari. See Hawkins 1983: 131-36.

40. Written ¹₁₅-BÀD DUMU ¹*sa-mir-a-a* (T. 13.24-25). Dalley 1996–1997: 82-84 + pl. 3 and fig. 6.

41. This reinforces Fales' assertion that a certain 'Assyrianization' was at work that is attested along 'generational' lines (fathers → sons) which witnesses to an assimilation toward Assyrian. See Fales 1991: 104-105.

42. The phrase in 2 Kgs 17 'Gozan on the Habur River' (lit. 'on the Habur, the river of Gozan') is unique and is apparently an Israelite designation (Cogan and Tadmor 1988: 197).

east, supplying rye, barley and livestock. But living in 'Assyria Proper' did not mean that all was well. Although they are described as 'healthy persons' (ZI[*napšutū*].MEŠ *sal-mu-te*), in an Assyrian letter the individual rations of deportees in Guzāna are mentioned: 1 *qa* of barley and 0.17 of a liter of oil per day—the 'minimum-survival' nutritional dosage![43] It is very probable that some Israelites who were settled in Guzāna received this type of treatment.

Such a daily 'minimum-survival' ration as 1 *qa* (i.e. roughly 1 liter), while supplying sufficient energy intake, would be accompanied by a marked nutritional imbalance over an extended period of time, especially manifesting deficiencies in vitamins A and C (Ellison 1981: 35-45; Younger 1998b: 121-32). The insufficiency in the latter can cause scurvy; while lack in the former can cause blindness.[44]

(2) *Forced Laborers.* In the building of Dūr-Šarrkīn, the bulk of the unskilled labor was done by deportees (Fuchs 1994: 339, ll. 424-426). As pointed out above, a fragmentary list of rations (Fales and Postgate 1995: no. 20) divides the laborers into two units: one (apparently the skilled workers) entitled to a 2-*qa* ration of barley, the other (the unskilled laborers) entitled to only a 1-*qa* ration—the absolute minimal daily ration. The plight of the unskilled laborers must have been very grievous.

(3) *Front Line/Border Towns/Forts.* Finally, some Israelites were deported to and suffered the hardships of living in a front-line region, described as the 'cities of the Medes' (*'ry mdy*) (2 Kgs 17.6; 18.11).[45] In the Assyrian sources, this would appear to be the area of Ḫarḫar[46] (renamed Kār-Šarrukīn by Sargon) and its neighboring townships. These Israelites could not have been deported before 716 BCE, simply because before that date Sargon had no 'cities of the Medes' within his provincial jurisdiction (Diakonoff 1991: 13). Living in such a front-line situation, the only way to survive was to find a common language (Assyrian[47] or perhaps Aramaic[48]), intermarry with everyone else, serve loyally the Assyrian

43. See Fales 1990: 29; Powell 1992: VI, 904. For the letter, see Parpola 1987: letter 257, ll. 5-16. This is following the interpretation of Fales of ll. 12-R.7.

44. Technically, the deficiency of vitamin A is the main cause of xerophthalmia and keratomalacia—conditions which, if not halted, produce permanent blindness.

45. Concerning the textual variants, see Becking 1992: 48 n. 7.

46. Concerning Ḫarḫar, see Levine 1974: 116-18.

47. Fuchs 1994: 44, ll. 72-73.

48. The recently discovered Bukān Inscription demonstrates that Aramaic may well have been the *lingua franca* for the region. See Lemaire 1998; Sokoloff 1999; Eph'al 1999.

king, do the labor required, adapt other religious deities and be receptive to other cultural practices (see Winter 1977: 371-86). While there was unquestionably influence by the West on the Assyrian culture (as documented admirably by Tadmor 1982), there should be little doubt that a certain 'Assyrianization' was at work (Fales 1991: 116).

c. *The Deportations to Samaria*

The deportations to Samaria follow the usual Assyrian bi-directional pattern. Sargon describes some of these deportations vividly in his Nimrud Prisms:

> I repopulated Samerina more than before. I brought into it people from countries conquered by my hands. I appointed my eunuch as governor over them. And I counted them as Assyrians (*COS*, II, 296).

The specific countries are not enumerated. But 2 Kgs 17.24 (+27-31) gives this information:

> The king of Assyria brought people from Babylon, Cuthah, Avva, Hamath and Sepharvaim and settled them in the towns of Samaria in the place of the Israelites; they took possession of Samaria, and settled in its cities...
>
> Then the king of Assyria commanded: 'Send there one of the priests whom you [pl.] deported from there; let him go back and live there, and teach them the rule (*mšpt*) of the god of the land'. So one of the priests whom they had deported from Samaria came; and lived in *Bethel* [*emphasis mine*]; and taught them how they should worship (*yr'*) Yahweh. But each nation still made its own gods and put them in the shrines of the high places that the people of Samaria had made, each nation in the cities in which they lived. The men of Babylon made Succoth-benoth (*sukkôt bᵉnôt*), the men of Cuthah made Nergal (*nērgal*), and the men of Hamath made Ashima (*'ᵃšîmā'*); the Avvites made Nibhaz (*nibḥaz*) and Tartak (*tartāq*), and the Sephravites burned their children in the fire to Adrammelech (*'adrammelek*) and Anammelech (*'ᵃnammelek*), the gods of Sepharvaim.

This passage has presented interpreters with a number of difficulties. Two major questions are: (1) Are these deportations the work of one Assyrian king (e.g. Sargon II), or the work of several?; and (2) What are the identifications of these peoples and who are the gods associated with them? To a certain extent, the questions are interrelated. To facilitate the discussion, the second question will be discussed first.

Initially, it might appear that the order of the entities in the lists in 2 Kgs 17 might be helpful in the identification process. Additionally some scholars have appealed to the additional listings in 2 Kgs 18.34 and 19.13 (‖ Isa. 36.19 and 37.13). However, a comparison of the lists demonstrates that the entities are not arranged according to any discernable geographic pattern:

2 Kgs 17.24:	Babylon, Cuthah, Avva, Hamath, Sepharvaim
2 Kgs 17.30-31:	Babylon, Cuth(a), Hamath, Avva, Sepharvaim (all gentilic forms)
2 Kgs 18.34:	Hamath and Arpad, Sepharvaim, Hena, Ivvah (var. + Samaria)
2 Kgs 19.13:	Hamath, Arpad, Lair, Sepharvaim, Hena, Ivvah
Isa. 36.19:	Hamath and Arpad, Sepharvaim
Isa. 37.13:	Hamath, Arpad, Lair, Sepharvaim, Hena, Ivvah

Moreover, there would be some question whether the Hamath of 2 Kings 17 is the same place as the Hamath mentioned in 2 Kings 18–19/Isaiah 36–37 (see discussion below). In addition, the listings in 2 Kings 17 are found in a very different type of passage,[49] and are serving a very different purpose, than all the other listings which are dominated by propagandistic contexts.

(i) *Babylon/Succoth-benoth*. The first place mentioned, Babylon, appears at first to be straightforward. But a problem arises as to whether the term *bābel* refers specifically to the city of 'Babylon' or is used as a collective noun or metonym for the region/country of Babylonia. If the city of Babylon is intended, then these deportees were most likely the result of Sennacherib's destruction of the city in 689 BCE (see, e.g., Cogan and Tadmor 1988: 209; for the text, see *COS*: II, 301).[50] On the other hand, if the latter nuance is intended, then this might well be a reference to the deportees from the region resulting from Sargon's campaigns against Merodach-baladan in 710–709 BCE (see, e.g., Na'aman and Zadok 1988: 44-46; 2000: 178). According to Sargon's inscriptions, he deported 90,580 people from the cities of Bīt Yakin and adjacent areas in the region. However, there is no mention of where they were deported to. Obviously, the way in which one understands this identification has a direct bearing on how one understands the answer to the first question above.

Unfortunately the identification of the deity Succoth-benoth (*sukkôt bᵉnôt*) is more complex. The identification remains uncertain. It is possible that the deity should be identified with ᵈSAG.KUD with a possible link to Amos 5.26 (Stol 1995). While this interpretation is in certain ways appealing, the explanation suggested by Lipiński (1973) it is also possible: namely, translating the MT *skwt bnwt* as 'image of Bānītu'. The term *skwt*

---

49. See the discussion of Viviano 1987 (esp. p. 554).
50. See also Esarhaddon Babel-Texts Episode 37 (Borger 1956: 25, ll. 12-24).

can be interpreted as a common noun meaning 'aspect, image' (Hallo 1977: 15). And Bānītu (*bnwt*) can be explained as a form of the divine name *dBānītu*, 'the creatress', sometimes an epithet of Ištar of Nineveh (see most recently Cogan 1995b).

(ii) *Cutha/Nergal*. The identifications of Cutha and the god Nergal are the most straightforward and certain of all the places and deities mentioned in 2 Kings 17. Cutha (Tall Ibrāhīm) was located about 25 km north of Kish (see Edzard and Gallery 1980–83). Unfortunately, the site has not been excavated.

It is not specifically mentioned in Sargon's royal inscriptions. Nevertheless, it might be inferred from Sargon's inscriptions that people from this city were deported as a result of his 710–709 BCE campaigns (see Na'aman 1993: 110-11). Furthermore, it might also be inferred from a letter of Sargon to Aššur-šarru-uṣur (see Parpola 1987: 4-7, ll. 66-71) that mentions citizens of Babylon, Borsippa, Kish, Nippur, Der, and at least one other city (lost in the break) who were residing in Que. Postgate (1973: 29) considers these people to be deportees (see also Na'aman and Zadok 2000: 178).[51] Unfortunately, these are only inferences and not direct evidence of a deportation of Sargon from Cutha.

On the other hand, the city of Cutha joined Merodach-baladan in his rebellion against Sennacherib; and it was punished by Sennacherib with a deportation in 703 BCE (see *COS*: II, 301). Consequently, since Cutha is specifically mentioned in Sennacherib's annals as a place from which he made a deportation, the probability is greater in favor of Sennacherib.

In the case of Nergal (*nērgal*), Cutha was holy to this deity, the god of plague and 'lord of the underworld' (ER.ERI₁₁.GAL). Cutha was 'the cult center par excellence for deities connected with the netherworld' (Edzard and Gallery 1980–83: 387). The worship of Nergal was an important part of the official Assyrian cult in Neo-Assyrian times (Livingstone 1995a).

(iii) *Avva/Nibhaz and Tartak*. The name Avva (*'awwā'*) is vocalized Ivvah (*'iwwāh*) in 2 Kgs 18.34, 19.12 and Isa. 37.13. It is a Semitic name, and two different locations have been proposed. Some scholars have proposed a location for the city in Syria (see Montgomery and Gehman 1951: 472;

---

51. Cole offers the option that these 'citizens' may have been merchants residing in the region (1996: 56 n. 2). His suggestion, however, is based on the assumption that Sargon or his predecessors never made deportations from any of these cities, except Der.

Gray 1977: 651). While Sargon's conquest of some of the Syrian states would appear to be the context, there is no mention of a Syrian city with this name. Other scholars have suggested locating the city on the Babylonian-Elamite border near the Uqnu River, equating Avva with the city of Amâ (^{URU}A-*ma-a*) (Zadok 1976: 120-21; Na'aman and Zadok 1988: 45; Becking 1992: 98). Amâ is mentioned in Sargon's annals during the 710 BCE campaign against Merodach-baladan and Šutruk-Nahhunte (the Elamite king), although no deportation of the city is mentioned.[52] The mention of Elamite deities significantly strengthens the identification with this area, since there is additional evidence of Elamite cultural and political influence on the West Semites who lived in this region (Zadok 1976: 121-23; for the campaign, see Waters 2000: 19-21).

This same city is also mentioned in Sennacherib's annals, spelled ^{URU}A-*ú-a-e* which is closer to the Aramaic and Hebrew spellings than the spelling in Sargon's annals. In a later document from Nippur, it is spelled ^{URU}A-*ú-a* (See Zadok 1976: 120). However, the fact that there is no mention in Sennacherib's inscriptions of a deportation from this city, and the fact that the city is mentioned in connection with 'Amate' (see n. 52, as well as discussion below) seem to strengthen the tie to Sargon.

The identification of the deities Nibhaz (*nibḥaz*) and Tartak (*tartāq*) is less problematic, though not problem free. Since some scholars have assumed a Syrian location for Avva, they have naturally sought a Syrian origin for this divine pair. Nonetheless, there does not appear to be any clear cut evidence for a Syrian origin of either of these two deities.[53] It is

52. The context reads (Fuchs 1994: 148-50, ll. 288b-295a): 'The rest of the hostile Arameans who dwelt in their district, and who had put their trust in Marduk-apal-iddina and Šutur-Naḫundi, and had occupied the Uqnû River, a distant abode, their dwellings like the deluge I overthrew, and the date palms, their sustenance and the gardens, the abundance of their province, I cut down, and (the contents of) their granaries I let my army eat. To the Uqnû River, the place of their concealment I sent my warriors, and they inflicted a defeat upon them...and the people together with their property they carried off.

The cities of Zamê, Aburê, Iaptiru, Maḫiṣu, Ḫilipanu, Dandan, Pattianu, Ḫaimanu, Gadiati, <u>Amate</u> (^{URU}A-*ma-te*), Nuḫânu, <u>Amâ</u> (^{URU}A-*ma-a*), Ḫiuru and Sa'ilu, 14 strong cities, together with towns in their environs along the Uqnû River that had feared the advance of my mighty weapons and had devastated their province, came out of the midst of the Uqnû River, a distant place, and seized my feet. That province more than before I caused to rest in safety, and I entrusted it into the hands of my governor of Gambulu.'

53. The attempt to drive Nibhaz from *mizbēaḥ* 'altar' by a series of phonological

considerably more likely that Nibhaz and Tartak should be identified with two Elamite deities (see Hommel 1912; 1926a; 1926b: 987; Cogan and Tadmor 1988: 212; Millard 1995c). Nibhaz has been identified with the Elamite deity ᵈ*Ibnahaza* who is associated with Ea in the Elamite god list (for this text, see King 1909: Pl. 24). Unfortunately, nothing else is known about this deity. Likewise, Tartak has been identified with the Elamite deity ᵈ*Dakdadra* who is listed immediately following ᵈ*Ibnahaza* in the Elamite god list.[54] Unfortunately, like ᵈ*Ibnahaza*, nothing is known about this deity.

(iv) *Hamath/Ashima*. While at first glance Hamath might seem to refer to the well-known city on the Orontes River in north Syria, conquered by Sargon in 720 BCE, this is very unlikely. There are two significant problems. First, Sargon's inscriptions specifically state that the Hamatheans were deported to Assyria. In particular, the Aššur 'Charter' states that the inhabitants were 'brought to my city, the city of Aššur' (Saggs 1975: ll. 25b-28; *COS*: II, 295).[55] While it is not impossible that the Assyrians deported the Hamatheans to multiple locations (as they did with Israel), there is no evidence presently to support this assumption. Second, it is also questionable whether the Assyrians would have put Samarians and Hamatheans together in Samaria, since they had just been allies against Sargon in the battle of Qarqar in 720 (Becking 1992: 99).

Therefore, it seems very likely that the Hebrew word *ḥᵃmāt* refers to Amate on the Uqnu river, taken in the battles of 710 BCE (see n. 52 above). Sargon's text does not specifically mention a deportation from the city of Amate—only a submission of the city. However, since serious doubt can be raised for the reference being to the Syrian city of Hamath, and since Amate is mentioned in conjunction with Amâ (Avva) in Sargon's annals,

---

shifts is very doubtful (proposed by Montgomery and Gehman 1951: 474). The proposal to identify Tartak with Atargatis is also doubtful. Again phonological shifts are necessary (though perhaps not as problematic as with Nibhaz and *mizbēah*). However, the identification is very unlikely since this would be the earliest attestation of this deity! (Cogan 1995c: 1586). See Younger (forthcoming b).

54. Hommel (1926a) proposed to read a transposed form of the name ᵈ*Dakdadra* in the Naram-Sin treaty as ᵈ*Dirtak* (which seemed even closer to the Hebrew transcription). But Hinz (1967: 74) has suggested that the reading of the cuneiform should be ᵈ*Siašum*. See Cogan 1995c: 1585. See Younger (forthcoming b).

55. In addition, see the Great Summary Inscription (Fuchs 1994: 200-201, ll. 33-36, *COS*: II, 296); the Iran Stela (Levine 34: 2-11); and various letters (see Becking 1992: 99 n. 23).

it seems more likely to be the correct identification (see Na'aman and Zadok 1988: 44).

Additionally, the city's name seems to be derived from the Aramaic tribe called 'Amatu'. In the Suhu and Mari area this tribe was one of the tribes that made up the Hatallu confederacy.[56] The tribe is also mentioned in the texts of Tiglath-pileser III. Thus, as pointed out by Zadok (1976: 117-22), 'Amatu' is an example of a toponym in eastern and western Babylonia that was named after the same Aramean tribe.

Interestingly, the people from Hamath/Amate are attributed with the worship of Ashima (*'šym'*), a West Semitic, and especially Aramaic deity, rather than the worship of Elamite deities like their counterparts from Avva (discussed above). Early on, Ashima (*'ašîmā'*) was identified by biblical scholars with Eshmun, a Phoenician god of healing whose name is written as ^{d}Ia-*su-mu-nu* in the treaty of Esarhaddon with Baal of Tyre (Parpola and Watanabe 1988: 27, ll. iv.14). However, in light of the growing number of attestations for the Aramaic deity Ashima, it is doubtful that there was any confusion with Eshmun (Cogan 1995a).[57]

Ashima, has been discovered on an Aramaic dedicatory inscription from Teima (Livingstone *et al.* 1983: 108-11, Pl. 96; Beyer and Livingstone 1987: 286-88). Teima is mentioned in the Suhu Annals and linked with the Arameans; and these are the same inscriptions that mention the Aramaic 'Amatu' tribe.[58] The deity may also be attested at Elephantine (Porten and Yardeni 1993: 234, 127; van der Toorn 1992). Finally, Ashima is very likely attested at Syrene in the Aramaic text written in Demotic script known today as *P. Amherst* 63 (Steiner 1997). Beside the mention of the deity elsewhere in this inscription, the text contains a mostly complete prayer to the deity designated as Ashim-Bethel (Steiner 1997: 321, ll. XV.13-17).

While some scholars have suggested that the text of Amos 8.14 should be emended from *bᵉ'ašmat šōmrôn*, 'by the guilt of Samaria', to either *bᵉ'ašimat*, 'by Ashima of Samaria', or *bᵉ'ašērat*, 'by the Asherah of Samaria' (Livingstone 1995b: 142; Dalley 1990: 30), J. Hadley (2000: 77) rightly comments:

56. Written: ^{lú}a-*mat-a-a*. 'Suhu Annals', text 2, I.17. See Cavigneaux and Ismail 1990: 343; *COS*: II, 279.

57. The resemblance of the divine names Ashima and Eshmun may be merely morphological, having no bearing upon their characters, powers or functions (Zadok 1976: 118-19). It seems very likely that Ashima ≠ Eshmun (Ribichini 1995).

58. See *COS*: II, 279-82, ll. i.7b-16a and iv.26b'-38'; Dion 1995: 68-69.

since the text as preserved has a perfectly good Hebrew word (*'ašmāh*) which admirably fits the context, there is no need whatsoever for emendation. One can only speculate upon the real meaning behind the 'guilt of Samaria', but if the asherah was still standing there, it is easy to believe that the phrase might bring it to mind.

(v) *Sepharvaim/Adrammelech and Anammelech.* This entity has been the most difficult one to identify. One suggestion has been to locate Sepharvaim (*sᵉparwayim*) in Phoenicia (see Kaufman 1978: 102 n. 9; cf. Becking 1992: 101-103). This identification has been based on two points: (1) the identifications of the deities Adrammelech and Anammelech with Phoenician deities, and (2) the geography implied by the serial order in 2 Kgs 17.24. The latter point is not a strong argument (see the discussion of the arrangement of the listings above). In the case of the former point, see the discussion below. Finally, although the Assyrian kings Sennacherib and Esarhaddon did deport Phoenicians, there is no evidence of any deportation of Phoenicians to Samaria, but rather to other locations.

Another suggestion is to locate Sepharvaim in Syria (Day 1989: 41-46). This understanding equates Sepharvaim with Sibraim (Montgomery and Gehman 1951: 472; van der Toorn 1992: 92). But Sibraim was located on the border between the lands of Hamath and Damascus, and it is thus likely to have belonged to one or the other's territory (Zadok 1976: 115-16).

A third suggestion is to equate Sepharvaim with the Babylonian city of Sippar (Driver 1958: 18-19). But Driver's proposal that Sepharvaim is a dual form reflecting the two parts which formed the city of Sippar is untenable (Zadok 1976: 155 n. 15).

Finally, it has been argued that 'Sepharvaim was probably a settlement in the Chaldean territory of Bīt Awukāni' (Na'aman and Zadok 1988: 44; Zadok 1976: 115-17). Bīt Awukāni is mentioned in the texts of Sargon. Zadok has pointed to the city of Sipra'ani (*ᵘʳᵘSi-pi-ra-i-ni*), a Chaldean toponym in the Murašû archive from Nippur (1976: 115-6). This city is apparently mentioned in Sennacherib's annals where it is spelled *ᵘʳᵘŠá-par-ri-e* (Luckenbill 1924: 53, l. 45). Thus this city of Saparrê/Sipra'ani would be located south of Nippur. This identification appears to be the most likely.

The first deity mentioned in connection with the people of Sepharvaim is Adrammelech (*'adrammelek*) (Millard 1995a).[59] Some scholars suggest

---

59. While one of Sennacherib's sons is called Adrammelech according to 2 Kgs 19.37, this should not be confused with the deity.

emending Adram to Adad (*'dd*) and linking the name Adrammelech to Adad-milki (an Assyro-Babylonian deity[60] supposedly known from personal names in the archive of Tell Halaf from the region of Harran and Gozan [Deller 1965: 382-83]). Some serious doubts about this identification have been voiced (Kaufman 1978: 101-109). Pedersén (1984–86: 313-16) has argued that the signs read Adad-milki (i.e. U.U) are simply to be read Dada or Dadda, caritative forms of Adad.[61] Millard (1995a: 18) comments:

> If the Sepharvites were Aramean or Phoenician, it is very unlikely that the name of their god would have lost its initial *h*, unless the Hebrew authors of Kings copied the information from a cuneiform text in Babylonian which would not express it.

The preferred interpretation of *'adrammelek* is to vocalize as an adjective + noun: *'dr + mlk*, 'the glorious one is king' (Millard 1995a: 18). This explanation would link the deity to a Phoenician origin, since the root *'dr* is absent in Aramaic. Nonetheless, the movement of peoples and cults by natural processes of migration and trade, as well as Assyrian deportations, could account for the movement of a group of Phoenicians who worshiped *'adrammelek* to a Babylonian context, only to see their descendents transplanted to Samaria (this is perhaps not dissimilar to the Aramaic tribe of 'Amatu' who worshiped Ashima discussed above). The worship of the deity (by burning of children) may indicate a link to Molech.

The second deity, Anammelech (*'anammelek*), has been understood as a composite of the Babylonian divine name *Anu(m)* + the West Semitic noun *melek*, 'king' (Gray 1977: 596; Montgomery and Gehman 1951: 476; Cogan and Tadmor 1988: 212). But the divine name Anu is written with an *'* in West Semitic transcription, never with an *'* (Millard 1995b: 58-59).

Preferably, the name should be understood as a composite of *'n + mlk*. The first element is the West Semitic male counterpart to the goddess, Anat (*'nt*). The second element would create the sentence name 'An is king'. Like Adrammelech above, this deity was worshiped by the burning of children which may suggest a relationship with Molech (Millard 1995b: 59).

---

60. First suggested by Jensen 1898: 333 n. 1; and then later by Ungnad 1940: 58; and accepted by many, e.g., Albright 1969: 157-58; Montgomery and Gehman 1951: 476; Cogan and Tadmor 1988: 212.

61. See now the 'Adad-milki-X' names in *PNA*: I, 28-29; and the 'Dādî', 'Dādi-X' names in *PNA*: I, 360-65.

(vi) *Synthesis*. Unfortunately the king responsible for the repopulation of Samaria is not identified in the text of 2 Kings 17. The only Assyrian monarch mentioned by name in the chapter is Shalmaneser V (v. 3), who can hardly be the king in view in v. 24.

Some scholars believe that these deportations were the work of Sargon II that occurred approximately from 716 to 708 BCE.[62] Certainly if these deportations were the work of only one Assyrian monarch, Sargon is the best candidate in light of the discussion of the identifications above. Of course, even if 2 Kings 17 refers only to deportations made by Sargon, this does not exclude any later waves of deportations to Samaria made by later Assyrian kings.

In fact, the biblical material alludes to some later deportations. For example, in Ezra 4.2, the deportees to Samaria implore Zerubbabel:

> Let us build (the temple) with you, because like you we seek your God, and we have been sacrificing to him ever since the days of Esarhaddon, king of Assyria, who brought us here.

The tradition preserved in Isa. 7.8[63] should probably be linked to this passage. Whether it is a gloss or not is not the issue here. Rather it is a witness to an additional tradition concerning the repopulation of Samaria. One more witness is found in Ezra 4.9-10 which mentions:

> ...the Persians, the people of Erech, the Babylonians, the people of Susa, that is, the Elamites, and the rest of the nations whom the great and honorable Osnappar (Assurbanipal) deported and settled in the city [var. cities] of Samaria and in the rest of (the province of) Beyond the River (Trans-Euphrates)...

P. Amherst 63, an Aramaic text in Demotic script,[64] contains an interesting New Year's festival liturgy of some exiles imported to Upper Egypt, probably Syrene, from Bethel. These exiles came originally from places called *rš* and *'rš* in the papyrus. These place names should most likely be identified with land between Babylonia and Elam known as Rāši and Arāšu in the Assyrian sources. R. Steiner suggests that the people of

---

62. Na'aman and Zadok 1988: 36-46. 'All these areas were conquered by Sargon II during his campaigns against Merodach-baladan in the years 710–709 BCE' (p. 44). See also Na'aman 1993: 110-12; Na'aman and Zadok 2000: 177-79.

63. 'Within sixty-five years (i.e. c. 669–667 BCE) Ephraim will be too shattered to be a people...'

64. See Steiner 1991; 1995; 1997; Steiner and Nimms 1984; 1985; Kottsieper 1997.

these two areas were captured by Assurbanipal during his campaign against Elam, and deported to the Assyrian province of Samaria. According to Steiner there is reason to believe that most if not all of them wound up in Bethel (cf. 2 Kgs 17.28 above), joining the foreign colonists settled there by earlier Assyrian kings (Steiner 1997: 310). Their subsequent migration to Egypt may be recorded in the text's account of the arrival of soldiers from Judah and Samaria (see *COS*: I, 321, ll. XVI.1-6).

While Steiner's reconstruction may remain the best explanation for all of the sources, it is important to note, as Na'aman correctly points out, that Sargon II attacked Rāši (see Fuchs 1994: 152, l. 302) and may have deported some of the inhabitants from this area to Bethel.

It is also important to note that the biblical text in 2 Kings 17 does not record all of the deportations made to Samaria, even by Sargon. Sargon claims to have defeated and deported some Arabs to Samaria (Samerina).[65]

> The Tamudi, Ibadidi, Marsima[ni] and Hayappâ, the land of distant Arabia, inhabitants of the desert, who knew[66] neither overseer nor commander, who never brought their tribute to any king—with the help of Aššur, my lord, I defeated them. I deported the rest of them. I settled (them) in Samaria/ Samerina.

Not much is known about these nomadic Arabian tribes. However, all of them, except for the Tamudi, can be regarded as Midianite tribes (Knauf 1988). The fact that the Hajapu[67] (who may be equated with the Old Testament *'ph*) had to pay tribute to Tiglath-pileser III (Tadmor 1994: 200-201, l. 9') exposes Sargon's claim to have conquered a people 'who never brought tribute to any king' to be a stereo-typed expression used for ideological purposes.

According to Eph'al (1982: 105-11), it is doubtful whether there were ever any military engagements between the Assyrians and these Arab tribes. He feels that the text reflects a spontaneous settlement of some Arab tribes in the territory of the Assyrian province Samerina which was

---

65. Annals, ll. 120b-123a. Fuchs 1994: 110; *COS*: II, 293. The same event is reported in Sargon II's Cylinder inscription: '...who conquered the Tamudi, the Ibadidi, the Marsimani and the Hayappâ, of whom the remainder I removed and settled in the land of Bīt-Ḫumria (Israel)' (Fuchs 1994: 34, ll. 19-20; *COS*: II, 298). For the date of this deportation, see the discussion of Na'aman and Zadok 1988: 43.

66. The Arab tribes are the subject and not the object of *idūma* (see Cogan and Tadmor 1988: 337; Becking 1992: 103).

67. It is often thought that they controlled the caravan routes on the Arabian peninsula.

simply tolerated by the Assyrians. The fact that there is no record of a campaign of Sargon II against the Arabs seems to support his view.

However, certain letters seem to indicate that some sort of military engagement between the Assyrians and the Arab tribes did indeed take place.[68] These letters describe Arab raids into Assyrian territory. While it is uncertain if these are the same Arabs as the ones mentioned in the annals from Khorsabad, it is possible that Sargon II would have reacted to these raids with military action—whether under his own command or under the command of an Assyrian officer (like in the case of the Yamani incident at Ashdod, see below). And this military action might have then led to their deportation to Samaria/Samerina (see Becking 1992: 102-104).

The recent discovery and publication of two cuneiform tablets from Tel Hadid provide additional knowledge about the deportations to Samaria (Na'aman and Zadok 2000). Since, in the first millennium BCE, cuneiform writing on tablets appeared in Palestine only after the Assyrian annexations and deportations, there can be little doubt that these tablets are the product of some of the Mesopotamian deportees to the region.

One tablet appears to be a real estate transaction and is dated by eponym to 698 BCE (only three years after Sennacherib's invasion of the Levant in 701 BCE). With the exception of one name, all of the personal names are Akkadian and most likely individuals who were part of the deportations to Samaria or their descendants.

The second tablet is a debt note with a pledge (the debtor pledges his wife and sister) and is dated by eponym to 664 BCE (during the earlier years of Assurbanipal). The debtor appears to be indigenous while the creditor probably belonged to the deportees or their descendants.

These tablets add to the small number of others documents that belonged to the deportees to Samaria (Na'aman and Zadok 2000: 176-77). 'On the whole, it is noteworthy that so far there is hardly any difference between the tiny group of neo-Assyrian deeds from Palestine and those from the Assyrian heartland: both display the same formulary and scribal conventions' (p. 177).

In conclusion, it is very evident from the biblical texts, as well as from the Neo-Assyrian royal inscriptions, that 2 Kings 17 does not give a

---

68. *SAA* 1.82 (= *ABL* 547) is a letter from Tabsil-Esharra, governor of Assur to Sargon II and reports Arab raids on the border near the Euphrates. *SAA* 1.84 (= *ABL* 88) is a letter from the same author, and reports the ravaging by Arabs of the city of Sippar. In other letters referring to the Arabs, the governor of Zobah reports on Arab penetration in the West. See Parpola 1987: 74.

complete account of all the deportations to Samaria. The text was, no doubt, written at least three generations after the first deportations (2 Kgs 17.41). Thus it telescopes many years into its presentation, perhaps covering the entire period of the Sargonid monarchs (Sargon, Sennacherib, Esarhaddon and Assurbanipal).[69]

2. *The 716/715 Campaign*

In 716 or 715 BCE Sargon campaigned again in Philistia as recorded in some prism fragments from Assur and Nineveh (newly edited by Fuchs 1998: 28-29). The relevant passage reads:

> Together with [...] and sheep [...] [I deported? ...] from the [land of...] in the land that [...] on the border of the city of the brook of Eg[ypt, a district which is on the shore of] the Western Sea I settled them. I assigned th[em into the hands of my official administrator] the sheikh of the city of Laban [...] (Ass 1-7, T 1-2).

> (As for) Šilkanni, king of Egypt, which [lies far away], the fear of the splendor of Aššur, my lord [...ov]erwhelmed him; and he brought to me as his present 12 big horses of Egypt, which their like is not to be found in the land of [Assyria] (Ass 8-11, T 3-7).

Unfortunately the events of this campaign are very incomplete. Sargon settled deportees at the Brook of Egypt, assigning them to the sheikh of Laban.[70] He may have wanted to create a clearly defined border between his empire and Egypt and have a local chief be responsible for it (Gallagher 1999: 115). With the Assyrian army in the region, Šilkanni, the king of Egypt (i.e. Osorkon IV), felt compelled to send Sargon 12 magnificent horses as a gift. These were probably Kushite horses from the Dongola Reach area, already an important horse-breeding center at this time (Heidorn 1997). This campaign was probably more commercial than military (Mattingly 1981: 47; Grayson 1991: 89). In fact, Isa. 19.23 may refer to this expedition. Although it is probable that Sargon replaced the king of

69. Cogan and Tadmor 1988: 208-13; Oded 1979: 66. An analogy can be drawn from the Aramaic Assur ostracon which contains a list of various ethnic groups deported to the region of Uruk in four successive reigns. See *KAI* 233 (ll. 15-16): 'Tiglath-pileser deported captives from Bit-Amukani; and Ululai (Shalmaneser V) deported [captives] from Bit-Adini; and Sargon deported captives from Dur-Sin; and [Sen]nacherib [deported cap]tives from Kish...'

70. For a discussion, see Eph'al 1982: 93, 104, 107-108.

Ashdod at this time (i.e. Azuri → Aḥimiti), there is no clear evidence for this. Sargon's Annals simply record the removal of Azuri on account of his plotting against Sargon and his replacement by his brother Aḥimiti, giving no indication as to when this occurred.

While Becking (1992: 54) has ascribed the Azekah inscription to this campaign, the evidence is quite insufficient; and hence unlikely.

3. The 712/711 Campaign:
The Yamani Affair at Ashdod (Isaiah 20.1)

Not very long after Sargon had returned to Assyria, the people of Ashdod rebelled once again. Traditionally, the campaign is dated to 712, but Fuchs (1998: 85-88) argues for a 711 date. This is recorded in a number of Sargon's inscriptions,[71] one of the more important being the Nineveh Prism fragments (Fuchs 1998: 44-46).[72] A translation of the relevant lines follows:

> In my ninth regnal year, I [marched] against [the city of Ashdod, which is on the coast of the Great Sea. [...] [the city] of Ashdod [...] [...] (VII.a: Sm 2022,II′ ll. 13-16).

> Because [he committed crimes...] from As[hdod ...] Aḥimiti [...]
> I promoted his favorite brother ov[er the people of Ashdod] and I [placed him on the throne of his father]. I imposed on him tribute and tax[es...] as on [former] kings [...] (VII.b: K.1668 + col. IV′ ll. 1-8a).

> Now the evil [Hittites] in [...] plotted evil [...] to withhold tribute [their heart] Their princes started a rebellion (and) insur[rection]; and they caused him to get out [of Ashdod] like a shedder of blood. Yamani, a *ḥupšu* man, [...] [...] [they plac]ed over them [...] They caused [him] to sit [on the throne] of his lord. Their city [...] [...] battle [...] [...] [...] [...] in its vicinity, a moat [...] 20 cubits (8.88 meters) in depth [they dug] that reached ground water (ll. 8b-25a).

---

71. For the Yamani affair in Sargon's inscriptions, see (1) *The Small 'Summary' Inscription*, Fuchs, 1994: 76, 308, ll. 11-15; Weißbach 1918: 178-79, ll. 11-15; and *COS*: II, 297; (2) *The Annals*, Fuchs 1994: 132-34, 326, ll. 241-51; *COS*: II, 294; (3) *The Great 'Summary' Inscription*, Fuchs 1994: 189-248, ll. 90-112a; *COS*: II, 296-97; (4) *The Nineveh Prism* (see text below) and (5) *The Tang-i Var Inscription*, Frame 1999, ll. 19-21; *COS*: II, 300.

72. Earlier publication: Winckler 1889: 186-89, taf. 44-46. Translations and studies: *ARAB* 2: §§190-218 (§214 and §§193-195); *ANET*[3] 287; *TUAT* 1/4: 381-82; Kapera 1972; 1976; 1987; Na'aman 1974: 32; 1994b; 1994c; Timm 1989: 344-45; Fuchs 1998: 73-74, 124-31; Tadmor 1958: 79.

To the [kings] of Philistia, Judah, E[dom], Moab, who live by the sea, bearers of tri[bute and] gifts to Aššur, my lord, <they sent> words of falsehood (and) treacherous speech to incite enmity with me.[73] To Pharaoh, king of Egypt, a prince who could not save them, they brought their good-will gifts and implored his alliance (ll. 25b-33a).

(But) I Sargon,[74] the legitimate ruler, who fears the oath of Šamaš (and) Marduk, who observes the commands of Aššur, I caused my troops to cross over the Tigris (and) Euphrates rivers at full springtime flood as though on dry land. Now Yamani himself, their king, who trusted in his own power, (and) did not submit to my lordship, heard the advance of my troops from afar, and the radiance of Aššur, my lord, overwhelmed him; and [...] on the bank of the river [...] deep water [...] he took? [...] [...] far away [...] he fled [...] [... A]shdod [...] [...] (ll. 33b-48).

Obviously the leaders of Ashdod disliked Aḫimiti and replaced him with a *ḫupšu* man (i.e. a commoner), Yamani, as their new king.[75] These leaders sent seditious messages to a number of southern Levantine states attempting to persuade them to join in an anti-Assyrian coalition. These included the rulers of Philistia, Judah, Edom,[76] and Moab.[77] These same leaders had also sent their good-will gifts (*šul-man-na-šú-nu iš-šu-ú-ma*) to Pir'u (Pharaoh), king of Egypt (*ᵐPi-ir-'u-u š[à]r* KUR *Mu-uṣ-ri*),[78] and implored his alliance (*e-ter-ri-šu-uš ki-it-ra*) (ll. 30b-33a). The leaders of the rebellion in Ashdod were attempting to create a *kitru*-alliance. Such unholy alliances (*kitru*)[79] are usually depicted with the enemies coming together against the Assyrian king. The weaker party often pays the stronger one with a 'bribe' or 'voluntary gift' (*ṭa'tu*). Unlike the *adê*, the *kitru* alliance is unholy since it is based on selfish motives. It always

73. For an explanation of this difficult sentence, see Fuchs 1998: 74; Younger 2002a.

74. A word play on the name of Sargon; hence: 'I, the-legitimate-king, the legitimate ruler'.

75. See also *ANET*: 287; *ARAB*: II, 193-95. For discussion on the issues, see Mattingly 1981; Spalinger 1973; Tadmor 1966; 1971; Kapera 1972; 1976; Galil 1992a; Na'aman 1993: 239-40. For Yamani, see K. Radner, 'Iāmānī', *PNA*: II, 491

76. On Edom's role, see now Millard 1992; Weippert 1987.

77. For Judah, Moab and Edom in 'the geography' of the Assyrian empire of Sargon's day, see Horowitz 1993. For the complete text see Grayson 1974–77.

78. Most likely this is a reference to Shabako (see Hoffmeier 2002).

79. For *kitru* alliances, cf. Liverani 1982. For another example of such an alliance, cf. the attempt by the leaders of Ekron to establish a *kitru* alliance in the days of Sennacherib (Rassam Cylinder 42-48). See Younger 2002a.

reflects misplaced 'trust'.[80] In contrast, the Assyrian king 'trusts' in Aššur. The *kitru* alliance normally consists of chaotic elements with unimaginable numbers of troops.

However, in this case, there is no clear indication that any kind of alliance formed or that any of these states lent support to the rebels in Ashdod, except for the Philistine city of Gath, which may have been simply part of Ashdod's territory (at least this is how the reference in Sargon's Great Summary Inscription is understood by many scholars). In fact, a few years earlier 'Azuri, the king of Ashdod, plotted in his heart to withhold tribute, and he sent (messages) to the neighboring kings, hostile to Assyria'.[81] But, as pointed out above, there was no support forthcoming in this instance, and Sargon states rather matter-of-factly that he simply removed Azuri and replaced him with Aḥimiti.[82] In any case, Sargon dealt with the Yamani rebellion apparently through his *turtānu* besieging and conquering Ashdod, Gath (Gimtu) and Ashdod-Yam.[83] These are the only places specifically mentioned in connection with this campaign against Ashdod.

Both Ashdod and Ashdod-Yam show clear archeological evidence of Assyrian conquest. At Ashdod, the destruction is most clearly revealed in the mass graves of Stratum VIII. Here approximately 3000 human individuals were buried in 16 loci within Area D (Mattingly 1981: 52). Furthermore, N. Haas noted that some of the skeletal remains display signs of decapitation (Dothan 1971: 212-13), something practiced by the Assyrian army after the capture of rebellious cities.[84]

The only biblical text to mention Sargon by name is Isa. 20.1 which refers to this 712/711 campaign stating: 'In the year that the commander-in-chief (*tartān*), who was sent by King Sargon of Assyria, came to Ashdod and fought against it and took it...' (NRSV). This is confirmed by the Eponym Chronicle which notes that Sargon stayed 'in the land' (Millard 1994: 47, 60). Sargon probably remained behind to supervise construction on his palace at Dūr-Šarrukin (Tadmor 1958: 92-94, 95-96).

---

80. The theme of the enemy's misplaced trust is pervasive in Assyrian royal inscriptions. See Cohen 1979: 39-41; Gonçalves 1986: 410-12.

81. Annals, ll. 249-50. Great Summary Inscription, ll. 90-92.

82. See Fuchs, 'Aḫi-Mīti', *PNA*: I, 65.

83. See the Annals (ll. 258b-259a) and the Great 'Summary' Inscription (ll. 103b-105a); Fuchs 1994: 197, 185; *COS*: II, 294, 296-97). See Grayson 1991: 89; Spalinger 1973.

84. For Ashdod-Yam see Kaplan 1993.

In his landmark article of 1958, H. Tadmor argued that the Assyrian army conquered Gath, Gibbethon and Ekron on its way to Ashdod and Ashdod-Yam; and that after the capture of Ashdod, Azekah was assaulted and captured (1958: 80-85).[85] Tadmor based his argument on two reliefs with epigraphs from Sargon's palace: Gabbutunu (Gibbethon) and 'Amqarruna (Ekron) (Room V, reliefs 5, 10). That the epigraphs identify these two cities is clear; that they belong to the 712 campaign rather than the 720 campaign is not clear. In fact, in contrast to Tadmor, in the most recent study of this matter, John Russell argues in favor of the one campaign per room hypothesis which understands the reliefs of Gabbutunu and 'Amqarruna to date to the 720 campaign (Russell 1999: 114-23).[86]

Recently it has been suggested that the Azekah Inscription depicts events in the context of Sargon's campaign against Ashdod in 712/711 BCE. Galil (1992a; 1992b; 1995) puts forth four arguments in favor of the Azekah inscription dating to Sargon's 712/711 campaign against Ashdod. First, he argues that in l. 5, the location of Azekah 'between my lan[nd] and Judah (*ina bi-* ⌈*riⁿ* [*áš*]-*ri-ia u* KUR *Ia-u-di*)' can only reflect a period between 712/711 and 701 BCE. But this reading is problematic as Frahm (1997: 230) points out (see also n. 18 above). Second, Galil argues that the spelling of Hezekiah in the Azekah inscription is different from the usual form of Hezekiah's name in Sennacherib's inscriptions: according to Galil, the Azekah Inscription read in ll. 4 and 11: [ᵐ*Ha-zaq-i*]*a-a-u* and ⌈ᵐ*Ha*⌉-⌈*zaq*]-[*i*]*a-a-u* (though note Frahm's comments 1997: 230); as opposed to Sennacherib's Annals (Rassam 42, 49): ᵐ*Ha-za-qi-a-ú*. But this is hardly a strong argument.[87] Scribes of the same Assyrian king could spell a foreign king's name more than one way, even in the same

85. Some of those following Tadmor by including Ekron and Gibbethon in Sargon's 712 campaign are: Tadmor 1966; Aharoni 1979; Galil 1988; 1992a; 1992b; 1995. Those who include these cities in the 720 campaign are: Na'aman 1979: 70; Russell 1999: 113-14. Those who link the Azekah inscription to Sargon's 712 campaign are: Tadmor 1966; Galil 1988; 1992a; 1992b; 1995. Some of those who link the Azekah inscription to Sennacherib's 701 campaign are: Rainey 1975; Na'aman 1974; 1979; Cogan 2000.

86. Russell (1999: 114) states: '...the relief decoration of each room is clearly concerned with the events in a single part of the empire, with none of the discontinuity or variety of settings that are seen in the battle reliefs of Assurnasirpal II or Tiglath-pileser III, who do mix several campaigns in a single room'. See also Younger 1999: 475-76 with bibliography; Albenda 1986; André-Salvini 1995; Becking 1997; Franklin 1994; Uehlinger 1997; 1998.

87. There is simply not enough evidence for this to be a diagnosic.

inscription. For example, in Shalmaneser III's Kurkh Monolith (*RIMA* 3: 11-24), the name of Asû/Asāu/Sūa the Gilzānean is spelled: ᵐ*a-su-ú* KUR *gil-za-na-a* (i.28) and ᵐ*a-sa-a-ú* MAN KUR *gil-za-a-ni* (ii.61). Moreover, in epigraph 1 of the Black Obelisk (*RIMA* 3: 149, text 87) the name is spelled: ᵐ*šu-ú-a* KUR *gil-za-na-a-a*.[88] Third, Galil argues (following Tadmor 1958: 82) that the rendering of Aššur's name by AN.ŠÁR started only in the days of Sargon, and since Sennacherib uses only the spelling *Aš-šur* in his historical texts, the inscription cannot be from Sennacherib's third campaign of 701 BCE. But if the Azekah Inscription is a type of literary text, then the use of AN.ŠÁR within it is entirely consistent with Sennacherib's usage of the name elsewhere (see Na'aman 1974: 31; Brinkman in Yurco 1991: 40 n. 34). Fourth, Galil argues that stylistically and lexically the Azekah Inscription is very close to Sargon's 'Letter to the God', which describes Sargon's campaign to Urartu in 714 BCE. While this is true, it obscures the fact that there are also similarities with Sennacherib's Annals—some of these are quite strong (Na'aman 1974; 1986). It must be admitted, however, that there are a greater number of literary similarities with Sargon's Letter to the God than Sennacherib's inscriptions.

None of these arguments proves that the inscription belongs to Sargon. Certainly none of them proves that the text dates to his 712/711 campaign. As stated above, there is no evidence that the campaign of 712/711 in any way involved Judah. The reference to the Judahite city of 'Azekah' in l. 5' of the inscription, as well as the name of Hezekiah (partially restored), demonstrate that part of the military action that the inscription portrays is set in Judah. Another city, whose name is not preserved, is described in l. 11' as a 'royal city of Philistines, which [Hezek]iah had captured and strengthened for himself'. The biblical text alludes to Hezekiah's activity in Philistia in 2 Kgs 18.8. Na'aman suggested the Philistine city of Gath (Tell eṣ-Ṣafi),[89] but recently Galil (1992a; 1992b; 1995) has proposed the city of Ekron.[90] Nevertheless, the city's description (if ll. 12'-20' continue with a description of the city mentioned in l. 11') does not seem to fit particularly well with Ekron.[91]

88. See K. Radner and R. Schmitt, 'Asû', *PNA*: I, 138-39.

89. Five limestone fragments of an Assyrian stela were found in the excavations of Tell eṣ-Ṣafi. See Bliss and Macalister 1902: 38, 41. However, Aren M. Maeir informs me that, on the basis of his personal inspection of the fragments, these fragments may not be part of a stela. Maeir's renewed excavations of Tell eṣ-Ṣafi seem to have added greater evidence, though not yet totally conclusive, that Tell eṣ-Ṣafi is ancient Gath.

90. Na'aman now concurs with this suggestion (personal communication).

91. Moreover, Ekron was a mere 10 acres in 701 with a population of approximately

But no matter what Philistine royal city may have been in view, it does not seem very likely that the Philistines of Ashdod would attempt to make a coalition with Judah in light of this circumstance. Furthermore, as noted above, Isa. 20.1 refers to the Assyrian action against Ashdod in 712/711. Surely the prophet would have mentioned the Assyrian conquest of the Judahite city of Azekah if it had actually occurred in this context, since it would have served as a more powerful object lesson than Ashdod regarding Isaiah's warning to the Judahites concerning any military action against the Assyrians (Frahm 1997: 231). As already argued above, the Nimrud Inscription recording the subjugation of Judah must be referring to the 720 BCE campaign on the basis of the inscription's date. Thus there is really no evidence of Judah's involvement in Ashdod's rebellion with the resultant, typical Assyrian reprisal.

Fortunately, the very recent publication of the Tang-i Var Inscription by G. Frame (1999) has clarified one important item of this campaign. Yamani, the rebel king of Ashdod, had, according to Sargon's inscriptions, fled at the very first sign of the approaching Assyrian army to the border of Egypt and Ethiopia (Meluḫḫa) where he consequently lived 'like a thief'. Prior to the publication of the Tang-i Var Inscription, all we knew was that the king of Ethiopia had been 'overwhelmed' by the fearful splendor of Sargon's majesty and in panic had chained Yamani and sent him to Sargon (Great Summary Inscription, ll. 109b-112; the Small Summary Inscription, l. 14). But now, with the publication of this new inscription, we know that the king who returned Yamani to Sargon was Shabataka/Shebitku (written Šapataku'). Thus the Tang-i Var inscription indicates, by naming Shabataka/Shebitku as the king who extradited Yamani from Egypt, that Shebitku was already ruler by 706, at least four years earlier than has generally been thought.[92]

4. *Conclusion*

Half a dozen years after the 712 campaign (i.e. 706 BCE), Sargon completed his new capital, Dūr-Šarrukin, and required the kings of the west to attend its dedication (Great Summary Inscription, ll. 177-179; Fuchs 1994:

1600 inhabitants. The identification of the city as Ekron would fit either with Sargon's 720 campaign or with Sennacherib's 701 campaign. The best fit historically is with the latter.

92. See the discussion of Frame 1999: 52-54; Redford 1999. For discussion of a possible coregency of Shabaka and Shabataka, see Hoffmeier 2002; Yurco 1991.

355). It is not improbable that Hezekiah, king of Judah, made the trek to visit this impressive new city (Gallagher 1999: 268). But only a year later, Sargon was suddenly and unexpectedly killed on the battlefield while campaigning in Anatolia. His death rocked the ancient world.

Within Assyria there was great consternation, not only because Sargon was the first and only Assyrian king killed on the battlefield, but also because he had not received a proper royal burial since his body was either in enemy hands or lost on the battlefield. This provoked an inquiry through extispicy by his son, Sennacherib, concerning 'Sargon's Sin'.[93] The result was the abandonment of Sargon's new capital of Dūr-Šarrukin (Tadmor, Landsberger and Parpola 1989: 28-29).

In the southern Levant, the impact was so great that the song of Isa. 14.4b-21, applied secondarily to a king of Babylon,[94] asserted that Sargon's fall was heard in the very depths of Sheol and roused the Rephaim into sarcastic rejoicing (Ginsberg 1968; Gallagher 1999: 87-90; 1994b). It is not surprising that revolts occurred almost immediately throughout the empire.

Thus Sargon greatly impacted the southern Levant, both in his life and through his death. It was an impact quite obviously felt in the political/ military history of the region—with Israel scattered through deportations, the Philistine states reduced to subjugation, and Judah in servitude as an Assyrian client; but it was also a literary impact that fortunately is preserved in the biblical literature.

BIBLIOGRAPHY

Aharoni, Y.
1979   *The Land of the Bible: A Historical Geography* (trans. A.F. Rainey; Phila-
              delphia: Westminster Press, rev. edn).

Albenda, P.
1986   *The Palace of Sargon, King of Assyria: Monumental Wall Reliefs at Dur-
              Sharrukin, from the Original Drawings Made at the Time of their Discovery*

93. For the text (a join of K. 4730 + Sm. 1876), see Tadmor, Landsberger and Parpola 1989: 9-24; Livingstone 1989: 77-79.

94. Isaiah himself may have called Sargon, king of Babylon, since Sargon spent 710–707 BCE ruling in Babylon—even reckoning his regnal years on this basis (Cyprus Stela, ll. 21-22; see Winckler 1889: 180-81). Although this may be very likely, the original taunt seems to be used in the present context of Isaiah as a prophetic judgment on Babylon.

                    in 1843–1844 by Botta and Flandin (Editions Recherche sur les Civilisa-
                    tions, Synthèse, 22; Paris: Editions Recherche sur les Civilisations).

Albright, W.F.
       1969   *Archaeology and the Religion of Israel* (Garden City, NY: Doubleday, 5th
                    edn).

André-Salvini, B.
       1995   'Remarques sur les inscriptions des reliefs du palais du Khorsabad', in
                    Khorsabad: 15-45.

Avigad, N.
       1993   'Samaria', in *NEAEHL*: IV, 1300-1310.

Becking, B.
       1992   *The Fall of Samaria: An Historical and Archaeological Study* (SHANE, 2;
                    Leiden: E.J. Brill).
       1997   'Assyrian Evidence for Iconic Polytheism in Ancient Israel', in K. van der
                    Toorn (ed), *The Image and the Book: Iconic Cults, Aniconism, and the Rise
                    of Book Religion in Israel and the Ancient Near East* (Leuven: Peeters): 157-
                    71.

Beyer, K., and A. Livingstone
       1987   'Die neuesten aramäischen Inschriften aus Taima', *ZDMG* 137: 285-96.
       1990   'Eine neue reicharamäische Inschrift aus Taima', *ZDMG* 140: 1-2.

Bliss, F.J., and R.A.S. Macalister
       1902   *Excavations in Palestine* (London: Palestine Exploration Fund).

Bordreuil, P.
       1996–97   'The Aramaic Documents from Til Barsib', *Abr-Nahrain* 34: 100-107.

Borger, R.
       1956   *Asarh*.
       1979   *BAL²*.

Botta P.E., and M.E. Flandin
       1849-50   *Monument de Ninive* (5 vols.; Paris: Imprimerie Nationale).

Brinkman, J.A.
       1984   *Prelude to Empire: Babylonian Society and Politics, 747–626 B.C.* (Occa-
                    sional Publications of the Babylonian Fund, 7; Philadelphia: University
                    Museum).

Cavigneaux, A., and B.K. Ismail
       1990   'Die Statthalter von Suhu und Mari im 8. Jh. v. Chr.', *BaM* 21: 321-456.

Christensen, D.L.
       1989   'The Identity of "King So" in Egypt (2 Kings XVII 4)', *VT* 39: 140-53.

Cogan, M.
       1995a   'Ashima', in *DDD*: 195-97.
       1995b   'Sukkoth-Benoth', in *DDD*: 1553-56.
       1995c   'Tartak', in *DDD*: 1584-86.
       2000   'Neo-Assyrian Inscriptions: Sennacherib', *COS*: II, 300-305.

Cogan, M., and H. Tadmor
       1988   *II Kings: A New Translation with Introduction and Commentary* (AB, 11;
                    Garden City, NY: Doubleday).

Cohen, Ch.
       1979   'Neo-Assyrian Elements in the First Speech of the Biblical Rab-Shaqeh',
                    IOS 9: 32-48.

Cole, S.W.
1996 *Nippur in Late Assyrian Times c. 755–612 BC* (SAAS, 4; Helsinki: The Neo-Assyrian Text Corpus Project).

Dalley, S.M.
1985 'Foreign Chariotry and Cavalry in the Armies of Tiglath-pileser III and Sargon II', *Iraq* 47: 31-48.
1990 'Yahweh in Hamath in the 8th Century B.C.: Cuneiform Material, and Historical Deductions', *VT* 40: 21-32.
1996–97 'Neo-Assyrian Tablets from Til Barsib', *Abr-Nahrain* 34: 66-99.
1998 'Yabâ, Atalya and the Foreign Policy of Late Assyrian Kings', *SAAB* 12: 83-98.

Dalley, S.M., and J.N. Postgate
1984 *The Tablets from Fort Shalmaneser* (CTN, 3; Oxford: British School of Archaeology).

Damerji, M.S.B.
1999 *Gräber assyrischer Königinen aus Nimrud* (Jahrbuch des Römisch-Germanischen Zentralmuseums, 45; Mainz: Verlag des Römisch-Germanischen Zentralmuseums).

Day, J.
1989 *Molech: A God of Human Sacrifice in the Old Testament* (Cambridge: Cambridge University Press).
1992 'The Problem of "So, King of Egypt" in 2 Kings xvii 4', *VT* 42: 289-301.

Deller, K.
1965 'Review of R. de Vaux, Les sacrifices de l'Ancien Testament', *Or* 34: 382-83.

Diakonoff, I.
1991 ' *'ry mdy* Cities of the Medes', in *Studies Tadmor*: 13-20.

Dion, P.-E.
1989 'Sennacherib's Expedition to Palestine', *Eglise et Théologie* 20: 5-26.
1995 'Les Araméens du moyen-euphrate au VIIIe siècle à la lumière des inscriptions des maîtres de Suhu et Mari', in J.A. Emerton (ed.), *Congress Volume. Paris, 1992* (VTSup, 61; Leiden: E.J. Brill): 53-73.

Donner, H.
1977 'The Separate States of Israel and Judah', in J.H. Hayes and J.M. Miller (eds.), *Israelite and Judaean History* (London: Westminster Press).

Dothan, M.
1971 *Ashdod II-III: The Second and Third Seasons of Excavations 1963, 1965. Soundings in 1967. I. Text. II. Figures and Plates* ('Atiqot. English Series, 9-10; Jerusalem: Department of Antiquities and Museums).
1993 'Ashdod', *NEAEHL*: I, 93-102.

Driver, G.R.
1958 'Geographical Problems', *EI* 5: 16*-20*.

Edzard, D.O., and M. Gallery
1980–83 'Kutha', *RlA* 6: 384-87.

Ellison, R.
1981 'Diet in Mesopotamia: The Evidence of the Barley Ration Texts (c. 3000–1400 BCE)', *Iraq* 43: 35-45.

Eph'al, I.
1982   *The Ancient Arabs* (Jerusalem: Magnes Press).
1999   'The Bukān Aramaic Inscription: Historical Considerations', *IEJ* 49: 116-21.
Fales, F.M.
1990   'Grain Reserves, Daily Rations and the Size of the Assyrian Army: A Quantitative Study', *SAAB* 4: 23-34.
1991   'West Semitic Names in the Assyrian Empire: Diffusion and Social Relevance', *SEL* 8: 99-117.
1994   'A Fresh Look at the Nimrud Wine Lists', in L. Milano (ed.), *Drinking in Ancient Societies: History and Culture of Drinks in the Ancient Near East. Papers of a Symposium held in Rome, May 17–19 1990* (HANES, 6; Padua: Sargon): 361-80.
Fales, F.M., and J.N. Postgate
1995   *Imperial Administrative Records. Part II. Provincial and Military Administration* (SAA, 11; Helsinki: Helsinki University Press).
Federn, W.
1960   'Daḫamunzu (KBo V 6 iii 8)', *JCS* 14: 33.
Forsberg, S.
1995   *Near Eastern Destuction Datings as Sources for Greek and Near Eastern Iron Age Chronology. Archaeological and Historical Studies: The Cases of Samaria (722 B.C.) and Tarsus (696 B.C.)* (Boreas; Uppsala Studies in Ancient Mediterranean and Near Eastern Civilizations, 19; Uppsala: Acta Universitatis Upsaliensis).
Frahm, E.
1997   *Einleitung in die Sanherib-Inschriften* (AfO Beiheft, 26; Vienna: Institut für Orientalistik der Universität).
Frame, G.
1999   'The Inscription of Sargon II at Tang-i Var', *Or* 68: 31-57 and Pls. i-xviii.
Franklin, N.
1994   'The Room V Reliefs at Dur-Sharrukin and Sargon II's Western Campaigns', *Tel Aviv* 21: 255-75.
Fuchs, A.
1994   *Die Inschriften Sargons II. aus Khorsabad* (Göttingen: Cuvillier Verlag).
1998   *Die Annalen des Jahres 711 v. Chr. nach Prismenfragmenten aus Ninive und Assur* (SAAS, 8; Helsinki: The Neo-Assyrian Text Corpus Project).
Gadd, C.J.
1954   'Inscribed Prisms of Sargon II from Nimrud', *Iraq* 16: 173-201 and pls. xlv, xlvi.
Gal, Z.
1992   *Lower Galilee during the Iron Age* (trans. by M.R. Josephy; Winona Lake, IN: Eisenbrauns).
1988–89 'Lower Galilee in the Iron Age II: Analysis of Survey Material and its Historical Interpretation', *Tel Aviv* 15-16: 56-64.
Galil, G.
1988   'Sennacherib versus Hezekiah: A New Look at the Assyrian Campaign to the West in 701 BCE', *Zion* 53: 1-12 (Hebrew).
1992a   'Judah and Assyria in the Sargonid Period', *Zion* 57: 111-33 (Hebrew).
1992b   'Conflicts Between Assyrian Vassals', *SAAB* 6: 55-63.

1995   'A New Look at the "Azekah Inscription"', *RB* 102: 321-29.
Gallagher, W.R.
1994   'On the Identity of Hêlēl Ben Šaḥar of Isa. 14.12-15', *UF* 26: 131-46.
1999   *Sennacherib's Campaign to Judah: New Studies* (SHCANE, 18; Leiden: E.J. Brill).
Galpaz-Feller, P.
2000   'Is That So? (2 Kings XVII 4)', *RB* 107: 338-47.
Ginsberg, H.L.
1968   'Reflexes of Sargon in Isaiah after 715 BCE', in *Studies Speiser*: 47-53.
Gonçalves, F.J.
1986   *L'expédition de Sennachérib en Palestine dans la littérature hébraïque ancienne* (Etudes bibliques, 7; Paris: J. Gabalda; Leuven: Peeters).
Gray, J.
1977   *I and II Kings* (OTL; Philadelphia: Westminster Press, 3rd edn).
Grayson, A.K.
1974–77   'The Empire of Sargon of Akkad', *AfO* 25: 56-64.
1986   'Assyria's Foreign Policy in Relation to Elam in the Eighth and Seventh Centuries B.C.', *Sumer* 42: 146-48.
1991   'Assyria: Tiglath-pileser III to Sargon II (744–705 B.C.)', in J. Boardman *et al.* (eds.), *The Cambridge Ancient History*, III/1 (Cambridge: Cambridge University Press, 2nd edn): 86-102, 762-64.
Green, A.R.W.
1993   'The Identity of King So of Egypt—An Alternative Interpretation', *JNES* 52: 99-108.
Hadley, J.M.
2000   *The Cult of Asherah in Ancient Israel and Judah: Evidence for a Hebrew Goddess* (University of Cambridge Oriental Publications, 57; Cambridge: Cambridge University Press).
Hallo, W.W.
1977   'New Moons and Sabbaths', *HUCA* 48: 1-18.
Hawkins, J.D.
1983   'The Hittite name of Til Barsip', *AnSt* 33: 131-36.
Heidorn, L.A.
1997   'The Horses of Kush', *JNES* 56: 105-14.
Hinz, W.
1967   'Elams Vertrag mit Narām-Sin von Akade', *ZA* 58: 66-96.
Hoffmeier, J.K.
2002   'Egypt's Role in the Events of 701 BCE in Jerusalem', in A. Killebrew and A.G. Vaughn (eds.), *Jerusalem: New Studies* (SBL Series) (forthcoming).
Hommel, F.
1912   'Die Götter Nibhaz und Tartak. 2 Kon. 17.31', *OLZ* 15: 118.
1926a   'Die Elamitische Götter-Siebenheit in CT 25,24', in *Paul Haupt Anniversary Volume* (Baltimore: The Johns Hopkins University Press): 159-68.
1926b   *Ethnographie und Geographie des Alten Orients* (Munich: C.H. Beck).
Horowitz, W.
1993   'Moab and Edom in the Sargon Geography', *IEJ* 43: 151-56.
Ikeda, Y.
1999   'Looking from Til Barsip on the Euphrates: Assyria and the West in Ninth

and Eighth Centuries B.C.', in K. Watanabe (ed.), *Priests and Officials in the Ancient Near East: Papers of the Second Colloquium on the Ancient Near East—The City and its Life held at the Middle Eastern Culture Center in Japan (Mitaka, Tokyo)* (Heidelberg: Universitätverlag C. Winter): 271-302.

Jensen, P.
1898   'Review of H.V. Hilprecht (ed.), *The Babylonian Expedition of the University of Pennsylvania*', *ZA* 13: 333 n. 1.

Kamil, A.
1999   'Inscriptions on Objections from Yaba's Tomb in Nimrud', in M.S.B. Damerji, *Gräber assyrischer Königinen aus Nimrud* (Jahrbuch des Römisch-Germanischen Zentralmuseums, 45; Mainz: Verlag des Römisch-Germanischen Zentralmuseums).

Kapera, Z.J.
1972   'Was Ya-ma-ni a Cypriot?', *Folia Orientalia* 14: 207-18.
1976   'The Ashdod Stele of Sargon II', *Folia Orientalia* 17: 87-99.
1987   'The Oldest Account of Sargon II's Campaign Against Ashdod', *Folia Orientalia* 24: 29-39.

Kaplan, J.
1993   'Ashdod-Yam'. *NEAEHL*: 1, 102-103.

Kaufman, S.
1978   'The Enigmatic Adad-milki', *JNES* 37: 101-109.

King, L.W.
1909   *Cuneiform Texts from Babylonian Tablets in the British Museum*, XXV (London: The British Museum).

Kitchen, K.A.
1986   *The Third Intermediate Period in Egypt (1100–650 BC)* (Warminster: Aris & Phillips, 2nd edn).

Kittel, R.
1933   *Geschichte des Volkes Israel* (2 vols.; Gotha, 4th edn).

Knauf, E.A.
1988   *Midian: Untersuchungen zur Geschichte Palästinas und Nordarabiens am Ende des 2. Jahrtausends v. Chr.* (Wiesbaden: Otto Harrassowitz).

Kottsieper, I.
1997   'Anmerkungen zu Pap. Amherst 63 Teil II-V', *UF* 29: 385-434.

Krauss, R.
1978   'Sō', König von ägypten—ein Deutungsvorschlag', *MDOG* 110: 49-54.

Lambert, W.G.
1981   'Portion of Inscribed Stela of Sargon II, King of Assyria', in O.W. Muscarella (ed.), *Ladders to Heaven: Art Treasures from Lands of the Bible* (Toronto: McClelland and Stewart): 125.

Leichty, E.
1970   *The Omen Series Šumma Izbu* (TCS, 4; Locust Valley, NY: J.J. Augustin).

Lemaire, A.
1998   'Une inscription araméenne du VIIIe s. av. J.-C. trouvée à Bukân', *Studia Iranica* 27: 15-30.

Levine, L.D.
1972   *Two Neo-Assyrian Stelae from Iran* (Toronto: Royal Ontario Museum).
1974   *Geographical Studies in the Neo-Assyrian Zagros* (Toronto: The Royal Ontario Museum; London: British Institute of Persian Studies).

Lipiński, E.
1973   '*Skn* et *sgn* dans le sémitique occidental du nord', *UF* 5: 202-204.
Liverani, M.
1982   '*Kitru, Katāru*', *Mesopotamia* 17: 43-66.
Livingstone, A.
1989   *Court Poetry and Literary Miscellanea* (SAA, 3; Helsinki: Helsinki University Press).
1995a   'Nergal', in *DDD*: 1170-72.
1995b   'New Light on the Ancient Town of Taimā'', in M.J. Geller, J.C. Greenfield, and M.P. Weitzman (eds.), *Studia Aramaica: New Sources and New Approaches* (JSSSup, 4; Oxford: Oxford University Press): 133-43.
Livingstone, A., *et al.*
1983   'Taima: Recent Sounding and New Inscribed Material', *Atlal* 7: 102-16 and pls. 87-97.
Luckenbill, D.D.
1924   *Annals of Sennacherib* (OIP, 2; Chicago: University of Chicago Press).
Machinist, P.
1983   'Assyria and its Image in the First Isaiah', *JAOS* 103: 719-37.
Mattingly, G.L.
1981   'An Archaeological Analysis of Sargon's 712 Campaign Against Ashdod', *NEASB* 17: 47-64.
Millard, A.R.
1976   'Assyrian Royal Names in Biblical Hebrew', *JSS* 21: 1-14.
1992   'Assyrian Involvement in Edom', in *EEM*: 35-39.
1994   *The Eponyms of the Assyrian Empire 910–612 BC* (SAAS, 2. Helsinki: The Neo-Assyrian Text Corpus Project).
1995a   'Adrammelech', in *DDD*: 17-19.
1995b   'Anammelech', in *DDD*: 58-60.
1995c   'Nibhaz', in *DDD*: 1172-74.
Montgomery, J.A., and H.S. Gehman
1951   *The Book of Kings* (ICC; Edinburgh: T. & T. Clark).
Na'aman, N.
1974   'Sennacherib's "Letter to God" on his Campaign to Judah', *BASOR* 214: 25-39.
1979   'The Brook of Egypt and Assyrian Policy on the Border of Egypt', *Tel Aviv* 6: 68-90.
1990   'The Historical Background to the Conquest of Samaria (720 BC)', *Bib* 71: 206-25.
1993   'Population Changes in Palestine Following the Assyrian Deportations', *Tel Aviv* 20: 104-24.
1994a   'Ahaz's and Hezekiah's Policy Toward Assyria in the Days of Sargon II and Sennacherib's Early Years', *Zion* 59: 5-30 (Hebrew).
1994b   'Hezekiah and the Kings of Assyria', *Tel Aviv* 21: 235-54.
1994c   'The Historical Portion of Sargon II's Nimrud Inscription', *SAAB* 8: 17-20.
1999   'Sargon's Khorsabad Inscriptions and the Nimrud Prisms', *UF* 31: 265-71.
2000   'The Number of Deportees from Samaria in the Nimrud Prisms of Sargon II', *NABU* 1.

Na'aman, N., and R. Zadok
    1988   'Sargon's Deportations to Israel and Philistia', *JCS* 40: 36-46.
    2000   'Assyrian Deportations to the Provine of Samerina in the Light of Two Cuneiform Tablets from Tel Hadid', *Tel Aviv* 27: 159-88.
Oded, B.
    1979   *Mass Deportations and Deportees in the Neo-Assyrian Empire* (Wiesbaden: Otto Harrassowitz).
Parpola, S.
    1987   *The Correspondence of Sargon II*. Part 1: *Letters from Assyria and the West* (SAA, 1; Helsinki: Helsinki University Press).
    1995   'The Construction of Dūr-Šarrukin in the Assyrian Royal Correspondence', in *Khorsabad*: 47-77.
Parpola, S., and K. Watanabe
    1988   *Neo-Assyrian Treaties and Loyalty Oaths* (SAA, 2; Helsinki: Helsinki University Press).
Pedersén, O.
    1984–86   'The Reading of the Neo-Assyrian Logogram U.U', *OrSu* 33-35: 313-16.
Porten, B., and A. Yardeni
    1993   *TAD*.
Postgate, J.N.
    1972–75   'Ḫalaḫḫa', *RlA* 4: 58.
    1973   'Assyrian Texts and Fragments', *Iraq* 35: 13-36.
    1989   'Ancient Assyria—A Multi-Racial State', *Aram* 1: 1-10.
    1992   'The Land of Assur and the Yoke of Assur', *World Archaeology* 23: 147-263.
    1995   'Some Latter-Day Merchants of Aššur', in *Studies von Soden*: 403-406.
Powell, M.A.
    1992   'Weights and Measures', in *ABD*: VI, 897-908.
Rainey, A.F.
    1975   in Aharoni 1979.
Reade, J.E.
    1972   'The Neo-Assyrian Court and Army: Evidence from the Sculptures', *Iraq* 34: 87-112.
Redford, D.B.
    1992   *Egypt, Canaan, and Israel in Ancient Times* (Princeton: Princeton University Press).
    1999   'A Note on the Chronology of Dynasty 25 and the Inscription of Sargon II at Tang-i Var', *Or* 68: 58-60.
Ribichini, S.
    1995   'Eshmun', in *DDD*: 583-87.
Russell, J.M.
    1999   *The Writing on the Wall: Studies in the Architectural Context of Late Assyrian Palace Inscriptions* (Winona Lake, IN: Eisenbrauns).
Russell, H.F.
    1987   'Archaeological Evidence for the Assyrians in South-East Turkey in the First Millennium B.C.', *Anadolu demir çağlari*: 56-64.

Saggs, H.W.F.
1975   'Historical Texts and Fragments of Sargon II of Assyria. I. The "Aššur Charter"', *Iraq* 37: 11-20 and pl. ix.

Schipper, B.
1998   'Wer war "Sô', König von Ägypten"', *BN* 92: 71-84.
1999   *Israel und Ägypten in der Königszeit: Die kulturellen Kontakte von Salomo bis zum Fall Jerusalems* (OBO, 170; Freiburg: Universitätsverlag Freiburg Schweiz; Göttingen: Vandenhoeck & Ruprecht).

Shea, W.H.
1992   'So, Ruler of Egypt', *AUSS* 30: 201-15.
1997   'The New Tirhakah Text and Sennacherib's Second Palestinian Campaign', *AUSS* 35: 181-87.
1999   'Jerusalem Under Siege: Did Sennacherib Attack Twice?', *BARev* 25/6: 36-44, 64.

Sokoloff, M.
1999   'The Old Aramaic Inscription from Bukān: A Revised Interpretation', *IEJ* 49: 105-15.

Spalinger, A.J.
1973   'The Year 712 B.C. and its Implications for Egyptian History', *JARCE* 10: 95-101.

Steiner, R.C.
1991   'The Aramaic Text in Demotic Script: The Liturgy of a New Year's Festival Imported from Bethel to Syene by Exiles from Rash', *JAOS* 111: 362-63.
1995   'Papyrus Amherst 63: A New Source for the Language, Literature, Religion, and History of the Arameans', in M.J. Geller, J.C. Greenfield and M.P. Weitzman (eds), *Studia Aramaica: New Sources and New Approaches* (JSSSup, 4; Oxford: Oxford University Press): 199-207.
1997   'The Aramaic Text in Demotic Script', *COS*: I, 309-27.

Steiner, R.C., and C.F. Nimms
1984   'You Can't Offer Your Sacrifices and Eat It Too: A Polemical Poem from the Aramaic Text in Demotic Script', *JNES* 43: 89-114.
1985   'Ashurbanipal and Shamash-shum-ukin: A Tale of Two Brothers from the Aramaic Text in Demotic Script', *RB* 92: 60-81.

Stol, M.
1995   'Sakkuth', *DDD* 1364-1365.

Sweeney, M.A.
1994   'Sargon's Threat against Jerusalem in Isaiah 10,27-32', *Bib* 75: 457-70.

Tadmor, H.
1958   'The Campaigns of Sargon II of Assur: A Chronological-Historical Study', *JCS* 12: 22-40; 77-100.
1966   'Philistia under Assyrian Rule', *BA* 29: 86-102.
1971   'Fragments of an Assyrian Stele of Sargon II', *'Atiqot* (English Series) 9: 192-97.
1982   'The Aramaization of Assyria: Aspects of Western Impact', in *Mesopotamien und seine Nachbarn*: 449-70.
1988   'The *urbi* of Hezekiah', *Beer-Sheva* (Moshe Held Memorial Volume) 3: 171-78 (Hebrew, English summary pp. 13*-14*).

1994   *The Inscriptions of Tiglath-pileser III King of Assyria* (Jerusalem: The Israel
               Academy of Sciences and Humanities).

Tadmor, H., B. Landsberger and S. Parpola
1989   'The Sin of Sargon and Sennacherib's Last Will', *SAAB* 3: 3-51.

Tappy, R.
1996   'Samaria', in *OEANE*: IV, 463-67.

Timm, St.
1989   *Moab zwischen den Mächten. Studien zu historischen Denkmählern und
               Texten* (AAT, 17; Wiesbaden: Otto Harrassowitz).

Toorn, K. van der
1992   'Anat-Yahu, Some Other Deities, and the Jews of Elephantine', *Numen* 39:
               80-101.

Uehlinger, C.
1997   'Figurative Policy, Propaganda und Prophetie', in J.A. Emerton (ed.),
               Congress Volume: Cambridge 1995 (VTSup, 66; Leiden: E.J. Brill): 297-
               349.

1998   '"...und wo sind die Götter von Samarien?" Die Wegführung syrisch-
               palästinischer Kultstatuen aut einem Relief Sargons II. in Ḫorṣābād/Dūr-
               Šarrukīn', in *Studies Loretz*: 739-76.

Ungnad, A.
1940   in J. Friedrich *et al.*, *Die Inschriften vom Tell Halaf* (AfO Beiheft, 6; Berlin).

Viviano, P.A.
1987   '2 Kings 17: A Rhetorical and Form-Critical Analysis', *CBQ* 49: 548-59.

Waters, M.W.
2000   *A Survey of Neo-Elamite History* (SAAS, 12; Helsinki: The Neo-Assyrian
               Text Corpus Project).

Weippert, M.
1987   'The Relations of the States East of the Jordan with the Mesopotamian
               Powers during the First Millennium B.C.', in A. Halidi (ed.), *SHAJ*, III
               (Amman: Department of Antiquities): 97-105.

Weißbach, F.H.
1918   'Zu den Inschriften der Säle im Palaste Sargon's II. von Assyrien', *ZDMG*
               72: 161-85.

Winckler, H.
1889   *Die Keilschrifttexte Sargons*. I. *Historisch-sachliche Einleitung, Umschrift
               und Übersetzung, Wörterverzeichnis* (Leipzig: E. Pfeiffer).

Winter, I.J.
1977   'Perspective on the "Local Style" of Hasanlu IVB: A Study in Receptivity',
               in L.D. Levine and T.C. Young, Jr (eds.), *Mountains and Lowlands: Essays
               in the Archeology of Greater Mesopotamia* (Bibliotheca Mesopotamica, 7;
               Malibu, CA: Undena Publications): 371-86.

Yeivin, S.
1952   'Who Was "Šō" the King of Egypt?' *VT* 2: 164-68.

Younger, K.L. Jr.
1996   'Sargon's Campaign Against Jerusalem—A Further Note', *Bib* 77: 108-10.
1998a   'The Deportations of the Israelites', *JBL* 117: 201-27.
1998b   'Two Comparative Notes on the Book of Ruth', *JANESCU* 26: 121-32.
1999   'The Fall of Samaria in Light of Recent Research', *CBQ* 61: 461-82.

2002a   'Assyrian Involvement in the Southern Levant at the End of the Eighth Century BCE', in A. Killebrew and A.G. Vaughn (eds.), *Jerusalem: New Studies* (SBL Series) (forthcoming).

2002b   ' "Give Us Our Daily Bread"—Everyday Life for the Israelite Deportees', in R.E. Averbeck, M.W. Chavalas and D. Weisberg (eds.), *Daily Life in the Ancient Near East* (Bethsaida, MD: CDL Press) (in press).

forthcoming a   'Yahweh at Ashkelon and Calaḫ?—Yahwistic Names in Neo-Assyrian', *VT*.

forthcoming b   'The Repopulation of Samaria (2 Kings 17:24, 27-31) in Light of Recent Study', in J.K. Hoffmeier and A.R. Millard (eds.), *The Future of Biblical Archaeology* (Winona Lake, IN: Eisenbrauns).

Yurco, F.J.
1991   'The Shabaka-Shebitku Coregency and the Supposed Second Campaign of Sennacherib against Judah: A Critical Assessment', *JBL* 110: 35-45.

Zadok, R.
1976   'Geographical and Onomastic Notes', *JANESCU* 8: 114-26.

Zevit, Z.
1991   'Yahweh Worship and Worshippers in 8th-Century Syria', *VT* 41: 363-66.

WHAT HAS NEBUCHADNEZZAR TO DO WITH DAVID?
ON THE NEO-BABYLONIAN PERIOD AND EARLY ISRAEL[*]

Bill T. Arnold

Comparative studies between Syria-Mesopotamia and the Bible have born much fruit and continue to give every indication that more will follow.[1] Nearly every genre of the Old Testament has found its parallel in Mesopotamian literature; law, poetry, wisdom, and historical texts. Genuinely objective comparisons help with the interpretation of both cultures. My purpose here is not to make direct comparisons or contrasts between any given texts from the Old Testament with one from Babylonia. But in this study, I am interested in institutional and socio-political analogies. These observations are less obvious than literary comparisons and are perhaps less satisfying initially. But I believe this approach has great potential for contributing to our understanding of both ancient Babylonia and early Israel.

The article will present two major aspects of Neo-Babylonian history for consideration, and draw a few similarities with early Israel. First, the period from 747 to 626 BCE is convenient for analyzing the rise of the empire, that is, from the rise of Nabonassar in Babylon to the accession of Nabopolassar. This period witnessed the rise of Babylonia from lethargy and political insignificance to one of the greatest empires of the ancient world. My focus in this first section will be on the ethnic heterogeneity of the inhabitants, and the relationship between tribal clans and settled urban culture.

[*]   I am grateful to the following colleagues who read this paper in various earlier forms and made many helpful suggestions: David W. Baker, Gary N. Knoppers, Alan R. Millard, John N. Oswalt and Brent A. Strawn. The ideas contained here are, as always, my own responsibility. I am also indebted to David Tillis of the Klau Library, Hebrew Union College, Cincinnati for his assistance.
1.   For definition of the 'contextual' approach, in which similarities as well as differences are examined, see Hallo 1980. Hallo has continued to lead the way in refining a genuinely balanced comparative method, see now Hallo 1991.

Second, the period of Neo-Babylonian empire itself (625 to 539) yields several interesting features for comparison and contrast with Israel. Despite the significant gap in time, there are several fascinating and instructive analogues with Israel's pre-monarchic and early monarchic periods.[2] This may be a particularly informative comparison since the Neo-Babylonian empire was the only *native* Semitic state of Iron Age Babylonia. All other rule was extraneously imposed on Babylon. As will be seen, southern Babylonia at this time was ethnically heterogeneous. Furthermore, the tribal groups I shall discuss were distant relatives of the early Israelites, since their language and culture reflect their West Semitic origins. These shared cultural features converge to make this survey of the rise, strength and social structure of the Neo-Babylonian empire a heuristic model for Old Testament studies.

1. *Southern Babylonia Prior to the Rise of Statehood*

A clear picture of the ethnic and socio-political conditions of Babylonia in the century and a half prior to Nabopolassar has only come to light in recent decades (Brinkman 1984a; Dietrich 1970; Frame 1992). The country was divided ethnically into three distinct groups. The first may be called 'native Babylonians', though they were native only in the sense that they had not *recently* migrated to southern Mesopotamia. They were an ethnic amalgam of several older groups which were by now indistinguishable. The second and third ethnic groups were West Semitic tribal inhabitants who were more recent arrivals into Babylonia; the Arameans and the Chaldeans. Such ethnic and cultural heterogeneity made unified resistance against Assyria to the north nearly impossible during this period.

The 'native Babylonian' group may also be referred to as 'Akkadians', since Assyrian sources referred to them as such when they wanted to distinguish them from the tribal groups (Frame 1992: 33; Brinkman 1984a: 11). These people were descendants of older groups that had been in southern Mesopotamia during the third and second millennia and who

2. The phrase 'early Neo-Babylonian' as used by Assyriologists to describe the earlier periods needs some clarification. In its broadest sense, it refers to that period between the end of the Kassite Dynasty and the beginning of the Neo-Babylonian Empire, or roughly 1155–625 BCE. However, my interest in this paper is more narrow in scope. I would like to focus specifically on the century and a half before the beginning of the empire under Nabopolassar and Nebuchadnezzar, and then look briefly at the empire itself.

were by now completely amalgamated culturally. Their heritage consisted predominantly of Akkadians and Sumerians of the third millennium, and Amorites and Kassites of the second.

This was the ethnic composition of the settled urban dwellers of southern Babylonia during this period. They made up the largest component of the old cult centers along the Euphrates corridor in the northwest (Babylon, Borsippa, Cutha, Dilbat and Sippar) and of the prestigious cities of the southwest (Ur and Uruk). Because of their long-standing presence in the country and their ethnic and cultural continuity with Babylonia's past, they were the bearers of traditional Babylonian culture, as witnessed by their personal names and their continued use of Akkadian as the language of choice against encroaching Aramaic influences (Greenfield 1982).

The fundamental social unit for the Babylonians was the family. Personal names using patronymics often reflect the importance of the nuclear family, for example, 'PN$_1$ son of PN$_2$', where PN$_2$ represents the father's name. Personal names occasionally also indicate the importance of broader kin-based groups among the Babylonians, where the name may be derived from an occupation (Potter, Smith, Fisher, etc.) or traced to a common eponymous ancestor. In the case of the latter, the individual usually bore three names, in which the last name was seen as the founder of the family: PN$_1$ son of PN$_2$, descendant of PN$_3$' (e.g. Mušēzib-Marduk *māršu ša* Kiribtu *mār* Sîn-nāṣir).[3]

The cities controlled by this Babylonian population formed the civil, religious, economic and judicial strength of Babylonia. These Babylonian cities were the intellectual and cultural centers of the country (Frame 1992: 35). Assyrian imperial ambitions were to a large degree dependent upon the support of the Babylonians in these cities during this period.[4] Since much of the documentation (especially the letters) for the period comes from the urban centers, more detail is known about this group than about the nomadic and semi-nomadic tribal groups.

The second ethnic constituent during this period was the Arameans. Arameans begin to appear in Assyrian literary sources in the late-twelfth and eleventh centuries BCE in central and northern Mesopotamia. Aramean groups existed in southern Babylonia from the beginning of the first

---

3. Frame 1992: 34; Brinkman 1984a: 11. Brinkman (1979) and Frame (1984) have also demonstrated how many of the important larger kin-groups came to dominate the civil and religious hierarchy of cities in northern Babylonia.

4. On the evidence for seventh century Uruk, see Arnold 1985.

millennium.[5] The origin and early development of the Arameans is shrouded in obscurity. The traditional scholarly interpretation has the Aramean hordes from the desert steppe sweeping across Syria and Upper Mesopotamia conquering the native populations.

But recent anthropological studies have questioned this massive invasion reconstruction for the appearance of the Arameans and other pastoral nomads in the ancient Near East. It now seems likely that these West Semitic-speaking peoples had lived in Syria and Upper Mesopotamia throughout the second millennium (Pitard 1994; Millard 1992). Though it seems clear the traditional invasion interpretation was overstated, there is nonetheless evidence of *some* degree of Aramean invasion eastward into Assyria and Babylonia in the early-eleventh century BCE due to general famine.[6] They seized cities by force and for much of the tenth century the western corridor of Babylonia was in a constant state of disruption because of the Aramean tribal groups who now controlled the important trade route along the Euphrates.

The Arameans settled principally along the Tigris or its tributaries and there is evidence of more than 40 such tribes (Brinkman 1979: 226). During the century and a half under consideration here, the most notable of these were the Gambulu along the Elamite border, the Puqudu also along the Elamite border and near Uruk (the 'Pekod' of Jer. 50.21 and Ezek. 23.23), the Ru'ua near Nippur,[7] and the Gurasimmu near Ur. The first two of these were the largest tribes and the only ones for which there is much information.

In general, these Aramean tribes were less sedentary than the Chaldeans (see below) and were less likely to assimilate Babylonian culture. Their economy seems to have been based on animal husbandry and they tended to occupy fewer cities and villages than the Chaldeans. Their personal names, unlike the Babylonian patronymics, consisted of the name followed by a gentilic adjective designating the specific tribe (e.g. PN LÚ *Puqūdaju*)

5.　On the Arameans of southern Babylonia generally, see Brinkman 1968: 267-85; 1984a: 12-14; Dietrich 1970. Dietrich's work is informative, but must be used with caution since he fails to distinguish adequately between the Arameans and Chaldeans; see Brinkman's critique in Brinkman 1977.

6.　In the eleventh century, Assyria herself was hard pressed by Aramean invaders, and in the ninth century, she campaigned vigorously against them in the west and in Babylonia. See Kupper 1957: 116-20; Brinkman 1968: 267; 1985.

7.　The location of this tribe is disputed. See Dietrich 1970: 101-102, where he argues for a location southeast of Uruk.

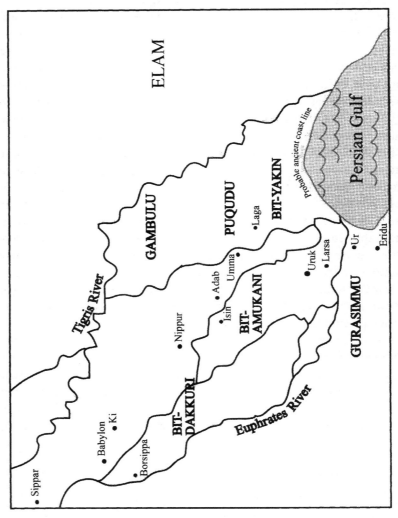

Fig. 1. *Southern Babylonia in the Seventh Century BCE*

(Brinkman 1977: 307). Also unlike the Chaldeans, the Aramean tribesmen were not generally inclined to become involved in the Babylonian political system and no known Aramean ever took the throne of Babylon.[8]

The Chaldean tribes of southern Babylonia made up the third ethnic constituent during this time period. They first appear in the Assyrian sources of the early-ninth century (Frame 1992: 36; Brinkman 1968: 260). Like the Arameans, they were West Semitic and many scholars have assumed they were in fact identical with the Arameans. But the native Assyrian and Babylonian sources consistently distinguished between them. Their differences in tribal organization, the dates of their respective appearances in history and contrasting levels of babylonization all lead one to conclude the Arameans and Chaldeans were two distinct groups, though perhaps ethnically related (Brinkman 1968: 266-67, 273-75).

There were five Chaldean tribes about which scholars have information, though only three of these played significant roles in the history of Babylonia. The largest and most influential were Bit-Dakkuri south of Borsippa, Bit-Amukani further south along the Euphrates, and Bit-Yakin to the east along the Tigris (see Figure 1) (Arnold 1994a: 57 n. 45; Brinkman 1984a: 15). The name of each tribe ('House of Dakkuri', 'House of Amukani', etc.) was taken from an eponymous ancestor. The tribes were larger and generally more unified than Aramean contemporaries. Each was under the control of a single Chaldean chieftain, unlike the Aramean tribes, which sometimes operated with numerous simultaneous sheikhs (*nasīku*) (Brinkman 1979: 226; 1984a: 13-14).

Despite their common tribalism and West Semitic ancestry, the Chaldeans and Arameans were different in many ways. The Chaldeans were in general more sedentary and more unified than the Arameans. They seem to have adapted quickly to Babylonian culture, taking Babylonian names and economic activities, all while maintaining their tribal structure and identity. They learned to control the trade routes of the Persian Gulf area and thereby accumulated considerable wealth with which they paid handsome tribute to the Assyrians. In addition to trade, they also engaged in agriculture and animal husbandry (Frame 1992: 37).

Also unlike their Aramean counterparts, the Chaldeans were deeply involved in Babylonian political life. Their submission and tribute to the Assyrians during the ninth and early-eighth centuries was a temporary ploy, since all the while they were growing in number and strength. Chal-

8. On the mistaken identity of Adad-apla-iddina, a ruler of Babylonia as an Aramean, see Walker 1982.

deans became contenders for the Babylonian throne by the middle of the eighth century. Sometime during the second and third decades of the eighth century a certain Eriba-Marduk of the Bit-Yakin tribe became the first powerful Chaldean monarch of Babylonia, taking advantage of a temporarily weakened Assyria in the north (Arnold 1994a: 58; Brinkman 1968: 221-24). His reign lasted only nine years, but set the stage for Chaldean resistance to the Assyrians for the next century and a half. There would be other Chaldean attempts to rule from a Babylonian base: Mukin-zeri from the Bit-Amukani tribe and the wealthy prince of the Bit-Yakin tribe, Merodach-baladan II, known also from Old Testament references.[9] The Chaldeans thus played a significant role in the movement in Babylonia to retain national autonomy free of Assyrian rule. The unity and spirit of independence growing among the Chaldean tribes culminated in the rise of the so-called 'Chaldean Dynasty', but more appropriately known as the Neo-Babylonian Empire (see n. 15 below).

These were the three primary ethnic groups of southern Babylonia during the last half of the eighth and the seventh centuries BCE. Though I have described three ethnic components,[10] it is clear that socially there were only two: the older Babylonian inhabitants of the larger cities and the more ethnic tribal groups who were relative newcomers (Arameans and Chaldeans). It should be noted that these two groups seldom acted in concert for matters of self-government or self-interest, and in fact, they were frequently in conflict with each other during this turbulent period. Especially during the internecine war between Ashurbanipal and Shamash-shum-ukin (652–648 BCE), the Babylonian cities of the south-land were typically pro-Assyrian, while the tribal groups were decidedly for independence.[11]

At this preliminary stage, I would like to highlight two sweeping comparisons between this picture of southern Babylonia and early Israel. First, the sociological constituents of Babylonia during the seventh century may be compared with those of pre-monarchic Israel, and second, the anthropological progression from tribalism to statehood is similar in these two cultures.

Like southern Mesopotamia during the century prior to the rise of the

9. 2 Kgs 20.12-19; Isa. 39; and see Brinkman 1964.

10. There was actually more ethnic diversity than this picture allows (Brinkman 1981).

11. On the relationship between the Babylonians of Uruk and the Puqudu-Arameans during this period, see Arnold 1985: 64-67.

Neo-Babylonian empire, early Israel was comprised of two distinct socio-logical groups. There were the settled urban-dwellers who were the bearers of the older, traditional culture—the Canaanites. There were also the pastoralist tribal groups, which in Palestine's case may or may not have been semi-nomadic—the tribes of Israel.[12] As in Babylonia, there was conflict between these groups and that conflict persisted over several centuries.

Current controversies among scholars of the Old Testament have to do with whether these two groups are ethnically distinct, and whether the tribal pastoralists were newcomers or long-standing inhabitants of the land (Hess 1993). But this simple comparison with Babylonia demonstrates that in antiquity it was possible for tribal pastoralists to enter an established culture, whether by sudden invasion (as some of the Arameans undoubtedly did) or by gradual infiltration (as some of the Chaldeans apparently did). One can also be quite certain of the ethnic and cultural distinctiveness of the two basic sociological constituents of southern Babylonia. On this comparison, it seems reasonable that the eventual population of Israel could have included tribes which originated outside of Palestine and were ethnically heterogeneous from the Canaanites.

The second comparison has to do with the phenomenon of loosely organized tribal confederations converging into statehood. At the beginning of the period under investigation here, Babylonia was under-populated, impoverished and politically fragmented. Brinkman (1984a: 123) has been able to demonstrate how the Neo-Babylonian Empire developed from such circumstances:

> Against the perduring threat of Assyrian domination, the Chaldeans forged far-reaching internal and external alliances, uniting previously discordant tribesmen (Arameans as well as Chaldeans) and the non-tribal populations of Babylonia into a common anti-Assyrian movement and joining to them their eastern and western neighbors, the Elamites and Arabs. This transformation of anti-Assyrian elements within Babylonia into a political coalition was to have consequences lasting beyond these decades and would eventually provide an effective power base for the development of the Neo-Babylonian state after 626 B.C.

12. A word of caution is in order here on oversimplifying ethnic and racial uniformity of ancient peoples. It is quite certain that all of these groups, Arameans, Chaldeans *and* Israelites, contained various admixtures of other ethnic components, and the groups we designate by these terms were defined less by race than by other sociological forces. Mendenhall (1973: 220) has warned against the tendency in biblical studies toward such racist ideas.

Because of the *pax Assyriaca*, the Babylonian economy improved dramatically through agriculture, animal husbandry and international trade. The Chaldeans especially benefited from the growth. Population levels rapidly increased, though the sources of the new residents are not entirely clear (Brinkman 1984b). Social organizations changed, as family-centered structures gradually gave way to broader kin-based groups. And ultimately, the role of the ever-present Assyrian threat from the north played a significant role in the rise of statehood. Again, Brinkman (1984a: 125) has summarized the effect Assyria had on the area:

> Anti-Assyrianism provided a rallying cry for the heterogeneous Babylonian populations and stimulated political unity... In effect, the history of these decades could be said to illustrate the rise of Babylonia to the threshold of her greatest political achievements and the paradoxical role of Assyria in facilitating that rise.

This portrait of rapid population increases, improved economics and the movement toward unified socio-political organization is exactly paralleled in early Israel. Surface surveys in the hill country of Ephraim located only five occupied sites in the Late Bronze Age, but 115 in Iron Age I (Finkelstein 1988–89: 167). Some archeologists interpret these data as shifts in the living patterns of inhabitants already in Canaan. Regardless of how the changes are explained, it is clear that the central hill region of Palestine witnessed a rapid population growth in Iron I, just as Babylonia did prior to the rise of the empire.

According to the biblical traditions, the other main features that gave rise to statehood in Babylonia were also present in Israel, that is, improved economics and external military threat. Due to the rise of iron technology and improved agricultural techniques, the early Israelites eventually saw improvement, though nothing as dramatic as the Chaldean advances in Babylonia (Borowski 1987). And just as the tribal groups of southern Mesopotamia were united politically by the long history of Assyrian aggression, so the Philistine threat attested in the Bible would have provided ample motivation for centralization of authority. Recent sociological and archeological studies have argued that the Philistine problem developed and intensified as the Israelite population grew and expanded westward, and these circumstances contributed to the rise of the Israelite monarchy (Gordon 1994a: 257-60; Finkelstein 1989: 59-61, 63).

Finally, before turning to the empire itself, we would be well served to remember that it currently lies beyond our grasp to understand thoroughly how tribal federations in antiquity governed themselves, and how some of these developed into larger states.[13] Such knowledge as scholars have from anthropological studies of similar cultures in modern times seems likely to be contaminated by contiguous advanced cultures. At the conclusion of his work on seventh century Babylonia, Brinkman laments the fact that modern scholarship lacks the knowledge needed to understand fully how these ancient tribal groups governed themselves and how they related to each other in larger kin-based groups (Brinkman 1984a: 124-25). This is even more true of early Israel, which may explain the plethora of current scholarly attempts to explain the socio-political conditions for Israel's appearance in Palestine and her rise to statehood. All dogmatism must be placed aside given the current lack of data.

2. *The Neo-Babylonian Empire*

A complete history of the Neo-Babylonian empire is still not possible due to the limited amount of detailed information. The broad outline, however, of the rise of Nabopolassar, his defeat of the Assyrians, the succession of Nebuchadnezzar and the subsequent splendor of his empire is documented well enough by the Babylonian Chronicle Series and various other sources.[14] It is not my purpose here to review that history, but merely to make a few observations apropos to the study of Israel. My comments are not directed toward political developments, but the sociological and ideological aspects of the empire, specifically the material and inscriptional remains of Nabopolassar (625–605 BCE) and Nebuchadnezzar II (604–562 BCE). This period of the empire's greatest strength was marked by military conquests, building activities and literary accomplishments.

As we have seen, the Assyrian threat contributed to the unification of tribal groups of southern Babylonia. Two of the largest Chaldean tribes had suffered most at the hands of the Assyrians, the Bit-Amukani and Bit-Yakin. The latter should be identified with at least part of the area of swamp-marsh around the lower courses of the Tigris–Euphrates valley at the head of the Persian Gulf known as the Sealand (Frame 1992: 36-43). In spite of numerous and repeated Assyrian actions against these groups, the Chaldean tribes provided the most important impetus and resources for independence in the anti-Assyrian movement. Ultimately, it was Bit-

13. Already in the book of Judges, there is evidence that the tribes of Israel viewed themselves as one nation (Block 1988: 41-45; 1984: 301-26).

14. Beaulieu 1995; Borger 1965; Grayson 1992; 1975: 10-24, 69-111; Wiseman 1956; 1985.

Yakin, or at least, the Sealand that provided the royal dynasty responsible for the nascent Neo-Babylonian empire, otherwise known as the Chaldean empire.[15]

As the state emerged, the need for unification grew greater, as did the need for a strong central authority. These needs were met partially by the massive rebuilding of Babylon undertaken by Nabopolassar, Nebuchadnezzar, and later and to a lesser extent, Nabonidus. The rebuilding efforts concentrated on public works—palaces, fortifications, streets and temples.[16] Without doubt, the early motivation for such rebuilding was the need to unify all Babylonia administratively and religiously. Earlier, Merodach-baladan had attempted to consolidate and centralize rule over the southern tribes at Babylon, and had been forced to accept Borsippa as his base of operations (Brinkman 1964: 14, 18). But Nabopolassar succeeded in establishing Babylon as the seat of a central government, ruling initially from a small palace near the Ishtar gate (Wiseman 1985: 42-43). New palaces and cult-centers were needed to unite Babylonia administratively and religiously.

The events of history portray Nebuchadnezzar as an especially capable military leader. The wealth and political stability provided by his military campaigns made it possible for him to pursue an extensive building program at Babylon. The majority of his surviving inscriptions may be called 'building inscriptions', and they emphasize the rebuilding he undertook at Babylon and 12 other cities throughout Babylonia (Wiseman 1985: 42). During his reign Babylon saw extensive replanning and new construction unparalleled in its history. He rebuilt the walls and joined the halves of the city on either side of the Euphrates with a bridge. In addition to a new royal palace on the Euphrates in the northern district, he focused on cult-centers. He continued the work of his father and completely restored the temple tower (*ziggurat*) named Etemenanki ('The building that is the Foundation of Heaven and Earth') and the temple of Esagil (Marduk's

---

15. The evidence is not unambiguous regarding the ethnic identity of the Neo-Babylonian kings. Though the Bible and classical authors designate this dynasty as 'Chaldean', the term in these sources is synonymous for 'Babylonian' and may not denote ethnic specificity. We still have no irrefutable proof, for example, that Nabopolassar was himself a Chaldean, and in this sense the term is strictly inappropriate when referring to the Neo-Babylonian empire. See Beaulieu 1995: II, 969; Brinkman 1984a: 110-11 n. 551; Wiseman 1985: 5-6.

16. For details on what follows here, see Wiseman 1985: 42-80; Arnold 1994a: 61-62.

shrine) adjacent to it, along with its subsidiary chapels. Well might Nebuchadnezzar take pride in his construction of Babylon (Dan. 4.30 [MT 4.27]), though such pride was his ultimate undoing.

The centrifugal forces of the diverse tribes of southern Babylonia created a need to unify the people in a central authority. Nebuchadnezzar described his new palace as 'a palace for my royal authority, for the admiration of my people, for the union of the land' (*ekal bīti tabrâti nīši markasa māti*).[17] The incredible reconstruction of the city of Babylon in general was motivated by the need to unify the confederation of Chaldean tribes, together with Arameans and native Babylonians.

I turn now from this discussion of material remains of Babylonia to a few observations on inscriptional remains. The evidence for Nabopolassar's and Nebuchadnezzar's direct contributions to Babylonian literature is much less overwhelming than for the previous point. Yet there is still room for some general observations. When considering written sources from ancient Babylonia, one must remember a basic distinction between 'literature' in the strict sense of the word vs. non-literary compositions such as lexical texts, prognostic texts, economic and administrative texts, and so on (Grayson 1992: 771-72). Documents of the last sort were a constant in Babylonian society throughout most of the first millennium (Brinkman and Kennedy 1983; 1986), and are not really a fair indication of royal strength. One may assume such texts were much more common in ancient Israel than current epigraphic finds would attest due to the perishable types of writing materials used in ancient Palestine and given the apparent widespread availability of writing in Israelite society (Millard 1972; 1985; 1995).

It is impossible to speak definitively about the amount of literary activity of the first degree, that is, the production of native Babylonian *belles lettres*, during the reigns of Nabopolassar and Nebuchadnezzar. Such artistic creations are rarely dated. Nonetheless, there is evidence that literary and artistic activity flourished during this period (Grayson 1992: 765-66).

There is an abundance of Neo-Babylonian archives, and beginning in the seventh century BCE (and in a few cases even the eighth century), many of these have Aramaic dockets scratched on the clay, or otherwise marked with black liquid. These dockets summarize the cuneiform texts for the benefit of secretaries who could not read cuneiform. It seems quite

17. Langdon 1912: 136, number 15, vii 36.

plausible that of the abundance of Neo-Babylonian economic and legal documents in our possession, we still have only a fraction of those produced because the bulk was written in Aramaic on leather or papyrus (Dandamaev 1986: 273; Oppenheim 1977: 94-95). Obviously the climatic conditions of southern Mesopotamia were not conducive to the preservation of these documents.

Yet, judging from the cuneiform records themselves, the Neo-Babylonian period was one of the most productive in all of Mesopotamian history. Over 4600 economic, business and legal documents (including letters) dated to the Neo-Babylonian kings have been published (Dandamaev 1986: 274; Weisberg 1980). The majority of these come from temple and private archives. With few exceptions we do not yet have state archives of the Neo-Babylonian period due apparently to the fact that state chanceries used Aramaic-speaking scribes who wrote on leather and papyrus (Dandamaev 1986: 275-76).

This period also produced a valuable historiographic source, the so-called Neo-Babylonian Chronicle Series, though it should probably not be treated as a 'series' (Brinkman 1990). These chronicles record outstanding events of each year beginning with the reign of Nabonassar (747–734 BCE) and continuing into the third century. Chronicles 2–7 deal with the Neo-Babylonian kings and complement each other internally (Grayson 1975: 10-24, 69-111; Wiseman 1956: 50-88). The chronicles are objective and are as close as the Babylonians came to genuine historiography (Grayson 1975: 8; Arnold 1994b: 129-48).

We currently know more about the organization and collection of Assyrian libraries than those from Babylonia because most Babylonian libraries were plundered in the nineteenth century CE before proper excavation techniques were being used (as was done at Ashur in the north). Nonetheless, we know of significant libraries at Babylon, Borsippa and Sippar from both the Old and Neo-Babylonian periods (Parpola 1983; Grayson 1992: 773). Recently, archeologists from the University of Baghdad discovered the library chamber in the Neo-Babylonian temple of Shamash at Sippar. Only a few of the texts have been published, but it appears that this find will shed light on the contents of Neo-Babylonian collections and on the physical arrangement of a Babylonian library. The tablets were shelved in deep cubicles with markings on the tablet edges for easy access to librarians ('call numbers') (Grayson 1992: 773; George 1993; 1987). It appears that the collection contains few new compositions, but rather represents a sampling of Mesopotamian literature. It was apparently meant to preserve the major products of the Babylonian literary tradition (Al-Rawi and George 1990; 1994). This would once again confirm Oppenheim's idea of the 'stream of tradition', which some scholars have referred to as 'canonical' texts for ancient Mesopotamia.[18]

In sum, the age of Nebuchadnezzar seems to have been one in which there was significant monumental and architectural achievement as well as increased literary activity and a renewed interest in the past. In addition to great productivity of economic and other non-literary texts, it seems likely that his reign witnessed a general renaissance of Babylonian literature. The ruins of his magnificent palace contained a museum in which he housed a large collection of 'antiquities', revealing his interest in archeology and history.[19] Though there is much less evidence of his direct involvement in the creation and preservation of literature, Nebuchadnezzar's interest in the great literary traditions of Babylonia's past may have been similar to that of Ashurbanipal's.

These observations on a specific Semitic empire of the first millennium—the Neo-Babylonian empire—may actually be true of a wider cultural milieu. Among ancient Semitic cultures in general, those that gave rise to a nationalistic empire tended to have a period of literary florescence and architectural accomplishments that occurred under the aegis of their most successful and dominant monarchs. Curiously, among Old Testament scholars such a possibility has been denied for ancient Israel. Some scholars deny Israel ever had dominant and successful monarchs like David and Solomon (Garbini 1988: 21-32). For those scholars who still admit the existence of David and Solomon, the age of literary greatness is nonetheless assumed to be the exile, though this would be an unparalleled situation among ancient Semitic peoples.

A close and unbiased comparison of these ancient Semitic cultures—Israel and Neo-Babylonia—suggests that the literary traditions of Israel preserved in the Old Testament genuinely reflect the architectural and literary activities of Israel's United Monarchy. The building of Jerusalem as a unifying factor for previously disparate tribes is socially and politically paralleled in the Chaldean use of Babylon. And just as the Neo-Babylonian monarchy preserved its great literary heritage from the past, and emphasized a previously little-used form of historiography (chronicle series), Israel appears to have preserved its own literary heritage (sources

18. Notwithstanding the caveats of Lieberman (1990) and Oppenheim (1977: 13).

19. Arnold 1994a: 64. An intense interest in the past was one of the leading characteristics of the Neo-Babylonian culture. See Beaulieu 1995: 970.

of the Pentateuch?) and created new forms of historiography (the earliest segments of the Deuteronomistic History).

3. *Implications for the Study of Early Israel*

I am now in a position to make a few general comments regarding current research on early Israel. Broadly speaking, there are five assertions common in current Old Testament scholarship[20] that may be called into question in light of these observations on the Neo-Babylonian period.

a. *Israelites Were Indigenous to Canaan*
Current approaches assume the Israelites originated within Canaan, namely the so-called 'peasant revolt' model and the 'pastoral Canaanites' model (Hess 1993: 129-32). But on this analogy with early Neo-Babylonian history, we cannot rule out the possibility of Semitic tribal groups originally extraneous to the indigenous culture and arriving centuries before they begin to play a significant role in the history of the region. The Arameans and Chaldeans arrived anywhere from two to four centuries prior to their unification and statehood in southern Babylonia. In the meantime, they lived nomadic and semi-nomadic lives as pastoralists and international merchants. Nor did their presence introduce a dramatically different material culture, especially in the case of the Chaldeans. This study shows that extraneous Semitic groups, newly arrived in an area, could have presence without visibility for centuries.

The initial arrival of the Chaldeans into southern Babylonia may have been peaceful, in which case the parallel reminds one of Alt's 'peaceful infiltration' model (Alt 1959). But such an infiltration may well have been impossible in the turbulent Levantine coast at the beginning of the Iron Age. Furthermore, the arrival of the Arameans into Assyria and Babylonia was certainly not peaceful. Assyrian sources reflect the pressure created by the invading Arameans of the eleventh century, and in the ninth century Assyria campaigned vigorously against Arameans in the west and in Babylonia.

b. *Israelites and Canaanites Were Culturally Continuous*
Related to the question of Israel's geographic origins are the issues of ethnicity and religion. Many scholars currently argue that the archeological

---

20. For further discussion of the current theories, see Younger 1999.

line of evidence proves a continuity of culture between the Canaanite Late Bronze Age and Iron I assemblages, making it impossible to accept the idea of an incursion of a new ethnic element. Most assume the ethical monotheism of the biblical story is a retrojection into the past from the time of the Josianic reforms or later. Thus the first Israelites were not distinct from the Canaanites, either in race or religious ideology.[21]

There can be no question that many archeologists have overstated the continuity between the hill country culture of Iron Age I and the preceding Late Bronze Age. One of the most ardent has stated:

> If you had been walking in the countryside of central Palestine...in the 12th or 11th century B.C.E. and had met several people, you could probably not have distinguished Israelites from Canaanites or Canaanites from Philistines. They probably looked alike and dressed alike and spoke alike (Dever 1992: 54).

But Israel Finkelstein has effectively shown that the continuity has been pressed too far. The pottery of the hill country, or 'Israelite Settlement sites' is in fact different from that of the Canaanite urban centers. The Israelite pottery was characterized by locally divergent subtypes, whereas Late Bronze pottery was uniform in appearance throughout the country (Finkelstein 1988: 313). This difference is significant, since, as Finkelstein argues, it would indeed be surprising if the Israelites had a radically different pottery type. Groups lacking an established ceramic culture commonly absorb traditions from the well-developed cultures in their vicinity when undergoing the process of sedentarization (Finkelstein 1988: 274).

Ancient history is replete with examples of tribal groups assuming a local culture upon sedentarizing in a region inhabited by a different ethnic group. Edwin Yamauchi has pointed out interesting cultural parallels with the Kassite descent from the Zagros Mountains into the fertile Mesopotamian alluvium and the destruction of numerous Mycenaean settlements by the Dorians, pastoralist Greeks from the north (Yamauchi 1994: 34). This study's comparison between early Israel and the tribal groups of seventh-century southern Babylonia yields further confirmation. There can be no question that the Aramean and Chaldean tribal groups were ethnically distinct *vis-à-vis* the urban Babylonians. Distinction of religious conviction is more difficult to prove, since all elements were polytheistic and presumably similar from the outset. Yet neither of the tribal groups

---

21. For a small sampling, Ahlström 1986: 3, 26; Coote and Whitelam 1987: 126; Dever 1983; 1990.

left a striking change in the material remains of southern Babylonia.

The ethnic heterogeneity of southern Babylonia is obvious from the onomastic, linguistic and socio-political evidence. The Chaldeans had become so 'babylonized' that they are difficult to distinguish linguistically or onomastically. But their tribal structure and organization was quite distinctive (Frame 1992: 37-38). The Arameans, on the other hand, were clearly distinguished by all three types of evidence. The onomastic evidence is impressive, since most retained West Semitic names and used gentilics instead of the Babylonian East Semitic names with patronymics. Sociologically, they too were tribal and less sedentary than the Chaldeans. Perhaps the most impressive indication of their ethnic distinctiveness is the linguistic evidence, since Aramaic began replacing the more cumbersome cuneiform script and the Akkadian language by the late-eighth century and probably became the common language in Babylonia by the late-seventh century (Frame 1992: 45-48; Greenfield 1982: 471).

The ethnic diversity of tribal groups of southern Babylonia in the seventh century is clearer because of the Neo-Assyrian sources describing them. The evidence for ancient Palestine is much less well documented by epigraphic sources. This is complicated further by the observation that Israel was closer to the Canaanites in language and culture than were the diverse groups of southern Babylonia to each other. Nonetheless, as the onomastic evidence helps preserve the ethnic diversity of Babylonia, so this type of evidence is revealing for early Israel. Theophoric elements in personal names provide insight into the religious culture of a people, and, given enough such evidence over a long period, is even suggestive of ethnic identity. The onomastic record for premonarchic Israel suggests the religious sentiment of the people was Yahwistic and remarkably distinct from Canaanite culture (Hess 1994a: 345-50). Evidence from the personal names seems to identify a cultural distinction between the Late Bronze Age inhabitants of Canaan and the Israelites of the premonarchic period. It is thus misleading to state that no feature distinguishes the Israelites from the Canaanites.

c. *Israel's Conquest Accounts Are Modeled on Late Mesopotamian Parallels*

Some have argued the narratives of Joshua 9–12 were modeled on Neo-Assyrian accounts and were therefore late in origin (Van Seters 1990). But recent research has shown that the form, structure and themes of these narratives were identical to other conquest accounts from the ancient Near

East, including Hittite and Egyptian exemplars from the second millennium BCE (Younger 1990: 197-237; Hoffmeier 1994: 165-79). To this it may now be added that certain of the Aramean tribes invaded eastward into Babylonia in the early-eleventh century because of famine.[22] Arameans seized cities and took control of communication routes by force, disrupting the old patterns of settled life. For much of the next century Babylonia was in a constant state of disruption because of the Aramean tribal groups, who now controlled the important trade route along the Euphrates. And over the next several centuries, the tribal population lived in an uncertain and tenuous symbiosis with the Babylonians of the urban centers. If this is a legitimate analogue for the Israelites and Canaanites of the thirteenth century, the conquest scenario cannot be eliminated as one viable explanation for Palestine.

d. *The Social Institutions of Israel's Premonarchic Period Are Unlikely*
Many Old Testament scholars are persistently skeptical of biblical narratives concerning early Israel, despite much corroborating extrabiblical evidence. Concerning the exodus and conquest narratives, one recent author states: 'These periods never existed' (Coote 1990: 3). Likewise the biblical picture of the judges period is considered highly unlikely.

Yet the socio-political situation in Palestine from 1200 to 1000 BCE has been illuminated substantially by archeological research. Israel Finkelstein has shown that the central hill country of Canaan witnessed the sudden appearance of many new village sites at the time of the transition from Late Bronze Age to Early Iron Age (approximately 1200 BCE) (Finkelstein 1988). Interestingly, the stele of Merneptah (or Merenptah), dating from the end of the thirteenth century BCE contains the first extrabiblical reference to Israel (*ANET*: 376-78; *COS*: II, 40-41). Rather than using the determinatives for city-states or lands and territories, the inscription uses the determinative for people or ethnic groups for Israel. It seems likely that the Israelites, as recent inhabitants of the central hill country, were not closely associated with any urban center. The Egyptian inscription described instead a people, an ethnic group, which it may be assumed was spread throughout the central hills. Indeed, it has recently been suggested that the biblical evidence describes 'a time when tribal identity was preminently important and when the topography of this identity, especially in the hill country, could be described only by means of natural landmarks

22. See n. 6 above.

and villages'.[23] In light of the Merneptah Stele, it is entirely possible to see the new assemblages of the central hill country in Iron I, not as the *emergence* of Israel, but as the *sedentarization* of Israel (Bimson 1991).

As has been seen, southern Babylonia prior to the rise of the Neo-Babylonian empire consisted of two basic ethnic and cultural groups, the continuation of the older culture populating the urban centers and the pastoralist tribal groups in the country, which were gradually settling new villages and towns. The city-state governments were not highly unified, but many were loosely aligned with Assyria in her struggle to control the area. The Arameans and Chaldeans were thus in conflict with the major power to the north and with the ethnically distinct inhabitants of the cities.

This situation is closely paralleled to Israel's judges period. The tribes of Israel were distinct from the long-standing inhabitants of the Canaanite cities, who were aligned with Egypt. As with the ethnic groups of Babylonia, the unity of the tribes of Israel was forged by their common need for defense and by their common ethnicity. It is also likely that a distinctive religious ideology contributed to the unity of the Israelite tribes. Though Noth's sociological parallel with the Greek amphictyonies is now almost universally rejected (Noth 1930), we should not dismiss the possibility of some sort of tribal league or confederation during Israel's premonarchic period.

There is also evidence that highland agriculture in the central hill country was combined with a rapidly expanding population during pre-monarchic Israel. We are now able to trace the rise in seventh century Babylonia of a combination of population increases, improved economics and a movement toward intertribal, socio-political organization. In early Israel agriculture based on terrace farming would have depended upon a large and stable population, which implies further that large families with long-term residence in the tribal territories would have begun to develop cooperation on the village level (Borowski 1987; Marfoe 1979: 20-23).

e. *Israel Had No 'Golden Age', or United Monarchy*

The Old Testament characterizes the time of David and Solomon as Israel's greatest period of material culture and monumental architecture. The textual witness also describes the United Monarchy as the age of Israel's literary creativity and productivity. Yet the guild of Old Testament

---

23. Hess 1994b: 199. He believes the boundary lists of Joshua probably originated in premonarchic Israel and served in the early stages of occupation and development (p. 205).

scholarship has dismantled this picture. Many deny the existence of the so-called Solomonic Enlightenment that produced Israel's earliest histori-ography and some historical minimalists doubt the existence of an Israelite 'kingdom' under David and Solomon (Garbini 1988; Ahlström 1986; Coote and Whitelam 1987). The problem is the total absence of archival and epigraphic material from their reigns. Until recently, we had no extrabiblical reference to either king.[24]

As we have seen, the Neo-Babylonian empire (especially the reigns of Nabopolassar and Nebuchadnezzar) witnessed significant monumental and architectural achievement in addition to increased literary activity. Specifi-cally we have seen how first Nabopolassar, but especially Nebuchadnezzar used a rebuilt Babylon to unify and govern centrally the diverse groups of Babylonia. These building activities included city walls, streets and even bridges, but the greatest fervor was reserved for palaces and cult-centers. The situation in Israel's United Monarchy is analogous. David's moti-vation for taking Jebus and making it the religious and administrative center of a diversified region is well attested. Immediately after taking the stronghold and naming it 'the City of David', he built up the city 'from the Millo inward' and enlisted the aid of Hiram of Tyre to build his royal palace (2 Sam. 5.9, 11). Solomon, of course, continued massive building activities (1 Kgs 6–8), not only the palace and temple in Jerusalem, but several other sites throughout the country.[25]

We have also seen how the Neo-Babylonian empire was a time of great literary activity. Besides the vast numbers of economic texts available from this period, the empire was a time for preserving the great literary traditions of Babylon's past (as illustrated by the recently discovered library at Sippar) and for producing historical records for the present (as with the Babylonian Chronicles).

In Israel we have little in the way of economic texts from the early periods, though this may be due to the accident of archeology, since the Israelites would have used less durable writing materials.[26] Though we

24. See now the reference to the 'house of David' in Biran and Naveh 1993; 1995; Halpern 1994; Schniedewind 1996; *COS*: II, 161-62. Millard has proposed a most plausible explanation for the absence of Israelite royal inscriptions. See Millard 1990; 1991.

25. For a useful survey of individual sites, fortifications and royal buildings, see Dever 1982; 1990.

26. By the ninth century, potsherds were used for such records. On the Samaria Ostraca, see Kaufman 1992.

have little extrabiblical testimony concerning the literary productivity of the United Monarchy, the Old Testament presents a situation analogous to the Neo-Babylonian empire. The royal courts of David and Solomon included an official scribe (or 'secretary', *sōpēr*) and a recorder (*mazkîr*, 2 Sam. 8.16-17; 20.24-25; 1 Kgs. 4.3). Though the precise nature of their roles is uncertain, they seem to have been responsible for record-keeping. The internal evidence of Samuel and Kings further favors the conclusion that many of the sources used in these books were written quite close to the events themselves (example, the Succession Narrative).[27]

One wonders if this is only scratching the surface. The Bible also draws a close association between David and Israelite hymnic literature on the one hand, and Solomon and Israelite wisdom literature on the other. Perhaps our parallels with Neo-Babylonian literary activity support the idea that David and Solomon were sponsors of the arts and writing crafts in early Israel. Certainly the transformation of Israel from a segmentary, tribal society into a territorial state ruled by a monarch was accompanied by significant economic, social, political and cultural changes, including innovations in state administration, taxation, extensive state building activity, state forced labor and cultural openness (Albertz 1994: 111-13). If this is so, then perhaps this is also the period in which Israel collected the ancient traditions of her heritage and rendered an account of her past (that is, the sources of the Pentateuch), just as the Neo-Babylonian empire became a time for preserving the great literature of Babylonia's past.

This scenario may be quite typical among ancient Semites whenever the tribal groups rose to statehood. Wherever nationalistic empires developed among Semites (Akkad, Ashur, Mari, etc.), the period of greatest military and political strength also became an age of literary florescence and architectural accomplishment. Such periods of enforced peace were the only times in the turbulent ancient Near East when monarchs and their state guilds had the time, inclination and resources to turn their attention to the architectural and literary crafts.[28] In Babylonia the use of durable writing materials and the fact that the royal city was later an unoccupied site yielding magnificent archeological testimony to the empire's building activities evinces greater evidence for the Neo-Babylonian Enlightenment. But we have no such luxury for ancient Israel. The archeological record for Solomon is impressive, but extrabiblical testimony for the United

27. Despite the persistent objections of Van Seters 1983; see now Gordon 1994b.

28. Anthropological studies support the correlation between the rise of bureaucratic states and the use of writing. See Goody 1986: 89-99.

Monarchy in general remains elusive. Nonetheless, these parallels with the Neo-Babylonian period suggest that in fact, Nabopolassar and Nebuchadnezzar have much in common with David and Solomon. Such institutional and socio-political analogies should provide limits to our skepticism[29] about early Israel and the biblical picture of the United Monarchy.

BIBLIOGRAPHY

Ahlström, G.
  1986   *Who Were the Israelites?* (Winona Lake, IN: Eisenbrauns).
Al-Rawi, F.N.H., and A.R. George
  1990   'Tablets from the Sippar Library II: Tablet II of the Babylonian Creation Epic', *Iraq* 52: 149.
  1994   'Tablets from the Sippar Library III: Two Royal Counterfeits', *Iraq* 56: 135-48.
Albertz, R.
  1994   *A History of Israelite Religion in the Old Testament Period. I. From the Beginnings to the End of the Monarchy* (trans. J. Bowden; Louisville, KY: Westminster/John Knox Press).
Alt, A.
  1959   'Die Landnahme der Israeliten in Palästina', in *idem, Kleine Schriften zur Geschichte des Volkes Israel* (Munich: Beck): I, 89-125 (originally published in *Reformationsprogramm der Universität Leipzig*, 1925; English translation available as 'The Settlement of the Israelites in Palestine', in A. Alt, *Essays on Old Testament History and Religion* [trans. R.A. Wilson; Oxford: Basil Blackwell, 1966]: 133-69).
Arnold, B.T.
  1985   'Babylonian Letters from the Kuyunjik Collection: Seventh Century Uruk in Light of New Epistolary Evidence' (PhD dissertation, Hebrew Union College).
  1994a   'Babylonians', *POTW*: 43-75.
  1994b   'The Weidner Chronicle and the Idea of History in Israel and Mesopotamia', in *FTH*: 129-48.
Beaulieu, P.-A.
  1995   'King Nabonidus and the Neo-Babylonian Empire', *CANE*: II, 969-79.
Bimson, J.J.
  1991   'Merenptah's Israel and Recent Theories of Israelite Origins', *JSOT* 49: 3-29.
Biran, A., and J. Naveh
  1993   'An Aramaic Stele Fragment from Tel Dan', *IEJ* 43: 81-98.
  1995   'The Tel Dan Inscription: A New Fragment', *IEJ* 45: 1-15.
Block, D.I.
  1984   '"Israel"—"Sons of Israel": A Study in Hebrew Eponymic Usage', *Studies in Religion* 13: 301-26.

29. To borrow an expression from Hallo 1990.

1988   'The Period of the Judges: Religious Disintegration under Tribal Rule', in *Studies Harrison*: 41-45.

Borger, R.
1965   'Der Aufstieg des neubabylonischen Reiches', *JCS* 19: 59-78.

Borowski, O.
1987   *Agriculture in Iron Age Israel: The Evidence from Archeology and the Bible* (Winona Lake, IN: Eisenbrauns).

Brinkman, J.A.
1964   'Merodach-baladan II', in R.D. Biggs and J.A. Brinkman (eds.), *Studies Presented to A. Leo Oppenheim* (Chicago: Oriental Institute): 6-53.

1968   *PKB.*

1977   'Notes on Arameans and Chaldeans in Southern Babylonia in the Early Seventh Century B.C.', *Or* 46: 304-25.

1979   'Babylonia under the Assyrian Empire, 745–627 B.C.', in *Power and Propoganda*: 237-38.

1981   'Hurrians in Babylonia in the Late Second Millennium B.C.: An Unexploited Minority Resource for Socio-Economic and Philological Analysis', in *Studies Lacheman*: 27-35.

1984a   *Prelude to Empire: Babylonian Society and Politics, 747–626 B.C.* (Occasional Publications of the Babylonian Fund, 7; Philadelphia: University Museum Press).

1984b   'Settlement Surveys and Documentary Evidence: Regional Variation and Secular Trend in Mesopotamian Demography', *JNES* 43: 169-80.

1985   'Babylonia and the Eastern Arameans', unpublished paper presented to the American Oriental Society, April 14, 1985.

1990   'The Babylonian Chronicle Revisited', in *Studies Moran*: 73-104.

Brinkman, J.A., and D.A. Kennedy
1983   'Documentary Evidence for the Economic Base of Early Neo-Babylonian Society: A Survey of Dated Babylonian Economic Texts, 721–626 B.C.', *JCS* 35: 1-90.

1986   'Supplement to the Survey of Dated Neo-Babylonian Economic Texts, 721–626 B.C.', *JCS* 38: 99-106.

Coote, R.B.
1990   *Early Israel: A New Horizon* (Minneapolis, MN: Fortress Press).

Coote, R.B., and K.W. Whitelam
1987   *The Emergence of Early Israel in Historical Perspective* (Sheffield: Almond Press).

Dandamaev, M.A.
1986   'The Neo-Babylonian Archives', in K.R. Veenhof (ed.), *Cuneiform Archives and Libraries* (RAI, 30; Uitgaven van het Nederlands Historisch-Archaeologisch Instituut te Istanbul, 52; Istanbul: Nederlands Historisch-Archaeologisch Instituut): 271-77.

Dever, W.G.
1982   'Monumental Architecture in Ancient Israel in the Period of the United Monarchy', in T. Ishida (ed.), *Studies in the Period of David and Solomon and Other Essays* (Winona Lake, IN: Eisenbrauns; = Dever 1990): 269-306.

1983   'Material Remains and the Cult in Ancient Israel: An Essay in Archaeological "Systematics"', *Studies Freedman*: 578-81.

1990   *Recent Archeological Discoveries and Biblical Research* (Seattle: University
            of Washington): 85-117.
1992   'How to Tell a Canaanite from an Israelite', in H. Shanks (ed.), *The Rise of
            Ancient Israel: Symposium at the Smithsonian Institution October 26, 1991*
            (Washington, DC: Biblical Archeology Society): 26-60.

Dietrich, M.
1970   *Die Aramäer Südbabyloniens in der Sargonidenzeit (700–648)* (AOAT, 7;
            Kevelaes: Butzon & Bercker Verlag).

Finkelstein, I.
1988   *The Archaeology of the Israelite Settlement* (Jerusalem: Israel Exploration
            Society).
1988–89   'The Land of Ephraim Survey 1980–1987: Preliminary Report', *Tel Aviv* 15-
            16: 167.
1989   'The Emergence of the Monarchy in Israel: The Environmental and Socio-
            Economic Aspects', *JSOT* 44: 59-61, 63.

Frame, G.
1984   'The "First Families" of Borsippa during the Early Neo-Babylonian Period',
            JCS 36: 67-80.
1992   *Babylonia 689–627 B.C.: A Political History* (Istanbul: Nederlands
            Historisch-Archaeologisch Instituut).

Garbini, G.
1988   *History and Ideology in Ancient Israel* (trans. J. Bowden; New York:
            Crossroad).

George, A.R.
1987   'Excavations in Iraq, 1985–86: Sippar (Abu Habba)', *Iraq* 49: 248-49, and
            pl. 47.
1993   'Review of K.R. Veenhof (ed.), *Cuneiform Archives and Libraries*', *JNES*
            52: 303.

Goody, J.
1986   *The Logic of Writing and the Organization of Society* (Cambridge: Cam-
            bridge University Press).

Gordon, R.P.
1994a   'Who Made the Kingmaker? Reflections on Samuel and the Institution of the
            Monarchy', in *FTH*: 257-60.
1994b   'In Search of David: The David Tradition in Recent Study', *FTH*: 285-98.

Grayson, A.K.
1975   *ABC*.
1992   'Mesopotamia, History of (Babylonia)', *ABD*: IV, 763-66.

Greenfield, J.
1982   'Babylonian-Aramaic Relationship', in *Mesopotamien und seine Nachbarn*:
            471-82.

Hallo, W.W.
1980   'Biblical History in its Near Eastern Setting: The Contextual Approach', *SIC*
            1: 1-26.
1990   'The Limits of Skepticism', *JAOS* 110: 187-99.
1991   'The Concept of Canonicity in Cuneiform and Biblical Literature: a
            Comparative Appraisal', *SIC* 4: 1-19.

Halpern, B.
    1994   'The Stela from Dan: Epigraphic and Historical Considerations', *BASOR*
                296: 63-80.
Hess, R.S.
    1993   'Early Israel in Canaan: A Survey of Recent Evidence and Interpretations',
                PEQ 125: 125-42.
    1994a   'Fallacies in the Study of Early Israel: An Onomastic Perspective', *TynBul*
                45: 345-50.
    1994b   'Asking Historical Questions of Joshua 13–19: Recent Discussion Concern-
                ing the Date of the Boundary Lists', *FTH*: 191-205.
Hoffmeier, J.K.
    1994   'The Structure of Joshua 1–11 and the Annals of Thutmose III', *FTH*:
                165-79.
Kaufman, I.T.
    1992   *ABD*: V, 921-26.
Kupper, J.-R.
    1957   *Les nomades en Mésopotamie au temps des rois de Mari* (Paris: Société
                d'édition 'Les belles lettres').
Langdon, S.H.
    1912   *Die neubabylonischen Königsinschriften* (VAB, IV; Leipzig: J.C. Hinrichs).
Lieberman, S.J.
    1990   'Canonical and Official Cuneiform Texts: Towards an Understanding of
                Assurbanipal's Personal Tablet Collection', in *Studies Moran*: 304-336.
Marfoe, L.
    1979   'The Integrative Transformation: Patterns of Socio-Political Organization in
                Southern Syria', *BASOR* 234: 1-42.
Mendenhall, G.
    1973   *The Tenth Generation: The Origins of the Biblical Tradition* (Baltimore: The
                Johns Hopkins University Press).
Millard, A.R.
    1972   'The Practice of Writing in Ancient Israel', *BA* 35: 98-111.
    1985   'An Assessment of the Evidence for Writing in Ancient Israel', *BAT 1985*:
                301-12.
    1990   'Israelite and Aramean History in the Light of Inscriptions', *TynBul* 41:
                261-75.
    1991   'The Uses of the Early Alphabets', in Cl. Baurain, C. Bonnet and V. Krings
                (eds.), *Phoinikeia Grammata: Lire et écrire en Méditerranée* (Namur:
                Société des études classiques): 101-14.
    1992   'Arameans', *ABD*: I, 345-50.
    1995   'The Knowledge of Writing in Iron Age Palestine', *TynBul* 46: 207-17.
Noth, M.
    1930   *Das System der Zwölf Stämme Israels* (repr., BWANT, 4.1; Darmstadt:
                Wissenschaftliche Buchgesellschaft).
Oppenheim, A.L.
    1977   *Ancient Mesopotamia* (Chicago: University of Chicago Press).
Parpola, S.
    1983   'Assyrian Library Records', *JNES* 42: 1-29.

Pitard, W.T.
  1994   'Arameans', *POTW*: 208-10.
Schniedewind, W.M.
  1996   'Tel Dan Stela: New Light on Aramaic and Jehu's Revolt', *BASOR* 302: 75-
              90.
Van Seters, J.
  1983   *In Search of History: Historiography in the Ancient World and the Origins
              of Biblical History* (New Haven: Yale University Press).
  1990   'Joshua's Campaign of Canaan and Near Eastern Historiography', *SJOT* 4:
              1-12.
Walker, C.B.F.
  1982   'Babylonian Chronicle 25: A Chronicle of the Kassite and Isin II Dynasties',
              in *Studies Kraus*: 414-15.
Weisberg, D.B.
  1980   *Texts from the Time of Nebuchadnezzar* (YOS, 17; New Haven: Yale
              University Press).
Wiseman, D.J.
  1956   *Chronicles of Chaldaean Kings (626–556 B.C.) in the British Museum*
              (London: British Museum).
  1985   *Nebuchadrezzar and Babylon* (Schweich Lectures, 1983; Oxford: Oxford
              University Press for the British Academy).
Yamauchi, E.
  1994   'The Current State of Old Testament Historiography', in *FTH*: 1-36.
Younger, K.L. Jr.
  1990   *Ancient Conquest Accounts: A Study in Ancient Near Eastern and Biblical
              History Writing* (JSOTSup, 98; Sheffield: JSOT Press).
  1999   'Early Israel in Recent Biblical Scholarship', in D.W. Baker and B.T. Arnold
              (eds.), *The Face of Old Testament Studies* (Grand Rapids: Baker Book
              House): 176-206.

The Eastern Jewish Diaspora under the Babylonians

Edwin Yamauchi

1. Introduction

The period covering the Babylonian Exile and the Postexilic era was a crucial epoch in Jewish history. As Salo Baron (1952: 102) remarks, the issues were: 'Would the Jews remain Jews even in exile and under a foreign monarch? Could a nationality exist without state or territory?'

The main sources for the history of the Jews during the Neo-Babylonian Empire (c. 612–539 BCE), and the Persian Empire (539–330 BCE) are the biblical books (2 Kings, 2 Chronicles, Isaiah, Jeremiah, Ezekiel, Daniel, Esther, Ezra, Nehemiah, Haggai, Zechariah, and Malachi), supplemented by important cuneiform texts (Assyrian and Babylonian Chronicles, the Yaukin [Jehoiachin] Tablets),[1] Old Persian inscriptions, the Cyrus Cylinder, the Murashu archive, and archeological excavations in Palestine, Mesopotamia, and Persia.[2] Some ostraca, seals, and bullae (seal impressions) (see Avigad 1965; 1974) also offer specific corroborative evidence of biblical figures. Later Greek sources such as Herodotus, Ctesias, Berossus, and Josephus provide some further information. The biblical texts remain the most important narrative sources.[3]

2. Assyrian Deportations

Whereas the population of Israel (the northern kingdom) in the eighth century has been estimated at 500,000 to 700,000, the population of Judah in the eighth to the sixth centuries has been estimated at between 220,000

---

1. These texts are the only direct evidence of the treatment of the Jewish exiles from Neo-Babylonian sources.

2. On the Jewish Diaspora under the Persians, see Davies and Finkelstein 1984; Yamauchi 1990; Grabbe 1992; Berquist 1995.

3. Smith 1989: 41 states: 'In sum, we are unable to make definite conclusions about exilic existence apart from the biblical text itself'.

and 300,000.[4] Population estimates for cities are made on the basis of 40 to 50 persons per dunam or 1000 square meters. As there are four dunams per acre, this would be an estimate of 160 to 200 persons per acre.

After the conquest of Samaria by Shalmaneser V in 722, Sargon II deported 27,280 (or 27,290) Israelites to Halah, Gozan on the Habor River, and Median cities (2 Kgs 17.6; 18.11) (see Younger 1998). When Sennacherib attacked Judah in 701, he deported numerous Jews especially from Lachish. His annals claim that he deported 200,150 from Judah.[5] Such a high figure is difficult to reconcile with the population estimates. Some scholars have argued that this must be an error for 2150 (Ungnad 1942–43). S. Stohlmann has suggested that the full number was counted, 'But not all of the 200,150 were deported, because there is no evidence of Assyrian resettlement of the conquered territory' (Stohlmann 1983: 157). Ezra 4.9-10 refers to the 'men of Tripolis, Persia, Erech and Babylon, the Elamites of Susa, and other people whom the great and honorable Ashurbanipal deported and settled in the city of Samaria and elsewhere in the Trans-Euphrates'.[6] These were probably settled there in 648.

An important difference between the deportations by the Assyrians and the Babylonians was that the latter did not replace the deportees with pagan newcomers. Thus Judah, though devastated, was not further contaminated with polytheism as was Israel.

3. *Israelite and Judahite Exiles under the Assyrians*

One must bear in mind that only a proportion of the population of the northern kingdom of Israel was deported by the Assyrians, perhaps only 5 per cent. Since these Israelites had already apostasized from an exclusive allegiance to Yahweh, many probably had no compunction about worshipping the alien gods of their new Mesopotamian homeland. Almost all eventually assimilated and intermarried (see Younger 2002), as did other exilic communities like the Egyptians. As M. Dandamaev observes:

4.   Weinberg 1972: 49-58. Albright 1963 comments: 'The population of Judah, which had probably passed 250,000 by the end of the eighth century, can scarcely have been over half that number during this interval [i.e. early sixth century]'.

5.   See *ANET*, 288; *COS*: II, 302-303. According to Oded 1979: 19: 'If Sennacherib claims that he deported more than 200,000 inhabitants from the cites of Judah, we take the number of deportees given in the document to be a "fact"'.

6.   All citations are from the NIV. On the mistranslation of the KJV, see Yamauchi 1988: IV, 630.

For a certain period of time the Egyptians maintained their ethnic identity
and even had their own popular assemblies. However, owing to mixed
marriages and under the influence of their surroundings, they usually gave
their children Babylonian names and were gradually assimilated with the
native population of the country (Danamaev 1992: 324).[7]

The prophets looked for a restoration not only of Judah but also of Israel
in the future. Ezekiel's famous vision of the dry bones coming to life has
the Lord revealing to the prophet, 'Son of man, these bones are the whole
house of Israel' (Ezek. 37.11). The Lord further instructed him to take two
sticks: on the one, writing 'Belonging to Judah and the Israelites associated with him', and on the other, 'Ephraim's stick, belonging to Joseph
and all the house of Israel associated with him' (Ezek. 37.16).

Jeremiah 31.37 has the Lord declaring, 'will I reject all the descendants
of Israel because of all they have done?' Jeremiah 50.4 promises, '"In
those days, at that time", declares the Lord, "the people of Israel and the
people of Judah together will go in tears to seek the Lord their God".'
After the punishment of Babylon, the Lord promised, 'But I will bring
Israel back to his own pasture and he will graze on Carmel and Bashan; his
appetite will be satisfied on the hills of Ephraim and Gilead' (Jer. 50.19).

These prophecies and references to 144,000 from the 12 tribes (Rev.
7.5-8) have spawned endless speculation about the tradition of 'The Ten
Lost Tribes'. E.J. Bickerman (1984: 343), comments:

What happened to the ten tribes in Assyria and Media?... We do not know.
The only book preserved by the Jews that refers to the life of the exiles
from Israel is the book of Tobit which represents the hero, a Galilean, as a
faithful worshipper at the Temple of Jerusalem.

The hope that the descendants of the Ten Tribes would be regathered
was at first fostered by Jewish circles (Ben-Zvi 1976). The idea was then
taken up by Europeans and eventually by Americans. The development of
the idea of Anglo-Israelism by Richard Brothers (1757–1824) popularized
the notion that the British were the remnants of the 'Ten Lost Tribes'.[8]
The idea has not only stimulated such important groups as the Mormons,
but even such radically racist groups as the Freeman, who were besieged
by Federal agents in Montana.[9]

7.   Cf. Wiseman 1966. Other expatriate communities included exiles from Asia
Minor, Syria, Phoenicia, Philistia, and Arabia. See Eph'al 1978.
8.   Godbey 1930; May 1943; Popkin 1986; Gross 1992; Goldman 1993; Gustafson
1994.
9.   'Hate is the Key to Ideology of Freemen', *New York Times* (April 12 1996),

4. *The Neo-Babylonians and the Last Kings of Judah*

The once invincible Assyrian Empire was toppled in 612 by a coalition of the Indo-European Medes and the Chaldeans.[10] The latter established the Neo-Babylonian dynasty under Nabopolassar, the father of the great king Nebuchadnezzar II (Wiseman 1985). Nebuchadnezzar (605–562) defeated the Egyptians at Carchemish (Jer. 46.2) and conquered Hatti (Syria-Palestine). It was he who vanquished rebellious Judah in 597 and again in 587 or 586, destroying Solomon's temple in the latter campaign. He was succeeded by a number of rather ephemeral kings such as Amel-Marduk (= biblical Evil-Merodach, 562–560) (Sack 1972), and Neriglissar (= biblical Nergalsharezer, 559–556) (Sack 1994). The last king of the Neo-Babylonians was Nabonidus (see Sack 1983; Yamauchi 1986a; Beaulieu 1989), whose son Belshazzar was depicted in Daniel as the de facto king at the time Babylon fell to the Persians under Cyrus in 539.

H. Tadmor has commented, 'No two other decades in the history of Judah are better documented than the years 609–586, for the most part spent under Babylonian suzerainty' (Tadmor 1976). Within these two decades four kings rapidly succeeded each other on the throne of Judah. After the death of the great reforming king Josiah, who attempted in vain to stop the Egyptian pharaoh Necho at the Megiddo Pass (2 Chron. 35.20-27), his son Jehoahaz, also known as Shallum, became king. Necho, however, carried him off to Egypt (Jer. 22.10-12). He was then succeeded by his unpopular brother Jehoiakim, also known as Eliakim (609–598). Despite the warnings of Jeremiah, Jehoiakim sought to ally himself with Egypt against Babylon, and persecuted those Jews who opposed his policies. In turning away from Babylon in 601, he was breaking his oath as a vassal to Nebuchadnezzar (2 Kgs 24.1).[11]

While the Babylonians were besieging Jerusalem, Jehoiakim died or was killed (Jer. 22.18-19). He was succeeded by his son, Jehoiachin (also

A8: 'So for four hours that mid-January day, Ms. Young was told that God created white gentiles as a superior race, descended directly from Adam and Eve, but that Jews descended from a sexual union between Eve and Satan. Moreover, they told her, whites were the true "Israelites," a lost tribe who had migrated to America, the new promised land, but that the Government was now corrupted by Jewish influence.'

10. On the Medes see Yamauchi 1990: ch. 1; on the Chaldeans, see Yamauchi 1983a: 123-25; Arnold 1994.

11. Mercer (1989: 190) proposes that Jehoiakim's three years of vassalage began after his brief deportation to Babylon in the winter of 604 (2 Chron. 36.6-7).

called Coniah), who was but 18 years old (2 Kgs 24.8). After only three months, Jehoiachin surrendered Jerusalem on 16 March 597 (2 Kgs 24.12). The Babylonian Chronicle laconically reports, 'Year 7, month Kislimu: The king of Akkad moved his army into Hatti land, laid siege to the city of Judah and the king took the city on the second day of the month Addaru. He appointed in it a king to his liking, took heavy booty from it and brought it into Babylon' (*ANET*: 564; *COS*: I, 468).[12] For surrendering without much resistance he was treated with relative leniency.

In place of Jehoiachin, his uncle Mattaniah, whose name was changed to Zedekiah, was appointed king by Nebuchadnezzar (2 Kgs 24.17). Though Zedekiah paid a visit to Babylon to affirm his loyalty (Jer. 51.59), he was probably swayed by Psammetichus II's visit in 591 to Judah to rely upon Egypt. When Zedekiah rebelled he broke his oath to Nebuchadnezzar (2 Chron. 36.13). Though Zedekiah tried to escape, he was captured near Jericho and brought to Nebuchadnezzar, his children were slain before his eyes and he himself was blinded (2 Kgs 25.5-7).

According to the biblical record, the Babylonian armies smashed Jerusalem's defenses (2 Kgs 25.10), destroyed the temple and palaces (2 Kgs 25.9, 13-17; Jer. 52.17-23), and devastated the country (Jer. 32.43; cf. Lamentations). Many of the leaders and priests were killed (2 Kgs 25.18-21). The temple vessels, which were carried off, were carefully inventoried (Jer. 27.16-22; 28.3-6; cf. Ezra 1.7-11) (Kalimi and Purvis 1994a; 1994b). As to the ark, it was never recovered (*m. Yoma* 5.2; cf. Josephus, *War* 1.152-53).[13]

5. *Jehoiachin in Exile*

Though Jehoiachin was carried away to Babylon, many of the people in Judah continued to recognize him as the legitimate king (Ezek. 1.2). This reference was questioned by C.C. Torrey, whose skepticism was countered by W.F. Albright's discovery of stamp seals of 'Eliakim steward of

---

12. Malamat (1968: 144) comments: 'The account in the Babylonian Chronicle for Nebuchadnezzar's 7th regnal year, devoted entirely to the conquest of Jerusalem, is a classical example of an external source serving to confirm the biblical narrative and to supplement it with important data'.

13. 2 Macc. 2.5 claims that Jeremiah hid the ark and the altar of incense in a cave. According to a tradition which arose in the Middle Ages, the Ethiopian Church claims that Solomon's son by the Queen of Sheba stole the ark from Jerusalem. See Isaac 1993.

Yaukin'.[14] Cuneiform texts, which were discovered by R. Koldewey in his excavations of Babylon (1899–1917), from an area which he misidentified as the site of the famous Hanging Gardens, indicate that Jehoiachin was maintained at the Babylonian court and provided with rations. The texts were sent to the Kaiser Friedrich Museum in Berlin, where they remained untranslated until they were published by E.F. Weidner in 1939.[15] One of four tablets is dated to 592/591 in the reign of Nebuchadnezzar. These tablets list oil and grain rations for a variety of different ethnic groups (Egyptians, Tyrians, Lydians, Greeks). These are the only Akkadian documents which refer to the ethnicon 'Judean' = $^{l\acute{u}}Ia$-$(a$-$)$-$u/\acute{u}$-da-a-a. Listed as recipients are Yaukin = biblical Jehoiachin, his five sons, eight anonymous and five named Jews (Albright 1942). The sons were evidently born to Jehoiachin in captivity.

Jehoiachin must have thereafter fallen into disfavor, because he was imprisoned. Some 30 years after the composition of Weidner ration tablets, Jehoiachin was released from captivity (2 Kgs 25.27-30; Jer. 52.31-34), when Evil Merodach (Amel-Marduk) became king (Sack 1972: 29). He was again at this time issued daily rations.

6. *Numbers Deported*

The biblical references to the numbers that were deported by the Babylonians under Nebuchadnezzar are incomplete and somewhat confusing. They have given rise to conflicting interpretations as to the actual number of Judeans and the percentage of the population deported.

Daniel 1.1 indicates that in Jehoiakim's third year, which would correspond to Nebuchadnezzar's first, Daniel, and his companions along with others, were carried off into captivity.[16] Until D.J. Wiseman published the Chaldean Chronicles in 1956 no extra-biblical evidence was available to document fully Nebuchadnezzar's early years (Wiseman 1956). The Chronicles speak of his conquest of Hatti (Syria–Palestine),[17] though there

---

14. Albright 1932; Orlinsky 1972: 200; However, Cogan and Tadmor (1988) commenting on 2 Kgs. 24.8, maintain that this is not a royal seal but one belonging to a class of private citizens.

15. Weidner 1939. See *ANET*: 308.

16. On the problems of this passage, see Collins 1993: 130-31; for proposed solutions, see Millard 1977: 69.

17. Mitchell (1991: 394) comments: ' "Khatti" was not a precise term, referring in the first millennium mainly to north Syria, but the fact that later in this document it is

is no explicit reference to a siege of Jerusalem in the Babylonian Chronicles in his first year (Malamat 1968: 137-55). Wiseman has attempted to address this difficulty (Wiseman 1965: 16-18). He has suggested that the phrase in Dan. 1.1, *wyṣr 'lyh*, ordinarily translated 'besieged it', may mean no more than 'showed hostility' or 'treated as an enemy' (Wiseman 1985: 23). Mercer suggests that the siege may not have been mentioned because it may have been short (Mercer 1989: 186).

According to Oded, in the Assyrian Empire, 'The state and legal documents make it clear that many foreigners, some of them deportees or their desendants, were serving as officials in the royal court, in the capital, in Assyria proper and in the provinces. Many foreign functionaries attained a very high position in the official hierarchy…' (Oded 1979: 104). Though we do not have extra-biblical evidence from the Babylonian Empire for Judeans like Daniel serving in high government offices (see below on the Murashu texts), we do have evidence of West Semites and Egyptians serving in such high positions (Zadok 1977: 87; Dandamaev 1992: 322).

In 597 Nebuchadnezzar carried off 'all the officers and fighting men, and all the craftsmen and artisans…a total of 10,000' (2 Kgs 24.14). 'The king also deported to Babylon the entire force of 7000 fighting men…and 1000 craftsmen and artisans' (24.16). If these figures represent only the heads of households, the total may have been closer to 30,000 (Malamat 1950: 223).

On the other hand, Jeremiah enumerates for 598 BCE only 3023 deportees (Jer. 52.28); this total evidently were from the countryside and not from Jerusalem, which was not conquered until 597. For the major campaign of 587 or 586 BCE[18] only 832 captives from Jerusalem (Jer. 52.29) are mentioned as deportees. In 581, after the murder of Gedaliah, 745 were deported for a grand total of 4600 (Jer. 52.30). The smaller figures of Jeremiah probably represent only men of the most important families. These figures are obviously very incomplete (Cogan and Tadmor 1988: 324).

Albright accepted only the figures of Jeremiah and explained the discrepancy with the larger figures as being due to losses suffered during

treated as including Judah suggests that Nebuchadnezzar's victorious march may have extended into Palestine.'

18. Jerusalem fell in the 11th year of Zedekiah (Jer. 52.5). Scholars, who believe that the regnal year began in Nisan (spring), date the beginning of the siege to 587 and the fall of Jerusalem after a siege of 18 months to 586. Other scholars, who believe that the regnal year began in Tishri (fall), date the fall of Jerusalem to 587.

the trek to Babylon (Albright 1963: 85). He furthermore estimated the total population of Judah when the exiles returned at between 20,000 and 50,000. Such a radically minimalist view makes it impossible to accept the large number of returnees listed in Ezra 2 (=Neh. 7).[19]

Other scholars assume that the numbers mentioned in 2 Kings and in Jeremiah are to be added, giving a total of about 15,000 deportees. Whitley estimated that the number was not less than 14,000 or 15,000 (Whitley 1957a: 66). Kreissig guesses a total of 15,600 deportees (Kreissig 1973: 22). Weinberg speculates that 10 per cent of the population or about 20,000 may have been deported (Weinberg 1972: 47; cf. Galling 1964: 51-52).

Impressed by the descriptions of widespread deportation found in 2 Kgs 25.11 and Jer. 39.9-10, earlier scholars had proposed very high figures by multiplying the numbers in Jeremiah and 2 Kings by a factor as high as five for family members. E. Meyer, R. Kittel, and E. Sellin calculated that as many as 40,000 to 70,000 were deported, or up to one-third of the population of Judah.

Whatever the numbers, it is clear that in addition to some of the poor, it was especially the upper classes who were deported (Dan. 1.3-4), leaving behind the poorest of the land (2 Kgs 25.12; Jer. 39.10; 52.16) to work the vineyards and the fields (Graham 1984). The Chronicler (2 Chron. 36.17-20), ignoring the people who remained in the land, gives the impression that all who were not killed were taken into exile in Babylon.

7. Jeremiah's Ministry

The great prophet Jeremiah began his career in 627 (Jer. 1.2), warning the people of Judah about invasions from the north, which may be interpreted as possible references to the nomadic Scythians from Russia (Yamauchi 1982), though most scholars believe they referred to the Chaldeans. Jeremiah's highly unpopular message was that the Lord was using the Babylonians under Nebuchadnezzar[20] to chastise his people for their un-faithfulness and sins.[21] They were to submit and not to rebel. Baruch, the scribe who recorded Jeremiah's bitter message and conveyed it to the

---

19. According to Ezra 2.64-65 about 50,000 responded. On the discrepancies between Ezra 2 and its parallel in Neh. 7, see Allrik 1954.

20. Nebuchadnezzar is mentioned 35 times in Jeremiah. See Fensham 1982.

21. 2 Kgs. 24.3-4, 13, also regards Nebuchadnezzar as God's agent to punish Judah for the sins of Manasseh.

royal court (Jer. 36), was himself probably once a royal scribe as indicated by the new evidence provided by his seal impressions.[22]

In his vision of two basket of figs Jeremiah implies that the people who submitted to deportation were superior to those who remained in the land (Jer. 24.1-10). In an important letter which he sent to the exiles (Jer. 29.4-7), he counseled:

> This is what the LORD Almighty, the God of Israel, says to all those I carried into exile from Jerusalem to Babylon: 'Build houses and settle down; plant gardens and eat what they produce. Marry and have sons and daughters; find wives for your sons and give your daughters in marriage, so that they too may have sons and daughters. Increase in number there; do not decrease. Also, seek the peace and prosperity of the city to which I have carried you into exile. Pray to the LORD for it, because if it prospers, you too will prosper'.

After the death of the last Judean kings, the Babylonians appointed a local leader, Gedaliah to govern from Mizpah (2 Kgs 25.22-24). Gedaliah, whose father had saved Jeremiah's life (Jer. 26.24), had been a royal steward as indicated by his seal impression (Orlinsky 1972: 202). A military officer, Ishmael ben Nethaniah, murdered Gedaliah, his family, and his Babylonian guards (2 Kgs 25.25-26; Jer. 40.7–41.3). Fearing Babylonian reprisals, many Judeans fled, some to various areas in Transjordan, and others to Egypt. The latter refugees took Jeremiah with them (Jer. 41.16–43.7).

8. *Life in Exile*

Initially, no doubt, the exiles were saddened and disoriented in their enforced exile, as memorably expressed in Ps. 137.1-6.[23]

> By the rivers of Babylon we sat and wept when we remembered Zion. There on the poplars we hung our harps, for there our captors asked us for songs, our tormentors demanded songs of joy; they said, 'Sing us one of the

22. Mitchell 1991: 395-96. The name on the seal and its patronymic (father's name) corresponds almost exactly with the Hebrew of Jer. 36.32: *lbrykyhw ben nryhw hspr* = biblical *brwk ben nryhw hspr*, 'Baruch ben Neriah, the scribe'. See Avigad 1978; Shanks 1987; 1996.

23. Ackroyd (1970: 57) comments, 'Among the psalms, Ps. 137 makes specific reference to this situation; it offers the only precise reference to the exile in the psalms, though there are other passages (e.g. Ps. 106.47) which refer to the gathering in of the scattered members of the people from among the nations'.

songs of Zion!' How can we sing the songs of the LORD while in a foreign land? If I forget you, O Jerusalem, may my right hand forget [its skill]. May my tongue cling to the roof of my mouth if I do not remember you, if I do not consider Jerusalem my highest joy.

Once the exiles were transported to their new homes, most were not reduced to a position of abject slavery. Though the Babylonians did use slaves, they had more than enough from natural reproduction (Dandamaev 1984: 457, 459, 652). Others became dependents of the palace or the temples. They worked upon lands which belonged to these institutions. From a careful study of not only the Israelites and the Judeans, but of a large variety of peoples who were exiled by the Assyrians, whose situation was probably similar to those deported by the Babylonians, Oded (1979: 87) has concluded:

> From the abundant administrative business and legal documents, and also from the Old Testament, one gets the impression that the deportees were not deprived of the rights of free persons. They lived a family life, had property (land, slaves, silver), were creditors and debtors, had the right to engage in litigation, in commerce and business transactions, and the right to witness contracts and suits, and to maintain their ancestral traditions.

The Judean exiles were settled in various communities in lower Mesopotamia. Judging from the place names, they were settled on the ruins of earlier cities such as at Tel-Abib (= 'the mound destroyed by a flood', Ezek. 3.15), Tel-Melah (= 'mound of salt'), and Tel Harsa (= 'mound covered with potsherds', Ezra 3.15). Other sites settled by the exiles included Cherub, Addan, Immer (Ezra 2.59), and Casiphia (Ezra 8.17). These lists also indicate that the exiles must have maintained some cohesion as members of local communities; those that returned, went 'each to his own town' (Ezra 2.1//Neh. 7.6). The descendants of the exiles evidently prospered, since those who returned brought with them numerous servants and animals, and were able to make contributions for the sacred services (Ezra 2.65-69; 8.26-27; Neh. 7.70-72).

An important source of what life was like in exile is provided by Ezekiel. His book was subject to much skepticism by earlier scholars.[24] Recent scholarship has restored respect for the integrity and authenticity of the book as an important source for the exile (Boadt 1992). Ezekiel, who was probably exiled with Jehoiachin, settled on the Kebar River, an irrigation canal near Nippur (Yamauchi 1983b). We note that he was

---

24. For a review of earlier scholarship see Whitley 1957a: 82-83; Rowley 1953.

married (Ezek. 24.18), and had his own house (8.1). He refers to both the elders of the house of Judah (8.1) and the elders of the house of Israel (14.1; 20.1), who met with him.

9. *The '70 Years'*

Jeremiah predicted that the captivity would last 70 years: 'But when 70 years are fulfilled, I will punish the king of Babylon' (Jer. 25.12). Again in Jer. 29.10, 'this is what the Lord says: When 70 years are completed for Babylon, I will come to you and fulfill my gracious promise to bring you back to this place'. Daniel (9.2) anticipated the completion of the 70 years predicted by Jeremiah.

Now 70 years was the span of a man's life (Ps. 90.10; Isa. 23.15). P. Grelot understands the 70 years as representing 10 periods of a sabbatical period of seven years (Lev. 25.1-7) (Grelot 1969). Assyrian texts of Esarhaddon speak of a 70-year period of devastation declared against Babylon in 689, which was reduced to 11 years by reversing two cuneiform signs (Saggs 1984: 105; see also *COS*: II, 306). Some scholars reckon the 70 years as the period of Babylonian sovereignty from 605 to 539. Others consider the 70-year period as being reckoned from the destruction of the temple to its rebuilding 586–516 (Whitley 1954; 1957b; Orr 1956). Commenting on 2 Chron. 36.20-21, H.G.M. Williamson suggests that as spoken originally by Jeremiah it may have been intended as a general period of punishment based on either an individual's life span or on three generations, but he believes that the Chronicler applied it to the period 586 to 516 (Williamson 1982: 418).

10. *Return from the Exile*

Cyrus was the founder of the Persian Empire and the greatest Achaemenid king. He reigned over the Persians from 559 to 530 BCE. He established Persian dominance over the Medes in 550, conquered Lydia and Ionia in 547–546, and captured Babylon in 539.

Isaiah 44.28 and 45.1 speak of Cyrus as the Lord's 'shepherd' and his 'anointed'.[25] Josephus (*Ant.* 11.4-5) has Cyrus declaring, 'I am persuaded

---

25. Conservative scholars cite these references as a remarkable example of explicit prophecy. Other scholars maintain that these references are evidence that the later chapters of Isaiah, should be assigned to an anonymous Deutero-Isaiah of the sixth century. See Yamauchi 1990: 72-73.

that he is the god whom the Israelite nation worships, for he foretold my name through the prophets and that I should build his temple in Jerusalem, the land of Judaea.' These things Cyrus supposedly knew from having read Isaiah.

Many scholars believe that Cyrus was an Iranian polytheist. A number of scholars, noting the continuity of religious thought between Cyrus and Darius, have sought to attribute the magnanimity of Cyrus to the teachings of Zoroaster.[26] Whether from religious motives or not, Cyrus reversed the policy of his predecessors—the Assyrians and the Babylonians. Instead of deporting the people he conquered, he permitted the Jews to return to their homeland. A Hebrew copy of the decree of Cyrus is found in Ezra 1.1-4, and a record of the Aramaic memorandum is given in Ezra 6.3-5. Ezra 1.1-4 reads:

> In the first year of Cyrus king of Persia, in order to fulfill the word of the LORD spoken by Jeremiah, the LORD moved the heart of Cyrus king of Persia to make a proclamation throughout his realm and to put in writing: This is what Cyrus king of Persia says: 'The LORD, the God of heaven, has given me all the kingdoms of the earth and he has appointed me to build a temple for him at Jerusalem in Judah. Anyone of his people among you— may his God be with him, and let him go up to Jerusalem in Judah and build the temple of the LORD, the God of Israel, the God who is in Jerusalem. And the people of any place where survivors may now be living are to provide him with silver and gold, with goods and livestock, and with freewill offerings for the temple of Jerusalem.'

Earlier scholars had questioned the authenticity of the decree because of the Jewish phraseology of the document. But documents from the Persian period and archeological evidence have provided convincing evidence of its authenticity (Bickerman 1946; de Vaux 1971). 'In the first year' means the first regnal year of Cyrus, beginning in Nisan 538, after his capture of Babylon in October 539. During these same months following the capture of Babylon, cuneiform texts record the Persian king's benefactions to Mesopotamian sanctuaries. Parallel to the phrase, 'The LORD, the God of heaven, has given me all the kingdoms of the earth' (Ezra 1.2), is the statement of an inscription of Cyrus from Ur, which reads, 'The great gods have delivered all the lands into my hand'.

Especially impressive corroborative evidence of Cyrus's policy of toleration is the 'Cyrus Cylinder', which indicates that he captured Babylon 'without any battle' (*ANET*: 315; *COS*: II, 314-16). One of the

---

26. On this issue, see Yamauchi 1990: 422-24.

first acts of Cyrus was to return the gods which had been removed from their sanctuaries by Nabonidus. A fragment of the Cyrus Cylinder, identified in 1970, also states that Cyrus restored Babylon's inner wall and moats. Excavations at Uruk and Ur reveal that Cyrus also made restorations in temples there.

According to the lists in Ezra 2//Nehemiah 7 about 50,000 responded to the opportunity Cyrus gave for them to return to the Holy Land. Many scholars have questioned whether such a large group would have joined the initial return under Sheshbazzar. They have suggested that the totals must include others who came later. But surely the initial response would have been indeed the greatest. The former Prime Minister of Israel, David Ben-Gurion, described the modern emigration of Jews from Iraq to Israel as follows: 'Almost the whole community of Babylonian exiles who stayed when Babylon was destroyed came to this country ten years ago—and their number was nearly thrice the number of those who returned to Zion in the days of Ezra and Nehemiah' (Ben-Gurion 1974: I, 133).

Salo Baron observes, 'in Ezra's list of those who participated in the first return under Zerubbabel, there are recorded among "the men of the people of Israel" many descendants of exiles from localities which formerly belonged to the northern kingdom' (Baron 1952: 343). In particular the names 'Pahath-Moab' and 'Elam' in Ezra 2.6-7, 14//Neh. 7.11-13, 19, may refer to Israelites exiled from Transjordan (1 Chron. 5.26) and those settled by the Assyrians in Media (2 Kgs 17.6) and in Elam (Isa. 11.11).

11. *Religious Developments during the Exile*[27]

Some of the Jewish deportees may have at first been awed by the great Ziggurat, the magnificent temple of Marduk, and the 50 other temples in Babylon (Ezek. 20.32) (Yamauchi 1985), but most Jews seem to have dismissed the thousands of idols in Mesopotamia (Isa. 46.1-2). The apocryphal *Letter of Jeremiah*, which may have been written between 300 and 100 BCE, purports to be the prophet's warning before the Exile:

> Now in Babylon you will see carried on men's shoulders gods made of silver, gold, and wood, which fill the heathen with awe. Be careful, then, never to imitate these Gentiles; do not be overawed by their gods when you see them in the midst of a procession of worshippers. But say in your hearts, 'To thee alone, Lord, is worship due' (NEB).

27. See Newsome 1971.

Deprived of the temple, the exiles laid emphasis on the observation of the Sabbath,[28] on the laws of purity, on prayer and confession (Dan. 9; Ezra 9; Neh. 9), and on fasting to commemorate the tragic events of the Babylonian attacks (Zech. 7.3, 5; 8.19). Great stress was played on studying and expounding the Torah, as we see in the calling of Ezra, the scribe (Ezra 7.6), 'a teacher well versed in the Law of Moses'.

It has often been surmised that the development of synagogues probably began in Mesopotamia during the Exile. The gatherings held under the auspices of Ezekiel (Ezek. 8.1; 14.1) have been seen as precursors to the synagogue assemblies. The reading, interpreting, and possibly the translating of the Scriptures into Aramaic—which were to be important features of the later synagogue service—were part of the great meeting described in Nehemiah 8.

The Babylonian Talmud (*Meg.* 29a) asserted that the Shekhinah, the glorious presence of Yahweh, rested in the third-century synagogue of Nehardea. In the tenth century CE, Sherira ben Hanina Gaon asserted:

> When Israel was exiled, Jehoiakin, the smiths, the craftsmen and some prophets among them, were brought to the city of Nehardea [in Babylonia] and Jehoiakhin, the king of Judah, and his entourage built there a synagogue (*bei-khenishta*) and used for its foundation stones and ashes, they had brought with them from the [site of] the [ruined] Temple [in Jerusalem] (Gutmann 1988: 209).

But archeological and inscriptional evidence for synagogues has not been found from the exilic period in Mesopotamia; the earliest evidence is from Ptolemaic Egypt (Hengel 1971; Yamauchi 1992a).

12. *Jews under the Achaemenids*

A fascinating light on the Jews in Mesopotamia during the later Persian period is shed by the Murashû Tablets, which were found in a room at Nippur in 1893. From 1898 to 1912 H.V. Hilprecht and A.T. Clay published 480 of these texts out of a reported total of 730 tablets. In 1974 Matthew Stolper wrote a dissertation using 179 hitherto unpublished Murashû texts from the University Museum in Pennsylvania and four from

---

28. The Sabbath is mentioned 15 times in Ezekiel. Individuals named Shabbethai appear in Ezra 10.15 and Neh. 8.7, in the Murashu texts (five individuals), and in the Elephantine papyri (three individuals). The latter are fifth-century Aramaic documents from a Jewish military colony on the Elephantine Island in the Upper Nile near Aswan. See Porten 1968: 124, 127. See also McKay 1994.

the British Museum. He reports that the total number of texts and fragments is now known to be 879 (Stolper 1985: 1). These texts date from the reigns of Artaxerxes I (464–424) and Darius II (423–404), mainly from the years 440 to 414—the era of Ezra and Nehemiah. This archive is the largest single source of conditions in Achaemenid Babylonia (Cardascia 1951).

Murashû and his sons, who managed agricultural land held as estates and fiefs, loaned out money, equipment and animals. They also collected taxes and rents. Studies of the names of their clients have demonstrated that some of their clients were Jews. Now no doubt many Jews adopted Babylonian names, particularly those in official positions such as Daniel and his companions (Dan. 1.5-7). Such individuals include the leaders Sheshbazar/Shenazzar (Ezra 1.8; 5.14; 1 Chron. 3.18) and Zerubbabel (Ezra 3.2), Bilshan (Ezra 2.2), Hattush, Nekoda, Esther (Est. 2.7) and Mordecai (Est. 2.6).[29] Extrabiblical evidence indicates that at times those with non-Jewish names gave their children Yahwistic names, and other parents with Yahwistic names gave their children non-Jewish (that is, Babylonian, West Semitic and even Iranian) names (Bickerman 1986: 316).

Yahwistic names, that is, names ending in the theophoric element *Yh/Yw/Yhw* for Yahweh (spelled in neo-babylonian *ia-a-ma*) are useful for identifying Jews and their families in the Murashû archive.[30] Examples include *Tobyaw* (= Tobiah), *Banayaw* (= Benaiah), and *Zabadyaw* (= Zebadiah). Of those identified as Jews, 38 bore Yahwistic names, 23 West Semitic names, six Akkadian names, and two Iranian names. The Jews, who were from 28 settlements, constituted only about 3 per cent of the 2500 individuals named in these records.[31] As these texts deal only with the countryside, they do not yield any information on the possible presence of Jews at Nippur itself.

The Jews appear as contracting parties, agents, witnesses, collectors of taxes, and royal officials. A Gedaliah served as a mounted archer, a Hanani managed the royal poultry farm, and a Jedaiah was an agent of a royal steward (Coogan 1974: 10). There seems to have been no social or

29. On the possibility that Mordecai may be identified with one of the individuals named *Marduka* in cuneiform texts, see Yamauchi 1992b.

30. For studies of comparable Yahwistic names in the Elephantine papyri, see Silverman 1970.

31. Zadok 1979: 78. Cf. also Zadok 1978 which is a critical review of Coogan 1976; Wallis 1980.

commercial barriers between the Jews and the Babylonians. Their prosperous situation may explain why some chose to remain in Meospotamia. At the same time their growing confidence may explain why, as Bickerman has shown in his analysis, the proportion of Yahwistic names grew larger in the second generation.[32]

13. *Jews in Arabia*

At the rise of Islam, Muhammad encountered strong Jewish communities especially at Yathrib (Medina) to which he fled in his Hejira of 622. Scholars have speculated that the ultimate origin of these colonies may be traced back to Nabonidus's extraordinary stay in Arabia for ten years (552–443), as many of the sites he visited (Teima, Dadanu, Padakku, Khibra, Iadikhu, Yathrib) were later centers of Jewish communities. C.J. Gadd first raised this possibility when he published in 1956 the funerary stele of Nabonidus's remarkable mother (Gadd 1958). Gadd reasoned that Nabonidus may have taken Jewish soldiers with him, some of whom remained in Arabia. This suggestion has been endorsed by I. Ben-Zvi (1960; 1961). Some scholars have cited the interesting 'Prayer of Nabonidus' found among the Dead Sea Scrolls as evidence that the Jews were aware of Nabonidus's sojourn in Teima.[33]

Late Yemenite Jewish traditions have their ancestors departing from Jerusalem 42 years before the destruction of the temple by Nebuchadnezzar. When Ezra asked them to return to Judah to help rebuild the temple, they refused because they foresaw the second destruction of the temple. Ezra then cursed them to a life of poverty, while they in turn cursed Ezra so he would not be buried in the Holy Land (Yamauchi 1986b; Newby 1988: 19 n. 12).

14. *Conclusion*

The Jews were hardly alone in experiencing the hardships of enforced exile. Nor were they alone in attempting to maintain their identity, inasmuch as groups like the Egyptians tried to do so. But all of them, with

---

32. Bickerman (1986: 322) states: 'The break with syncretism occurred in the generation of Ezra, who, probably, was born about 500'.

33. García Martínez 1994: 289. Many scholars have concluded that this document underlies what has been confused in Dan. 4 as the madness of Nebuchadnezzar, but there are major differences between the two texts.

the exception of the Jews, were eventually assimilated and disappeared as a recognizable entity. Eph'al remarks: 'The outstanding survival of the Jews in Babylonia as an entity-in-exile in the subsequent period—in contrast to the disappearance of all the other foreign ethnic groups there—remains, however, a problem demanding a fuller explanation' (Eph'al 1978: 88). No doubt the key to their survival was their faith in a God, who, though he momentarily punished them, was nonetheless a faithful covenant-keeping Lord, who would watch over them even in a foreign Diaspora and restore them to their Holy Land.

BIBLIOGRAPHY

Ackroyd, P.R.
    1970   *Israel under Babylon and Persia* (London: Oxford University Press).
Albright, W.F.
    1932   'The Seal of Eliakim and the Latest Pre-exilic History of Judah, with Some Observations on Ezekiel', *JBL* 51: 77-106.
    1942   'King Joiachin in Exile', *BA* 5: 49-55 (reprinted in D.N. Freedman and G.E. Wright [eds.], *The Biblical Archaeologist Reader* [Garden City, NY: Doubleday]: 106-12).
    1963   *The Biblical Period from Abraham to Ezra* (New York: Harper and Row).
Allrik, H.L.
    1954   'The Lists of Zerubbabel (Nehemiah 7 and Ezra 2) and the Hebrew Numeral Notations', *BASOR* 136: 21-27.
Arnold, B.T.
    1994   'Babylonians', *POTW*: 43-75.
Avigad, N.
    1965   'Seals of the Exiles', *IEJ* 15: 223-30.
    1974   'More Evidence on the Judean Post-Exilic Stamps', *IEJ* 24: 52-58.
    1978   'Baruch the Scribe and Jerahmeel the King's Son', *IEJ* 28: 52-56.
Baron, S.W.
    1952   *A Social and Religious History of the Jews.* I. *Ancient Times to the Beginning of the Christian Era* (New York: Columbia University Press, 2nd edn).
Beaulieu, P.-A.
    1989   *The Reign of Nabonidus, King of Babylon 556–339 B.C.* (New Haven: Yale University Press).
Ben-Gurion, D.
    1974   'Cyrus, King of Persia', in *Commémoration Cyrus* (Leiden: E.J. Brill).
Ben-Zvi, I.
    1960   'The Origins of the Settlement of Jewish Tribes in Arabia', *EI* 6: 35*-37*.
    1961   'Les origines de l'établissement des tribus d'Israël en Arabie', *Le Muséon* 74: 143-90.
    1976   *The Exiled and the Redeemed* (Jerusalem: Yad Izhak Ben-Zvi Publications).

Berquist, J.L.
1995   *Judaism in Persia's Shadow* (Minneapolis: Fortress Press).
Bickerman, E.J.
1946   'The Edict of Cyrus in Ezra 1', *JBL* 65: 249-75.
1984   'The Babylonian Captivity', in W.D. Davies and L. Finkelstein (eds.),
        Cambridge History of Judaism. I. *Introduction: The Persian Period* (Cam-
        bridge: Cambridge University Press): 342-58.
1986   *Studies in Jewish and Christian History*, III (Leiden: E.J. Brill; = 'The
        Generation of Ezra and Nehemiah', *Proceedings of the American Academy
        of Jewish Research* [1978: 1-28]): 113-40.
Boadt, L.
1992   'Ezekiel, Book of', *ABD*: II, 711-22.
Cardascia, G.
1951   *Les archives des Muraŝû* (Paris: Imprimerie Nationale).
Cogan, M., and H. Tadmor
1988   *II Kings* (AB, 11; Garden City, NY: Doubleday).
Collins, J.J.
1993   *Daniel* (Minneapolis: Fortress Press).
Coogan, M.D.
1974   'Life in the Diaspora', *BA* 37: 10.
1976   *West Semitic Personal Names in the Muraŝû Documents* (Missoula, MT:
        Scholars Press).
Dandamaev, M.A.
1984   *Slavery in Babylonia* (trans. M.A. Powell; Dekalb, IL: Northern Illinois
        University Press).
1992   'Egyptians in Babylonia in the 6th–5th Centuries B.C.', in D. Chapin and F.
        Joannès (eds.), *La circulation des biens, des personnes et des idées dans le
        Proche-Orient ancien* (RAI, 38; Paris: Éditions Recherche sur les Civili-
        sations, 1992): 321-25.
Davies, W.D., and L. Finkelstein (eds.)
1984   *The Cambridge History of Judaism*. I. *Introduciton; The Persian Period*
        (Cambridge: Cambridge University Press).
Eph'al, I.
1978   'The Western Minorities in Babylonia in the 6th–5th Centuries B.C.:
        Maintenance and Cohesion', *Or* 47: 74-90.
Fensham, F.C.
1982   'Nebukadrezzar in the Book of Jeremiah', *JNSL* 10: 53-65.
Gadd, C.J.
1958   'The Harran Inscription of Nabonidus', *AnSt* 8: 35-92.
Galling, K.
1964   *Studien zur Geschichte Israels im persischen Zeitalter* (Tübingen: J.C.B.
        Mohr, 1964).
García Martínez, F.
1994   *The Dead Sea Scrolls Translated* (Leiden: E.J. Brill).
Godbey, A.H.
1930   *The Lost Tribes—A Myth* (New York: Ktav, 1974 repr. of 1930 edn).

Goldman, S. (ed.)
 1993 *Hebrew and the Bible in America* (Hanover: University Press of New England).
Grabbe, L.L.
 1992 *Judaism from Cyrus to Hadrian I: The Persian and Greek Periods* (Minneapolis: Fortress Press).
Graham, J.N.
 1984 ' "Vinedressers and Plowmen": 2 Kings 25.12 and Jeremiah 52.16', *BA* 47: 55-58.
Grelot, P.
 1969 'Soixante-dix semaines d'années', *Bib* 50: 175.
Gross, A.
 1992 'The Expulsion and the Search for the Ten Tribes', *Judaism* 41: 130-47.
Gustafson, S.
 1994 'Nations of Israelites', *Religion and Literature* 26: 31-53.
Gutmann, J.
 1988 'Sherira Gaon and the Babylonian Origin of the Synagogue', in R. Dán (ed.), *Occident and Orient* (Leiden: E.J. Brill): 209-12.
Hengel, M.
 1971 'Proseuche und Synagoge', in G. Jeremias, H.-W. Kuhn and H. Stegemann (eds.), *Tradition und Glaube* (Göttingen: Vandenhoeck & Ruprecht): 157-84.
Isaac, E.
 1993 'The Legend of Solomon and Sheba', *BARev* 19: 62-63.
Kalimi I., and J. Purvis
 1994a 'King Jehoiachin and the Vessels of the Lord's House in Biblical Literature', *CBQ* 56: 449-57.
 1994b 'The Hiding of the Temple Vessels in Jewish and Samaritan Literature', *CBQ* 56: 679-85.
Kreissig, H.
 1973 *Die sozialökonomische Situation in Juda zur Achämenidenzeit* (Berlin: Akademie Verlag).
Malamat, A.
 1950 'The Last Wars of the Kingdom of Judah', *JNES* 9: 218-27.
 1968 'The Last Kings of Judah and the Fall of Jerusalem', *IEJ* 18: 137-55.
May, H.G.
 1943 'The Ten Lost Tribes', *BA* 6: 55-60.
McKay, H.A.
 1994 *Sabbath and Synagogue* (Leiden: E. J. Brill).
Mercer, M.K.
 1989 'Daniel 1.1 and Jehoiakim's Three years of Servitude', *AUSS* 27: 179-92.
Millard, A.R.
 1977 'Daniel 1–6 and History', *EvQ* 49: 67-73.
Mitchell, T.C.
 1991 'Judah until the Fall of Jerusalem (c. 700–586 B.C.', in J. Boardman *et al.* (eds.), *The Cambridge Ancient History*, III/2 (Cambridge: Cambridge University Press, 2nd edn): 371-91.

Newby, G.D.
1988   *A History of the Jews of Arabia* (Columbia, SC: University of South Carolina Press).

Newsome, J.D. Jr
1971   *By the Waters of Babylon: An Introduction to the History and Theology of the Exile* (Atlanta: John Knox Press).

Oded, B.
1979   *Mass Deportations and Deportees in the Neo-Assyrian Empire* (Wiesbaden: Ludwig Reichert Verlag).

Orlinsky, H.M.
1972   *Understanding the Bible through History and Archeology* (New York: Ktav).

Orr, A.
1956   'The Seventy Years of Babylon', *VT* 6: 304-306.

Popkin, R.H.
1986   'The Lost Tribes, the Caraites and the English Millenarians', *JJS* 37: 213-27.

Porten, B.
1968   *Archives from Elephantine* (Berkeley: University of California Press).

Rowley, H.H.
1953   'The Book of Ezekiel in Modern Study', *BJRL* 36: 146-90.

Sack, R.H.
1972   *Amel-Marduk 562–560 B.C.* (Kevelaer: Butzon & Bercker).
1983   'The Nabonidus Legend', *RA* 77: 59-67.
1994   *Neriglissar—King of Babylon* (Kevelaer: Butzon & Bercker).

Saggs, H.W.F.
1984   *The Might That Was Assyria* (London: Sidgwick & Jackson).

Shanks, H.
1987   'Jeremiah's Scribe and Confidant Speaks from a Hoard of Clay Bullae', *BARev* 13.5: 58.
1996   'Fingerprint of Jeremiah's Scribe', *BARev* 22.2: 36-38.

Silverman, M.H.
1970   'Hebrew Name-Types in the Elephantine Documents', *Or* 39: 465-91.

Smith, D.
1989   *The Religion of the Landless: The Social Context of the Babylonian Exile* (Bloomington, IN: Meyer Stone Books).

Stohlmann, S.
1983   'The Judaean Exile after 701 B.C.E.', in *SIC* 2: 147-75.

Stolper, M.
1985   *Entrepreneurs and Empire* (Leiden: Nederlands Historisch-Archaeologisch Instituut te Istanbul).

Tadmor, H.
1976   'The Period of the First Temple, the Babylonian Exile and the Restoration', in H.H. Ben-Sasson (ed.), *A History of the Jewish People* (Cambridge, MA: Harvard University Press): 91-182.

Ungnad, A.
1942-43   'Die Zahl der von Sanherib deportierten Judäer', *ZAW* 59: 199-202.

Vaux, R. de
1971   'The Decrees of Cyrus and Darius on the Rebuilding of the Temple', in *The Bible and the Ancient Near East* (Garden City, NY: Doubleday).

Wallis, G.
1980   'Jüdische Bürger in Babylonien während der Achämeniden-Zeit', *Persica* 9: 129-85.
Weidner, E.F.
1939   'Jojachin, König von Juda, in babylonischen Keilschrifttexten', *Mélanges Syriens offerts à Monsieur René Dussaud* (Paris: Geuthner): II, 923-35.
Weinberg, J.P.
1972   'Demographische Notizen zur Geschichte der nachexilischen Gemeinde in Juda', *Klio* 54: 49-58.
Whitley, C.F.
1954   'The Term Seventy Years Captivity', *VT* 4: 60-72.
1957a   *The Exilic Age* (Philadelphia: Westminster Press).
1957b   'The Seventy Years Desolation—A Rejoinder', *VT* 7: 416-18.
Williamson, H.G.M.
1982   *1 and 2 Chronicles* (Grand Rapids: Eerdmans).
Wiseman, D.J.
1956   *Chronicles of Chaldaean Kings* (London: British Museum).
1966   'Some Egyptians in Babylonia', *Iraq* 28: 154-58.
1985   *Nebuchadrezzar and Babylon* (London: Oxford University Press).
Wiseman, D.J. *et al.* (eds.)
1965   *Notes on Some Problems in the Book of Daniel* (London: Tyndale Press).
Yamauchi, E.
1982   *Foes from the Northern Frontiers* (Grand Rapids: Baker Book House).
1983a   'Chaldea, Chaldeans', in E.M. Blaiklock and R.K. Harrison (eds.), *The New International Dictionary of Biblical Archeology* (Grand Rapids: Zondervan): 123-25.
1983b   'Nippur', in E.M. Blaiklock and R.K. Harrison (eds.), *The New International Dictionary of Biblical Archeology* (Grand Rapids: Zondervan): 339-41.
1985   'Babylon', in R.K. Harrison (ed.), *Major Cities of the Biblical World* (Nashville: Thomas Nelson): 46-47.
1986a   'Nabonidus', in *ISBE*: III, 468-70.
1986b   'Postbiblical Traditions about Ezra and Nehemiah', in *Studies Archer*: 167-76.
1988   'Ezra–Nehemiah', in F.E. Gaebelein (ed.), *The Expositor's Bible Commentary* (Grand Rapids: Zondervan).
1990   *Persia and the Bible* (Grand Rapids: Baker Book House).
1992a   'Synagogue', in J.B. Green, S. McKnight and I.H. Marshall (eds.), *Dictionary of Jesus and the Gospels* (Downers Grove, IL: InterVarsity Press): 781-84.
1992b   'Mordecai, the Persepolis Tablets, and the Susa Excavations', *VT* 42: 272-75.
Younger, K.L. Jr
1998   'The Deportations of the Israelites', *JBL* 117: 201-27.
2002   ' "Give Us Our Daily Bread"—Everyday Life for the Israelite Deportees', in R.E. Averbeck, M.W. Chavalas and D. Weisberg (eds.), *Daily Life in the Ancient Near East* (Bethsaida, MD: CDL Press) (in press).

Zadok, R.
1977   *On West Semites in Babylonia during the Chaldean and Achaemenian Periods: An Onomastic Study* (Jerusalem: H.J. and Z. Wanaarta and Tel Aviv University).
1978   'West Semitic Personal Names in the Murašû Documents', *BASOR* 231: 73-78.
1979   *The Jews in Babylonian during the Chaldean and Achaemenian Periods according to the Babylonian Sources* (Haifa: University of Haifa Press).

INDEXES

INDEX OF REFERENCES

OLD TESTAMENT

INDEX OF AUTHORS

JOURNAL FOR THE STUDY OF THE OLD TESTAMENT
SUPPLEMENT SERIES